IN DEFENSE OF
MIRACLES

A COMPREHENSIVE CASE FOR GOD'S ACTION IN HISTORY

EDITED BY R. DOUGLAS GEIVETT
& GARY R. HABERMAS

InterVarsity Press
Downers Grove, Illinois

InterVarsity Press® is the book-publishing division of InterVarsity Christian Fellowship®, a student movement active on campus at hundreds of universities, colleges and schools of nursing in the United States of America, and a member movement of the International Fellowship of Evangelical Students. For information about local and regional activities, write Public Relations Dept., InterVarsity Christian Fellowship, 6400 Schroeder Rd., P.O. Box 7895, Madison, WI 53707-7895.

Scripture quotations, unless otherwise noted, are from the New Revised Standard Version of the Bible, copyright 1989 by the Division of Christian Education of the National Council of the Churches of Christ in the U.S.A., and are used by permission.

Cover photograph: Christie's Images, London/SuperStock. Morning of the Resurrection by Burne-Jones.

ISBN 0-8308-1528-7

Printed in the United States of America ⊗

Library of Congress Cataloging-in-Publication Data

In defense of miracles : a comprehensive case for God's action in
  history / edited by R. Douglas Geivett and Gary R. Habermas.
    p. cm.
    Includes bibliographical references.
    ISBN 0-8308-1528-7 (alk. paper)
    1. Miracles.   2. Apologetics.   I. Geivett, R. Douglas.
II. Habermas, Gary R.
BT97.2.I5 1997
231.7'3—dc21   96-46653
                                                                    CIP

21	20	19	18	17	16	15	14	13	12	11	10	9	8	7	6	5	4	3	2	1
13	12	11	10	09	08	07	06	05	04	03	02	01	00	99	98	97				

Introduction/R. Douglas Geivett and Gary R. Habermas ——————— 9

PART 1: THE CASE AGAINST MIRACLES ———————— 27

1/Of Miracles/David Hume (d. 1776) ————————————— 29

2/Neo-Humean Arguments About the Miraculous/Antony Flew ——— 45

PART 2: THE POSSIBILITY OF MIRACLES ———————— 59

3/Defining Miracles/Richard L. Purtill ————————————— 61

4/Miracles & the Modern Mind/Norman L. Geisler ——————— 73

5/History & Miracles/Francis J. Beckwith ——————————— 86

6/Recognizing a Miracle/Winfried Corduan ——————————— 99

PART 3: A THEISTIC CONTEXT FOR MIRACLES ————— 113

7/Miracles & Conceptual Systems/Ronald H. Nash ——————— 115

8/Science, Miracles, Agency Theory & the God-of-the-Gaps/

    J. P. Moreland ————————————————————— 132

9/God's Existence/W. David Beck ————————————— 149

10/God's Actions/Stephen T. Davis ————————————— 163

11/The Evidential Value of Miracles/R. Douglas Geivett ————— 178

PART 4: CHRISTIAN MIRACLES—CASE STUDIES ————— 197

12/Miracles in the World Religions/David K. Clark ——————— 199

13/Fulfilled Prophecy as Miracle/Robert C. Newman ————— 214

14/The Incarnation of Jesus Christ/John S. Feinberg ————— 226

15/The Empty Tomb of Jesus/William Lane Craig ————————— 247

16/The Resurrection Appearances of Jesus/Gary R. Habermas ——— 262

Conclusion: Has God Acted in History?/R. Douglas Geivett and

    Gary R. Habermas ————————————————————— 276

Notes ————————————————————————————— 281

Bibliography ————————————————————————— 321

Contributors ————————————————————————— 329

Introduction

The possibility that miracles have happened—that God has acted in history—continues to fascinate. Every year at Easter, major news magazines feature cover stories on the Christian belief in the resurrection of Jesus Christ. And every year academic conferences are convened, more sermons are preached, scholars from various traditions are queried, laypersons—believers and unbelievers—are polled, and the perception that a verdict remains uncertain is reinforced.

Contemporary interest in miracles is not merely an armchair phenomenon. Millions of infirm journey to Lourdes and other places each year, not only desiring but expecting a miracle of physical healing. Countless others trek to Eastern Europe to witness alleged apparitions of the Virgin Mary at Medjugorje. Religious believers regularly speak quite literally of "smaller-scale" miracles happening in their everyday experience: answers to prayer, remarkable provisions of basic needs and a variety of strange coincidences that seem to betoken the interference of some divine agent or agents in the world.

Within the academy, the whole subject of miracles has recently undergone a strange reversal of fortune. While theologians and biblical scholars of liberal persuasion perpetuate a virulent skepticism about the miraculous, many professional philosophers openly affirm God's miraculous involvement in human affairs. As David Shatz has observed, "A religious philosopher can exude greater tranquility and confidence today than at any other time in recent decades."[1]

As it happens, many of the most fundamental questions about miracles are philosophical in nature. These questions can be usefully organized into two categories. The first category relates to concerns about whether it is reasonable to think that miracles have occurred. Six specific concerns fit into this category: (1) Can Christianity be credible if miracles are not possible?[2] (2) Even if miracles have happened in the past, can it be reasonable for anyone other than eyewitnesses to believe in miracles? (3) May not the distinguishing features of a miracle be so difficult to discern that even eyewitnesses to miraculous events would not be able to identify them as miraculous? (4) Are not the grounds for concluding that miracles are actual different from the grounds for concluding that miracles are possible? (5) Is the concept of a miracle even intelligible? (6) Is the idea of "divine intervention" compatible with the nature of a perfect God?[3]

The second category focuses on the role that miracles might play in supporting other religious beliefs. Here are some questions that might be asked in this regard: (1) Can miracles be used in an independent argument for the existence of God? (2) Do miracles add confirmation to the proposition that God exists? (3) Can miracles be employed as evidence for other religious beliefs besides the belief that God exists? (4) Do miracles confirm divine revelation? (5) Do the miracle traditions of competing religions cancel each other out so that no tradition can rely on miracles as evidence?

Both sets of questions are the focus of close critical attention in this book. With the exception of part one, all chapters are written by Christian intellectuals; and with the exception of Robert Newman, whose training is in astrophysics, all contributors are professional philosophers. In this introduction we first present a sketch of the recent history of intellectual interest in miracles within three disciplines. We then describe the overall organization of the book, illustrating the logical progression of each chapter and its contribution to a comprehensive argument that God has indeed acted in history.

One problem with brief discussions of intellectual trends, especially when they cover more than a century of thought, is that such overviews regularly require much generalizing. Realizing that gaps in coverage are unavoidable, we nevertheless attempt to give here an accurate, if sketchy, summary of some major movements in theology, philosophy and historical studies as they relate to current scholarly discussion of the miracles question.

Theological Trends

As with most topics, critical theological scholarship has never been uniform in its conclusions about the topic of miracles. This applies not only to the subject of the historicity of such occurrences, which has probably occasioned the most controversy, but also to such other issues as the relation between miracles and faith on the one hand, and between miracles and mythology on the other. Even a consensus about how best to define a miracle has proven elusive.

While many notable intellectuals have produced intricate arguments for the factuality of miracles, the last few centuries have also witnessed numerous attempts to disallow on various grounds any divine intervention in history. A brief survey of a few of the more notable attempts to deny the actuality of miracles illustrates the general character of such critical approaches.

In the seventeenth and eighteenth centuries, deism was popular in England, while certain similar trends could be found also in France and Germany. Classical deists generally opposed belief in divine intervention in history, whether in the form of prophecy or miracles, for such belief seemed to them to violate the canons of reason. Divine intervention was often regarded as superfluous or gratuitous in that it implied that God's original creation was somehow defective. Sometimes alternative schemes were advanced in order to explain the supernatural components of traditional beliefs.[4]

In the nineteenth century, deistic polemics gave way to classical Protestant liberalism. During this period, the chief examples of naturalistic responses to Jesus' miracles evolved. This century also witnessed a crescendo of published "lives of Jesus," which typically construed Jesus as a great example for living while repudiating all supernatural elements associated with Jesus, along with traditional dogmatic theology.

Continuing a number of earlier deistic tendencies, the predominant approach to miracles in the early liberalism of the nineteenth century was rationalistic in nature. Heinrich Paulus (1761-1851), for instance, who published his two-volume life of Jesus in 1828, accepted as historical a fair amount of the New Testament text, but substituted naturalistic explanations for the miraculous element.

In his watershed publication *Life of Jesus Critically Examined* (1835), David Friedrich Strauss (1808-1874) presented a serious challenge to the classic approach of Paulus. Strauss replaced the rationalist method with a mythical strategy that called into question many Gospel reports concerning the historical Jesus. He held that the Gospels were mythological in nature, depicting transcendental ideas in seemingly historical garb in order to articulate essentially inexpressible truths. This mythical approach popularized by Strauss and others denied the basic historicity of the Gospels. It also undermined earlier rationalist strategies, since they assumed the factual reliability of much of the Gospels.[5]

Deism and liberalism manifested a common impulse to modify orthodox Christianity. Traditional miracle claims were cleverly reinterpreted rather than simply cast aside. This practice exemplified a type of methodological naturalism, which acknowledged the reality of God in some general (perhaps mystical) sense, without assigning any role to God in the production of the tradition. Thus, these scholars presumed to conduct their investigations as if there were no supernatural realm. It was but a short step from such a perspective to full-blown metaphysical naturalism that altogether denied anything beyond the natural order.

The demise of liberalism occurred in the early twentieth century. An optimistic anthropology, which held that humankind was gradually evolving to ever higher levels of sophistication, was crushed by the stark realities of World War I and the realization that something was seriously amiss within human nature. Those who clung tenaciously to the earlier idealism surmounted the horrific implications of the greatest slaughter of human lives in history, only to be confronted by World War II and a repetition of the carnage.

This troublesome climate was furthered by the publication in 1918 of *Epistle to the Roman*.[6] by Karl Barth (1886-1968). This work, calling for renewed belief in the sovereignty of God and the sinfulness of persons, struck a theological nerve that called an entire generation of theologians away from groundless trust in the goodness of human faculties back to a revitalized focus on God. Neo-orthodoxy, the movement inspired by Barth, surged to the forefront of theological discussions. Though this movement replaced several liberal theological emphases, Barth and those who followed him expressed less interest in the historicity of miracles. They favored instead a strict divorce between the demand for evidence and concern for a purified religious faith. Ensuing decades saw a decline of interest in the search for the historical

Jesus in general and in the examination of his miracles in particular.[7]

Rudolf Bultmann (1884-1976), in his 1941 essay "New Testament and Mythology," popularized the theological methodology of demythologization, taking the discussion of miracles into a new arena.[8] Biblical descriptions of supernatural events came to be regarded as crucial indicators of early Christian belief that should be viewed separately from the issue of their historicity. So the transcendent language of the Bible was not to be discarded; rather, it was to be reinterpreted in terms of its existential significance for living and decision-making in the modern world.[9]

Many theologians in the grip of Bultmann's existential approach continued his research program for some years. But by the mid-1950s, signs of dissatisfaction appeared and new strategies emerged, acknowledging the importance of at least a minimum number of historical facts from the life of Jesus. A particularly influential movement both rejected the nineteenth-century quest for the historical Jesus and presented a modest critique of contemporary mythical approaches.[10]

Other scholars went further in their critique of the dominant research of the first half of the century. Some reached conclusions that seemed more sympathetic to the stance of traditional Christian approaches to certain supernatural elements contained in the Gospels. Wolfhart Pannenberg (b. 1928) led a group of thinkers who argued forcefully for the concept of God's revelation in time-space history.[11] Jürgen Moltmann (b. 1926) and others emphasized a new eschatological perspective, one that acknowledged the importance of God's part in both past and present history.[12]

While the last few decades of the twentieth century have witnessed the efflorescence of various approaches to the study of miracles, much of recent critical theological thought has been more open to some sense of God's acting in history. Although there is no identifiable consensus among current scholars, there has been a somewhat positive assessment of the need to investigate the historicity of Jesus. This is due in no small measure to a fresh awareness of and appreciation for the Jewish background and context of Jesus' life and teachings.[13] One notable exception to this trend is the position adopted by the controversial Jesus Seminar. Acknowledging the need for further research into the historical Jesus, these scholars favor a return to a mythical approach to the Gospels, more in concert with the methodologies of Strauss and Bultmann.[14]

Philosophical Trends
While the above developments dominated the theological landscape

during the period we have been considering, other emphases were prominent in philosophical environs. Logical positivism emerged on the European continent (namely, in Austria) in the first third of the twentieth century and quickly gained influence, especially in England. Inspired by such earlier thinkers as David Hume (1711-1776), Immanuel Kant (1724-1804) and Auguste Comte (1798-1857), the Austrian philosopher Moritz Schlick (1882-1936) provided leadership to the fledgling group, called the Vienna Circle, in the 1920s.

British philosopher A. J. Ayer (1910-1989) popularized many similar ideas with his 1936 volume *Language, Truth and Logic*. This small book acquainted many with the "verification principle." According to this standard, a meaningful statement was either analytic—a statement expressing a necessary truth known strictly a priori (as in deductive logic, mathematics or tautological statements)— or empirically verifiable (such as many scientific statements). Any statements that could not be deemed meaningful by one or the other of these standards were counted as altogether meaningless pseudostatements because they were incapable of the requisite verification.[15]

Early positivists, applying this criterion, judged that there was no room for the disciplines of theology or normative ethics, or for the study of traditional topics in the philosophy of religion and metaphysics. The subject of miracles, accordingly, was judged unfit for serious philosophical discussion and analysis. Religious discourse and inquiry were sealed off from scholarly discussion, since these activities did not conform to the requisite standard of meaningfulness.[16]

Positivism, however, soon suffered several debilitating setbacks within philosophical ranks. One problem in particular plagued the postivist method: its own verification principle was self-referentially defeating. That is, the principle itself could not be counted as meaningful on its own terms, since the statement expressing the principle was neither empirically verifiable nor analytically true![17] As a result, many philosophers who still thought that positivism had made beneficial contributions to the enterprise of epistemology turned to less rigid applications of the verificationist criterion. Others dispensed with the positivist criterion altogether, replacing it with more realistic and practicable principles for the rational regulation of belief. Today much work in philosophy is devoted to the problem of improving our stock of beliefs, or exercising responsibility in our belief-forming practices, or meeting our obligations as seekers of truth.[18]

There is currently no consensus among contemporary philosophers regarding the significance and evidential value of the concept of miracles. While every conceivable position is represented by some philosopher or other, attempts to defend belief in the existence of God, the reality of miracles and personal immortality have been vigorously resumed by many.[19] The founding of the large and influential Society of Christian Philosophers in 1978 illustrates the resurgence of Christian philosophy in recent decades. Theological topics "banned" under the aegis of positivism now enjoy frank discussion and forthright defense by avowedly orthodox philosophers who are prominent in the American Philosophical Association. The subject of miracles is favored with fruitful discussion, much of it in support of a traditional Christian understanding of these supernatural events.[20]

Historical Trends

A half-century before the logical positivism of the Vienna Circle, a different sort of positivism had infiltrated the discipline of historiography.[21] This version emphasized painstaking analysis and objective research, and was believed to culminate in the discovery of the hard, cold facts of history. It was thought that by strict adherence to the available data, the past could be reconstructed in the same unbiased fashion that was practiced in the other sciences. Some even believed that there were historical laws just as surely as there were other natural laws.

Leading the positivist charge was German historian Leopold von Ranke (1795-1886), who held that the study of history was a science and that it therefore needed to employ scientific methods suitably adapted to its own subject matter. Von Ranke boldly envisioned the reconstruction of the past in exact terms, without interference from prejudice or other subjective biases.

By the end of the nineteenth century, however, a relativist tendency began to sweep historical studies, in strict opposition to this objectivist trend. Over against positivism, this later emphasis was characteristically embedded in philosophical idealism, often explicitly associated with the traditions of Immanuel Kant and G. W. F. Hegel (1770-1831). Over the next few decades this more recent movement criticized the view that historical inquiry was a science. Wilhelm Dilthey (1833-1911) was an early proponent of this emerging position.

In contrast to positivism, the new outlook not only enumerated several differences between historical and scientific techniques but also emphasized the more subjective role of the historian. Factors such as one's personal preferences, preconceptions, moral opinions and overall worldview were thought to contribute much more to the writing of history than was previously believed. And while it was thought that history could often be reconstructed in factual terms, especially where historians of differing views agreed, the interpretation of past events was regarded as a realm where the subjective tendencies were paramount. One prominent trend among historians such as Benedetto Croce (1866-1952) and Robin Collingwood (1889-1943) was to view all history as contemporary, to be relived in the modern historian's own thoughts.[22]

Since the middle of the current century, a kind of synthesis has taken place, with historians pursuing the facts of the past by utilizing the more objective tools of historical research on the one hand, while also attempting to take seriously the limitations imposed by various sorts of subjective factors on the other hand. Thus, always mindful of the limiting influence of contemporary cultural biases and preoccupations, as well as other considerations that restrict the perception of historical reality, it is now widely agreed that historians may fruitfully investigate the past and make reasonable (if sometimes provisional) judgments about what really happened.[23]

The question of miracles has not generally been directly considered in this specific debate about historical practice. But certainly there are major ramifications here for any thesis that encourages the examination of the past in order to determine whether reliable data point to such events in history. One large question is whether this discipline can undertake the investigation of alleged miracles in a responsible manner.

Critical Approaches to Miracles

Springing directly from theological, philosophical and historiographical trends like those delineated above are a number of critical attitudes toward miracles that deserve independent discussion. Six such approaches will be set forth in this section. These responses to the miracle question often are made by more than one group, and there is some evidence of overlap between them. The critical approaches set forth here are addressed in various places throughout this volume.

Miracles rationalized. One of the most common responses to miracle claims is to attempt to explain them away. As long as there have been miracle reports, there have been efforts to provide thoroughly naturalistic explanations for the alleged supernatural elements of these reports.

Often the scenario for the nonsupernatural portion of a report is readily accepted, but elaborate descriptions of "what really happened" are imposed on the more contentious "miraculous" material.

Miracles as myth. A more radical approach, frequently the reverse of the previous position, is to question the entire report in which a miracle claim is embedded. In other words, not only the miracle component of a tradition but even the surrounding so-called historical material is seen as something other than an accurate, historical description. Often the supposition is that mythology is the telling of seemingly factual events in terms that could not otherwise be expressed without resorting to transcendent terminology, especially in ancient cultures.

Miracles and sense experience. Most would agree that empirical data are needed to reach reliable conclusions about scientific and historical matters. But some researchers insist on the more radical claim that *only* the evidence of empirical facts is admissible in the assessment of scientific and historical theories. Miracle claims are expected to meet this same restrictive and ultimately specious standard. Such an approach is occasionally combined with the suggestion that while the historian's discipline is an excellent vehicle for seeking knowledge about the past, this discipline must resist investigations of the supernatural, since there can be no empirical access to it.

Miracles and interpretation. It has also been popular to assert, in contrast to the previous view, that even when the data of the past can be known, the correct *interpretation* of historical facts may not be. And to know the actual significance of an event regarded by some to be a miracle is doubly difficult, for both factual and interpretive reasons. Miracles are, by definition, acts of God. But to know the mind of God or his purposes is the most challenging interpretive activity in which a scholar could engage.

Miracles and faith. Regardless of whether or not we can have knowledge of the past, some hold that historical information is irrelevant to the act of faith. No proof of any kind can justify the sort of belief required for the religious life, which is a private, inward, subjective affair. It is sometimes claimed that faith is opposed to evidence, and perhaps even opposed to a factual basis of any sort. Faith, properly speaking, launches out into the unknown, stepping out without a known foundation.

Miracles and evidence. A final approach emphasizes the value of evidence in assessing miracle claims. Many scholars think that in some sense philosophical arguments and/or historical evidence can (or should) be offered in favor of miracles. One version of this approach maintains that the evidence is great enough to establish a strong probability for miracles (or for a particular miracle), even for interested unbelievers who are willing to look at the data. Others hold that belief in miracles is at least rational, whether or not there is enough evidence to compel assent.

These six contemporary attitudes toward the subject of miracles coincide with a wide variety of critical positions, both scholarly and popular. Keeping them in view, as well as the trends that preceded them, will be useful in following the discussion of miracles in this volume.

The Organization of the Book

Many individuals have been commissioned to prepare chapters for this volume. In order to forestall the impression that the contributions are arranged haphazardly, we include the following explanation of their order. It would doubtless be possible to benefit from this book without reading the chapters in consecutive order. Nevertheless, there is a logic to the sequence that the reader should be aware of. The placement of each chapter reflects the natural ordering of topics, and it also advances the argument here developed on behalf of miracles.

The chapters of part one introduce the reader to the problem of miracles by letting two famous antagonists present the case against miracles. Writing in the eighteenth century, David Hume boldly confessed:

I flatter myself, that I have discovered an argument of a like nature, which, if just, will, with the wise and learned, be an everlasting check to all kinds of superstitious delusion, and consequently, will be useful as long as the world endures. For so long, I presume, will the accounts of miracles and prodigies be found in all history, sacred and profane.[24]

Hume's influence on the contemporary attitude toward miracles cannot be overstated. As American philosopher C. S. Peirce observed, "The whole of modern 'higher criticism' of ancient history in general, and of Biblical history in particular, is based upon the same logic that is used by Hume."[25] Chapter one is an unabridged reprint of Hume's essay "Of Miracles," first published in 1748 as Section X of his *Philosophical Essays Concerning the Human Understanding* (better known by its 1758 title, *An Enquiry Concerning Human Understanding*). This selection is the most widely reprinted piece of literature on miracles of all time. There is a notable tendency among contemporary critics of miracles to rehabilitate arguments first launched by Hume over two centuries ago. That is only one indication that Hume's essay constitutes a remarkably complete summary of the polemic against miracles. Any reflective person prepared to read the other chapters in this book should therefore be familiar with Hume's own brief "treatise" on miracles.[26]

Hume's negative evaluation of miracles is extended by contemporary British philosopher Antony Flew in chapter two. While Flew does not hesitate to criticize Hume when he thinks the arguments are misguided, he also is quite generous in his praise for the genius of Hume's attack on miracles. In Flew, David Hume has found an influential twentieth-century voice. The material in chapter two updates Flew's extensive critical work on miracles. In many respects, the chapters by Hume and Flew set the agenda for the rest of the book. The chapters in parts two through four develop a systematic case for miracles that can be regarded as a collective response to the challenge thrown down in part one. The chapters in part two deal primarily with conceptual issues, including the definition and possibility of miracles. Several of these chapters interact explicitly and in detail with the arguments of chapters one and two.

No adequate exploration of the topic can begin without a thorough investigation of the concept of a miracle. In chapter three, Richard Purtill identifies several defining features of a miracle and examines the crucial relationship between a miracle and the laws of nature. He explains why influential definitions proposed by David Hume and Alastair McKinnon are inadequate. Purtill concludes by describing the theoretical advantages of a theistic understanding of natural laws over the perspective of metaphysical naturalism (the view that there is nothing outside of nature).

Whereas Purtill focuses on Hume's definition of miracle—and on one question-begging argument against miracles implicit in Hume's definition—Norman Geisler presents a thorough critique of Hume's argument that belief in miracles is irrational because miracles are, by definition, too rare to overcome the evidence of experienced regularities. Geisler's essay in chapter four also responds to Flew's contention that repeatable events have greater evidential value than nonrepeatable events and that miracles are therefore devoid of evidential value.

Every historian knows about "the mischief wrought by time."[27] The accurate reconstruction of the past from data available in the present is always a tricky business. But the challenge is compounded when the object of historical inquiry is an alleged miracle of great religious significance. In chapter five, Francis Beckwith considers the question, Can history be inspected for the occurrence of miracles? He begins with an examination of two arguments about the historian's craft. One argument is that since miracles refer to the agency of a supernatural being and a supernatural being is empirically inaccessible, it transcends the limits of properly historical investigation to conclude that a miracle has happened. The other argument requires a subjectivist conception of the historian's practice, according to which all historical judgments are relativized to the historian's own subjective evaluations of the meaning and importance of alleged events of history.

Beckwith then sympathetically weighs the claim that belief in the past occurrence of a miracle requires greater evidence than belief in the past occurrence of ordinary events. He is careful, however, to point out that the threshold of evidence appropriate for belief in past miracles is not in principle unattainable. Finally, he examines a worry that was famously articulated by Ernst Troeltsch (1865-1923) and has more recently been emphasized by Antony Flew: if no miracle could be identified in the present, then there can be no basis for judging that a miracle occurred in the past.

The very specific difficulty of identifying a miracle, whether past or present, is the focus of chapter six, written by Winfried Corduan. Having a satisfactory definition of miracle should not be confused with having a reliable method for determining whether a given event is or was a miracle. The concept of a miracle may be coherent without being exemplified, and the concept of a miracle may be exemplified without being identifiable as a miracle by some human observer. Corduan's criteria for the identification of an act of God in history emphasize the significance and implications of a believer's worldview. He suggests that a religious believer is in a better position than an unbeliever to recognize a bona fide act of God, especially if the unbeliever accepts a naturalistic worldview (according to which miracles are impossible) and the evidence for the reality of a miracle is not strong enough to overcome the naturalistic prejudice. He allows, however, that the evidence that an event is a miracle may be so strong that even the naturalist may be able to identify the event as miraculous. Thus, much depends on (1) the degree of evidence that a miracle has occurred and (2) the specific character of one's worldview.

The relevance of one's worldview for assessing miracle claims is further explored by Ronald Nash in chapter seven. Nash extends the discussion, however, by setting forth the basic features of a worldview and then contrasting the worldviews of theism and metaphysical naturalism in terms of these features. He thus begins the general task of constructing a theistic context for thinking about miracles, which is the central thrust of part three. His chapter includes an argument that metaphysical naturalism is internally inconsistent and is therefore an inadequate general basis for repudiating miracles. While he acknowledges that problems internal to metaphysical naturalism do not entail that theism is true, he observes that a proper appreciation of the weak justification for naturalism should encourage a greater openness to the possibility of rational belief in miracles.

It has been widely assumed, among believers and unbelievers alike, that the concept of a miracle can play no useful role in the practice of science. J. P. Moreland argues in chapter eight that this is a mistake. He extends the earlier discussion of naturalism and miracles by arguing that *methodological* naturalism, no less than metaphysical naturalism, is an unacceptable position. The methodological naturalist holds that all scientifically investigated events must be explained strictly in terms of the operation of natural laws, so that no reference can be made to divine action in order to explain events that occur in the natural world, even by scientists who believe in God.

Central to Moreland's case for "theistic science" is the idea that divine action, like human action, is to be understood in terms of libertarian agency. God's free acts leave scientifically detectable gaps in the natural world—gaps that cannot be eliminated by the procedures of methodological naturalism. Thus, the scientist may, precisely as a scientist interested in explaining events that occur in the natural world, infer that God is the direct agent-cause of at least some of those events. This result is important not only for the practice of science but also for the general problem of identifying certain events as miraculous.

The discussion through chapter eight illustrates the value of natural theology for supporting belief in miracles, but no direct argument for theism is attempted until chapter nine. In this chapter, David Beck sketches an argument for the existence of God that is especially germane to the question, Has God acted in history? Beck observes that any argument for the existence of God that would support the possibility of miracles must be an argument for the existence of a personal agent with sufficient power, intelligence and moral concern to produce a miracle. He then arranges three traditional arguments for the existence of God in linear fashion, with each consecutive argument contributing to an increasingly rich conception of God. Beck concludes that this type of case for theism shows that miracles are *possible*. He leaves open the question whether miracles may be considered *probable* on theism.

One potential repudiation of the claim that miracles are possible, even assuming that theism is true, is the argument that God could not be an agent that causes events to take place in the natural physical and temporal world. The idea is that because God does not have a body and does not exist in time, God cannot be meaningfully thought to act in the physical world at a particular time. Stephen Davis takes up this challenge in chapter ten. Davis develops a model of divine action that makes sense of the possibility of an immaterial and timeless agent acting in the spatio-temporal context of human history.

With chapter eleven a distinct shift takes place. Whereas earlier chapters are concerned with defending the possibility of miracles, Douglas Geivett focuses on two new questions: Are there good reasons to think that miracles have happened? and, Can miracles count as evidence for other religious beliefs? These questions concern the evidential value of miracles, and Geivett describes two very different ways of thinking about this issue.

One approach holds that miracles provide evidence that God exists. According to this approach, if there is good evidence to believe that an event which cannot be explained naturalistically has actually taken place, then that is evidence that the event is a miracle and that God therefore exists. The other approach moves in the other direction, arguing that background evidence that God exists may justify the expectation that God would produce a miracle. This is because a benevolent deity of sufficient power and intelligence can be expected to alleviate features of the human condition by producing a revelation that provides the requisite religious knowledge. Miracles help to confirm that this expectation has been satisfied by a particular candidate revelation.

Even with this decided shift away from questions about the mere possibility of miracles to questions about the actual occurrence of miracles, there is no detailed consideration of evidence for specific miracles until part four. Chapters twelve through sixteen complete this investigation of miracles by focusing on the specific evidence for miracles within the Christian tradition. David Clark begins this task in chapter twelve. He evaluates the claim that because competing religious traditions appeal to the evidential support of miracles, the peculiar miracle claims of a particular religious tradition cannot be used to confirm the truth of that tradition. This is the suggestion that the evidential force of the miracles of one tradition would cancel the evidential force of the miracles of another tradition.

Clark explores the relation between the concept of miracle and the thought structures of the world's various religions, arguing that many religious traditions lack the conceptual space for miracle. He also develops criteria for comparing the relative strength of competing miracle claims within alternative religious perspectives, even when they have room conceptually for miracle. Finally, he suggests that Christianity, with its miracle of the resurrection of Jesus Christ, occupies a superior position epistemically vis-à-vis other religious traditions. This judgment invites close attention to the detailed evidence for the resurrection.

Before this evidence for the crowning miracle of Christianity is considered, however, two other miracles of the Christian tradition are brought into focus: fulfilled prophecy and the Incarnation. As Stuart Hackett has remarked, "An unusually provocative subset of the miraculous in general confronts us in the phenomenon associated with predictive prophecy."[28] This is confirmed by the sampling of evidence for fulfilled prophecy conducted by Robert Newman in chapter thirteen. To be sure, fulfilled predictions are a type of miracle. First there is the prediction and then there is the fulfillment. But what precisely is the miraculous component of a fulfilled prediction? Both the prediction and the fulfillment are needed in order to identify the operation of divine agency and conclude that a miracle has occurred. We should not conclude that a miracle had happened if the predictive component was not complemented by fulfillment; and certainly no event could count as "fulfillment" if the event was not first "pre-dicted." In some sense, then, it is the combination of prediction and fulfillment that constitutes the phenomenon of fulfilled prophecy as miraculous.

It is possible, however, that both the prediction and the fulfillment are discrete miraculous events. First, if the predictive "insight" is itself caused by God—such that the prophet's knowledge of future events is not the result of the operation of human cognitive faculties—then the foresight of the prophet, quite apart from the fulfillment of his prophecy, would itself be miraculous, though the procurement of such knowledge about the future could not be identified as a miracle without the fulfillment.[29]

Second, the fulfillment of the prophet's predictive message may be miraculous, even if the prophet did have some purely human faculty of predictive insight. Such fulfillment would be most easily identifiable as miraculous in those cases where, as Newman says, the detailed fulfillment of the prediction could not have been staged by clever human actors. While both the prediction (or knowledge) of future events and their fulfillment may require explanation in terms of miracle, Newman concentrates on the fulfillment aspect. He considers three classes of fulfilled prophecies: (1) historical parables, such as the prophet Hosea's marriage to Gomer, which functioned as a large-scale object lesson describing God's covenant relationship with Israel and Israel's future in relation to that covenant; (2) "twin cities prophecies" that allow a comparison of the historical destinies of two ancient cities mentioned together in the same passage of Scripture (for example, Tyre and Sidon, Babylon and Nineveh, Memphis and Thebes, Ekron and Ashkelon); and (3) prophecies concerning the Messiah of Israel fulfilled in the historical figure Jesus of Nazareth.

Newman's arrangement of material is important. For if the fulfillment of messianic prophecy by Jesus is the crucial test case for fulfilled prophecy,[30] then one must answer the charge that Israel's doctrine of the Messiah does not anticipate literal fulfillment in a future historical figure like Jesus.[31] To the degree that a prejudice against the miraculous nature of fulfilled prophecy lies behind this charge, the objection may be rebutted by appealing to evidence for other types of fulfilled prophecy (such as the "twin cities" fulfillments).

Since Newman's chapter focuses on the evidence of fulfillment and not on epistemological questions about fulfilled prophecy, we make two additional observations. First, the fulfillment of predictive prophecy is empirical evidence against the a priori claim that even divine knowledge of future contingents (including counterfactuals of human freedom) is impossible. Thus, any argument for this impossibility must respond to the counterexamples embodied in evidence of fulfilled prophecy.

Second, there are at least three values peculiar to fulfilled prophecy construed as miraculous: (1) it confirms God's production of a revelation for humanity in the Old and New Testaments, (2) it confirms God's sovereign involvement in historical contingencies affecting individuals and nations in considerable detail, and (3) it builds confidence in God's Word about future events that remain to be fulfilled (for example, the Second Coming of Jesus Christ and the general resurrection of both believers and unbelievers). These promises ought to be taken seriously and their personal significance weighed carefully in light of the past fulfillment in detail of prophecy recorded centuries earlier.

Turning to the doctrine of the Incarnation of Jesus Christ in chapter fourteen, John Feinberg argues that the classical Chalcedonian formulation regarding the two natures of Jesus Christ is coherent. While he does not attempt to produce evidence that this traditional doctrine of the Incarnation is true, he does seek to demonstrate that a plausible account of the doctrine can be spelled out. Feinberg relies heavily on the work of Christian philosopher Thomas V. Morris, adopting his two-minds thesis but revising his position on Jesus' temptation as a man.

In chapter fifteen, William Lane Craig presents the historical evidence for the empty tomb of Jesus and shows how this evidence supports belief in the resurrection of Jesus from the dead. Craig begins with the evidence for the historicity of the burial tradition. He then turns to the historicity of the empty-tomb tradition, marshaling no fewer than six independent arguments that support this tradition. He concludes with a careful consideration of the question, If the tomb of Jesus was found empty, how did this situation come to be? Naturalistic replies are discovered to be wholly inadequate.

The case for the resurrection of Jesus is further strengthened by the material presented by Gary Habermas on the postresurrection appearances of Jesus in chapter sixteen. Habermas produces nine lines of evidence for the historicity of the resurrection appearances reported in the New Testament. Four of these derive from the historically reliable testimony of the apostle Paul; the other five consist in independent corroborations of Paul's testimony. It is argued that Jesus did appear alive again to his followers after his death and that these were bodily appearances in the most literal sense. Throughout this chapter, emphasis is placed on the historical support for these claims.

As the reader can see from this survey of the contents, close consideration has been given in this book to the sequencing of chapters. This arrangement was part of the original conception of this project, and the authors for each chapter were commissioned because of their expertise in each case. We count it a great privilege to have worked so closely with such fine scholars and experienced authors. We recognize that each chapter is the result of many years of careful scholarship, and we are grateful for the valuable contributions of these faithful individuals.

Our families also deserve special acknowledgment here. As authors and editors of past publications, we have had occasion before to praise them for the extra measure of support they have provided. This time around, however, the strength of family has been particularly meaningful to us. Finally, we wish to thank those who helped in the production of the manuscript—John Bloom, Marti Chavarria, Carolyn Crawford, Jim Hoover and others at IVP, Jeff Lehman, Steve Porter and Dan Yim.

PART 1
THE CASE
AGAINST
MIRACLES

ONE

OF MIRACLES[1]

DAVID HUME
(d. 1776)

Part 1

There is, in Dr. Tillotson's writings, an argument against the *real presence*, which is as concise, and elegant, and strong as any argument can possibly be supposed against a doctrine, so little worthy of a serious refutation. It is acknowledged on all hands, says that learned prelate, that the authority, either of the scripture or of tradition, is founded merely in the testimony of the apostles, who were eyewitnesses to those miracles of our Savior, by which he proved his divine mission. Our evidence, then, for the truth of the *Christian* religion is less than the evidence for the truth of our senses; because, even in the first authors of our religion, it was no greater; and it is evident it must diminish in passing from them to their disciples; nor can any one rest such confidence in their testimony, as in the immediate object of his senses. But a weaker evidence can never destroy a stronger; and therefore, were the doctrine of the real presence ever so clearly revealed in scripture, it were directly contrary to the rules of just reasoning to give our assent to it. It contradicts sense, though both the scripture and tradition, on which it is supposed to be built, carry not such evidence with them as sense; when they are considered merely as external evidences, and are not brought home to every one's breast, by the immediate operation of the Holy Spirit.

Nothing is so convenient as a decisive argument of this kind, which must at least *silence* the most arrogant bigotry and superstition, and free us from their impertinent solicitations. I flatter myself, that I have discovered an argument of a like nature, which, if just, will, with the wise and learned, be an everlasting check to all kinds of superstitious delusion, and consequently, will be useful as long as the world endures. For so long, I presume, will the accounts of miracles and prodigies be found in all history, sacred and profane.

Though experience be our only guide in reasoning concerning matters of fact; it must be acknowledged, that this guide is not altogether infallible, but in some cases is apt to lead us into errors. One, who in our climate, should expect better weather in any week of June than in one of December, would reason justly, and conformably to experience; but it is certain, that he may happen, in the event, to find himself mistaken. However, we may observe, that, in such a case, he would have no cause to complain of experience; because it commonly informs us beforehand of the uncertainty, by that contrariety of events, which we may learn from a diligent observation. All effects follow not with like certainty from their supposed causes. Some events are found, in all countries and all ages, to have been constantly conjoined together: Others are found to have been more variable, and sometimes to disappoint our expectations; so that, in our reasonings concerning matter of fact, there are all imaginable degrees of assurance, from the highest certainty to the lowest species of moral evidence.

A wise man, therefore, proportions his belief to the evidence. In such conclusions as are founded on an infallible experience, he expects the event with the last degree of assurance, and regards his past experience as a full *proof* of the future existence of that event. In other cases, he proceeds with more caution: He weighs the opposite experiments: He considers which side is supported by the greater number of experiments: to that side he inclines, with doubt and hesitation; and when at last he fixes his judgment, the evidence exceeds not what we properly call *probability*. All probability, then, supposes an opposition of experiments and observations, where the one side is found to overbalance the other, and to produce a degree of evidence, proportioned to the superiority. A hundred instances or experiments on one side, and fifty on another, afford a doubtful expectation of any event; though a hundred uniform experiments, with only one that is contradictory, reasonably beget a pretty strong degree of assurance. In all cases, we must balance the opposite experiments, where they are opposite, and deduct the smaller number from the greater, in order to know the exact force of the superior evidence.

To apply these principles to a particular instance; we may observe, that there is no species of reasoning more common, more useful, and even necessary to human life, than that which is derived from the testimony of men, and the reports of eyewitnesses and spectators. This species of reasoning, perhaps, one may deny to be founded on the relation of cause and effect. I shall not dispute about a word. It will be sufficient to observe that our assurance in any argument of this kind is derived from no other principle than our observation of the veracity of human testimony, and of the usual conformity of facts to the reports of witnesses. It being a general maxim, that no objects have any discoverable connection together, and that all the inferences, which we can draw from one to another, are founded merely on our experience of their constant and regular conjunction; it is evident, that we ought not to make an exception to this maxim in favor of human testimony, whose connection with any event seems, in itself, as little necessary as any other. Were not the memory tenacious to a certain degree; had not men commonly an inclination to truth and a principle of probity; were they not sensible to shame, when detected in a falsehood: Were not these, I say, discovered by *experience* to be qualities, inherent in human nature, we should never repose the least confidence in human testimony. A man delirious, or noted for falsehood and villainy, has no manner of authority with us.

And as the evidence, derived from witnesses and human testimony, is founded on past experience, so it varies with the experience, and is regarded either as a *proof* or a *probability*, according as the conjunction between any particular kind of report and any kind of object has been found to be constant or variable. There are a number of circumstances to be taken into consideration in all judgments of this kind; and the ultimate standard, by which we determine all disputes, that may arise concerning them, is always derived from experience and observation. Where this experience is not entirely uniform on any side, it is attended with an unavoidable contrariety in our judgments, and with the same opposition and mutual destruction of argument as in every other kind of evidence. We frequently hesitate concerning the reports of others. We balance the opposite circumstances, which cause any doubt or uncertainty; and when we discover a superiority on any side, we incline to it; but still with a diminution of assurance, in proportion to the force of its antagonist.

This contrariety of evidence, in the present case, may be derived from several different causes; from the opposition of contrary testimony; from the character or number of the witnesses; from the manner of their delivering their testimony; or from the union of all these circumstances. We entertain a suspicion concerning any matter of fact, when the witnesses contradict each other; when they are but few, or of a doubtful character; when they have an interest in what they affirm; when they deliver their testimony with hesitation, or on the contrary, with too violent asseverations. There are many other particulars of the same kind, which may diminish or destroy the force of any argument, derived from human testimony.

Suppose, for instance, that the fact, which the testimony endeavors to establish, partakes of the extraordinary and the marvelous; in that case, the evidence, resulting from the testimony, admits of a diminution, greater or less, in proportion as the fact is more or less unusual. The reason why we place any credit in witnesses and historians, is not derived from any *connection,* which we perceive *a priori,* between testimony and reality, but because we are accustomed to find a conformity between them. But when the fact attested is such a one as has seldom fallen under our observation, here is a contest of two opposite experiences; of which the one destroys the other, as far as its force goes, and the superior can only operate on the mind by the force, which remains. The very same principle of experience, which gives us a certain degree of assurance in the testimony of witnesses, gives us also, in this case, another degree of assurance against the fact, which they endeavor to establish; from which contradiction there necessarily arises a counterpoise, and mutual destruction of belief and authority.

I should not believe such a story were it told me by Cato, was a proverbial saying in Rome, even during the lifetime of that philosophical patriot.[2] The incredibility of a fact, it was allowed, might invalidate so great an authority.

The Indian prince, who refused to believe the first relations concerning the effects of frost, reasoned justly; and it naturally required very strong testimony to engage his assent to facts, that arose from a state of nature, with which he was unacquainted, and which bore so little analogy to those events, of which he had had constant and uniform experience. Though they were not contrary to his experience, they were not conformable to it.[3]

But in order to increase the probability against the testimony of witnesses, let us suppose, that the fact, which they affirm, instead of being only marvelous, is really miraculous; and suppose also, that the testimony considered apart and in itself, amounts to an entire proof; in that case, there is proof against proof, of which the strongest must prevail, but still with a diminution of its force, in proportion to that of its antagonist.

A miracle is a violation of the laws of nature; and as a firm and unalterable experience has established these laws, the proof against a miracle, from the very nature of the fact, is as entire as any argument from experience can possibly be imagined. Why is it more than probable, that all men must die; that lead cannot, of itself, remain suspended in the air; that fire consumes wood, and is extinguished by water; unless it be, that these events are found agreeable to the laws of nature, and there is required a violation of these laws, or in other words, a miracle to prevent them? Nothing is esteemed a miracle, if it ever happen in the common course of nature. It is no miracle that a man, seemingly in good health, should die on a sudden: because such a kind of death, though more unusual than any other, has yet been frequently observed to happen. But it is a miracle, that a dead man should come to life; because that has never been observed in any age or country. There must, therefore, be a uniform experience against every miraculous event, otherwise the event would not merit that appellation. And as a uniform experience amounts to a proof, there is here a direct and full *proof*, from the nature of the fact, against the existence of any miracle; nor can such a proof be destroyed, or the miracle rendered credible, but by an opposite proof, which is superior.[4]

The plain consequence is (and it is a general maxim worthy of our attention), "That no testimony is sufficient to establish a miracle, unless the testimony be of such a kind, that its falsehood would be more miraculous, than the fact, which it endeavors to establish; and even in that case there is a mutual destruction of arguments, and the superior only gives us an assurance suitable to that degree of force, which remains, after deducting the inferior." When anyone tells me, that he saw a dead man restored to life, I immediately consider with myself, whether it be more probable, that this person should either deceive or be deceived, or that the fact, which he relates, should really have happened. I weigh the one miracle against the other; and according to the superiority, which I discover, I pronounce my decision, and always reject the greater miracle. If the falsehood of his testimony would be more miraculous, than the event which he relates; then, and not till then, can he pretend to command my belief or opinion.

Part II

In the foregoing reasoning we have supposed, that the testimony, upon which a miracle is founded, may possibly amount to an entire proof, and that the falsehood of that testimony would be a real prodigy: But it is easy to show, that we have been a great deal too liberal in our concession, and that there never was a miraculous event established on so full an evidence.

For *first*, there is not to be found, in all history, any miracle attested by a sufficient number of men, of such unquestioned good sense, education, and learning, as to secure us against all delusion in themselves; of such undoubted integrity, as to place them beyond all suspicion of any design to deceive others; of such credit and reputation in the eyes of mankind, as to have a great deal to lose in case of their being detected in any falsehood; and at the same time, attesting facts performed in such a public manner and in so celebrated a part of the world, as to render the detection unavoidable: All which circumstances are requisite to give us a full assurance in the testimony of men.

Secondly. We may observe in human nature a principle which, if strictly examined, will be found to diminish extremely the assurance, which we might, from human testimony, have, in any kind of prodigy. The maxim, by which we commonly conduct ourselves in our reasonings, is, that the objects, of which we have no experience, resemble those, of which we have; that what we have found to be most usual is always most probable; and that where there is an opposition of arguments, we ought to give the preference to such as are founded on the greatest number of past observations. But though, in proceeding by this rule, we readily reject any fact which is unusual and incredible in an ordinary degree; yet in advancing farther, the mind observes not always the same rule; but when anything is affirmed utterly absurd and miraculous, it rather the more readily admits of such a fact, upon account of that very circumstance, which ought to destroy all its authority. The passion of *surprise* and *wonder*, arising from miracles, being an agreeable emotion, gives a sensible tendency toward the belief of those events, from which it is derived. And this goes so far, that even those who cannot enjoy this pleasure immediately, nor can believe those miraculous events, of which they are informed, yet love to partake of the satisfaction at second-hand or by rebound, and place a pride and delight in exciting the admiration of others.

With what greediness are the miraculous accounts of travelers received, their descriptions of sea and land monsters, their relations of wonderful adventures, strange men, and uncouth manners? But if the spirit of religion join itself to the love of wonder, there is an end of common sense; and human testimony, in these circumstances, loses all pretensions to authority. A religionist may be an enthusiast, and imagine he sees what has no reality: he may know his narrative to be false, and yet persevere in it, with the best intentions in the world, for the sake of promoting so holy a cause: or even where this delusion has not place, vanity, excited by so strong a temptation, operates on him more powerfully than on the rest of mankind in any other circumstances; and self-interest with equal force. His auditors may not have, and commonly have not, sufficient judgment to canvass his evidence: what judgment they have, they renounce by principle, in these sublime and mysterious subjects: or if they were ever so willing to employ it, passion and a heated imagination disturb the regularity of its operations. Their credulity increases his impudence: and his impudence overpowers their credulity.

Eloquence, when at its highest pitch, leaves little room for reason or reflection; but addressing itself entirely to the fancy or the affections, captivates the willing hearers, and subdues their understanding. Happily, this pitch it seldom attains. But what a Tully or a Demosthenes could scarcely effect over a Roman or Athenian audience, every *Capuchin*, every itinerant or stationary teacher can perform over the generality of mankind, and in a higher degree, by touching such gross and vulgar passions.

The many instances of forged miracles, and prophecies, and supernatural events, which, in all ages, have either been detected by contrary evidence, or which detect themselves by their absurdity, prove sufficiently the strong propensity of mankind to the extraordinary and the marvelous, and ought reasonably to beget a suspicion against all relations of this kind. This is our natural way of thinking, even with regard to the most common and most credible events. For instance: There is no kind of report which rises so easily, and spreads so quickly, especially in country places and provincial towns, as those concerning marriages; insomuch that two young persons of equal condition never see each other twice, but the whole neighborhood immediately join them together. The pleasure of telling a piece of news so interesting, of propagating it, and of being the first reporters of it, spreads the intelligence. And this is so well known, that no man of sense gives attention to these reports, till he find them confirmed by some greater evidence. Do not the same passions, and others still stronger, incline the generality of mankind to believe and report, with the greatest vehemence and assurance, all religious miracles?

Thirdly. It forms a strong presumption against all supernatural and miraculous relations, that they are observed chiefly to abound among ignorant and barbarous nations; or if a civilized people has ever given admission to any of them, that people will be found to have received them from ignorant and barbarous ancestors, who transmitted them with that inviolable sanction and authority, which always attend received opinions. When we peruse the first histories of all nations, we are apt to imagine ourselves transported into some new world; where the whole frame of nature is disjointed, and every element performs its operations in a different manner, from what it does at present. Battles, revolutions, pestilence, famine and death, are never the effect of those natural causes, which we experience. Prodigies, omens, oracles, judgments, quite obscure the few natural events, that are intermingled with them. But as the former grow thinner every page, in proportion as we advance nearer the enlightened ages, we soon learn, that there is nothing mysterious or supernatural in the case, but that all proceeds from the usual propensity of mankind toward the marvelous, and that, though this inclination may at intervals receive a check from sense and learning, it can never be thoroughly extirpated from human nature.

It is strange, a judicious reader is apt to say, upon the perusal of these wonderful historians, *that such prodigious events never happen in our days.* But it is nothing strange, I hope, that men should lie in all ages. You must surely have seen instances enough of that frailty. You have yourself heard many such marvelous relations started, which, being treated with scorn by all the wise and judicious, have at last been abandoned even by the vulgar. Be assured, that those renowned lies, which have spread and flourished to such a monstrous height, arose from like beginnings; but being sown in a more proper soil, shot up at last into prodigies almost equal to those which they relate.

It was a wise policy in that the false prophet, Alexander, who though now forgotten, was once so famous, to lay the first scene of his impostures in Paphlagonia, where, as Lucian tells us, the people were extremely ignorant and stupid, and ready to swallow even the grossest delusion. People at a distance, who are weak enough to think the matter at all worth enquiry, have no opportunity of receiving better information. The stories come magnified to them by a hundred circumstances. Fools are industrious in propagating the imposture; while the wise and learned are contented, in general, to deride its absurdity, without informing themselves of the particular facts, by which it may be distinctly refuted. And thus the impostor above mentioned was enabled to proceed, from his ignorant Paphlagonians, to the enlisting of votaries, even among the Grecian philosophers, and men of the most eminent rank and distinction in Rome: nay, could engage the attention of that sage emperor Marcus Aurelius; so far as to make him trust the success of a military expedition to his delusive prophecies.

The advantages are so great, of starting an imposture among an ignorant people, that, even though the delusion should be too gross to impose on the generality of them *(which, though seldom, is sometimes the case)* it has a much better chance for succeeding in remote countries, than if the first scene had been laid in a city renowned for arts and knowledge. The most ignorant and barbarous of these barbarians carry the report abroad. None of their countrymen have a large correspondence, or sufficient credit and authority to contradict and beat down the delusion. Men's inclination to the marvelous has full opportunity to display itself. And thus a story, which is universally exploded in the place where it was first started, shall pass for certain at a thousand miles distance. But had Alexander fixed his residence at Athens, the philosophers of that renowned mart of learning had immediately spread, throughout the whole Roman empire, their sense of the matter; which, being supported by so great authority, and displayed by all the force of reason and eloquence, had entirely opened the eyes of mankind. It is true; Lucian, passing by chance through Paphlagonia, had an opportunity of performing this good office. But, though much to be wished, it does not always happen, that every Alexander meets with a Lucian, ready to expose and detect his impostures.

I may add as a *fourth* reason, which diminishes the authority of prodigies, that there is no testimony for any, even those which have not been expressly detected, that is not opposed by an infinite number of witnesses; so that not only the miracle destroys the credit of testimony, but the testimony destroys itself. To make this the better understood, let us consider, that, in matters of religion, whatever is different is contrary; and that it is impossible the religions of ancient Rome, of Turkey, of Siam, and of China should, all of them, be established on any solid foundation. Every miracle, therefore, pretended to have been wrought in any of these religions (and all of them abound in miracles), as its direct scope is to establish the particular system to which it is attributed; so has it the same force, though more indirectly, to overthrow every other system. In destroying a rival system, it likewise destroys the credit of those miracles, on which that system was established; so that all the prodigies of different religions are to be regarded as contrary facts, and the evidences of these prodigies, whether weak or strong, as opposite to each other. According to this method of reasoning, when we believe any miracle of Mahomet or his successors, we have for our warrant the testimony of a few barbarous Arabians: And on the other hand, we are to regard the authority of Titus Livius, Plutarch, Tacitus, and, in short, of all the authors and witnesses, Grecian, Chinese, and Roman Catholic, who have related any miracle in their particular religion; I say, we are to regard their testimony in the same light as if they had mentioned that Mohammedan miracle, and had in express terms contradicted it, with the same certainty as they have for the miracle they relate. This argument may appear over subtle and refined; but is not in reality different from the reasoning of a judge, who supposes, that the credit of two witnesses, maintaining a crime against any one, is destroyed by the testimony of two others, who affirm him to have been two hundred leagues distant, at the same instant when the crime is said to have been committed.

One of the best attested miracles in all profane history, is that which Tacitus reports of Vespasian, who cured a blind man in Alexandria, by means of his spittle, and a lame man by the mere touch of his foot; in obedience to a vision of the god Serapis, who had enjoined them to have recourse to the Emperor, for these miraculous cures. The story may be seen in that fine historian;[5] where every circumstance seems to add weight to the testimony, and might be displayed at large with all the force of argument and eloquence, if anyone were now concerned to enforce the evidence of that exploded and idolatrous superstition. The gravity, solidity, age, and probity of so great an emperor, who, through the whole course of his life, conversed in a familiar manner with his friends and courtiers, and never affected those extraordinary airs of divinity assumed by Alexander and Demetrius. The historian, a contemporary writer, noted for candor and veracity, and withal, the greatest and most penetrating genius, perhaps, of all antiquity; and so free from any tendency to credulity, that he even lies under the contrary imputation, of atheism and profaneness: The persons, from whose authority he related the miracle, of established character for judgment and veracity, as we may well presume; eyewitnesses of the fact, and confirming their testimony, after the Flavian family was despoiled of the empire, and could no longer give any reward, as the price of a lie *Utrumque, qui interfuere, nunc quoque memorant, postquam nullum mendacio pretium.* To which if we add the public nature of the facts, as related, it will appear, that no evidence can well be supposed stronger for so gross and so palpable a falsehood.

There is also a memorable story related by Cardinal de Retz, which may well deserve our consideration. When that intriguing politician fled into Spain, to avoid the persecution of his enemies, he passed through Saragossa, the capital of Arragon, where he was shown, in the cathedral, a man, who had served seven years as a doorkeeper, and was well known to everybody in town, that had ever paid his devotions at that church. He had been seen, for so long a time, wanting a leg; but recovered that limb by the rubbing of holy oil upon the stump; and the cardinal assures us that he saw him with two legs. This miracle was vouched by all the canons of the church; and the whole company in town were appealed to for a confirmation of the fact; whom the cardinal found, by their zealous devotion, to be thorough believers of the miracle. Here the relater was also contemporary to the supposed prodigy, of an incredulous and libertine character, as well as of great genius; the miracle of so *singular* a nature as could scarcely admit of a counterfeit, and the witnesses very numerous, and all of them, in a manner, spectators of the fact, to which they gave their testimony. And what adds mightily to the force of the evidence, and may double our surprise on this occasion, is, that the cardinal himself, who relates the story, seems not to give any credit to it, and consequently cannot be suspected of any concurrence in the holy fraud. He considered justly, that it was not requisite, in order to reject a fact of this nature, to be able accurately to disprove the testimony, and to trace its falsehood, through all the circumstances of knavery and credulity which produced it. He knew, that, as this was commonly altogether impossible at any small distance of time and place; so was it extremely difficult, even where one was immediately present, by reason of the bigotry, ignorance, cunning, and roguery of a great part of mankind. He therefore concluded, like a just reasoner, that such an evidence carried falsehood upon the very face of it, and that a miracle, supported by any human testimony, was more properly a subject of derision than of argument.

There surely never was a greater number of miracles ascribed to one person, than those, which were lately said to have been wrought in France upon the tomb of Abbé Paris, the famous Jansenist, with whose sanctity the people were so long deluded. The curing of the sick, giving hearing to the deaf, and sight to the blind, were everywhere talked of as the usual effects of that holy sepulcher. But what is more extraordinary; many of the miracles were immediately proved upon the spot, before judges of unquestioned integrity, attested by witnesses of credit and distinction, in a learned age, and on the most eminent theater that is now in the world. Nor is this all: a relation of them was published and dispersed every where; nor were the *Jesuits,* though a learned body, supported by the civil magistrate, and determined enemies to those opinions, in whose favor the miracles were said to have been wrought, ever able distinctly to refute or detect them.[6] Where shall we find such a number of circumstances, agreeing to the corroboration of one fact? And what have we to oppose to such a cloud of witnesses, but the absolute impossibility or miraculous nature of the events, which they relate? And this surely, in the eyes of all reasonable people, will alone be regarded as a sufficient refutation.

Is the consequence just, because some human testimony has the utmost force and authority in some cases, when it relates the battle of Philippi or Pharsalia for instance; that therefore all kinds of testimony must, in all cases, have equal force and authority? Suppose that the Caesarean and Pompeian factions had, each of them, claimed the victory in these battles, and that the historians of each party had uniformly ascribed the advantage to their own side; how could mankind, at this distance, have been able to determine between them? The contrariety is equally strong between the miracles related by Herodotus or Plutarch, and those delivered by Mariana, Bede, or any monkish historian.

The wise lend a very academic faith to every report which favors the passion of the reporter; whether it magnifies his country, his family, or himself, or in any other way strikes in with his natural inclinations and propensities. But what greater temptation than to appear a missionary, a prophet, an ambassador from heaven? Who would not encounter many dangers and difficulties, in order to attain so sublime a character? Or if, by the help of vanity and a heated imagination, a man has first made a convert of himself, and entered seriously into the delusion; who ever scruples to make use of pious frauds, in support of so holy and meritorious a cause?

The smallest spark may here kindle into the greatest flame; because the materials are always prepared for it. The *avidum genus auricularum,*[7] the gazing populace, receive greedily, without examination, whatever soothes superstition, and promotes wonder.

How many stories of this nature have, in all ages, been detected and exploded in their infancy? How many more have been celebrated for a time, and have afterwards sunk into neglect and oblivion? Where such reports, therefore, fly about, the solution of the phenomenon is obvious; and we judge in conformity to regular experience and observation, when we account for it by the known and natural principles of credulity and delusion. And shall we, rather than have a recourse to so natural a solution, allow of a miraculous violation of the most established laws of nature?

I need not mention the difficulty of detecting a falsehood in any private or even public history, at the place, where it is said to happen; much more when the scene is removed to ever so small a distance. Even a court of judicature, with all the authority, accuracy, and judgment, which they can employ, find themselves often at a loss to distinguish between truth and falsehood in the most recent actions. But the matter never comes to any issue, if trusted to the common method of altercation and debate and flying rumors; especially when men's passions have taken part on either side.

In the infancy of new religions, the wise and learned commonly esteem the matter too inconsiderable to deserve their attention or regard. And when afterwards they would willingly detect the cheat, in order to undeceive the deluded multitude, the season is now past, and the records and witnesses, which might clear up the matter, have perished beyond recovery.

No means of detection remain, but those which must be drawn from the very testimony itself of the reporters: and these, though always sufficient with the judicious and knowing, are commonly too fine to fall under the comprehension of the vulgar.

Upon the whole, then, it appears, that no testimony for any kind of miracle has ever amounted to a probability, much less to a proof; and that, even supposing it amounted to a proof, it would be opposed by another proof; derived from the very nature of the fact, which it would endeavor to establish. It is experience only, which gives authority to human testimony; and it is the same experience, which assures us of the laws of nature. When, therefore, these two kinds of experience are contrary, we have nothing to do but subtract the one from the other, and embrace an opinion, either on one side or the other, with that assurance which arises from the remainder. But according to the principle here explained, this subtraction, with regard to all popular religions, amounts to an entire annihilation; and therefore we may establish it as a maxim, that no human testimony can have such force as to prove a miracle, and make it a just foundation for any such system of religion.

I beg the limitations here made may be remarked, when I say, that a miracle can never be proved, so as to be the foundation of a system of religion. For I own, that otherwise, there may possibly be miracles, or violations of the usual course of nature, of such a kind as to admit of proof from human testimony; though, perhaps, it will be impossible to find any such in all the records of history. Thus, suppose, all authors, in all languages, agree, that, from the first of January 1600, there was a total darkness over the whole earth for eight days: suppose that the tradition of this extraordinary event is still strong and lively among the people: that all travelers, who return from foreign countries, bring us accounts of the same tradition, without the least variation or contradiction: it is evident, that our present philosophers, instead of doubting the fact, ought to receive it as certain, and ought to search for the causes whence it might be derived. The decay, corruption, and dissolution of nature, is an event rendered probable by so many analogies, that any phenomenon, which seems to have a tendency toward that catastrophe, comes within the reach of human testimony, if that testimony be very extensive and uniform.

But suppose, that all the historians who treat of England, should agree, that, on the first day of January 1600, Queen Elizabeth died; that both before and after her death she was seen by her physicians and the whole court, as is usual with persons of her rank; that her successor was acknowledged and proclaimed by the parliament; and that, after being interred a month, she again appeared, resumed the throne, and governed England for three years: I must confess that I should be surprised at the concurrence of so many odd circumstances, but should not have the least inclination to believe so miraculous an event. I should not doubt of her pretended death, and of those other public circumstances that followed it: I should only assert it to have been pretended, and that it neither was, nor possibly could be real. You would in vain object to me the difficulty, and almost impossibility of deceiving the world in an affair of such consequence; the wisdom and solid judgment of that renowned queen; with the little or no advantage which she could reap from so poor an artifice: All this might astonish me; but I would still reply, that the knavery and folly of men are such common phenomena, that I should rather believe the most extraordinary events to arise from their concurrence, than admit of so signal a violation of the laws of nature.

But should this miracle be ascribed to any new system of religion; men, in all ages, have been so much imposed on by ridiculous stories of that kind, that this very circumstance would be a full proof of a cheat, and sufficient, with all men of sense, not only to make them reject the fact, but even reject it without further examination. Though the Being to whom the miracle is ascribed, be, in this case, Almighty, it does not, upon that account, become a whit more probable; since it is impossible for us to know the attributes or actions of such a Being, otherwise than from the experience which we have of his productions, in the usual course of nature. This still reduces us to past observation, and obliges us to compare the instances of the violation of truth in the testimony of men, with those of the violation of the laws of nature by miracles, in order to judge which of them is most likely and probable. As the violations of truth are more common in the testimony concerning religious miracles, than in that concerning any other matter of fact; this must diminish very much the authority of the former testimony, and make us form a general resolution, never to lend any attention to it, with whatever specious pretense it may be covered.

Lord Bacon seems to have embraced the same principles of reasoning. "We ought," says he, "to make a collection or particular history of all monsters and prodigious births or productions, and in a word of every thing new, rare, and extraordinary in nature. But this must be done with the most severe scrutiny, lest we depart from truth. Above all, every relation must be considered as suspicious, which depends in any degree upon religion, as the prodigies of Livy: And no less so, every thing that is to be found in the writers of natural magic or alchemy, or such authors, who seem, all of them, to have an unconquerable appetite for falsehood and fable."[8]

I am the better pleased with the method of reasoning here delivered, as I think it may serve to confound those dangerous friends or disguised enemies to the *Christian Religion,* who have undertaken to defend it by the principles of human reason. Our most holy religion is founded on *Faith,* not on reason; and it is a sure method of exposing it to put it to such a trial as it is, by no means, fitted to endure. To make this more evident, let us examine those miracles, related in scripture; and not to lose ourselves in too wide a field, let us confine ourselves to such as we find in the *Pentateuch,* which we shall examine, according to the principles of these pretended Christians, not as the word or testimony of God himself, but as the production of a mere human writer and historian. Here then we are first to consider a book, presented to us by a barbarous and ignorant people, written in an age when they were still more barbarous, and in all probability long after the facts which it relates, corroborated by no concurring testimony, and resembling those fabulous accounts, which every nation gives of its origin. Upon reading this book, we find it full of prodigies and miracles. It gives an account of a state of the world and of human nature entirely different from the present: Of our fall from that state: Of the age of man, extended to near a thousand years: Of the destruction of the world by a deluge: Of the arbitrary choice of one people, as the favorites of heaven; and that people the countrymen of the author: Of their deliverance from bondage by prodigies the most astonishing imaginable: I desire any one to lay his hand upon his heart, and after a serious consideration declare, whether he thinks that the falsehood of such a book, supported by such a testimony, would be more extraordinary and miraculous than all the miracles it relates; which is, however, necessary to make it be received, according to the measures of probability above established.

What we have said of miracles may be applied, without any variation, to prophecies; and indeed, all prophecies are real miracles, and as such only, can be admitted as proofs of any revelation. If it did not exceed the capacity of human nature to foretell future events, it would be absurd to employ any prophecy as an argument for a divine mission or authority from heaven. So that, upon the whole, we may conclude, that the *Christian Religion* not only was at first attended with miracles, but even at this day cannot be believed by any reasonable person without one. Mere reason is insufficient to convince us of its veracity: And whoever is moved by *Faith* to assent to it, is conscious of a continued miracle in his own person, which subverts all the principles of his understanding, and gives him a determination to believe what is most contrary to custom and experience.

TWO

NEO-HUMEAN ARGUMENTS ABOUT THE MIRACULOUS

ANTONY FLEW

DAVID HUME, THE FIRST OF THE TWO GREAT PHILOSOPHERS OF THE eighteenth-century Age of Enlightenment, was also the first thinker of the modern period to develop systematically a world outlook that was thoroughly skeptical, this worldly, and human centered. A friend and admirer of Benjamin Franklin, living just long enough to hear of and to welcome the American Declaration of Independence, Hume was the philosophical founding father of what is in the United States today so widely and so fiercely denounced as "secular humanism."

Our present concern, however, is with only twenty or so pages of all Hume's writings. These pages, reprinted as chapter one in this volume, constitute Section X, entitled "Of Miracles," in *An Enquiry Concerning Human Understanding*. They provoked in Hume's own lifetime more protest and controversy than all the rest of those writings put together. Hume himself, like his contemporary critics, was most interested in "the accounts of miracles and prodigies" found in what in those days people still distinguished as sacred (as opposed to profane) history. Both he and they were above all concerned with the application of his supposed "everlasting check" to accounts of what was believed to be the supremely significant "miracle and prodigy"—the alleged physical resurrection of Jesus bar Joseph, hailed as the Christ.

Miracles and the Rationality of Faith

During the lifetime of Hume and for a century and more thereafter there was a standard, two-stage, systematic program of rational apologetic for the Christian religion.[1] Apologists began by trying to establish, while appealing only to natural reason and secular experience, the existence and certain minimal characteristics of God. From that first conclusion they proceeded to argue that this somewhat sketchy "religion of nature" can and should be supplanted and enriched by a more abundant revelation. This second part of the case for Christianity rested on the contention that there is ample historical evidence to show that the New Testament miracles, including crucially the physical resurrection of Jesus, did actually occur. Since miracles necessarily constitute achievements by exercises of supernatural power of what is naturally impossible, it was argued that these New Testament miracles constitute supernatural endorsements of the teachings thus endorsed.

1. Hume's main purpose in Section X of this *Enquiry*, a purpose in which he believed that he was successful, is to establish that "a miracle can never be proved, so as to be the foundation of a system of religion." This contention threatens to abort the whole project of a rational apologetic for a revealed religion. For there would seem to be no other way of showing that the Christian revelation, or any rival candidate, constitutes an authentic self-revelation of the true God. To serve as the key term in such a demonstration, the word *miracle* has to be construed (as both Hume himself and all his contemporary opponents did construe it) in a very strong sense. It must involve an overriding of a law of nature, a doing of what is known to be naturally impossible by a Power which is, by this very overriding, shown to be supernatural.

Only if this is given can the occurrence of a miracle under the auspices of some particular system of belief constitute an inexpungible divine endorsement of that system. Without appreciating the rationality and the straightforwardness of this approach to the settling of disputes between the protagonists of incompatible sets of religious beliefs, we cannot hope to understand either Hume's insistence that the miracle stories of rival religions must be assessed as not merely different but contrary or the delighted attention that he gives to the then-recent affair of the Abbé Paris. It was precisely and only because both the Jansenists and the Jesuits did accept these principles that both parties were so keen to show, the former that miracles had occurred at that cleric's tomb, and the latter that they had not.

2. In 1870, during the third session of the First Vatican Council, the beliefs that both parts of this two-stage program of rational apologetic could indeed be fulfilled became defined dogmata of the Roman Catholic Church, and hence essential elements of its faith. The canon defining the first part reads:

If anyone shall say, that the one and true God, our creator and Lord, cannot be known for certain through the creation by the natural light of human reason: let them be cast out *[anathema]*.[2]

The canon defining the second part reads:

If anyone shall say, that miracles cannot happen, and hence that all accounts of them, even those contained in holy Scriptures, should be relegated to the category of fables or myths; or that miracles can never be known for certain nor the divine origin of the Christian religion be proved thereby: let them be cast out *[anathema]*.[3]

It is important to recognize—credit where credit is due—the fundamental rationality of this traditional apologetic. It is in this respect so different from many of its degenerate and irrationalist successors. For it is not here proposed to demand faith either against all reason or without sufficient reason both for making any leap of faith at all and for making one particular, approved leap as opposed to all the other available alternatives. Thus, if we turn to chapter six of book one of the *Summa contra Gentiles*[4] we find St. Thomas arguing in Section 1:

Those who place their faith in this truth . . . "for which the human reason offers no experiential evidence" . . . do not believe foolishly, as though following artificial fables (2 Peter 1:16). For these "secrets of divine Wisdom" (Job 11:6) the divine Wisdom itself, which knows all things to the full, has deigned to reveal to men. It reveals its own presence, as well as the truth of its teaching and inspiration, by fitting arguments; and in order to confirm those truths that exceed natural knowledge, it gives visible manifestation to works which surpass the ability of all nature.

In Section 4 of the same chapter St. Thomas goes on to dispose of rival candidate revelations, and in particular Christianity's then and now most formidable contemporary competitor, Islam. Simply plumping for a faith that has not been endorsed by miracles is dismissed as frivolous *(levis):*

On the other hand, those who founded sects committed to erroneous doctrines proceeded in a way that is opposite to this. The point is clear in the case of Mohammed. . . . He did not bring forth any signs produced in a supernatural way, by which alone divine inspiration is appropriately evidenced. . . . On the contrary, Mohammed said that he was sent in the power of his arms—which are signs not lacking to robbers and tyrants. . . . It is thus clear that those who place any faith in his words believe frivolously.

3. At least in my own country appeals to the alleged occurrence of miracles have long since gone out of fashion as evidences to be offered for the authenticity of an allegedly divine self-revelation. Thus, for instance, the 1922 Commission Report on *Doctrine in the Church of England*[5] proclaimed:

It has to be recognized that legends involving abnormal events have tended to grow very easily in regard to great religious leaders, and that in consequence it is impossible in the present state of knowledge to make the same evidential use of the narratives of miracles in the Gospels that appeared possible in the past.

The commission's contention was both right and rational. But it was also, on two counts, rash. In the first place, and more generally, if a candidate is not identifiable as an authentic divine revelation by reference to the occurrence of endorsing miracles, then how else, if at all, is it to be so identified? The second reason for accounting that commission contention rash is more particular. It is what used to be called the scandal of particularity. This consists in the fact that Christianity, alone among the great world religions, centers on what is supposed to have happened during a particular period, in a particular country, and upon this particular planet, Earth. The Christian is, in the words of the Apostles' Creed, defined as one who believes "in God the Father Almighty, Maker of heaven and earth: and in Jesus Christ his only Son our Lord, who was conceived by the Holy Ghost, born of the Virgin Mary, suffered under Pontius Pilate, was crucified, dead, and buried," and who on "the third day . . . rose again from the dead."

The scandalous particularity consists here in the fact that one particular alleged miracle, occurring at one particular time and place on one particular planet, is not just one part of the evidence for identifying Christianity as a revelation of and from God, but is itself the crucial element in the essential content of that putative revelation. For, absent that resurrection, there remains no sufficient reason for accepting either that the man Jesus is to be incomprehensibly identified with "God the

Father Almighty, Maker of heaven and earth," or that his actual teachings, whatever they may have been, are thereby revealed to be supremely authoritative. As was so incisively and correctly argued by the apostle Paul, "If Christ be not risen, then is our preaching vain, and your faith is also vain."[6]

The Presuppositions of Critical History
The argument to be presented now is epistemological rather than ontological. It is directed not at the question of whether miracles occur but at the question of whether—and, if so, how—we could know that they do, and when and where they have. This argument is fundamentally the same as that deployed by Hume in Section X of *An Enquiry Concerning Human Understanding.* But it has been substantially strengthened. Strengthening is needed mainly but not only because, by denying earlier in that *Enquiry* that we either do or even can have experience of physical necessity and physical impossibility, Hume disqualified himself from making the crucially necessary distinction between the merely marvelous and the genuinely miraculous.

1. The heart of the matter is that the criteria by which we must assess historical testimony, and the general presumptions that alone make it possible for us to construe the detritus of the past as historical evidence, must inevitably rule out any possibility of establishing, on purely historical grounds, that some genuinely miraculous event has indeed occurred. Hume himself concentrated on testimonial evidence because his own conception of the historian, later to be illustrated in his bestselling *History of England from the Invasion of Julius Caesar to the Revolution in 1688,*[7] was of a judge assessing, with judicious impartiality, the testimony set before him. But, in the present context, this limitation is not immediately important.

The basic propositions are, first, that the present relics of the past cannot be interpreted as historical evidence at all unless we presume that the same fundamental regularities obtained then as still obtain today. Second, that in trying as best they may to determine what actually happened, historians must employ as criteria all their present knowledge, or presumed knowledge, of what is probable or improbable, possible or impossible. Third, that, since the word *miracle* has to be defined in terms of physical necessity and physical impossibility, the application of these criteria inevitably precludes proof of the actual occurrence of a miracle.

Hume illustrated the first proposition in *A Treatise of Human Nature,* urging that it is only on such presumptions of regularity that we can justify the conclusion that ink marks on old pieces of paper constitute testimonial evidence (2.3.1).[8] Earlier in this same *Enquiry* he had urged the inescapable importance of the criteria demanded by the second. Without such criteria there can be no critical discrimination, and hence no history worthy of the name. The application of both the second and the third contention can be seen most sharply in the footnote in which Hume quotes with approval the reasoning of the famous physician De Sylva in the case of Mlle. Thibaut: "It was impossible that she could have been so ill as was 'proved' by witnesses, because it was impossible that she could, in so short a time, have recovered so perfectly as he found her."[9]

2. We need at this point to ask and to answer a question that Hume himself was in no position to press. What, if anything, justified De Sylva in rejecting a proposition apparently proved true by the testimony of eyewitnesses? What, if anything, justified him in thus stubbornly continuing to maintain that the miraculous cure did not in fact occur, since it could not have done so?

It is a matter of what evidence there is or can be, a matter of verifiability and of verification. The two crucial and conflicting propositions are of very different and quite disproportionate orders of logical strength, of confirmability and confirmation. For the proposition or propositions asserted by the putative witnesses were singular and in the past tense— "once upon a time, on one particular occasion, this or that actually happened." The days are, therefore, long past when these claims could be directly confirmed or disconfirmed. But the proposition or propositions that rule out the alleged miraculous occurrences as physically impossible must be open and general. They are either of the form "It is physically necessary for every so-and-so to be such-and-such," or of the form "It is physically impossible for any so-and-so to be such-and-such." Nomological propositions, as these are called, propositions asserting the subsistence of laws of nature and/or of causal connections, can in principle therefore, if not necessarily and always in practice, be tested and retested anywhere and at any time.

Historical reasoning of the form here exemplified by the physician De Sylva, like reasoning in all other valid forms, will sometimes, if its premises are false, lead to false conclusions. Hume himself, by dismissing reports of phenomena that the progress of abnormal psychology has since shown to be entirely possible, became exposed to Hamlet's too often quoted rebuke to overweening philosophy. What is physically or, if you like, naturally impossible is what is logically incompatible with true laws of nature. So, if you mistake some proposition to express such a law when in fact it does not, then you are bound to be wrong also about the consequent practical impossibilities. But that a form of argument must sometimes lead to false conclusions is no sufficient reason to reject it as invalid.

Nor is there for the Christian apologist any escape through contending either that there is something wrong with the concept of a miracle as a kind of naturally impossible event or that we can never in fact know what is and is not naturally impossible. For Christian apologetics absolutely presupposes that we all know a physical resurrection to be naturally impossible, that its occurrence would—as must have been thunderously maintained in a million Easter sermons[10]—be the miracle of miracles. Were such events known to be merely marvelous and extremely unusual, then the physical resurrection of Jesus bar Joseph, even had it actually occurred, would amount to at best the weakest of reasons for holding to the Apostles' Creed.

3. To make clearer what is involved, consider an example derived from the work of the acknowledged father of critical history. This example has the advantage of being far removed from any ideologically sensitive area. Herodotus knew that, except where it is joined to Asia by an isthmus, Africa is surrounded by sea. But he did not know either that Earth is in fact—roughly—spherical and suspended in space, or all the consequences of these first facts. So, in chapter forty-two of book four of his account of ancient Greece's Great Patriotic War, he writes, "Necos, the Egyptian king . . . desisting from the canal which he had begun between the Nile and the Arabian Gulf, sent to sea a number of ships manned by Phoenicians with orders to make for the Straits of Gibraltar, and return to Egypt through them, and by the Mediterranean." This in due course they succeeded in doing. "On their return they declared—I for my part do not believe them, but perhaps others may—that in sailing round Africa they had the sun on their right hand."

The incredulity of Herodotus on this particular point was, as we know, mistaken. Indeed, the very feature of the whole tradition that provoked his suspicion constitutes for us the best reason for believing that a Phoenician expedition did indeed circumnavigate Africa. But that Herodotus here went wrong on a point of fact does not show that his method was unsound. On the contrary, his verdict on this point is only discovered to have been mistaken when later historians, employing the same fundamental principles of assessment, reconsider it in the light of subsequent advances in astronomy and geography. It was entirely proper and reasonable for Herodotus to measure the likelihood of this Phoenician tale against the possibilities suggested by the best astronomical theory and geographical information available to him in the fifth century B.C., as well as against what he knew of the veracity of travelers in general, and of Phoenician sailors in particular. It was one thing to believe that they had set off and returned as reported. For he presumably had further confirming evidence for this in addition to the unsupported testimony of Phoenician sailors. And, if they had done these things, then they must have circumnavigated Africa, since it would have been physically impossible for them to overland their ships. It would have been quite another matter to believe a traveler's tale unsupported by other evidence, and not made probable by any promising theory.

Similar considerations and principles apply whether, as here, attention centers on an alleged impossibility, or whether, as more usually, it is a matter of what, granted always some presupposed framework of known possibilities and impossibilities, is only probable or improbable.

Possible Counters to Such Methodological Objections

1. Faced by this Humean argument, apologists are likely to respond in various ways. They may, for instance, recall that Hume himself was so imprudent as to dismiss stories of two wonders allegedly wrought by the Roman emperor Vespasian, stories that we now have excellent reason to believe were substantially true. Thus in Section X of his first *Enquiry* Hume mentions and contemptuously dismisses allegations that the Roman emperor Vespasian wrought two miracles of healing. Thirty years ago I went back to Hume's two stated authorities—which apparently no one else during the two preceding centuries had ever done. I found that Tacitus, recognized as the better of these two authorities, had recorded that before finally acting as the two partially paralyzed patients were asking him to act, Vespasian had ordered his army doctors to examine them. They reported finding no organic lesions.

Vespasian calculated that he had something to gain and nothing to lose. If he acted as the partially paralyzed patients wished, and his action was without effect, then everyone would allow that he had made a cheap but kindly concession to Egyptian ignorance and superstition. But if he acted in the same way, and it appeared that he had effected two miraculous cures, then the word would go out that there was no possibility of a successful rebellion, since the emperor was an invincible miracle worker. It appears that when Vespasian did so act, and the patients were duly healed by faith, the natives were appropriately impressed.

2. The temptation here is to suggest that further advances in our scientific knowledge may verify several of the miracle stories in the Bible in the same sort of way. But this is not a bit of help to the apologist if the progressive verification is achieved—as in fact in that case it was, and always has to be—only at the price of showing that, although what was said to have happened did indeed happen, its happening was not after all miraculous. Suppose that all the miracle stories in the New Testament were true, but that none of the events that occurred were genuinely miraculous. Then we would be left with no evidencing reason for believing the fundamental, essential, defining Christian dogma, that Jesus bar Joseph was God incarnate.

The important distinction between evidencing and motivating reasons for believing that some proposition is true is here most appropriately explained by referring to the Wager Argument of Blaise Pascal.[11] He begins by asserting that "reason can decide nothing here." By this Pascal means evidencing reason. He then proceeds to argue that prudence provides an overwhelmingly strong motivating reason for self-persuasion.

3. Again there is no apologetic profit to be had here from maintaining what may or may not be true, that the characteristically biblical notion is that of a sign, not necessarily involving any overriding of an established natural order. For, insofar as there now becomes nothing intrinsically remarkable and discernibly out of this world about the occurrences themselves, these putatively revealing signs will have to be identified and interpreted as such by reference to precisely that system of supposed divine self-revelation, the claims of which require authentication.

4. Someone is sure to want to remind us of Hume's own contention that we have and could have no experience of, no Humean impressions of (physical as opposed to logical) necessities and impossibilities. The consequence, on Hume's view, is that these are not legitimate ideas. Others will be eager to assert, however implausibly, that modern science has had to jettison the notions both of causality and of laws of nature. There is, however, no need to try to refute such teachings here. For if Christian apologists are to produce good evidencing reasons for believ-

ing that they have a hold on an authentic revelation, then they have to presuppose the existence of a strong natural order, an order the maintenance of which is physically necessary and which it is humanly impossible to violate. If truly there is no such order, then there can be no question of any overridings of it and hence no question of referring to any alleged overridings in order to validate anything.

Could Natural Theology Probabilify Revelation?

Hume was, I contend, correct in the main contention of Section X of this *Enquiry,* namely, that "a miracle can never be proved so as to be the foundation of a system of religion." But it is essential to realize that this conclusion depends on two things: first, an understanding of the methodological presuppositions of critical history, and second, a recognition of the impossibility of supplementing these by appealing to natural theology. Neither alone could be decisive. To ignore either, or not to appreciate how they complement one another, is to fail to take the measure of the force and the generality of the Humean offensive. We have, therefore, to appreciate that Sections X and XI of this *Enquiry* are complementary; the former recognizing the presuppositions of critical history and drawing out relevant implications, and the latter confronting the project of a natural theology at its apparent strongest and laboring to show it to be fundamentally misconceived.[12]

1. Cardinal Newman was perhaps Hume's most worthy opponent with respect to the thesis of Section X. Yet even he appears to have failed to appreciate the complementarity between it and the subsequent Section XI. While he is prepared to allow the general soundness of Hume's principles for the assessment of testimonial evidence, he nevertheless challenges their application to "these particular miracles, ascribed to the particular Peter, James, and John." What we have to ask, according to Newman, is whether such miraculous events really are "unlikely supposing there is a Power, external to the world, who can bring them about; supposing they are the only means by which He can reveal himself to those who need a revelation; supposing that He is likely to reveal himself; that He has a great end in doing so."[13]

If these suppositions could indeed be granted, then perhaps it would be reasonable to draw the conclusions desired. But Hume had in that subsequent Section XI developed a most powerful argument for saying not only that we do not have any natural knowledge of the existence of such a power, but also, and here perhaps even more relevantly, that we could have no warrant for conjectures as to what upon that supposition might reasonably be expected. For what Hume loved to call "the religious hypothesis"[14] is that of "a single being . . . not comprehended under any species or genus." God is therefore not a being from whose experienced attributes or qualities we can, by analogy, make reasonable inferences. The response to Newman's rhetorical questions should therefore be that any such conclusions about either likelihoods or unlikelihoods on that hypothesis must necessarily be altogether groundless and arbitrary. As Hume himself argued, "It must evidently appear contrary to all rules of analogy to reason, from the intentions and projects of men, to those of a Being so different, and so much superior."

2. So what reason do we have, what reason could we have, for believing that "there is a Power, external to the world" which is likely to produce "these particular miracles" or indeed any miracles at all, and for supposing that "He is likely to reveal himself; that He has a great end in doing so"?

Suppose that we did have sufficient evidencing reason to believe in the existence of a God discovered to be the omniscient and omnipotent ultimate sustaining cause of everything that exists and of everything that happens in the universe. Would it not, absent any revelation to the contrary, be reasonable to presume that God would see to it that everything in the universe is always as that God[15] wishes it to be? And if that God has made some creatures of a kind that can and cannot but make choices, but nevertheless wants some or all of those choices to be freely made in certain particular senses and no others, then presumably that God ensures that those particular choices are in fact always made in those desired senses and no others,[16] however deplorable many of the choices actually may seem to many of us.

The step from the existence of an omniscient and omnipotent Creator to the conclusion that the Creator is any sort of partisan in the created universe is as big as it is crucial. Because they have taken their concept of God to be one and indivisible, illicitly assuming that anything possessing any of the defining characteristics must possess them all, many even of the greatest thinkers have made this step without noticing, and in consequence without anxiously seeking, some justification for the making of it.

Joseph Butler, who held the senior see of Durham in the days when a Christian commitment was still a precondition for securing such appointments, was certainly one of the two finest philosophical minds ever to adorn the Church of England's bench of bishops. Yet even he could argue:

> There is no need to abstruse reasonings and distinctions, to convince
> an unprejudiced understanding, that there is a God who made and
> governs the world, and will judge it in righteousness . . . to an
> unprejudiced mind ten thousand instances of design cannot but prove
> a designer.[17]

To Butler it thus seemed utterly obvious that a proof of a designer and
maker of the universe must at the same time be a proof that the designer
and maker will also be a righteous judge, rewarding and punishing. Yet
earlier Butler had himself suggested that this conclusion is, prima facie,
scarcely plausible:

> Upon supposition that God exercises a moral government over the
> world, the analogy of this natural government suggests and makes it
> credible that this moral government must be a scheme quite beyond
> our comprehension, and this affords a general answer to all objections
> against the justice and goodness of it.[18]

This crucial and very remarkable move from omnipotent and omniscient
creator to judge who will judge the world "in righteousness" seemed
even to Butler so easy and so obvious that it required for its justification
neither "abstruse reasonings" nor apparently any reasonings at all. That
this should have been so is no doubt to be explained by reference to the
fact that Butler—like almost everyone else who has ever essayed to seek
out and examine evidencing reasons for believing in the Mosaic God of
Judaism, Christianity, and Islam—was raised among what Islam knows
as "peoples of the Book." He was thus misled to take the concept of that
God absolutely for granted throughout his examination of those reasons.
Apparently it never occurred to Butler that if he could prove the existence
of an omnipotent and omniscient creator, he would not thereby have
shown that it is certain or even likely that the creator is a just judge. He
was thus unwittingly prejudiced, like the rest of us, by teachings handed
down through generations of parents and pedagogues, priests and
rabbis, imams and ayatollahs.

The crux here is the historical development of a finite, one-among-
many, worldly, tribal god into the unique, omnipotent, omniscient
creator God of "the peoples of the Book." It is entirely natural to think
of tribal gods as devoted to the best interests of the tribe, endorsing its
established norms and providing support in its wars. But would anyone
who was not prejudiced by influences from that book, and who was
open-mindedly and for the first time entertaining the idea of an omnipotent, omniscient creator, ever think of such a being as possibly interven-

ing as a partisan in conflicts within (his or her or its) creation?

It would, surely, appear obvious to such a person that everything that occurs or does not occur within a created universe must, by the hypothesis, be precisely and only what its creator wants either to occur or not to occur. What scope is there for creatures to defy the will of their creator? What room even for a concept of such defiance? For a creator to punish creatures for what, by the hypothesis, he necessarily and as such (ultimately) causes them to do would be the most monstrous, perverse and sadistic of performances. Absent revelation to the contrary, the expectations of natural reason must surely be that such a creator god would be as detached and uninvolved as the gods of Epicurus. Indeed, some Indian religious thinkers, not prejudiced by any present or previous Mosaic commitments, are said to describe a creator god as being, essentially and in the nature of the case, "beyond good and evil."[19]

PART 2
THE POSSIBILITY OF MIRACLES

THREE

DEFINING
MIRACLES

RICHARD L. PURTILL

NOT LONG AGO I BEGAN HAVING CHEST PAINS, AND MY DOCTOR prescribed nitroglycerin tablets. When I went to the local pharmacy to get the prescription filled, I spoke with the pharmacist about how the pills work. He said something that stuck in my mind: "If the pills don't take away the pain at the first try, wait a little and then take a second dose. If that doesn't take away the pain, take a third dose and immediately call 911 for the paramedics." He explained that paramedics would much rather be called unnecessarily than be called too late to help.

Not too long afterward I was awakened early in the morning by chest pain. One dose of nitroglycerin didn't help. I got up and went downstairs, my wife accompanying me. I took a second dose and there was no improvement. My wife said, "Perhaps I ought to drive you to the hospital emergency room." I asked her to call 911 instead, then took a third dose of medication, which did not affect the pain. After what seemed hours, but was actually about ten minutes, the paramedics arrived. By this time I was being crushed by the greatest pain I had ever experienced. They rushed me to the hospital, where a dose of anticoagulant was administered to dissolve the clot that was causing the heart attack. I had a triple bypass operation from which I recovered slowly but completely. Soon I felt as good as ever.

Sometime later, when I thought I had recovered completely, I drove to Seattle, about ninety miles from my home. About a third of the way to Seattle a tire went flat. I pulled onto the shoulder of the freeway and began changing the tire, when I lost consciousness. (I later learned that my heart actually stopped beating.) I was found lying by my car, with my head on the freeway. Two passing motorists stopped. Both knew how to administer CPR, and one used his car phone to call the paramedics at a nearby fire station. With the assistance of two highway patrolmen, the paramedics restarted my heart. I subsequently had another operation, this time to plant a defibrillator in my chest.

Now the point of this anecdote is that although these happenings were wonderful and I am duly grateful to God and to the people who assisted me during these events, I would not call any of these events miraculous. There is a wider sense of "miracle" according to which events such as the one I experienced are miraculous; some writers have defined a miracle as "an extraordinary event that creates or confirms faith," and the events I have described certainly meet that description. But there was nothing in the events to suggest any nonnatural causes. The pharmacist's remarks, the training of the people who helped me, the medical technology are all things that seem to need no nonnatural explanation. Of course, if I thought that the pharmacist's remarks were directly inspired by God or that one of the passing motorists was an angel in disguise, I would have to rethink the judgment.

I do indeed believe that God was, as usual, hiding divine action in plain sight amid the ordinary course of events. The various elements in my experience—my conversation with the pharmacist, the fact that my good Samaritans had medical expertise, and so on—can all be explained in terms of purely natural factors. My preservation was a "coincidence" in the sense in which Aristotle defines it: the (humanly) unforeseen result of causes acting for other ends.

The Defining Features of a Miracle

How God acts through the coincidence of circumstances, how God, as C. S. Lewis said, adapts "the whole spiritual universe to the whole corporeal universe,"[1] is a fascinating topic: the providence, or, as the Greeks charmingly say, "the economy" of God. But although all miracles are part of the divine "economy," not all providential events are miracles. I propose to define a miracle as an event in which God temporarily makes an exception to the natural order of things, to show that God is acting. Each part of the definition is important.

First, the exception to the natural order is *temporary*: the raising of Lazarus and the resurrection of Jesus Christ are *exceptional* events. They do not in any way affect our practical certainty that dead men stay dead. As C. S. Lewis pointed out, once a miracle has been performed, the subsequent events follow natural laws. "If events ever come from beyond nature altogether she will [not] be incommoded by them. Be sure that she will rush to the point where she is invaded as the defensive forces rush to a cut on our finger, and there hasten to accommodate the newcomer. The moment it enters her realm it will obey all the natural laws."[2]

Second, it is an *exception* to the ordinary course of nature. Since it was Lazarus's *nature* to die in the circumstances of his illness, his resurrection was, in the strict sense, *supernatural,* going beyond what was natural for him. It was, therefore, a miracle. Some writers prefer the term *resuscitation* for miracles such as the raising of Lazarus. There are some good grounds for this; the person restored to life must eventually undergo a natural death, and certain effects of resurrection seem to be absent. However, using the word *resuscitation* for what happened to Lazarus implies that this event is of the same general type as my own case: my heart had stopped beating, but was able to be started again as a result of natural causes. Also, the idea of the raising of Lazarus as a prophetic forerunner of Christ's own resurrection is lost. So I prefer to speak of such events as "resurrections," not "resuscitations."

Third, unless we have the idea of a way things ordinarily happen—*the natural order of things,* some idea of "laws of nature"—then the idea of a miracle cannot be made clear. It is basically a "contrast idea." Without the idea of natural law to which miracles are an exception we cannot explain the basic idea of a miracle in this sense. If nature were chaotic, if "anything could happen," then miracles could not be contrasted with what we ordinarily expect. Some authors[3] have suggested that the Hebraic worldview had no formal notion of "laws of nature" and that defining a miracle as a "temporary exception to the natural order of things" is anachronistic, especially if we explain the "natural order of things" in terms of natural laws. But that is precisely why I have used the phrase "the natural order of things." The Hebrews at the time of the crossing of the Red Sea knew perfectly well what naturally happened to the sea. The fact that the Red Sea parted to enable the children of Israel to cross dry shod could be seen by them as exceptions to the way things naturally occurred. Similarly, the miraculous healings and the raising of dead people accomplished by Christ could be seen by the people who witnessed them not merely as unlikely events but as events that were contrary to all natural expectations. They did not need a sophisticated concept of a law of nature to see this.

Fourth, a miracle must be caused *by the power of God*. If for some reason we find that some apparently wonderful event can be accounted for by some power less than the power of God, then we withhold the designation "miracle."

The fifth part of the definition addresses the purpose of miracles. Even if we could imagine God simply "showing off" his power by temporarily suspending a law of nature, if this suspension caused no effects on the human witnesses we might not be willing to call it a miracle. We must include within our definition, then, the idea of miracle as a *sign* of God's action. One possible purpose of miracles is to take a hint from our wider sense of miracles and say that miracles are intended to "create or confirm faith." This, however, may be a little narrow: some miracles may not confirm faith since the people with faith at the time of the miracle may not need it confirmed, and it may not create faith because those nonbelievers on hand during the miracle may *refuse* to believe, despite the miracle. So perhaps a wider sense of the purpose of miracle is needed: I suggest "to show that God is acting."

Once again, then, a miracle is "an event in which God temporarily makes an exception to the natural order of things, to show that God is acting."

Clearly, no attempt to define a miracle can be deemed satisfactory if it does not seek to clarify the relationship between miracles and laws of nature. Certain long-standing conceptions of miracle falter precisely because they depend on misunderstandings of this relationship. And this has led to a facile acceptance of altogether irrelevant objections to belief in miracles.

David Hume's Definition of Miracle
In his famous argument against miracles, for example, David Hume defines a miracle in this way:

> Nothing is esteemed a miracle, if it ever happen in the common course of nature. It is no miracle that a man, seemingly in good health, should die on a sudden: because such a kind of death, though more unusual

than any other, has yet been frequently observed to happen. But it is a miracle, that a dead man should come to life; because that has never been observed in any age or country. There must, therefore, be a uniform experience against every miraculous event, otherwise the event would not merit that appellation.[4]

Hume's definition begins rather like my own: his "common course of events" can be taken as equivalent to "the natural order of things." He goes on, however, to argue circularly against the possibility of miracles. The question at issue is whether such miracles as the resurrection of Jesus Christ or the raising of Lazarus have in fact occurred. To assume at the outset of framing a definition that the sort of event being defined has "never been observed in any age or country" assumes as a premise what is supposed to be proved as the conclusion and is therefore guilty of begging the question.

Nor is defining a miracle as something against which there is uniform experience at all useful. It would be an argument against the possibility of any unique event that has not happened, for example, landing a human being on Mars. We would not argue that it is impossible to land a person on Mars "because there is uniform experience against it." In deciding whether something is possible, we do not consult past experience in this sense: what is physically possible is what is not forbidden by the laws of nature, whether or not it has ever happened.

Some people have argued that what Hume is giving here is not an argument against the existence or possible existence of miracles, but an argument that no kind of evidence available to us would be sufficient to *show* that a miracle has occurred. This will be discussed further in chapters four and five of this book, but my own opinion is that Hume gives *both* a question-begging argument against miracles *and* an argument that no evidence available to us is sufficient to show that a miracle has occurred. But we need not settle this here. The point is that the definition of miracles as "that which has never been observed in any age or country" is basic to both arguments: against the possibility of miracles and against the idea that we could ever have evidence for them.

Many modern defenders of Hume, such as Antony Flew, acknowledge the question-begging character of Hume's own argument.

Since to say that *A* is the cause of *B* is in his view to say that all *A*'s are followed by *B*'s, and that we habitually associate *A*'s with *B*'s, he would presumably have to say that a law of nature holds wherever *A*'s are constantly conjoined with *B*'s, and a similar habitual association obtains. Since to the logical analysis of the conceptions of either cause or law such habitual psychological associations are clearly quite irrelevant, this must reduce statements of lawful connection to statements of a merely numerical universal conjunction. But if that were indeed all that a law of nature asserted then it would give no ground at all for saying that the occurrence of an exception to such a law is physically impossible. Any attempt to use our knowledge, or presumed knowledge, of such a merely numerical universal proposition as an evidential canon by which to justify the outright rejection of any testimony to the occurrence of a falsifying exception would be a preposterous piece of question begging.

In one deservedly notorious passage Hume seems to be doing just that: "It is no miracle that a man, seemingly in good health, should die on a sudden, because such a kind of death, though more unusual than any other, has yet been frequently observed to happen. But it is a miracle that a dead man should come to life, because that has never been observed in any age or country." Hume can provide no conception of a law of nature sufficiently strong to allow for any real distinction between the miraculous and the extremely unusual. For if a law of nature really was no more than an epitome and an extrapolation of a long and uninterruptedly uniform series of observations, then an exception to the law—a breach in the uniformity of the series—could be only an unusual, and no doubt unexpected, event. While if in laws of nature we had only what we have called merely numerical universal propositions, then to dismiss out of hand all testimony to the occurrence beyond the range of our observations of a counter example, on the sole ground that such an occurrence would falsify the universal generalization based upon our observations to date, would indeed be arbitrary and bigoted. This particular remark of Hume's, if nothing else, provides some justification for the harsh interpretation: "He first answers, 'Yes,' to the question whether Nature is absolutely uniform: and then uses this 'Yes' as a ground for answering, 'No,' to the question, 'Do miracles occur?' " [C. S. Lewis, *Miracles,* rev. ed. (London: Collins Fontana, 1960)].

Once the essential nomological element in the meaning of statements of laws of nature is recognized, then it becomes clear that knowledge—or presumed knowledge—of a law of nature could be a ground for dismissing as in fact impossible the occurrence of anything inconsistent with that law.[5]

This may suggest that we should interpret Hume's argument against the existence of miracles in the following charitable way. Miracles are to be defined as "something forbidden by the laws of nature." Here is where experience, which shows that laws of nature are never violated, comes in. The argument may be spelled out as follows:

1. A miracle is a violation of the laws of nature.
2. We have uniform experience that the laws of nature are never violated.
3. Therefore, miracles cannot occur.

As Flew has said, Hume is in a particularly bad position to give an argument like this. For him, "laws of nature" are simply observed regularities that embody no necessity. (Necessity lies purely in the realm of ideas.) Thus to say that miracles violate laws of nature is simply to say that there is uniform experience against them, a return to the question-begging argument.

Alastair McKinnon's Conception of Miracle and Natural Law

Another view of what a miracle is comes from Alastair McKinnon. If laws of nature are simply "whatever occurs," then it makes no sense to speak of the *violation* of "laws" of nature. This has obvious implications for miracles:

> Natural laws bear no similarities to civil codes and they do not in any way constrain the course of nature. They exert no opposition or resistance to anything, not even to the odd or exceptional. They are simply highly generalized shorthand descriptions of how things do in fact happen. . . . Hence there can be no suspensions of natural law rightly understood. Or, as here defined, *miracle* contains a contradiction in terms. . . . This contradiction may stand out more clearly if for *natural law* we substitute the expression *the actual course of events*. Miracle would then be defined as "an event involving the suspension of the actual course of events."[6]

This view, that natural laws are simply "generalized shorthand descriptions of how things . . . happen," is quite broad in its conception of natural laws, and it is compatible with the view that the regularities we observe are only a matter of chance. In fact, this conception is so broad that, as McKinnon points out, it provides no suitable contrast to the idea of miracle. Because it is so broad it is an extremely weak conception of natural law, since nothing in the definition of natural law would exclude such events as the resurrection of the dead. In other words, a resurrection from the dead would be as "natural" as any other event. If it can be ascertained, on the basis of historical research, that a resurrection from the dead once occurred several centuries ago, then that event, like all events, falls under the "generalized shorthand description" of "the actual course of nature."

Surely this is not the sense of "laws of nature" that most people have in mind when they define a miracle as a suspension of or a violation of or an exception to natural law. Most people, regardless of their attitude toward miracles, hold that natural laws do in fact "constrain the course of events." McKinnon's definition of natural laws permits no way of contrasting "accidental generalizations" with laws, or of distinguishing between a universe ruled by chance and one ruled by natural laws. Arguably, then, McKinnon's definition of a natural law is mistaken as an analysis of how we use the term "natural law." In fact, McKinnon's position is an attempt to cut off an interesting argument by definition: on his view, no question of miracles can arise, since whatever happens, natural laws must include it. Since miracles are unique events, not necessarily repeatable in the same circumstances, a "natural law" about human death would have to take the form "when human beings are dead they stay dead, *except* Jesus, Lazarus, the son of the widow at Nain and so on." This is not the place to critique McKinnon's full proposal. I focus on issues related to his definition of miracles and leave for other chapters the task of answering additional philosophical problems that McKinnon and others have raised for the rational acceptance of miracles as I have defined them in this chapter.[7]

A Theistic Conception of Natural Law

A further view, that natural laws are ordinances passed by the creator of nature for its regulation, certainly delivers the required contrast. Legal ordinances and moral ordinances are such that although it would be better if they were not violated, they can in fact be violated. A natural law, on the other hand, cannot be violated; no amount of effort on our part (or on the part of any finite creature) will be sufficient to violate a law of nature. Such ordinances can, however, be suspended, temporarily and for a particular purpose, by the creator of nature; on this view an exception to the laws of nature can be permitted only by the creator of nature, just as an exception to a legal ordinance can be permitted only by the authority that passed the law (or some higher authority).

We thus have a contrast between what can be accomplished by any finite creature and what could only be accomplished by God. This shows why scientists as a rule are not professionally (i.e., as scientists) interested in miracles: they tend to confine their investigations to the ordinary course of nature and to ignore such exceptions as might be made to the course of nature by God, since exceptions brought about by personal agency cannot be predicted from a study of what normally happens. Of course, by defining miracles as exceptions to the natural order of things, we deprive miracles of any *scientific* interest only if science is *essentially* concerned with what happens as *part of* the natural order of things. In chapter eight, "Science, Miracles, Agency Theory and the God-of-the-Gaps," J. P. Moreland argues that miracles do not lie outside the bounds of scientific investigation.

As an event caused by divine will acting from outside this natural order, a miracle neither confirms nor disconfirms any generalization about the natural order of things. In fact, as Richard Swinburne argues, there is a good reason in this context to define a miracle as "a non-repeatable counter-instance to a law of nature."[8] What this means is that the phenomenon (or event type) is nonrepeatable by us, or by any finite creature, not that God could not repeat the same type of event. (Swinburne seems to think that scientists must regard nature as a "closed system" and make predictions on that basis. If something from outside of nature operates to change the natural order of things, the scientist, as scientist, has no professional concern with it.)

Theism Versus Metaphysical Naturalism on the Concept of Miracle

The system of thought known as "metaphysical naturalism" holds that there is nothing outside of nature: everything in our experience can be accounted for by purely natural forces. A certain conception of laws of nature complements this attitude: natural laws are inherent tendencies in matter/energy. On this conception of natural law it is impossible to envision an exception to it: nothing in nature could cause such an exception, and by hypothesis there is nothing outside of nature.

The argument goes like this:

1. Metaphysical naturalism is true.

2. If metaphysical naturalism is true, then laws of nature are inherent tendencies within matter/energy.

3. Such inherent tendencies do not allow for exceptions.

4. Nothing outside of nature can cause such an exception, since there is nothing outside of nature.

5. Thus there *cannot* be exceptions to the laws of nature, and if miracles are defined as exceptions to the laws of nature, then miracles are impossible.

But of course premises one and four of the above argument are not scientific statements: they are philosophical positions that would have to be judged philosophically. It comes as no great surprise to discover that a position assuming naturalism leaves no room for miracles and that a position affirming the existence of a creator of the natural order allows for miracles, or that a position that describes natural laws as simply a summary of what happens cannot even make the contrast between miracles and nonmiraculous events.

As a consequence of this analysis, it may be doubted that any sort of argument from miracles to the existence of God can succeed, for one must have some prior reason to assume the existence of God before one can even make sense of the idea of miracle. Nevertheless, it might be possible to form the idea of a miracle by reflecting on the highly recalcitrant nature of some events (the resurrection of Jesus Christ, for example), inferring the existence and activity of God in order best to explain the occurrence of those events, and labeling such acts of God "miracles," as Douglas Geivett explains in chapter eleven. Furthermore, the proposition that God exists, should it be independently supported by other types of arguments for the existence of God, may be further confirmed by historical evidence that miracles have happened. The occurrence of miraculous events may be one of the many features of the universe that makes better sense on the hypothesis that God exists.

At any rate, the concept of a miracle should make perfectly good *sense* to critics of theism. The metaphysical naturalist could say, "I see that what the theist means by a law of nature is an ordinance established by God for the regulation of the universe. Given the theist's account of natural laws, the idea of an exception to that ordinance by the creator of nature makes sense. I, on the other hand, regard laws of nature as inherent tendencies in matter/energy that do not allow exceptions. That basic difference concerns what laws of nature are. Underlying this basic difference is a question about whether my naturalistic scheme will account for our total experience of the world better than the theistic scheme. It is no use arguing about whether miracles *can* occur before we settle these questions."

Certainly theism's concept of a miracle, and its correlative understanding of the laws of nature, make sense only within a religious context. This does not mean that one must *accept* the truth of theism in order to understand the concept of a miracle. Rather, one must see that *given* the truth of theism the concept of natural law that goes with theism follows naturally, and so does the concept of miracles. None of this rules out the possibility of disagreement among theists about whether God *would* make exceptions to his ordinances for the regulation of the universe. Nor, for that matter, are disagreements among naturalists excluded. Not all metaphysical naturalists accept premise three in the above argument. Nevertheless, the basic choice is between theism and naturalism. In this contest, theism enjoys certain advantages. As C. S. Lewis observed:

> If we admit God, must we admit Miracle? Indeed, indeed, you have no security against it. That is the bargain. Theology says to you in effect, "Admit God and with Him the risk of a few miracles, and I in return will ratify your faith in uniformity as regards the overwhelming majority of events." The philosophy which forbids you to make uniformity absolute is also the philosophy which offers you solid grounds for believing it to be general, to be *almost* absolute. The Being who threatens Nature's claim to omnipotence confirms her in her lawful occasions. Give us this ha'porth of tar and we will save the ship. The alternative is really much worse. Try to make Nature absolute and you find that her uniformity is not even probable. By claiming too much, you get nothing. You get the deadlock, as in Hume. Theology offers you a working arrangement, which leaves the scientist free to continue his experiments and the Christian to continue his prayers.[9]

If we adopt the theistic view of natural laws, then we have a *reason* for thinking that such laws will hold in most cases. A Humean view, on the other hand, permits no such assurance. Of course the scientist, requiring this sort of assurance, would be better off adopting the theistic view of natural law, for it provides the philosophical background needed in the practice of good science. The theistic scientist has a philosophical reason for expecting laws to be discovered in nature: he thinks that such laws are the product of a mind, namely, the mind of God. The nontheistic scientist, however, can have no such assurances. For him the fact that nature functions in lawlike fashion is ultimately a "brute fact," completely unexplainable on his own views. This and other problems for naturalism are developed by Norman Geisler (chapter four), Ronald Nash (chapter seven) and J. P. Moreland (chapter eight).

Conclusion

The definition of miracle developed in this chapter is analyzed into five components. A miracle is an event (1) brought about by the power of God that is (2) a temporary (3) exception (4) to the ordinary course of nature (5) for the purpose of showing that God has acted in history. Central to this definition of miracle is its conception of the relationship between miracles and laws of nature. I have therefore focused on this aspect of the concept of miracle. I have argued that some conceptions of the relationship between miracles and natural laws (David Hume's, for example) beg the question against the possibility of miracles, and that other conceptions of this relationship eliminate the possibility of religiously significant miracles by adopting a very weak account of natural laws according to which any event that happens (including a dead man's rising) is perfectly "natural" (as in the case of Alastair McKinnon).

Over against these inadequate conceptions of the relationship between miracles and natural laws I have suggested that both miracles and natural laws be understood theistically. Natural laws are ordained by God for the typical governance of phenomena in the natural world, such that events in the natural world follow a regular and predictable pattern. God, however, may wish to act directly in the world in a way that temporarily suspends the operation of natural laws in order to permit the identification of an event as uniquely and specially caused by God. Such an event, which does not fit the lawlike pattern of events in the natural order, is a miracle. Finally, I have argued that a theistic conception of natural laws enjoys certain advantages over the conception normally associated with metaphysical naturalism.

The entire discussion in this chapter has been limited to conceptual analysis. Developing a working definition of miracle is only the first step in answering the question: Has God acted in history in an identifiably miraculous fashion? It is to other interesting and important features of this question that the remaining chapters in this volume are directed.

FOUR
MIRACLES &
THE MODERN
MIND

NORMAN L. GEISLER

THE MODERN ATTITUDE TOWARD MIRACLES HAS BEEN MOLDED largely by David Hume (chapter one). Antony Flew's argument against the miraculous (chapter two) can be viewed as an extension of Hume's position. The basic reason for modern antisupernaturalism is simple: miracles are incredible. And David Hume provided what many believe to be the most formidable assault against the credibility of belief in miracles.[1] Hume actually has three arguments against miracles: one philosophical, one historical and one religious. The first is an argument *in principle,* which does not question the credibility of witnesses to an alleged miracle. The second is an argument *in practice,* which holds that no miracle enjoys enough support by credible witnesses to be believed. The last argues that miracle claims from competing religious traditions cancel each other out. Since my concern here is only with the possibility of miracles, I confine my discussion to Hume's first argument.[2]

Hume's Philosophical Argument That Miracles Are Incredible
In Section X of his famous *An Enquiry Concerning Human Understanding,* Hume introduces his argument with these words: "I flatter

myself, that I have discovered an argument . . . which, if just, will, with the wise and learned, be an everlasting check to all kinds of superstitious delusion, and consequently, will be useful as long as the world endures."[3] Just what is this "final" argument against miracles? In Hume's own words the reasoning goes like this:[4]

[1] A wise man . . . proportions his belief to the evidence. [2] In such conclusions as are founded on an infallible experience, he expects the event with the last degree of assurance, and regards his past experience as a full *proof* of the future existence of that event. . . . [3] As the evidence, derived from witnesses and human testimony, is founded on past experience, so it varies with the experience, and is regarded either as a *proof* or a *probability*, according as the conjunction between any particular kind of report and any kind of object has been found to be constant or variable. [4] There are a number of circumstances to be taken into consideration in all judgments of this kind; and the ultimate standard, by which we determine all disputes, that may arise concerning them, is always derived from experience and observation. [5] Where this experience is not entirely uniform on any side, it is attended with an unavoidable contrariety in our judgments and with the same opposition and mutual destruction of argument as in every other kind of evidence. . . . [6] We entertain a suspicion concerning any matter of fact, when the witnesses contradict each other; when they are but few, or of a doubtful character; when they have an interest in what they affirm; when they deliver their testimony with hesitation, or . . . with too violent asseverations. . . . [7] But when the fact attested is such a one as has seldom fallen under our observation, here is a contest of two opposite experiences; of which the one destroys the other, as far as its force goes, and the superior can only operate on the mind by the force, which remains. [8] A miracle is a violation of the laws of nature; and as a firm and unalterable experience has established these laws, [9] the proof against a miracle, from the very nature of the fact, is as entire as any argument from experience can possibly be imagined. . . . [10] And as a uniform experience amounts to a proof, there is here a direct and full *proof,* from the nature of the fact, against the existence of any miracle.

Again, using his own words, Hume's argument can be abbreviated in the following way:

1. "A miracle is a violation of the laws of nature."

2. "Firm and unalterable experience has established these laws."

3. "A wise man . . . proportions his belief to the evidence."

4. Therefore, "the proof against a miracle . . . is as entire as any argument from experience can possibly be imagined."

Hume concludes, "There must, therefore, be a uniform experience against every miraculous event, otherwise the event would not merit that appellation." So "nothing is esteemed a miracle, if it ever happened in the common course of nature."[5]

Two Ways to Understand Hume's Argument

Hume's argument against miracles can be understood in two ways, the "hard" and the "soft" interpretations. According to the "hard" interpretation of the argument, Hume would be claiming that (1) miracles by definition are a violation of natural law; (2) natural laws are unalterably uniform; (3) therefore, miracles cannot occur. Despite the fact that Hume's argument can be understood to follow this pattern, it may not be what he has in mind. If this is his argument, then it clearly begs the question by simply defining miracles as impossible. For if miracles are a "violation" of what cannot be "altered," then miracles are, in the nature of the case, impossible. Further, a supernaturalist could easily avoid this dilemma. For instance, he could refuse Hume's definition of miracle as a "violation" of fixed law and consider it an "exception" to a general rule. That is, he could define natural law as the regular (normal) pattern of events but not as a universal or unalterable pattern, as suggested by Richard Purtill in chapter three of this volume.

A Restatement of Hume's Argument Against Miracles

This would, however, be an easy way out of the problem for the supernaturalist. Hume's underlying argument is much more difficult to answer, for it is compatible with a "softer" view of natural law. He argues not for the impossibility of miracles but for the *incredibility* of accepting miracles. The argument can be stated this way:

1. A miracle is by definition a rare occurrence.

2. Natural law is by definition a description of regular occurrence.

3. The evidence for the regular is always greater than that for the rare.

4. A wise man always bases his belief on the greater evidence.

5. Therefore, a wise man should never believe in miracle.

Notice that on this "soft" form of the argument miracles are not ruled out entirely; they are simply held to be always incredible given their nature and the constraints of evidence on rational belief. The wise person does not claim that miracles cannot occur; he simply never *believes* they happen because he never has enough evidence for that belief—and that is because of what a miracle is. One indication that Hume is emphasizing credibility (or believability) rather than possibility is his use of such terms as "belief" and "is esteemed." But even on this "soft" interpretation of the argument, the rationality of belief in miracles is eliminated, since by the very nature of the case no thoughtful person should ever hold that a miracle has indeed occurred. Thus, Hume seems to avoid begging the question while successfully eliminating the possibility of reasonable belief in miracles.

Antony Flew's Neo-Humean Argument Against Miracles

Variations of Hume's in-principle argument against miracles are still deployed by widely respected contemporary philosophers. In his article "Miracles" in *The Encyclopedia of Philosophy,* Antony Flew argues that miracles are unrepeatable. As he sees it, Hume's argument really amounts to something like this:

1. Every miracle is a violation of a law of nature.

2. The evidence against any violation of a law of nature is the strongest possible evidence.

3. Therefore, the evidence against miracles is the strongest possible evidence.[6]

Flew claims that "Hume was primarily concerned, not with the question of fact, but with that of evidence. The problem was how the occurrence of a miracle could be proved, rather than whether any such events had ever occurred." However, adds Flew, "our sole ground for characterizing the reported occurrence as miraculous is at the same time a sufficient reason for calling it physically impossible." Why, we may ask, is this so? Because "the critical historian, confronted with some story of a miracle, will usually dismiss it out of hand."[7]

On what grounds are miracles dismissed by critical historians? Flew answers, "To justify his procedure he will have to appeal to precisely the principle which Hume advanced: the absolute 'impossibility or miraculous nature' of the events attested must, 'in the eyes of all reasonable people . . . alone be regarded as a sufficient refutation.' "[8] In short, even though miracles are not logically impossible, they are scientifically impossible, "for it is only and precisely by presuming that the laws that hold today held in the past . . . that we can rationally interpret the detritus [remains] of the past as evidence and from it construct our account of what actually happened."[9]

As to the charge that this uniformitarian approach to history is "irrationally dogmatic," Flew answers with what is truly the heart of his amplification of Hume's argument. First, "as Hume was insisting from first to last, the possibility of miracles is a matter of evidence and not of dogmatism." Further, "the proposition reporting the (alleged) occurrence of the miracle will be singular, particular, and in the past tense." Propositions of this sort "cannot any longer be tested directly. It is this that gives propositions of the first sort [i.e., of the general and repeatable] the vastly greater logical strength."[10] In view of this, Flew's argument can now be restated as follows:

1. Miracles are by nature particular and unrepeatable.
2. Natural events are by nature general and repeatable.
3. In practice, the evidence for the general and repeatable is always greater than that for the particular and unrepeatable.
4. Therefore, in practice, the evidence will always be greater against miracles than for them.

With this statement it becomes clear that for Flew generality and repeatability (in the present) are what give natural events greater evidential value than miracles. And since, of course, it will always be this way in the future, the evidence against miracles will always be greater than the evidence for them.

An Evaluation of Hume's Argument Against Miracles

There is a central thread to the Hume-Flew argument against miracles: both are based on what may be called the "repeatability principle," that evidence for what occurs over and over always outweighs evidence that does not. But since miracles by their very nature are singularities, the evidence against them is always greater. Since there are distinctive features in each of Hume's and Flew's presentations, however, we need to evaluate them separately.

Since the "hard" form of Hume's in-principle argument clearly begs the question and is easily rehabilitated by redefining the terms, let us concentrate on the "soft" form. Many believe the "soft" version is what Hume intended. We begin with Hume's claim about "uniform experience."

The assumption of uniform experience. Hume speaks of "uniform" experience against miracles, but this seems either to beg the question or else to be special pleading. It begs the question if Hume presumes to know the whole field of experience to be uniform in advance of looking at the evidence for uniformity. For how can one know that all possible experience will confirm naturalism, unless one has access to all possible experiences, including those in the future? If, on the other hand, Hume simply means by "uniform" experience the select experiences of *some* persons (who either have not or believe they have not encountered a miracle), then this is special pleading. For there are others who claim to have experienced miracles. Why should their testimony be inferior to that of others who report uniformity? As Stanley Jaki observes, "Insofar as he [Hume] was a sensationist or empiricist philosopher he had to grant equal credibility to the recognition of any fact, usual or unusual."[11]

In the final analysis, then, the debate over miracles cannot be settled by supposed "uniform" experience. For this either begs the question in advance of investigation or else opens the door for a factual analysis of whether indeed there is sufficient evidence to believe that a miracle has occurred. As C. S. Lewis observed,

> Now of course we must agree with Hume that if there is absolutely "uniform experience" against miracles, if in other words they have never happened, why then they never have. Unfortunately we know the experience against them to be uniform only if we know that all the reports of them are false. And we can know all the reports to be false only if we know already that miracles have never occurred. In fact, we are arguing in a circle.[12]

The alternative to this circular arguing is *to be open to the possibility that miracles have occurred.*

Adding evidence versus weighing evidence. Hume does not really *weigh* evidence for miracles; rather, he *adds* evidence against them. Since death occurs over and over again and resurrection occurs only on rare occasions at best, Hume simply adds up all the deaths against the very few alleged resurrections and rejects the latter. In Hume's own words, "It is no miracle that a man, seemingly in good health, should die on a sudden: because such a kind of death, though more unusual than any other, has yet been frequently observed to happen. But it is a miracle, that a dead man should come to life; because that has never been observed in any age or country." Hence, it is "more than probable, that all men must die."[13] But this does not involve weighing evidence to determine whether or not a given person, say Jesus of Nazareth (see chapters fifteen and sixteen), has been raised from the dead. It is simply adding up the evidence of all other occasions where people have died and have not been raised and using it to overwhelm any possible evidence that some person who died was brought back to life.

There are additional problems with Hume's policy of adding up events to determine what to believe in general. First, even if a few well-attested resurrections actually occurred, on Hume's principles no rational person should believe them, since deaths would always outnumber resurrections. Rational beliefs should not, however, be determined by majority vote. Hume seems to commit a kind of *consensus gentium* fallacy, an informal logical fallacy arguing that something should be believed to be true simply because it is believed by most people.

Second, this argument equates quantity of evidence and probability. It says, in effect, that we should always believe what is most probable (in the sense of "enjoying the highest odds"). But this is silly. On these grounds a dice player should not believe the dice show three sixes on the first roll, since the odds against it are 216 to 1. Or, we should never believe we have been dealt a perfect bridge hand (though this has happened) since the odds against it are 1,635,013,559,600 to 1! What Hume seems to overlook is that wise people base their beliefs on facts, not simply on odds. Sometimes the "odds" against an event are high (based on past observation), but the evidence for the event is otherwise very good (based on current observation or reliable testimony). Hume's argument confuses *quantity* of evidence with the *quality* of evidence. Evidence should be *weighed*, not *added*.

Third, Hume's policy of "adding" evidence would eliminate belief in any unusual or unique event from the past, to say nothing of miracles. Richard Whately satirized Hume's thesis in a famous pamphlet, *Historical Doubts Concerning the Existence of Napoleon Bonaparte*. Whately reasoned from Humean principle that since Napoleon's exploits were so fantastic, so extraordinary, so unprecedented, no intelligent person should believe that these reported events ever happened. After recounting Napoleon's amazing and unparalleled military feats, Whately queried, "Does anyone believe all this and yet refuse to believe a miracle? Or rather, what is this but a miracle? Is not this a violation of the laws of nature?" If skeptics do not deny the existence of Napoleon, they "must at least acknowledge that they do not apply to that question the same plan of reasoning which they have made use of in others."[14]

Proving too much. In fact, Hume's argument seems to prove too much. It proves that we should not believe in a miracle even if it happens!

For this argument does not hold that miracles have not occurred but only that we should not believe they have occurred simply because the evidence for the regular is always greater than that for the rare. But on this logic, if a miracle did occur—rare as it may be—one should still not believe in it. It is patently absurd, however, to claim that an event should be disbelieved, even if it has occurred, that is, when the evidence is overwhelming that the purported miracle has occurred.

What often happens is that antisupernaturalists change their claims as to whether such an event is really a miracle. Hume, for example, claimed that a resurrection would be a miracle, since he was convinced there was no sufficient evidence that a resurrection had occurred. Flew, on the other hand, perhaps perceiving that the evidence for a resurrection is greater than Hume thought, would not agree that a resurrection is a miracle. But this changes the rules in the middle of the game. Further, from an epistemic point of view (see chapters six and eleven) it argues that we should not believe in miracles even if we have good evidence that they have occurred. But surely no rational person should disbelieve an event for which there is good evidence.

Evidence for the past cannot determine the present. Hume admonishes the wise person always to believe in advance that miracles will never occur. Anyone who examines the evidence for an allegedly miraculous event should come "prearmed" with the "uniform" and "unalterable" testimony of the past, so that even if the event should seem highly miraculous, it should be presumed not to be a miracle. For "in such conclusions as are founded on an infallible experience, he expects the event with the last [i.e., highest] degree of assurance, and regards his past experience as a full *proof* of the future existence of that event."[15]

Here again Hume's uniformitarian prejudice is evident. Only if one approaches the world with a kind of invincible bias—that one should believe only in accordance with what has been experienced in the past—can one discount in principle all claims for the miraculous. There are two important objections to this reasoning. First, Hume is inconsistent with his own epistemology. He himself recognized the fallacy of this kind of reasoning when he argued that based on past conformity, nothing can be known with certainty about the future. We cannot even know for sure that the sun will rise tomorrow morning.[16] Hence, for Hume to deny future miracles based on past experience is inconsistent with his own principles and is a violation of his own system.

Second, if it were true that no present exception can overthrow supposed "laws" of nature based on our uniform experience in the past, then there could be no true progress in our scientific understanding of the world. For established or *repeatable* exceptions to past patterns are precisely what force a change in scientific belief. When an observed exception to a past "law" is established, that "law" ($L1$) is revised and a new "law" ($L2$) replaces it. This is precisely what happened when certain outer-spatial "exceptions" to Newton's law of gravitation were found and Einstein's theory of relativity was considered broader and more adequate. Without established exceptions, no progress can be made in science. In short, Hume's objections to miracles seem to be unscientific! Exceptions to "laws" have a heuristic (discovery) value; they are goads to progress in our understanding of the universe. Miracles as *unrepeatable* exceptions do not call for a covering law and, hence, would meet the necessary conditions for being supernatural. Of course, in order to meet the sufficient conditions for a miracle, something needs to be more than a thus far unrepeated event (see chapter three). Otherwise it may just be an anomaly. However, the fact that there are unrepeated events (whether anomalies or not) severely undermines Hume's argument against miracles.

This criticism does not entail that all exceptions to a known law call for another natural law to explain them. Since scientific understanding is based on regular and repeated events, one must be able to show how the exception is repeatable before one can claim it has a natural cause rather than a supernatural one. No single exception to a known scientific law calls for another broader natural law to explain it. Only *repeatable* exceptions call for natural causes. An unrepeated exception may have a supernatural cause. Indeed, if it has the earmarks of intelligent intervention from beyond the natural world, then it is reasonable to posit a supernatural cause, not a natural one (see chapter eight).[17]

Confusing basis of knowledge and object of knowledge. Hume argued convincingly that all our empirical knowledge is based on repetition. From this it is reasoned that the evidence for what is repeatable is always greater than the evidence for what is rare (like a miracle). But this confuses the basis of our knowledge and the object of our knowledge. Simply because a rational or "scientific" understanding of the world is *based on* observation of regularly recurring events, it does not follow that the *object* of this understanding must be a regular event. Our understanding that the painting on the Sistine Chapel was done by a great artist is based on the experience of seeing numerous similar paintings by other great artists. Yet the object of this understanding (the creation scene on the chapel ceiling, for example) is an unrepeated singularity. Similarly, the SETI scientist will accept a single message from outer space on a radio telescope as an indication that there are intelligent beings out there only because that scientist has repeatedly observed the production of similar messages by intelligent beings.[18] Likewise, the basis for believing that an event has a supernatural cause is the regular observation of certain kinds of events that result from intelligent causes.[19] But the *object* of that understanding can be an unrepeated *singularity* (namely, a miracle).[20] One requires but a single piece of ancient pottery to infer an intelligent cause of it, even though one must have seen *many* potters (or the like) make pottery (or the like) in order to know that only intelligent beings produce things of this kind. Likewise, the *basis* of our understanding that an event has an intelligent supernatural cause is our observation that intelligent beings (agents) *regularly* produce events of a similar kind within the natural world. The *object* of this understanding, however, may be a *singular* event (for example, a miracle).

Indeed, if the scientist, *based on* observation of regular causal conjunctions in the present, can conclude that the weight of the evidence points to a big bang *singularity* in which the material, space-time universe exploded into being out of nothing some billions of geological years ago, then not only are miracles possible, but the big one has already been confirmed! It remains to be seen whether any other miraculous events have occurred (see chapters twelve through sixteen in this volume). What is seldom appreciated, however, is that the very basis for asseverating the possibility (and even actuality) of miracles is David Hume's own principle of "constant conjunction" (the "repeatability principle"). So, far from eliminating miracles, Hume's own principle provides the grounds for identifying them (see chapter six).

An Evaluation of Flew's Argument Against Miracles

In addition to the critique of Hume's argument against miracles, much of which applies to Flew's argument, there are distinctive problems with Flew's view. All of these are internal to his naturalistic system.

Naturalistic unrepeatabilities. Most modern naturalists, like Flew, accept some unrepeatable singularities of their own. Many contemporary astronomers believe in the singular origin of the universe by a "(really) big bang." And nearly all scientists believe that the origin of life on this planet also was a singular event that has never been repeated here. But if Flew's argument against miracles is correct, then it is a mistake for scientists to believe in either of these singularities, which many of them consider to be natural events. Since the big bang involves the whole universe's coming into existence out of nothing, a theist might want to claim this is a miracle (something only God can do). But even if it is only a natural event, its existence as an unrepeated singularity refutes Flew's argument against miracles. Thus, Flew's argument against supernaturalism must also undermine the rationality of some basic naturalistic belief(s) of contemporary scientists.

Naturalism's unfalsifiability. Flew's view is subject to his own familiar criticism of theism; namely, it is an unfalsifiable position. For no matter what state of affairs actually occurs (even a resurrection), Flew (contrary even to Hume's claims) would be obliged to believe it was not a miracle. For Flew argued that "it often seems to people who are not religious as if there was no conceivable event or series of events the occurrence of which would be admitted by sophisticated religious people to be a sufficient reason for conceding 'there wasn't a God after all.' "[21] In short, their belief is actually unfalsifiable.

But in like manner, we may ask Flew (rephrasing his own words), "What would have to occur or to have occurred to constitute for you a disproof of your antisupernaturalism?"[22] Flew must answer that no event in the world would falsify his naturalism because in practice he believes the evidence is always greater against miracles than for them. So his assertion that miracles do not happen is unfalsifiable. It does not help for Flew to claim that his antisupernaturalism is falsifiable in principle but never in practice, on the grounds that in practice the evidence will always be greater for what is repeatable. For surely he would then have to allow the theist the claim that in principle the existence of God is falsifiable but that in practice no event could disconfirm God's existence! The fact that Flew and other atheologians busy themselves with attempts to disprove the existence of God (by arguing, for example, from the fact of evil in the world) reveals their belief that falsification in practice is that with which they are ultimately concerned.

Surely the antisupernaturalist cannot have it both ways. If Flew and others countenance the practical unfalsifiability of naturalism, why should not the unfalsifiability of belief in God (or in miracles) also be permitted? On the other hand, if supernaturalism can never be established in practice, why should that matter if naturalism can never be so established either? It is always possible for the theist to claim of every alleged natural event that "God is the ultimate cause of it." The theist may insist that all "natural" events (that is, naturally repeatable ones) are the way God normally operates while "miraculous" events are the way God works on special occasions. There is no way in practice to falsify this theistic belief, and the unfalsifiability of this belief is as innocuous as the unfalsifiability of Flew's naturalism. For just as Flew acknowledges that naturalism is unfalsifiable in practice, so too the theist could claim the same for theism. For any event in the natural world (whether it is repeatable or unrepeatable), the theist can always claim "God is the ultimate cause of it," and on Flew's grounds no naturalist can disprove this theistic claim.[23]

Finally, the theist denies that God is the direct cause of evil. The immediate cause of evil is some free agent(s) whom God permits to operate with a good power called free choice and for an ultimate good known at least to God (even if we do not know it).[24] Hence the argument from God's causality (or permission) of natural evil does not eliminate the possibility of his doing miracles. Indeed, his permission of certain evils may even explain some of his miraculous actions. For example, the miracles of the incarnation and of the resurrection of Jesus Christ (discussed in chapters fourteen through sixteen) serve his good purposes to rescue human persons from the evils of human sinfulness and its consequences (see chapter eleven).

Evidence for the repeatable is not always greater. Flew's assumption that the repeatable always evidentially outweighs the unrepeatable is subject to serious challenge. If this assumption is correct, then, as Whately pointed out, one should not believe in the historicity of any unusual events from the past (since none are repeatable). Likewise, even historical geology is unrepeatable in practice, since the fossil record was formed only once and has not been repeated. So also is the history of our planet unrepeatable. Yet it has happened. Hence if Flew is right, the science of geology should be eliminated too!

As the noted physicist Stanley Jaki has observed, scientists do not reject unrepeated singularities out of hand. "Luckily for science, scientists relatively rarely brush aside reports about a really *new* case with the remark: 'It cannot be really different from the thousand other cases we have already investigated.' The brave reply of the young assistant, 'But, Sir, what if this is the thousand and first case?' . . . is precisely the rejoinder that is to be offered in connection with facts that fall under suspicion because of their miraculous character."[25] So if the naturalist pushes his arguments far enough to eliminate miracles, by implication he thereby eliminates the grounds for his own beliefs about numerous other matters. If he qualifies his arguments so as to include all the natural and scientific data he wishes, then he reopens the door for miracles.

Summary and Conclusion

Hume and Flew have offered a forceful argument against miracles. But strong as it may seem, the evaluation here offered suggests that Hume was overly optimistic to believe that this argument could be "an everlasting check" and "useful as long as the world endures" to refute any claim for the miraculous. In point of fact, for several reasons Hume's argument is not successful. First, in the "hard" form it begs the question by assuming that miracles are by definition impossible. Second, in the "soft" form the argument engages in special pleading, begs the question, proves too much (such as that even Napoleon did not exist!), is inconsistent with Hume's own epistemology and makes scientific progress impossible. In brief, to repudiate miracles in advance of considering the evidence for their occurrence seems wholly prejudicial. If they are not thus repudiated, however, the door remains open to their possibility and to reasonable belief in their actuality. The wise do not *legislate* in advance that miracles cannot be believed to have happened; rather, they *look* at the evidence to see if God has indeed acted in history. Further, as the analysis of Flew's reasons reveals, the evidence for the rare is sometimes greater than that for the regular. Indeed, Flew's naturalism seems to be trapped by its own falsifiability principle, since there may be no way in practice to falsify his belief that every event is a natural event.

In view of the foregoing analysis, we must distinguish between the "modern" mind and the rational mind. The "modern" mind seems to be conditioned by an incurable naturalistic bias that has failed to justify itself rationally. Despite all efforts, it has failed to demonstrate the irrationality of belief in miracles. In the next chapter, Francis Beckwith addresses another modern objection to miracles, namely, that historians are unable to investigate reports of past miracles for the purposes of confirming that they actually happened.

FIVE

HISTORY &
MIRACLES

FRANCIS J. BECKWITH

IMAGINE A FRIEND TELLS YOU THAT HE HAD LUNCH WITH HIS FATHER last week. You gasp with amazement, not because you think there is anything particularly unusual about having lunch but because you think there is something particularly unusual about your friend's luncheon: his father has been deceased for about two years, or at least so you thought. In fact, you were a pallbearer at the man's open-casket funeral. Because you are a reasonable person, you begin to reflect on what was just told to you. You consider ways to reconcile your friend's testimony with what you know. You think to yourself, *Maybe he's gone mad or he's joking with me or he's mistaken.* But it's interesting to note what probably does not cross your mind as an option: *Since my friend's father has risen from the dead, I will have to return his name to my Christmas list.*

Your restraint in this regard would, according to David Hume, be quite reasonable: "When anyone tells me, that he saw a dead man restored to life, I immediately consider with myself, whether it be more probable, that this person should either deceive or be deceived, or that the fact, which he relates, should really have happened."[1] According to Hume, it is more likely in such a case that deception has occurred than that the testimony is authentic. After all, you would not doubt your friend's testimony if his father were alive and well. This is because you base your expectations and your judgments on your previous experience and what you know about the world: dead people remain dead.

This story, to which I will refer throughout this essay, may help us to understand better a central philosophical question for Christians who believe that their faith rests on the historicity of particular claims of the miraculous: Can history be inspected for the occurrence of miracles? Let us call this "the history question.". Since other conceptual problems surrounding the miraculous are addressed elsewhere in this volume (see chapters three, ten and eleven), this chapter will answer the history question by addressing three objections: (1) given the nature of the historian's craft, it is not within the bounds of historical study to investigate a miracle, especially when historians are bound by the limitations of historical relativism and subjectivism; (2) if miracle claims must be supported by greater evidence than ordinary claims, it can never be rational to claim that a miracle has occurred; and (3) if we cannot identify present miracles, then we are not justified in believing that miracles occurred in the past, since without uniformity between the past and the present it is not possible for historians to record with accuracy anything from the past (Ernst Troeltsch's *principle of analogy*).

Some scholars challenge the historicity of the miraculous by arguing that history as a discipline is not equipped to handle the task. This challenge, though much wider in scope than can possibly be covered here,[2] has two primary components, which will be addressed in this chapter: *(a)* it is not within the bounds of the historical endeavor to investigate a miracle, since historians do not possess the proper tools; and *(b)* historical inquiry is too limited by historians' own subjective limitations to yield a reliable objectivist account of historical events.

Miracles and the Limits of Historical Research

Those who defend *(a)* argue in the following way: miracles cannot be the object of historical research, since the agent to which a miracle is ascribed is a nonempirical, supernatural being (namely God, or perhaps an angel), and historians do not have the proper tools by which to detect such an agent.[3] There are at least three problems with this argument. First, historians can investigate the facts surrounding an alleged miracle without addressing its supernatural agency. Take the resurrection of Jesus, which Christians claim was performed by God. Although historians may have no interest in this theological interpretation of the event, it does not follow from this that historical research is completely incapable of addressing any aspect of the alleged event. That is to say, the claim that Jesus rose from the dead, because it is associated with other historical phenomena, can be checked out by historians. Such phenomena include (1) the claim by Jesus of Nazareth, a first-century Jewish carpenter, that he was the Son of God and that his resurrection from the dead would establish the truth of this claim; (2) the crucifixion, death and entombment of Jesus (c. A.D. 33); (3) Jesus' tomb discovered to be empty a few days after his death; and (4) the claim by Jesus' followers that they saw their leader alive several days after the burial.[4]

Second, it seems that believers in miracles do not have to concede one of the premises of this objection—that historians do not have the proper tools by which to detect the supernatural agent who is said to have performed the miracles. A number of scholars,[5] including Winfried Corduan (chapter six, "Recognizing a Miracle"), persuasively argue that one can detect through the investigation of history various aspects of the supernatural agency of an alleged miraculous event.

Third, even opponents of miracles seem implicitly to reject this objection, since the possibility of disproving the historicity of a miracle would be something they would not want to give up. But disproving the historicity of a miracle is only possible if it is within the bounds of the historical endeavor to investigate a miracle. For example, suppose archaeologists discover conclusive proof that the tomb of Jesus of Nazareth was not empty after his burial, that he did not consider himself to be the Son of God, and that his followers never claimed to have seen him alive after he died. Opponents of miracles would rightfully conclude that such evidence counts against the claim that Jesus was resurrected from the dead by God. But this implies that historians can investigate miraculous claims.

Historians' Subjective Limitations

Defenders of *(b)*, such as Carl Becker and Charles Beard,[6] argue that the craft of history is too subjective due to limitations within historians themselves. That is to say, there can be no objective history that can tell us how events in the past *really happened*, since historians' work is shaped by their own ideas, value judgments, worldview, prejudices and perspective. This is why Becker writes, "The event itself, the facts, do not say anything, do not impose any meaning. It is the historian who speaks, who imposes a meaning."[7] If this position is correct, then Christian apologists' appeal to historical facts is flawed from the outset, since there are no historically objective facts out there. There are just the writings of historians who are limited by their time, place, beliefs and worldview.

There is something to be said for this position if it is merely saying that nobody is absolutely objective. Christian apologists can agree with relativists that people often permit their biases and prejudices to influence how they look at facts. For instance, Christian apologists may believe that some people who reject miracles do not do so because of a lack of evidence, but rather because of their a priori commitment to a nontheistic worldview such as naturalism.[8] However, if defenders of this objection are saying that the limitations of historians are all-encompassing and for that reason our knowledge of history is completely relative, there are a number of problems with such a view. First, the position is self-refuting. As Norman L. Geisler points out:

> If relativity is unavoidable the position of the historical relativists is self-refuting. For either their view is historically conditioned and, therefore, unobjective or else it is not relative but objective. If the latter, then it thereby admits that it is possible to be objective in viewing history. On the contrary, if the position of historical relativism is itself relative, then it cannot be objectively true. It is simply subjective opinion which has no basis to claim to be objectively true about all of history. In short, if it is a subjective opinion it cannot eliminate the possibility that history is objectively knowable; and if it is an objective fact about history then objective facts can be known about history. In the first case objectivity is not eliminated and in the second relativity is self-defeated. Hence, in either case, objectivity is possible.[9]

Second, if history is not objective, then there is no such thing as an objectively bad history or interpretation of historical events. But such a view seems absurd. Consider this example. Suppose historian X argues that Adolf Hitler killed six million Jews because he had a fondness for Jews and wanted to make sure they would get to heaven more quickly. On the other hand, historian Y maintains that Hitler killed six million Jews since he was an anti-Semite who was obsessed with accomplishing a complete genocide of the Jewish people because he believed outrageous and false things about them. It would seem that the historical relativist would have to say that there are no objective facts that could help us to determine who is correct between X and Y, since each is locked within a private perspective. But there are a host of facts, including Hitler's own writings, which clearly indicate that Y is correct and that X is completely mistaken.

Third, those who defend historical relativism because of the presence of historians' own ideas, value judgments, worldview, prejudices and perspective ignore the important distinction between *logical process* and *psychological process*. That is to say, though it is certainly true that historians' judgments are psychologically influenced by all these factors, it does not follow from this that historians cannot test or justify their judgment by comparing it to the objective facts. As Ronald H. Nash points out:

> It is one thing to study the *psychological process* by which a historian formulates his beliefs and another thing to study the *logical process* by which those beliefs can be justified. . . . It is important not to confuse the process of discovery and justification. The process of discovering the past may be influenced by any number of psychological and social factors. But when the historian turns to the matter of justifying his interpretations, his psychological quirks and prejudices, his background, and his interests should become irrelevant. . . . The historian's work can always be challenged; and when it is, his evidence, reasoning, and interpretations will be subject to critical revision.[10]

Fourth (which follows from my third criticism), "the constant rewriting of history is based on the assumption that objectivity is possible."[11] Consider the 1994 publication and release of the diaries of former White House aide to President Richard Nixon, H. R. Haldeman. Historians and journalists were enthusiastic about these diaries because they would provide them with facts that could shed more light on the Watergate scandal and the Nixon presidency. But if history cannot be objective, in what sense can these diaries increase our knowledge or help us assess and make more accurate our record of past events? Geisler develops this point:

> Why strive for accuracy unless it is believed that the revision is more objectively true than the previous view? Why critically analyze unless improvement toward a more accurate view is the assumed goal? Perfect objectivity may be practically unattainable within the limited resources of the historian on most if not all topics. But be this as it may, the inability to attain 100 percent objectivity is a long way from total relativity. Reaching a degree of objectivity which is subject to criticism and revision is a more realistic conclusion than the relativist's arguments.[12]

Fifth, there is a common core of incontrovertible facts to which even historical relativists admit. For example, E. H. Carr, a relativist, claims that "there are basic facts which are the same for all historians," and that it is the historian's duty to present them accurately.[13] Although Becker maintains that facts have no objective meaning, he concedes that "some things, some 'facts' can be established and agreed upon," such as the assassination of Abraham Lincoln, the date of the Declaration of Independence, the selling of indulgences in 1517, and Caesar's crossing of the Rubicon.[14]

To summarize this section, I have argued that skeptical historians' objections to the miraculous fail. First, miracles can be the object of historical research even if the agent to which a miracle is ascribed is a nonempirical, supernatural being because (1) historians can investigate the facts surrounding a miracle claim without referring directly to supernatural agency, (2) believers may very well be able to detect the supernatural agency behind an alleged miraculous event, and (3) opponents of miracles implicitly assume the applicability of historical research to miracles whenever they try to *disprove* their occurrence. Second, historical relativism is seriously flawed since it (1) is self-refuting, (2) is incapable of making sense of judgments of bad and good history, (3) confuses logical process with psychological process, (4) cannot discount the objectivity assumed in the rewriting of history as our knowledge of the past apparently increases and (5) cannot call into question a common core of historical facts.

Miracle Claims, Ordinary Events and Rational Justification

Believers in miracles disagree about whether one needs more evidence for a miracle than one needs for an ordinary event.[15] But it seems to me that if one looks carefully at the above story about the alleged resurrection of your friend's father, more evidence is required to be rational in believing that an ordinary event has occurred. After all, a miracle is by definition at least a highly unusual event (see Richard Purtill's discussion of the nature of a miracle in chapter three). And even if one thinks that there is rational justification to believe in the existence of a deity with the means and motive to perform miracles (see chapters nine, ten and eleven), thus raising the probability that a miracle would occur, miracles would still be exceptional (or rare) occurrences.

David Hume (whose famous tract against miracles appears in chapter one) and other opponents of miracles have used the comparative improbability of miraculous events vis-à-vis ordinary events to argue that one is never justified in believing that a miracle has occurred in history.

Antony Flew, a contributor to this volume (chapter two), explains: "But now, clearly, the evidence for the subsistence of such a strong order of Nature will have to be put on the side of the balance opposite to that containing the evidence for the occurrence of the exceptional overriding."[16] Consequently, one is never justified in believing in the occurrence of a miracle in history since the "strong order of Nature" will *always* outweigh the evidence for a miracle.

Evidence and knowing that improbable events have occurred. Opponents of miracles maintain that we should always believe what is more probable, usually adding that whatever has occurred more frequently has greater probability in its favor. We must weigh as evidence the improbability of a miracle occurring against the evidence for an alleged miraculous event. This leads, of course, to the conclusion that we are never justified in believing that a miracle has occurred. This argument can be put in the form of a conditional assertion:

(1) If E is a highly improbable event, no evidence is sufficient for one to be justified in believing it has occurred.

This assertion, however, seems to be incorrect. Is it not perfectly reasonable occasionally to believe, because there is sufficient evidence, that an improbable event has occurred? How could the possibility of sufficient evidence for the improbable be ruled out a priori? Consider the following example:

Life magazine once reported that all 15 people scheduled to attend a rehearsal of a church choir in Beatrice, Neb., were late for practice on March 1, 1950, and each had a different reason: a car wouldn't start, a radio program wasn't over, ironing wasn't finished, a conversation dragged on. It was fortunate that none arrived on schedule at 7:15 p.m.—the church was destroyed by an explosion at 7:25. The choir members wondered whether their mutual delays were an act of God. . . . Weaver estimated there was a one-in-a-million chance that all 15 would be late the same evening.[17]

According to the conditional assertion (1), opponents of miracles claim that we should reject the reliable testimony and circumstantial evidence that has substantiated the event described in this anecdote, even though it would seem perfectly reasonable to believe that the event has occurred. Consider two more examples. It is highly unlikely that my friend Mark will be dealt a royal flush while playing poker in Las Vegas. That is, the odds are that he will be dealt a less promising hand—the odds of being dealt a royal flush are 0.15×10^{-5}.[18] But according to opponents of miracles, if Mark is dealt the highly improbable hand, a royal flush, none of us would be justified in accepting as true the testimony of several reliable witnesses who report that they had seen the hand.

Imagine next the case of a woman accused of murder and brought to trial. Testifying against her are five upstanding and responsible citizens who have no reason to lie. Each testifies to having seen the accused commit the murder. Suppose, however, that the defendant's attorney, a strong supporter of (1), calls 875 people to testify that they have known the defendant for more than twenty years and have never seen her murder anybody. Following this procession of witnesses, the defense attorney argues, "Ladies and gentlemen of the jury, your job as rational agents is to weigh the testimonies of 875 people who say that they have never witnessed my client commit a murder. Because the 'evidence' of her not murdering anyone in the past is greater than the evidence of her recently murdering someone, and because a person's belief is not justified unless he or she believes on the basis of the greater evidence, my client is *not* guilty." The problem with this reasoning, as any intelligent jury or judge would quickly recognize, is that it mistakenly assumes—as the advocate of (1) mistakenly assumes— that what is most probable (what is more likely to occur, like not murdering) cannot be used perpetually to trump any evidence, however powerful, for the occurrence of a rare event (like murdering).

Evidence and knowing that miraculous events have occurred. It is possible, however, that I have misunderstood opponents of miracles, since the above instances of improbable events are perfectly *natural* events. Though they are like miracle claims in virtue of being improbable, they are unlike miracle claims in that they occur in accordance with the regular course of nature (Hume and others would call miracles "violations of natural law"). For this reason, perhaps opponents of miracles are claiming that we are not justified in believing the testimonial and circumstantial evidence for those improbable events as long as those events are thought to be miracles that violate natural law. (For more on this, see chapter three.) This claim can be put in the form of the following conditional assertion:

(2) If E is a miracle that violates natural law, no evidence is sufficient for one to be justified in believing it has occurred.

Purtill argues in chapter three of this volume that it is perfectly coherent to hold that a miracle (an improbable event) violates, or in some sense supersedes, natural law. Nevertheless, as I have argued, sufficient testimony and evidence can make it reasonable to believe that an improbable event has actually occurred. Hence to say that no testimony or evidence is sufficient for us to be justified in believing a miracle has occurred is to beg the question in favor of naturalism. In other words, in order to claim that no evidence is sufficient to prove a miraculous event has occurred, opponents of miracles must assume the truth of naturalism, the view which if true would make any evidence for a miracle de facto insufficient, a point that Ronald Nash develops more fully in chapter seven.

It seems, however, that the only way for opponents of miracles to claim correctly that no historical or contemporary evidence is sufficient to warrant belief that a miracle has occurred is if violations of natural law are *maximally improbable*. In other words, there are no events more improbable than miracles, which is to say that miracles are the most improbable events that can be conceived. But we can know that miracles are maximally improbable *only if* we already *know* that miracles could or have never occurred, or that they are logically impossible (that is, conceptually impossible, like a "square circle" or a "married bachelor"). Opponents of miracles must therefore maintain that miracles are maximally improbable because they already know that miracles could or have never occurred. But Alvin Plantinga is right to ask:

> Why should a theist think that such a proposition [namely, *E has occurred and E is a violation of a law of nature*] is maximally improbable? (Indeed, why should anyone think so? We aren't given *a priori* that nature is seldom interfered with.) Even if a theist thinks of miracles as a violation of laws of nature . . . she needn't think it improbable *in excelsis* that a miracle occur; so why couldn't she perfectly sensibly believe, on the basis of sufficient testimony, that some particular miraculous event has occurred?[19]

Consequently, opponents of miracles beg the question if they claim that miracles are maximally improbable. Nevertheless, this should not be interpreted to mean that we should never be skeptical about firsthand testimonies affirming that a miracle has occurred (see chapter twelve, where David Clark evaluates the miracle claims of non-Christian traditions). J. C. A. Gaskin has made the point, however, that "there is an uncomfortable sense that by means of it [i.e., the historical argument against miracles] one may well justify disbelieving reports of things which did in fact happen—like your disbelief in my report of seeing water turned into wine if my report had also been vouched by numerous other good and impartial witnesses."[20] Gaskin continues:

While it is certainly true that when something altogether extraordinary is reported, the wise man will require more evidence than usual and will check and re-check the evidence very carefully, nevertheless at some stage in his accumulation of respectable evidence the wise man would be in danger of becoming dogmatic and obscurantist if he did *not* believe the evidence.[21]

Miraculous Events, Probability and the Nature of Evidence

Let us return to the story I presented at the beginning of this chapter. After hearing your friend tell you that he had lunch with his father, who had been dead for about two years, it would seem reasonable that you assume a posture similar to Hume's: it is more likely that deception is involved at some level than that your friend's testimony reports the truth.[22] Let us suppose, however, that seventy-five reliable witnesses over the past year corroborate your friend's testimony. Moreover, the mortuary, which had embalmed the body, reports that the body disappeared a year ago and is nowhere to be found, and forensic experts determine that the fingerprints of the man with whom your friend had lunch perfectly match the fingerprints of his dead father. Furthermore, your friend's father was a religious man deeply committed to serving God and had prayed prior to his death for God to resurrect him in order to establish the truth of his religious convictions for the benefit of his skeptical relatives.

Assuming that the evidence in this story is well founded, the dismissal of historical evidence for the miraculous becomes highly artificial as well as woefully inadequate. In this case, it is not a weighing of *a* probability L (the regularity of nature's laws) against *a* probability T (your friend's testimony that L had been violated), but a weighing of L against what Cardinal Newman called a "convergence of independent probabilities," T_1, T_2, T_3, . . . T_n (for example, diverse and reliable testimonies, fingerprints, circumstantial evidence such as the missing embalmed body and his prayer to God).[23]

It has been pointed out by some that just as our formulations of natural law are based on certain regularities, our standards of evaluating historical testimony and evidence are also based on certain regularities (for example, "witnesses in such-and-such a situation are more apt to tell the truth"; justification of the principles of historiography, forensic pathology, document analysis and detective work).[24] Since these standards individually do not have the same probative strength as a natural law, a single piece, or even several strands, of testimonial evidence is in most cases insufficient to justify one's claim that a miracle has occurred.

A single testimony, however, is usually sufficient in most everyday situations (such as "It is raining outside"). But it seems to me that the testimonial evidence might be multiplied and reinforced by circumstantial and other considerations, as in the case of your friend's father, and the explanation of the event as a miracle that violates natural law might connect the data simply and coherently (just as we expect a natural law to do),[25] while a denial of either the occurrence of the event or its miraculous nature appears to be an ad hoc naturalism-of-the-gaps.[26] Then the believer in miracles is justified in believing that a miraculous event has occurred. The authors of the essays included in part four ("Christian Miracles—Case Studies") accept this burden and make the case for certain Christian miracles by providing historical evidence that is sufficient to warrant a belief that miracles have occurred. In this overall case, the data are multiplied and reinforced.

Ernst Troeltsch's Principle of Analogy

German theologian Ernst Troeltsch, in explaining what he considers the principles and methods of historiography (the writing of history), suggests the principle of analogy: "On the analogy of the events known to us we seek by conjecture and sympathetic understanding to explain and reconstruct the past."[27] That is, without uniformity between the past and the present, it is not possible for one to record with accuracy anything from the past. The implication of this principle for miracles is obvious: if one cannot identify present miracles, then one cannot be justified in believing that miracles occurred in the past. One of the most powerful uses of Troeltsch's principle is developed in an argument by Antony Flew, though Troeltsch's name is not mentioned by Flew in the immediate context:

> The basic propositions are: first, that the present relics of the past cannot be interpreted as historical evidence at all, unless we presume that the fundamental regularities obtained then as still obtain today; second, that in trying as best he may determine what actually happened the historian must employ his present knowledge of what is probable or improbable, possible or impossible; and third, since *miracle* has to be defined in terms of practical impossibility the application of these criteria precludes proof of a miracle.[28]

A number of objections can be raised against this argument. First, it begs the question by assuming an antimiraculous worldview to quash a priori all evidence for the miraculous. Flew and Troeltsch are certainly correct if they are merely saying that we must assume some continuity and consistency between the present and the past in order to acquire any historical knowledge. After all, in order to justify their belief that a miracle has occurred, believers in miracles rely on criteria developed in a number of disciplines—archaeology, forensic medicine, law, literary theory, psychology, for example—which all depend on the assumption that the regularities of the present are the regularities of the past. However, if Flew and Troeltsch are saying that historians cannot have historical knowledge unless they assume that *regular* events (that is, nonmiraculous events) are the only ones that have ever occurred, then their position begs the question. That is, they assume the truth of a nonmiraculous worldview in order to prove that one cannot justify a miraculous worldview. It is one thing to make the uncontroversial claim that historians must assume some continuity of regularities between the present and the past in order to have historical knowledge. It is quite another thing, however, to claim, as do Flew and Troeltsch, that we must assume a nonmiraculous worldview in order to have historical knowledge. Such a position calls for the automatic rejection of new data, regardless of how well grounded evidentially, which may support the historicity of the miraculous and count against the nonmiraculous worldview.

A second objection to the Flew-Troeltsch argument follows closely behind the first: this argument confuses analogy as a *basis* for studying the past with the *object* of the past that is studied. That is to say, we assume consistency and continuity when studying the past, but it does not follow that what we discover about the past (that is, the object of our inquiry) cannot be a unique singularity. Geisler provides an example:

> The SETI (Search for Extra-Terrestrial Intelligence) is believed to be scientific for believing that receipt of a single message from space will reveal the existence of intelligent life. For even if the object of pursuit is the reception of only one message, nevertheless, the basis of knowing that it was produced by intelligence is the regular conjunction of intelligent beings with this kind of complex information. So, while knowledge of the past is based on analogies in the present, the object of this knowledge can be a singularity.[29]

Third, the argument assumes without proof that miracles are not occurring in the present.[30] That is to say, defenders of this argument must show that there are no present miracles and not merely assume there are not. After all, if miracles are presently occurring, then Troeltsch's principle of analogy could be granted and used to *support* the reality of past miracles.

As I have pointed out already, since the standards by which we judge evidence and testimony are based on certain regularities, which are true in both the past and the present, the possibility that one can be justified in believing in the historicity of a miracle cannot be ruled out in principle, since its historicity can be based on the convergence of independent probabilities. Understood in this way, *regularity* can yield a unique and singular result, since regularity is the basis and not the object of historical investigation.

Consider again the example of the apparent resurrection of your friend's father, but let us further suppose that the event occurred twenty years ago. Assuming the truth of these features of the account, it would seem that if Flew and Troeltsch maintained that the event did not occur because the historian must assume that the regularities of the past are continuous with the regularities of the present, they would be missing the whole point of historical investigation. It would also appear that they would be engaging in special pleading for one sort of regularity (natural laws) that would require the historian to use that regularity to always trump and completely disregard other sorts of regularity (the bases of evidential criteria).

The pieces of evidence in this fictional tale are themselves based on certain regularities (for example, "It is highly improbable that forensic scientists should be wrong about fingerprints in a properly conducted laboratory setting"). The pieces of evidence are independent probabilities that converge on the event and provide a basis for being justified in believing that the event had actually happened. Additionally, the radical law-violating nature of the resurrection, as well as the timing and context of the occurrence, make appeals to coincidence and psychosomatic explanations clearly question-begging and ad hoc.

Conclusion

In responding to three of the most important objections to the historicity of the miraculous, three conclusions have been reached: (1) the historical investigation of the miraculous is consistent with historians' craft and cannot be refuted by appeals to historical relativism and subjectivism; (2) even if miracle claims need support from more evidence than ordinary claims in order to be held rationally, it can sometimes be the case that one has sufficient evidence to believe that a miracle has occurred; and (3) Ernst Troeltsch's principle of analogy fails to undermine belief in the miraculous.[31]

SIX

RECOGNIZING
A MIRACLE

WINFRIED CORDUAN

Numerous questions surround the matter of miracles, but many of them are meaningless if it is in principle impossible ever to recognize a miracle when one has occurred. What would be the point of studying the issues surrounding miracles if one had already decided in advance that all alleged miracles are simply unusual events of nature? In other words, even if we had a clear definition of what a miracle is, and even if it were possible to believe the witnesses to them, one would still have to decide for each event that it was a natural event, and thus the evidence for there being miracles could in principle never come in.

In this chapter I begin by stating the skeptic's case, according to which the very nature of science rules out the possibility of identifying any event as miraculous. I then shift gears by focusing not on what a skeptic might require to identify a miracle, but on what is involved when a believer claims to have identified a miraculous event. From there I will show how those insights transfer back to the argument against the skeptic, primarily by making the case that for some events a prima facie presumption may be that they are miracles.

Miracles Not Identifiable

A number of writers have argued that it is indeed impossible ever to recognize a miracle. This position needs to be distinguished from the well-known argument, which David Hume includes in his critique, that the probability of a miracle's having occurred is never as high as the probability that the witnesses to an alleged miracle were mistaken.[1] This argument concerns the evidence for miracles, but the issue of the recognition of miracles renders the question of evidence irrelevant, at least for the moment. Obviously, if it is in principle impossible to recognize a miracle, then no amount of evidence could ever justify the event as a miracle. The essence of the skeptic's argument is that the methodological objection to including the miraculous will make it impossible ever to call an event a miracle. Such is the challenge laid down by Antony Flew. In his article "Miracles" in *The Encyclopedia of Philosophy,* Flew makes the following points:[2]

1. The occurrence of a miracle is frequently used to attest a particular doctrinal point or system, for example, the way in which a believer in God may use miracles to make a case for theism.

2. If a miracle is to serve as genuine evidence for a belief, it must be recognizable as a miracle by someone not already committed to the belief in question. To use miracles as evidence for a belief and then require that the belief be stipulated so as to make miracles plausible would simply beg the question. Thus "the method of identification must be logically independent of that system."[3]

3. There is no natural faculty that human beings have for recognizing when the normal limits of nature have been exceeded.

4. The very essence of the work of the scientist demands being open to new possibilities in observations of nature. If new observations conflict with present theories, the scientist needs to revise his or her theories, not blame the event on something supernatural.

5. Thus the best approach to understanding an anomalous event, which might otherwise be regarded as a miracle, is always to expand our understanding of the potentialities of nature. Rather than claiming we saw something supernatural, we should recognize that nature is capable of doing more than we had expected. And so it becomes impossible a priori ever to identify an event as a miracle.

6. Consequently, the very fact of an event's having happened, no matter how strange, is sufficient to identify it as nonmiraculous. Let us call such strange anomalous occurrences "natural miracles." Flew asserts, "If ever we became able to say that some account of the ostensibly miraculous was indeed veridical, we can say it only because we now know

that the occurrences reported were not miraculous at all."[4]

Similar thoughts are echoed by Guy Robinson.[5] He argues against a "miracles-in-the-gaps" understanding of the miraculous. According to Robinson, it is commonly (but mistakenly) thought that where science is at a loss for an explanation, the notion of the miraculous may be invoked. He maintains that there is no basis for allowing religious categories to play a role in scientific explanation. "Science and religion have no common frontier and no disputed territory."[6] Science does not recoil before anomalies, but is always a priori disposed to broaden its understanding of nature in order to accommodate them. Thus, the suggestion that miracles should take over where science leaves off is incoherent. In a real sense science never leaves off.[7]

Essentially the same case has been proposed by Patrick Nowell-Smith[8] and Stephen J. Wykstra.[9] Refutations have been attempted by Margaret Boden,[10] John Warwick Montgomery[11] and George I. Mavrodes.[12] Briefly put, these attempted refutations intend to show that scientists, in describing and collating their observations, are violating empirical methodology by not retaining openness for miraculous events. They thereby try to beat the naturalists at their own game, but it is not at all clear that those arguments go to the heart of the issue, because the skeptics maintain that their very methodology must rule out supernatural events.

Let us review the logic of the naturalists' position:

1. An unusual event has been observed or reported.

2. Some people infer that the cause of the event is supernatural.

3. But inferences to the supernatural may not be made unless any possibility of a natural cause has been completely eliminated.

4. A scientist may never consider the possibility of a natural cause to have been completely eliminated.

5. Therefore, an inference to the supernatural on the basis of such an unusual event is never justified.

In short, the naturalist skeptics claim that theists may identify an event as a miracle only if they can convince the naturalists that it is a miracle. By virtue of their assumptions about the nature of science, however, the naturalists will never be convinced that a miracle has actually occurred. Therefore, not even theists can identify an event as miraculous.

We can now see that the naturalists have laid out the rules of the game in such a way that they cannot possibly lose. Of course, they will reply that they are right to insist on those rules if the alleged miracles are intended to convince them that there is something supernatural. It hardly makes sense to expect the naturalists to concede the reality of miracles so that they can become convinced of the reality of the supernatural. But neither is it rational to forbid the possibility of the supernatural and yet demand that believers use the miraculous as evidence for the supernatural (which appears to be the requirement placed on believers by Flew).

Are we then at a standoff? The answer is yes only if we continue to play on the same old turf. We need to return to the question of the evidential value of miracles later on in this chapter (see also chapter eleven), but first we must reconsider the naturalists' constraints on the possibility of identifying a genuine miracle. It would be a mistake for theists to accept the naturalists' own requirements regarding the identifiability of a miracle in order to show that some event is genuinely miraculous. A crucial consideration is that beliefs about many matters of fact are embedded within larger worldviews, and evidence for miraculous events is evaluated in terms of broader conceptual schemes.[13] Let us then consider first what it means for someone who is open to the supernatural to recognize a miracle. Then we may ask how to approach the naturalist for whom the identification of a miracle is an a priori impossibility.

Inside the Believer's Circle

Let us call a person with the disposition to allow the possibility of miracles a "believer." For our purposes, this term has a fairly restricted sense; it refers to the belief in miracles and not necessarily to all that would be involved in being a religious believer. Therefore, in the sense in which we are using the term it refers only to someone who will accept some miracles as having happened without necessarily having to accept all alleged miracles or one miracle in particular.

As we begin our look at the recognition of miracles by believers, we find that they do not necessarily agree on the identification of particular miracles. This observation suggests that any attempt to specify a convenient formula or absolute criterion for identifying a genuine miracle will only lead to disappointment.

Let us consider a particular example. In Luke 4:16-30 we read that a mob in Nazareth attempted to kill Jesus by throwing him down a cliff. Then we read, "But passing through the midst of them he went away" (v. 30 RSV). It is natural to ask whether Jesus performed a miracle with this escape from the angry crowd. It turns out that commentators who are well disposed toward accepting miracles disagree. On the one hand, H. A. Ironside claims that it was a miracle,[14] while the popular German

Bible teacher Fritz Rienecker does not think so,[15] and the NIV Study Bible leaves the matter open: "Luke does not explain whether the escape was miraculous or simply the result of Jesus' commanding presence."[16]

This small example, clearly an exception to the usual depiction of miracles in the Gospels, can nevertheless serve as an entry point for a crucial observation about the believer in miracles. The disposition to accept some events as miraculous does not entail having an unequivocal set of criteria to decide whether a miracle has occurred. This point becomes even clearer if we inventory the attitudes of some believers toward purported miracles, such as healings in a revival. Believers who were present at the event might interpret such a miracle as a psychosomatic event, not something supernatural. The believers do believe in miracles, but not in this particular one. We can also observe that believers who identify the event as a miracle may not be particularly inclined to invoke the idea that a natural law has been broken, either because they do not conceptualize the issue in these terms or even because they are ignorant of the matters in question.

On what grounds do believers actually assert that an event is a miracle rather than a natural event? Given the above remarks, it is not possible to give a universally applicable answer, but the chances are good that the believer is going to answer something along the lines of "because only God could have done this," or "because it would take supernatural intervention by God to bring this about." For believers, the first criterion is whether the occurrence is due to a direct act of God.

But to say that an event is a miracle if it is an act of God seems to be both circular and ambiguous. Whether the event is a direct act of God, and therefore a miracle, is precisely the point at issue. What the believer apparently means is that explaining the event as an act of God is the best available option. But this explanation implies that the event has to be extremely unusual, for the believer will be parsimonious with his identification of an event as miracle.

Levels of Divine Intervention and Types of Miracles

To identify an event as a miracle because it appears to be an act of God is also ambiguous. Believers are typically already committed to various levels of divine acts. We can point out three possibilities:

a. Providence. Believers may give credit to God in a situation in which nothing discernibly supernatural occurred. For example, they may say that "God brought it about that I have this job." God worked through natural processes; thus this sort of divine action would be perfectly compatible with Flew's argument against miracles.

b. Direct nonmiraculous intervention. Believers may say that God has acted in answering a prayer, even when the answer to prayer followed completely natural and unsurprising processes. "I prayed for a good job, applied for this position and was hired." Again, there is no incompatibility with Flew's objection here.

c. Direct miraculous intervention. Believers would probably say that a *miracle* had occurred if an event happened which could be best explained as a direct act of God.

As already alluded to, an event that fit into category c would have to be very unusual, even for believers to label it as a miracle. The whole reason for the concept of a miracle is to distinguish miracles from ordinary, natural events. The question, then, comes up as to how unusual an event would have to be for such an explanation to seem best to the believer's mind. Believers may explain why they regard a particular event as a miracle by pointing out that it seems to be a violation of a law of nature. But it is unlikely that they would do this in all cases. We can identify two possible instances in which a miracle might be said to have occurred.

1. "Constellation miracles." Sometimes an event can be explained in terms of natural laws, and yet believers may claim that it was a miracle. In many such cases, it is the coming together of certain natural events— their "constellation"—that makes the event unusual. Let us say that a believer— call him Bill Smith—loses his application for employment on the way to mailing it. A strong wind carries it across town, where it gets stuck between the cab and bed of a produce truck that happens to be going to the very city where Bill's prospective employer is headquartered. As the truck is parked at its destination overnight, vandals ransack the truck and so dislodge the letter. The letter lies on the sidewalk until the next morning, when it is picked up by a jogger, the daughter of the company president. She presents it to her father, who reads the application and hires Bill.

Meanwhile, Bill has been asking God to intervene on his behalf since he lost the application. When Bill gets a phone call from the president of the company, he thanks God for a miracle. As a believer in God, he is justified in this assessment, though it would admittedly not satisfy a naturalist. Bill recognizes that the event is highly unusual; the fact that he prayed clinches it for him that God intervened, and so he feels justified in identifying the event as miraculous.

This type of miraculous event is what R. F. Holland has called a "contingency" miracle.[17] Norman Geisler refers to it as a "class two" miracle.[18] The aspect of the situation that calls special attention to divine agency is nothing inherently unlikely, let alone physically incongruous. It is, rather, the coming together of a number of events that are in themselves physically possible (perhaps even somewhat probable) to form a constellation of events that is highly improbable. What prevents Bill from thinking of this constellation of events merely as a massive coincidence? It is the fact the sequence occurred within a context of his expectation of divine agency on his behalf (which fact reminds us again that we are still within the circle of believers—a skeptic need not be convinced).

2. *"Violation miracles."* The label for this type of miracle refers to the idea that apparently a law of nature has been violated. We are here concerned with events that go counter to what is normally expected or considered to be plausible. Water does not turn into wine, and people who have been dead for three days do not come back to life. A believer might claim that a miracle has occurred if her hand had been severed in an accident, she prayed, and a new hand "grew back" instantaneously. Of course, for this to count as a miracle, it must be an act of God. Leaving all supernatural agency out of the picture would result in an unusual manifestation of human regenerative powers, not a miracle. On the other hand (no pun intended), granted divine agency, believers might still thank God for the healing even if the event were explicable in terms of known natural processes (i.e., a constellation miracle).

The Necessity of Divine Agency

Both of these two types of miracles have this in common: believers identify an event as a miracle when two features come together—the event is unusual enough to point them in the direction of expected divine agency, and (given their worldview) there is enough reason to believe that God has in fact intervened in this particular case.

Some recent writers have taken a similar approach to the identification of a miracle primarily when it is recognized as an act of God. Douglas K. Erlandson maintains that believers recognize a miracle primarily because they see God involved in an event as agent, not because the possibility of scientific explanation has been circumvented, but alongside all scientific investigations.[19] Similarly, Robert Young states that "when a miracle occurs, God is an active agent-factor in the set of factors . . .

which actually was causally operative. His presence (ceteris paribus) alters the outcome from what it (perhaps) would have been if, contrary to fact, he had not been present."[20]

Under this criterion, persons trying to decide whether or not an event is a miracle engage in a kind of hypothesis testing. They ask themselves what the outcome would have been if God had not acted and contrast that hypothesis with what actually did occur, given God's act. If God's direct intervention is an indispensable causal factor in the event, then the believers recognize the event to be a miracle. Thus, we identify a miracle on the basis that the hypothesis of God as necessary agent-factor is the most plausible. Young claims that believers need not introduce the additional concepts of violation or constellation miracles since all that is necessary is to recognize God's agency.

However, when we return to the question of how to identify an event as a miracle, a criticism of Young's concept presents itself. It centers on Young's contention that his understanding of the miraculous is categorically distinct from the violation or the constellation concept. It is hard to see how one would come to identify God as agent-factor if some prior violation or constellation was not at least the occasion for such a recognition. In order to convince believers that a miracle has occurred, something extremely unusual needs to have taken place.

In sum, believers recognize a miracle when they see God acting directly in some unusual way. There is no absolute test as to when this occurs, but there need not be one. Believers will operate with informal criteria, by which they recognize God's intervention. Christian believers agree, for example, that Jesus' turning water into wine is a miracle, even if they do not have a definite recognition formula at their disposal.

Speaking Outside the Circle

Now we need to address ourselves to the tricky matter of unbelievers' or skeptics' recognition of a miracle. Let us draw a loose distinction between these two groups of people. We can define unbelievers as those who do not accept the idea of the supernatural but are theoretically willing to be convinced that a miraculous event could have occurred. They have never seen one and expect never to see one, but do not say dogmatically that such an event could never occur. Let us call skeptics those who believe that the supernatural does not exist and hold that miracles are therefore a priori impossible. It appears that Flew and Robinson qualify as skeptics.

Let me begin with two observations. First, there is no good reason to stipulate that being able to persuade unbelievers or skeptics delineates the single or even the crucial test for the possibility of recognizing a miracle. Many observers may fail to recognize the aurora borealis, the symptoms of diabetes or the invalid character of an AAA-2 categorical syllogism. But that fact does not mean that people trained to recognize such things are not entitled to make the identification. It is quite possible that believers are more expert when it comes to recognizing miracles because their worldview enables them to recognize them more easily and accurately. The fact that someone with a different worldview cannot recognize miracles need not be fatal to the possibility of any such recognition.

Second, if we allow for the theoretical possibility that unbelievers could or should be capable of miracle recognition, believers should be able to produce some criteria that would help unbelievers become convinced. However, believers cannot be obligated to persuade people of the reality of miracles against their will. If skeptics do not in some way leave a door open to the possibility of miracles, then it makes no sense to insist that believers be able to persuade them before believers can identify a miracle as such. Skeptics who repudiate even the possibility of the miraculous thereby remove themselves from genuine dialogue about the availability of evidence for the occurrence of miracles.

Concern about the possibility of unbelievers' recognition of a miracle does, however, arise in connection with one type of claim made by some theists: a miraculous event may serve as evidence for some supernatural reality, for example, the existence of God. But do miracles ever function this way? From the function of miracles for many religious believers we can see that miracles are widely thought to carry evidential significance. To be sure, there is considerable debate concerning the evidential value of miracles; some writers warn against the idea that miracles compel belief in the supernatural. Thus Colin Brown writes that in prescientific times "miracles were not thought of as a basic ground for belief in God."[21] In contrast, John Warwick Montgomery argues that "from earliest Christian history—indeed from the pages of the Bible itself—miracles have been the mainstay of Christian apologetics."[22] If there is mediating ground here, it is in the suggestion that miracles contribute to part of the case for the authentication of claims about the supernatural. The apostle John wrote that "these [signs] are written that you may believe that Jesus is the Christ, the Son of God, and that believing you might have life in his name" (Jn 20:31 RSV). Similarly, Thomas Aquinas considered the authority of Scripture to be "divinely confirmed by miracles."[23] If these expressions are true, then miracles must contribute to the process of eliciting belief where that belief would otherwise be absent or not as strong.[24]

And so we come back to the question of how someone not already in the circle of faith can even recognize a miracle. At this point we need to be aware of two levels of explanation of unusual events. On one level, a miracle receives an interpretation within a belief system; for example, the resurrection of Christ confirms his claims to deity and saviorhood. But on a more basic level, the event itself is explained as an instance of a supernatural miracle. The point is this: the recognition of a miracle is not merely an empirical observation, but an explanatory hypothesis.

Having said as much, another point follows immediately: not all explanatory hypotheses are created equal. C. S. Peirce observed that scientific hypotheses arise neither out of thin air nor out of the facts themselves, but out of the total reciprocal interaction between the data and scientists' theories. He called this process of deriving and verifying theories "abduction."[25] For our purposes we can draw the following implication: a good explanatory hypothesis is one that is (1) accurate with regard to the facts and plausible within the total circumstances, and (2) consistent with the worldview of the theorist.

To illustrate the inequality of explanations with a simple example, let us imagine that I notice a cup of coffee by my side as I am writing this chapter. How did the cup get there? The number of possible explanations is endless. Here are only a few of the possibilities:

(1) My wife brought the cup of coffee.

(2) A Boy Scout seeking to do his good deed for the day sneaked into my house and brought me the coffee.

(3) A scientist on the other side of town who is working with laser rays has projected a hologram of the cup onto my desk.

(4) Our Lady of Guadalupe, in an effort to convert me to Roman Catholicism, has materialized the coffee by my side.

(5) Alien invaders are baiting me with a cup of coffee containing a substance that will transport me to a planet on the other side of the galaxy if I drink it.

Given the appropriate presuppositions, each of these interpretations could explain the cup of coffee by my side. But the numbered explanations do not have equal standing. For me, at least, there is a prima facie presumption in favor of (1) because it best fits my total circumstances, as well as my prior intellectual commitments.

But what if I lived alone as a confirmed bachelor? Suddenly the prima facie presumption would have to switch. Of course, I could describe a set of circumstances whereby the possibility of explanation (1) is preserved. Perhaps someone drugged me a few weeks ago, married me while I was out of touch with reality, and recently entered my house surreptitiously to bring me coffee.

While it may always be possible to come up with a way of justifying any explanation, the attempt to do so may torture our capacities for credulity beyond what is reasonable. Although the number of possible explanations for any event is in theory boundless, there will be one or more explanations which will be immediately more plausible than most others. That fact does not guarantee their truth, but they enjoy an advantage in competition with other explanations because they are more reasonable. This explanation is a prima facie presumption.

Prima Facie Presumption for Miracles

The same kind of reasoning applies to the problem of identifying a miracle. It may be possible, by a series of mental gymnastics, to interpret any event in terms of the laws of nature—even if the application of natural laws is not yet fully understood. But there comes a point at which the prima facie presumption has to go the other way—in favor of the miracle explanation.

Take the case of a man who, in various direct and indirect ways, claims to be God. He heals people of various diseases, including some that are currently thought to be irreversibly degenerative. He predicts his own death and resurrection, which then comes to pass exactly as predicted.[26] It still is possible to refuse to recognize anything miraculous here. The skeptical naturalist could say, "I refuse to recognize any of these events as miraculous. They are all expressions of yet-to-be-discovered scientific laws." But the prima facie presumption has to be against this attitude because it appeals to something we do not have while we do have something else, namely a cogent supernatural explanation.

If one insists on adopting a position against any possibility of recognizing miracles, then, with a little creativity, it may always be possible to contrive sufficient ad hoc revisions of current patterns of naturalistic explanation to cling to such an understanding in all cases. It is interesting that Antony Flew should virtually hoist himself by his own petard; he violates the same epistemological concern that won him acclaim in connection with the issue of religious language. In his celebrated article on falsification, Flew accuses believers of allowing the belief in God's love to "die the death of a thousand qualifications." He asks, "What would have to occur or to have occurred to constitute for you a disproof of the love of, or the existence of, God?"[27] With similar exasperation, we might ask, What would an event have to be like in order for skeptics to recognize that event as something that is not entirely "natural"?

In fact, Flew has responded to this particular challenge. When asked by Gary Habermas, during a debate about the resurrection of Jesus, whether incontrovertible evidence for the historicity of the resurrection would not have to force the naturalist to reconsider his position concerning the deity of Jesus Christ, Flew responded, "You'd have to be open to it."[28] Nevertheless Flew continued, "What would happen next, I don't know. But clearly there would have to be some ears opened to some radical new thinking." If having such evidence for the resurrection would actually make Flew more open to the deity of Jesus Christ, it is to his credit.

But perhaps Flew also had in mind the idea of a natural "nonmiraculous miracle," an event that cannot be deemed a miracle simply because it happened. The problem with "natural miracles" is that they are an attempt by the naturalistic skeptic to have it both ways. For as Flew stated, and Nowell-Smith also strongly endorsed, the scientific enterprise involves not merely description but the subsumption of events under laws. Nowell-Smith insists that an explanation apart from regularity is no explanation at all.[29] But surely this is a two-edged sword that undercuts the idea of "natural miracle" as well. The idea of a natural event that violates the natural order can be maintained only on the basis of dogmatic antisupernaturalism.

The skeptics' dogmatic position must ultimately degenerate into the fallacy of the appeal to ignorance: no one has proven that an event could not be the result of some unknown scientific law; therefore the event is the result of an unknown scientific law. Such a line of reasoning is not convincing.

As I observed earlier, the actual identification of an event as a miracle may not always be clear, even for the believer. Obviously, even more latitude must be granted unbelievers; they are entitled to a reasonable amount of caution and reservation.[30] But that allowance does not get them off the hook when the evidence is overwhelmingly in favor of an event's being a miracle. In general, it seems fair to say that when the evidence for the occurrence of an event is beyond reasonable doubt and there is no other plausible explanation available, unbelievers need to start at least to entertain the possibility of a miracle. This obligation may even be stronger if cautious and intelligent believers identify the event as a miracle.

Consider, for example, how I might, as a Christian believer, react to a Buddhist or Muslim miracle story. When presented with Gautama's alleged flipping of a huge elephant for two miles with his big toe, or Muhammad's professed ride from Mecca to Jerusalem and back in one night, I assume the role of the unbeliever. If I intend to withhold belief in these alleged miracles, it would be appropriate for me to locate problems with the evidence thought to support them or with the reliability of reports about them. But it would be improper for me to acknowledge the evidence for one or the other of these miracle claims and then refuse to recognize the event as miraculous. If the evidence seemed to me to be quite strong, then I would have an obligation to become more open to the possibility that these events are miracles, even though they are embedded within religious traditions at odds with my own.[31]

Thus we can see that believers and unbelievers cannot be expected to agree on a correct identification of a genuine miracle if the evidence itself is ambiguous. Furthermore, the question of worldviews is of particular importance. When we encounter a true skeptic whose worldview prevents the recognition of a miracle, we should not be led to tinker with our definition of miracle or to seek compromises that neither side can accept. At this point, a defense of the theistic worldview must be conducted on independent grounds. This is one of the reasons for including chapter nine in this volume.

Conclusion

In this chapter I have attempted to make two contributions to the discussion of how to recognize a miracle. First, I have argued that the recognition of a miracle is initially the prerogative of believers, for whom it is not necessarily, however, an unproblematic task. Second, I have argued that in response to unbelievers (as opposed to confirmed skeptics, for whom the matter is beyond rational evidence) Christian theists must emphasize prima facie presumptions that sometimes favor the judgment that God has indeed acted in history.

PART 3
A THEISTIC CONTEXT FOR MIRACLES

SEVEN

MIRACLES & CONCEPTUAL SYSTEMS

RONALD H. NASH

There are few things more important in defending the possibility of miracles than understanding the role played by conceptual frameworks in setting the limits of possibility in this area. Religious believers who affirm the possibility of miracles need to understand how our general perspective on the world (that is, our "worldview") controls our attitude toward miracle claims. People who disagree about the reality of miracles often find themselves talking past each other simply because they do not appreciate each other's underlying convictions that make their respective attitudes about miracles seem reasonable to them.

A conceptual framework is the pattern or arrangement of our concepts (ideas) that enables us to make sense of the world by organizing all that we believe. This framework, or worldview, is a comprehensive, systematic view of life and of the world as a whole. The philosophical systems of great thinkers such as Plato and Aristotle, Thomas Aquinas and Bonaventure, René Descartes and Immanuel Kant are all worldviews. Every mature, rational human being, each reader of this book, has a worldview just as surely as Plato did. Most people, however, have no idea what a worldview is. Consequently, they are not aware of the specific contours of their worldview, or even that they have one. But all thoughtful persons should pay attention to the structure of their own worldview, for that worldview inevitably influences what they believe and how they live.

Conceptual frameworks function like eyeglasses to bring the world into clearer focus. Naturally, a realistic view of the world—a view that is true to the way the world is—requires the proper conceptual framework. When someone views the world through the lens of an inaccurate worldview, the world may seem to make sense to that person. But the sense that person makes of the world will be wrong in important and potentially dangerous respects. Having the right worldview, that is, viewing the world through the right conceptual lens, is vital to the proper appraisal of miracle claims and their significance for our lives.

Fortunately, only a handful of worldviews present themselves for acceptance to reasonable people. Within the current cultural climate, it is the worldview of *naturalism* that creates the greatest problems for belief in miracles. Before turning to naturalism, let us outline a perspective called Christian theism that affirms the reality of miracles. With the exception of David Hume and Antony Flew, all the contributors to this book share this perspective.

The Framework of Christian Theism

There is a tendency on the part of many people to think of Christianity as a collection of unrelated beliefs and claims. This is a mistake. We should approach the Christian faith as a conceptual system, as a total world-and-life view. Once people understand that both Christianity and its adversaries in the world of ideas are worldviews, they will be in a better position to judge the relative merits of the total Christian system.

Worldviews contain at least five clusters of beliefs, namely, beliefs about God, ultimate reality, knowledge, morality and human nature. While worldviews may include other important beliefs that need not concern us here, these five are usually the ones that define the most important differences among competing conceptual systems. The Christian worldview is theistic in the sense that it affirms the existence of one supremely powerful and personal God. Theism differs from polytheism in its affirmation that there is only one God (Deut 6:4). It parts company with the various forms of pantheism by insisting that God is personal and must not be confused with the world that is God's creation. Theism must also be distinguished from panentheism, the position that regards the world as an eternal being needed by God in much the same way a human soul needs a body. Theists also reject panentheistic attempts to limit God's power and knowledge, which have the effect of making the God of panentheism a finite being.[1] Other important attributes of God, such as his holiness, justice and love, are described in Scripture.

Historical Christian theism is also Trinitarian. The doctrine of the Trinity reflects the Christian conviction that the Father, the Son and the Holy Spirit are three distinct centers of consciousness sharing fully in the one divine nature and in the activities of the other persons of the Trinity. An important corollary of the doctrine is the Christian conviction that Jesus Christ is both fully God and fully man.[2] Christians use the word *Incarnation* to express their belief that the birth of Jesus Christ marked the entrance of the eternal and divine Son of God into the human race.

The Bible begins with the words "In the beginning God created the heavens and the earth." Many early Christian thinkers found it important to draw out certain implications of the biblical view of God and stipulate that God created the world ex nihilo (from nothing), which is an important metaphysical tenet of the Christian worldview. This was necessary, they believed, in order to contrast the Christian understanding of creation and Plato's speculation about the origin of the world. Plato had suggested that a godlike being, the craftsman, had brought the world into being by fashioning an eternal stuff or matter after the pattern of eternal ideas that existed independently of the craftsman. Moreover, this creative activity took place in a space-time receptacle or box that also existed independently of the craftsman. Such early Christian thinkers as Augustine (A.D. 354-430) wanted the world to know that the Christian God and the Christian view of creation differed totally from this Platonic picture. Plato's god (if indeed that is an appropriate word for his craftsman) was not the infinite, all-powerful and sovereign God of the Christian Scriptures. Plato's god was finite and limited. In the Christian account of creation, nothing existed prior to creation except God. There was no time or space, there was no preexisting matter. Everything else that existed besides God depended totally on God for its existence. If God did not exist, the world would not exist. The cosmos was not eternal, self-sufficient or self-explanatory. It was freely created by God.

The existence of the world, therefore, is not a brute fact, nor is the world a purposeless machine, in the Christian understanding of things. The world exists as the result of a free decision to create by a God who is eternal, transcendent, nonmaterial, omnipotent, omniscient, omnibenevolent, loving and personal. Because there is a God-ordained order to the creation, human beings can discover that order. It is this order that makes science possible; it is this order that scientists attempt to describe in their laws.

Every worldview includes important presuppositions about human knowledge. For example, almost all of them maintain that knowledge is attainable by the human mind. Consider the absurdities involved in claiming to know that *no one* can know anything. A well-formed Christian worldview will exclude views suggesting that humans cannot attain knowledge about God. Christianity clearly teaches that God has revealed information about God.[3] While Christian thinkers may disagree about many issues in this area, it should be clear that the Christian worldview is no ally of skepticism. Human beings can know God's creation; they are also capable of attaining knowledge about God.

The fact that all human beings bear the image of God (another of Christianity's basic beliefs about human nature) explains why we are capable of rational thought, love and God-consciousness; it also explains why we are moral creatures. Of course, sin (yet another of Christianity's important notions) has distorted this image of God and explains why humans turn away from God and the moral law—why we sometimes go wrong with regard to our emotions, conduct and thinking. Because of the image of God, we should expect to find that the ethical principles of the Christian worldview reflect what all of us at the deepest level of our moral being know to be true.

According to the Christian worldview, God is the ground of the laws that govern the physical universe and that make possible the order of the cosmos. God is also the ground of the moral laws that ought to govern human behavior and that make possible order between humans. Christian theism insists on the existence of universal moral laws; the laws of morality must apply to all humans, regardless of when or where they have lived. They must also be objective in the sense that their truth is independent of human preference and desire. David Beck stresses this in chapter nine of this volume.

William J. Abraham provides us with an introduction to the complex subject of what the Christian worldview teaches about humankind:

Human beings are made in the image of God, and their fate depends on their relationship with God. They are free to respond to or reject God and they will be judged in accordance with how they respond to him. This judgment begins now but finally takes place beyond death in a life to come. Christians furthermore offer a diagnosis of what is wrong with the world. Fundamentally, they say, our problems are spiritual: we need to be made anew by God. Human beings have misused their freedom; they are in a state of rebellion against God; they are sinners. These conclusions lead to a set of solutions to this ill. As one might expect, the fundamental solution is again spiritual.[4] The Christian worldview recognizes that human beings are more than physical beings; there is more to them than their bodies. No system that reduces humans to the lowest common material denominator, that denies the wonder and glory of the human mind, that rejects the possibility of redemption from sin and eternal life can be consistent with the worldview that Christians draw from God's revealed truth in Scripture. Thus, Christianity is a conceptual system, a worldview. Once people understand that both Christian theism and its adversaries in the world of ideas are worldviews, they will be in a better position to judge the relative merits of the total Christian system.

The case for or against Christian theism should be made and evaluated in terms of total systems. The Christian faith has important things to say about the whole of human life. Once Christians understand in a systematic way how the alternatives to Christianity are also worldviews, they will be in a better position to justify their choice of Christianity rationally. The reason many people reject Christianity is not due to their problems with one or two isolated issues; it is the result of their anti-Christian conceptual scheme, which leads them to reject information and arguments that for believers provide support for the Christian worldview.

Metaphysical Naturalism

At this stage of human history there are hundreds, perhaps thousands of conceptual systems that influence various people around the world. Every world religion is a worldview, as are the countless number of sects within each religion. In other parts of the world, Christianity's major challenges come from such worldviews as Islam, Buddhism, Hinduism and Shintoism, as well as such nonreligions as communism. But in Europe and the United States, the competing worldview that Christians encounter most frequently is metaphysical naturalism. The relevance of this kind of naturalism to the question of miracles will become obvious in short order.

The central claim of metaphysical naturalism is that nothing exists outside the material, mechanical (that is, nonpurposeful), natural order.[5] S. D. Gaede explains:

The naturalistic world view rests upon the belief that the material universe is the sum total of reality. To put it negatively, naturalism holds to the proposition that the supernatural, in any form, does not exist. . . . The naturalistic world view assumes that the matter or stuff which makes up the universe has never been created but has always existed. This is because an act of creation presupposes the existence of some reality outside of, or larger than, the world order—incompatible with the tenet that the material universe is the sum total of reality. Naturalism normally assumes that always-existing matter has developed into the ordered universe which we see by a blind, timeless process of chance. . . . Within the context of the naturalistic world view, miracles, as such, do not exist; they are natural events which have yet to be explained.[6]

Metaphysical naturalism obviously implies a certain view of miracles: not only are they not *actual,* they are not *possible.* In his book *Miracles,* C. S. Lewis brilliantly shows that most Westerners who object to the Christian belief in miracles do so because they have made a prior commitment to the naturalistic worldview. In that book, Lewis says of naturalism:

What the Naturalist believes is that the ultimate Fact, the thing you can't go behind, is a vast process in space and time which is *going on of its own accord.* Inside that total system every particular event (such as your sitting reading this book) happens because some other event has happened; in the long run, because the Total Event is happening. Each particular thing (such as this page) is what it is because other things are what they are; and so, eventually, because the whole system is what it is. All the things and events are so completely interlocked that no one of them can claim the slightest independence from "the whole show." None of them exists "on its own" or "goes on of its own" except in the sense that it exhibits at some particular place and time, that general "existence on its own" or "behaviour of its own accord" which belongs to "Nature" (the great total interlocked event) as a whole. Thus no thoroughgoing Naturalist believes in free will: for free will would mean that human beings have the power of independent action, the power of doing something more or other than what was involved by the total series of events. And any such separate power of originating events is what the Naturalist denies. Spontaneity, originality, action "on its own," is a privilege reserved for "the whole show," which he calls *Nature.*[7]

For a naturalist, the universe is analogous to a sealed box. Everything that happens inside the box (the natural order) is caused by or is explicable in terms of other things that exist within the box. *Nothing* (including God) exists outside the box; therefore, nothing outside the box that we call the universe or nature can have any causal effect within the box. The resulting picture of metaphysical naturalism looks like figure 1.

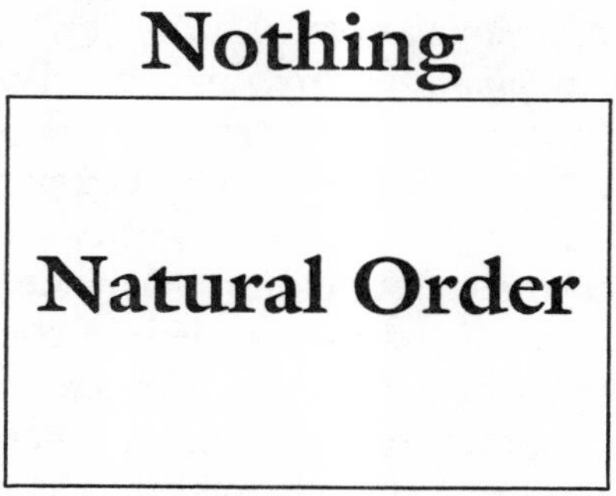

Nothing

Natural Order

Figure 1. Metphysical Naturalism

It is important to notice that the box (the natural order) is closed and sealed tightly. Even if something did, *per impossibile*, exist outside the box, it could not serve as the cause of any event that occurs within the box. *Everything* that happens within nature has its cause in something else that exists within the natural order. As philosopher William Halverson explains, metaphysical naturalism claims

> that what happens in the world is theoretically explicable without residue in terms of the internal structures and the external relations of these material entities. The world is . . . like a gigantic machine whose parts are so numerous and whose processes are so complex that we have thus far been able to achieve only a very partial and fragmentary understanding of how it works. In principle, however, everything that occurs is ultimately explicable in terms of the properties and relations of the particles of which matter is composed.[8]

A metaphysical naturalist, then, is someone who believes the following propositions:

1. Only nature exists. By *nature* I mean, following Stephen Davis, "the sum total of what could in principle be observed by human beings or be studied by methods analogous to those used in the natural sciences."[9] Anyone who adopts a naturalist worldview holds that God does not exist.

For by definition anything that exists is part of the box.

2. *Nature is a materialistic system.*[10] The basic components of existing things are material entities. This does not mean that metaphysical naturalists deny the existence of such things as human memories of the past and hopes for the future, or plans, intentions and logical inferences. Whatever such things as thoughts, beliefs and inferences are, they are either material things or reducible to or explainable in terms of material things or caused by something material.

3. *Nature is a self-explanatory system.* Any and everything that happens within the natural order must, at least in principle, be explainable in terms of other elements of the natural order. It is never necessary to seek the explanation for any event within nature in something beyond the natural order. In general, the naturalist holds that only the *parts* and not the *whole* require explanation in terms of something else (which brings us back to the brute factuality of the universe, whether it has an absolute beginning or not). Furthermore, not only is it not *necessary* to seek explanation in terms of something beyond the natural order; it is not even *possible* to find ultimate explanations for objects and events in the natural order. It is interesting that there is, first, an insistence on explanation for all individual entities and events in the system, but, second, the denial of both the necessity and the possibility of explaining the whole system in terms of something else.[11]

In this connection, it would be easy to assume that metaphysical naturalists must also believe that the natural order (the box) is eternal. But naturalism is more complex than this. It is true that many naturalists prefer to think of the universe as always existing in some state or other. Many of them, however, reserve the right to claim that the universe is a brute fact, that it had a beginning but that it simply sprang into existence uncaused. The naturalist position about the age of the natural order amounts to the claim that *either the universe has always existed, or it sprang into existence without a cause.* It should be noted, however, that one does not need to be a theist to have trouble understanding or accepting the belief that an uncaused universe sprang into existence from absolutely nothing at all.

4. *Nature is characterized by total uniformity.* This uniformity is apparent in the regularity of the natural order, something that scientists attempt to capture in the natural laws they formulate. Many philosophers mistakenly rush to judgment at this point and infer that a belief in miracles is incompatible somehow with the order and regularity of the

natural order.

5. Nature is a deterministic system. Determinism is the belief that every event is made physically necessary by one or more antecedent causes. Because the metaphysical naturalism under consideration here is also a kind of physicalism, those antecedent causes must either be matter or be reducible to matter. In this view of things, there is no room for any theory of agency whereby either God or human beings acting apart from any totally determining causes can function as causes in the natural order.[12]

Clearly, any people in the grip of these naturalistic habits of mind could not be expected to believe in the miraculous, for it would be inconsistent for them to do so. For such people, evidence of putative miracles can never be persuasive. Indeed, since miracles are, by definition, impossible, it is impossible that there should ever be evidence for a miracle. Thus, no arguments on behalf of the miraculous can possibly succeed with naturalists *on the naturalists' own terms*. The only proper way to address their disbelief is to *begin* by challenging the elements of their naturalism.

Naturalism and Theism Contrasted

What are the important ways that Christian theism differs from naturalism? Figure 2, depicting the Christian worldview, is a good place to start.

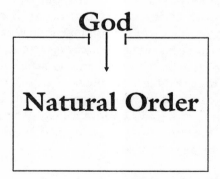

Figure 2. The Christian Worldview

This figure illustrates three important elements of the Christian worldview:

1. God exists outside the box.
2. God created the box.

3. God acts causally within the box.

Christian theism rejects naturalists' contention that nothing, including God, exists outside the natural order. It also denies that the natural world of physical objects has always existed. God created the world freely and ex nihilo. The universe is contingent in the sense that it could not have begun to exist without God's creative act and it could not continue to exist without God's sustaining activity.

It is especially important to note that aside from the fact that the box is "open" to causes existing outside the box, Christians' scientific understanding of the natural order need not differ in any way from the naturalists'.[13] Christians believe that nature exhibits patterns of order and regularity. Of course, they also believe that this uniformity results from God's free decision to create the universe in a particular way. Christian theism recognizes the same cause-and-effect order within the natural order as do naturalists. But Christians believe that the natural order depends on God for both its existence and its order. When Christians assert that God is capable of exerting causal influence within the natural order, they do not mean necessarily that such divine action results in a suspension or violation of the natural order.[14] But whether miracles are exceptions to the laws of nature or not, the essential point here is that the world is not closed to God's causal activity. In the next chapter, by J. P. Moreland, this issue is examined in detail.

Finally, Christian theism denies that nature is a self-explanatory system. The very existence of the contingent universe requires that we seek the cause of its being in a necessary being, one that does not depend on anything else for its existence. (For an argument from the contingency of the universe to the existence of a nonnatural cause of the universe, see chapter nine by David Beck.[15]) Laws operating within the natural order owe their existence to God's creative activity. And many things that happen within the natural order are affected by or influenced by or brought about by free acts of the personal God.

The Case Against Naturalism

A careful analysis of naturalism reveals a problem so serious that it fails one of the major tests that rational persons can expect any worldview to pass.[16] In order to see how this is so, it is necessary first to recall that naturalism regards the universe as a self-contained and self-explanatory system. There is nothing outside the box we call nature that can explain or that is necessary to explain anything inside the box. Naturalism claims that every individual object or event can be explained in terms of something else within the natural order. This dogma is not an accidental or nonessential feature of the naturalistic position. All that is required for naturalism to be false is the discovery of one thing that cannot be explained in the naturalistic way. C. S. Lewis set up this line of argument as follows:

> If necessities of thought force us to allow to any one thing any degree of independence from the Total System—if any one thing makes good a claim to be on its own, to be something more than an expression of the character of Nature as a whole—then we have abandoned Naturalism. For by Naturalism we mean the doctrine that only Nature—the whole interlocked system—exists. And if that were true, every thing and event would, if we knew enough, be explicable without remainder . . . as a necessary product of the system.[17]

With a little effort, we can see that no thoughtful naturalists can ignore at least one thing. Lewis explains:

> All possible knowledge . . . depends on the validity of reasoning. If the feeling of certainty which we express by words like *must be* and *therefore* and *since* is a real perception of how things outside our minds really "must" be, well and good. But if this certainty is merely a feeling *in* our minds and not a genuine insight into realities beyond them—if it merely represents the ways our minds happen to work—then we have no knowledge. Unless human reasoning is valid no science can be true.[18]

And, we might add, unless human reasoning is valid, no arguments by any metaphysical naturalist directed against Christian theism or offered in support of naturalism can be sound.

The human mind, as we know, has the power to grasp contingent truths, that is, things that *are* the case though they might not have been the case. But the human mind also has the power to grasp *necessary connections,* that is, what *must* be the case. This latter power, the ability to grasp *necessary* connections, is the hallmark of human *reasoning.* What I am here calling a necessary connection may be illustrated by the following familiar syllogism. If it is true that all men are mortal and if it is true that Socrates is a man, then it *must* be true that Socrates is mortal. Nearly anyone can see, even without special training in logic, that the conclusion, *Socrates is mortal,* must be true if the other two propositions are true. All students taking an introductory course in logic are able, on the first day of class, to supply the correct conclusion the instant they see the two premises. Grasping such necessary connections is quite natural.

Naturalists themselves must appeal to this kind of necessary connection in their own arguments for naturalism; indeed, in their reasoning about everything. But can naturalists account for this essential element of the reasoning process that they utilize in their arguments for their own position? Lewis thinks not, and for good reason. As Lewis sees it, naturalism "discredits our processes of reasoning or at least reduces their credit to such a humble level that it can no longer support Naturalism itself."[19] Why is that? Because

> no account of the universe [including metaphysical naturalism] can be true unless that account leaves it possible for our thinking to be a real insight. A theory which explained everything else in the whole universe but which made it impossible to believe that our thinking was valid, would be utterly out of court. For that theory would itself have been reached by thinking, and if thinking is not valid that theory would, of course, be itself demolished. It would have destroyed its own credentials. It would be an argument which proved that no argument was sound—a proof that there are no such things as proofs—which is nonsense.[20]

Lewis is careful to point out that his argument is *not* grounded on the claim that metaphysical naturalism affirms that every human judgment (like every event in the universe) has a cause. He understands that even though my belief about a matter may be caused by nonrational factors, my belief may still be true.[21] In the argument before us, Lewis is talking about something else, namely, the logical connection between a belief and the ground of that belief. It is one thing for a belief to have a nonrational cause; it is something else for a belief to have a reason or ground. The ravings of a madman may have a cause but lack any justifying ground. The reasoning of a philosopher may have a cause, but it also possesses a justifying ground.[22] What metaphysical naturalism does, according to Lewis, is sever what should be unseverable: the link between conclusions and the grounds or reasons for those conclusions. As Lewis says, "Unless our conclusion is the logical consequent from a ground it will be worthless [as an example of a *reasoned* conclusion] and could be true only by a fluke."[23] Therefore naturalism "offers what professes to be a full account of our mental behaviour; but this account, on inspection, leaves no room for the acts of knowing or insight on which the whole value of our thinking, as a means to truth, depends."[24]

In metaphysical naturalism, "acts of reasoning are not interlocked with the total interlocking system of Nature as all its other items are interlocked with one another. They are connected with it in a different way; as the understanding of a machine is certainly connected with the machine but not in the way the parts of the machine are connected with each other. The knowledge of a thing is not one of the thing's parts. In this sense something beyond Nature operates whenever we reason."[25] Thus, the thrust of Lewis's argument against naturalism becomes clear. By definition, metaphysical naturalism excludes the possible existence of anything beyond nature, anything outside the box. But the process of reasoning *requires* something that exceeds the bounds of nature, namely, the laws of logical inference.

A Further Difficulty with Metaphysical Naturalism

In a book first published in 1963, American philosopher Richard Taylor presented an argument that, while similar to Lewis's, points to an additional problem with metaphysical naturalism. Taylor introduced his argument with an interesting example that bid his reader imagine herself in a coach on a British train. Looking out the window, the passenger sees a large number of white stones on a hillside lying in a pattern that spells out the letters THE BRITISH RAILWAYS WELCOMES YOU TO WALES. Should such a passenger be in a reflective mood on such an occasion, she might well begin to contemplate how those stones happened to be in that particular arrangement. It is possible that without any intelligent being having anything to do with it, the stones simply rolled down the hillside over a period of many years and just happened to end up in an arrangement that resembled the letters noted above. However implausible we find the hypothesis that the arrangement of the stones was a purely accidental happening, we must admit that such a thing is logically possible. Of course, Taylor admits, the most natural reaction to seeing the stones would be a conviction that the arrangement of stones was brought about by one or more humans who intended that it communicate a message. Thus Taylor admits that there are at least two explanations for the arrangement of the stones: a natural, nonpurposive explanation and an explanation in terms of the intentions of at least one intelligent being.

Taylor's next step in the development of his argument is critical. Suppose, he suggests, that the passenger decides, solely on the basis of stones she sees on the hillside, that she is in fact entering Wales. Taylor is not insisting that the purposive account of the stones is in fact the true one. His argument is purely hypothetical. *If* the passenger infers that the stones communicate a true message (and she therefore believes that she really is entering Wales), it would be quite unreasonable for her also to assume that the positioning of the stones was an accident. Once you conclude that the stones really do convey an intelligible message, Taylor continues,

> you would, in fact, be presupposing that they were arranged that way by an intelligent and purposeful being or beings for the purpose of conveying a certain message having nothing to do with the stones themselves. Another way of expressing the same point is that it would be *irrational* for you to regard the arrangement of the stones as evidence that you were entering Wales, and at the same time to suppose that they might have come to have that arrangement accidentally, that is, as the result of the ordinary interactions of natural or physical forces. If, for instance, they came to be so arranged over the course of time, simply by rolling down the hill, one by one, and finally just happening to end up that way, or if they were strewn upon the ground that way by the forces of any earthquake or storm or what-not, then their arrangement would in no sense constitute evidence that you were entering Wales, or for anything whatever unconnected with themselves.[26]

Taylor's analysis thus far seems correct. If I were the passenger and if I thought the arrangement of the stones were a result of chance, purely natural forces, there would be something quite bizarre about my also believing, solely on the evidence provided by the stones, that I was indeed entering Wales. But if I concluded, solely on the evidence provided by the stones, that I was entering Wales, consistency would seem to require that I also believe that the arrangement of the stones was not an accident. What does all this have to do with making an intelligent choice between theism and metaphysical naturalism? Taylor invites us to consider similar reasoning about our cognitive faculties:

> Just as it is possible for a collection of stones to present a novel and interesting arrangement on the side of a hill . . . so also it is possible for such things as our own organs of sense to be the accidental and unintended results, over ages of time, of perfectly impersonal, nonpurposeful forces. In fact, ever so many biologists believe that this is precisely what has happened, that our organs of sense are in no real sense purposeful things, but only appear so because of our failure to consider how they might have arisen through the normal workings of nature.[27]

In the case of the stones, the simple fact that they exhibit a particular shape or pattern does not constitute proof that there is purpose or intention behind the arrangement. Likewise, Taylor observes, "the mere complexity, refinement, and seemingly purposeful arrangement of our sense organs do not, accordingly, constitute any conclusive reason for supposing that they are the outcome of any purposeful activity. A natural, nonpurposeful explanation of them is possible, and has been attempted—successfully, in the opinion of many."[28] It certainly appears as though metaphysical naturalists would have to pursue this kind of nonpurposeful account of human cognitive faculties.

Taylor then points to the problem in the antitheists' position. Even persons who view their sense organs as the products of chance, natural and nonpurposeful forces depend on them to deliver information about the world that they regard as true. "We suppose, without even thinking about it, that they [our sense organs] reveal to us things that have nothing to do with themselves, their structures, or their origins."[29] Such people, Taylor thinks, are just as inconsistent as the person who derives a true message from a nonpurposeful arrangement of stones.

It would be irrational for one to say *both* that his sensory and cognitive faculties had a natural, nonpurposeful origin and *also* that they reveal some truth with respect to something other than themselves, something that is not merely inferred from them. *If* their origin can be entirely accounted for in terms of chance variations, natural selection, and so on, without supposing that they somehow embody and express the purposes of some creative being, then the most we can say of them is that they exist, that they are complex and wondrous in their construction, and are perhaps in other respects interesting and remarkable. We cannot say that they are, entirely by themselves, reliable guides to any truth whatever, save only what can be inferred from their own structure and arrangement. If, on the other hand, we do assume that they are guides to some truths having nothing to do with themselves, then it is difficult to see how we can, consistently with that supposition, believe them to have arisen by accident, or by the ordinary workings of purposeless forces, even over ages of time.[30]

Thus naturalists seem to be caught in a trap. If they are consistent with their naturalistic presuppositions, they must assume that our human cognitive faculties are a product of chance, purposeless forces. But if this is so, they appear grossly inconsistent when they place so much trust in those faculties. But like Taylor's train passenger, if they assume that their cognitive faculties are trustworthy and do provide accurate information about the world, they seem compelled to abandon one of the cardinal presuppositions of metaphysical naturalism and to conclude that their cognitive faculties were formed as a result of the activity of some purposeful, intelligent agent.[31]

Concluding Comments About the Critique of Naturalism

It is difficult to see how metaphysical naturalism can provide an adequate reason why anyone controlled by naturalistic presuppositions should suppose that human reasoning can ever be valid or that our sense organs can be trusted. Why should we not conclude that naturalism is incompatible with attitudes of trust in either our rational or our empirical faculties? Why should we not think, following Richard Purtill, that naturalism destroys "our confidence in the validity of *any* reasoning—including the reasoning that may have led us to adopt these [naturalistic] theories! Thus they [the naturalistic theories] are self-destructive, rather like the man who saws off the branch he is sitting on. The only cold comfort they [metaphysical naturalists] hold out is that some of our thought might happen to agree with reality."[32] But on naturalistic grounds, we can never know that it does. And when we are honest about the probabilities, it appears to be enormously improbable that such agreement would ever occur.

One of naturalism's major problems is explaining how mindless forces give rise to minds, knowledge, sound reasoning and moral principles that really do report how human beings ought to behave.[33] Not surprisingly, all naturalists want the rest of us to think that *their worldview,* their naturalism, is a product of *their* sound reasoning. All things considered, it is hard to see why naturalism is not self-referentially absurd. Before any person can justify accepting naturalism on rational grounds, it is first necessary to reject a cardinal tenet of the naturalist position. In other words, the only way people can provide rational grounds for believing in naturalism is to cease being naturalists. I am not suggesting that this self-defeating feature of naturalism proves by itself that theism is true. There are enough other alternatives to naturalism that the falsity of naturalism does not entail the truth of theism. Nevertheless, the incoherence of naturalism holds an important implication for a study of miracles.

Most opposition to the possibility of miracles in the West comes from people controlled by the presuppositions of naturalism. Most such people refuse even to consider evidence that appears to support the actuality of miracles, such as the incarnation or the resurrection of Jesus Christ, because—consciously or unconsciously—their minds are closed on that subject. Miracles are judged to be impossible *before the fact.*[34]

I have two suggestions for metaphysical naturalists. First, they need to recognize the extent to which their conclusions about miracles are dictated by their naturalistic presuppositions. Their opposition to miracles is not a result of their greater intelligence or enlightenment; it is a function of their worldview. And, to the extent that their worldview is a function of their education, perhaps they should go back and reflect on those times in their education when they uncritically accepted the presuppositions of their mentors. Second, they need to consider the self-defeating nature of naturalism. If they pursue these two recommendations, they have a fair chance of seeing that God really has acted in history.

EIGHT

SCIENCE, MIRACLES, AGENCY THEORY & THE GOD-OF-THE-GAPS

J. P. MORELAND

MANY ASPECTS OF THE RELATIONSHIP BETWEEN SCIENCE AND MIRacles are worthy topics of study. Currently, there is a heated dialogue about the proper way to integrate science and theology. Much of this dialogue focuses on the question, Must science presuppose methodological naturalism? Related to this question are different ways of viewing the nature of a direct, miraculous act of God and the relationship between such an act and the practice of science. Given the ideological importance of science in contemporary culture, it is not surprising to see naturalists claim that miracles, even if they happened, are totally outside the limits of science. For example, atheist philosopher Michael Ruse claims that "the Creationists believe the world started miraculously. But miracles lie outside of science, which by definition deals with the natural, the repeatable, that which is governed by law."[1]

Surprisingly, numerous Christian intellectuals agree with this position against what I shall call "theistic science." According to theistic science:

1. There is a personal, transcendent agent—God—who has, through immediate, primary agency and mediate, secondary causation, created/designed the world and has acted through immediate, primary

agency in "natural" history.

2. Commitment to (1) has a proper place in the practice of science.

3. This commitment can appropriately enter into the practice of science through various uses in scientific methodology of gaps in the natural world (for example, their postulation, discovery and explanation) that are essential features of immediate, primary divine agency properly understood.

Those rejecting theistic science claim that it adopts an inappropriate god-of-the-gaps strategy. Scientists, they say, must assume methodological naturalism and study natural entities from a natural point of view, seeking explanations for things in terms of natural events and laws that are part of the natural causal fabric. Thus, scientists' theological beliefs lie outside of science. On this view, science and theology are noninteracting, complementary perspectives of the same reality that focus on different levels of description. As authentic but incomplete perspectives on the world, science and theology must be integrated into a coherent whole. But each level of description (for example, the chemical versus the theological) is complete at its own level, with no gaps at that level for other perspectives to fill.

As a total account of integration, this perspective is unacceptable. Theistic science is a legitimate research program. Since I have defended my views about this controversy elsewhere,[2] I shall concentrate here on proposition (3) above by arguing that a certain understanding of agency theory shows that the complementarity view is inadequate and that libertarian, agent acts (human or divine) result in gaps in the causal fabric of the natural world that should be acknowledged in the practice of science. After stating the complementarity view, I shall contrast libertarian and compatibilist models of action, and show why "gaps" are best explained in terms of agency. My goal is to demonstrate the relevance of a libertarian model of agency for the practice of science.

The Complementarity View

The complementarity view enjoys wide popularity among both Christian and non-Christian intellectuals. While these thinkers differ regarding the details of their approach, there is broad agreement about the general features of the model. The goal of natural science is to seek natural explanations of the physical properties, behavior and formative history of the physical universe. Science is inherently committed to methodological naturalism—the idea that explanations of phenomena are to be sought within the nonpersonal causal fabric of processes in the created order. In general, an appeal to the personal intentions or actions of an agent, especially a supernatural one, violates the commitment to methodological naturalism constitutive of good science. Methodological naturalism is unrelated to metaphysical naturalism (the natural world is all there is), for philosophical theses about the existence, nature and acts of God are beyond the limits of science.

In nature, wholes are often more than the sum of their parts. Reality consists in a hierarchy of different levels of systems or things that are parts of and give rise to wholes at higher levels of organization due to the complex interaction of the parts at lower levels. For example, ascending from bottom to top through one sort of hierarchy we have the following sequence: energy, subatomic entities, atoms, molecules, constituents of cells (e.g., organelles), cells, biological systems (e.g., the respiratory system), whole biological organisms, the psychological level, the sociological level, the theological level. As one ascends, each new level comes to be, not because some new entity has been added "from the outside," but because it emerges from lower levels due to the complex interaction of parts that give rise to the higher level. Thus psychological states emerge (or supervene) upon neurophysiological states when the latter reach an appropriate level of complexity. In this view, human persons are not genuine substances with natures, but rather property-things (ordered aggregates)—structured collections of externally related parts with emergent properties.

Each level in the hierarchy is capable of an exhaustive description at that level using only concepts appropriate to that level with no gaps to be bridged by notions referring to entities at higher levels. Each level is an authentic, though partial, perspective, and the whole truth emerges when all the complementary levels are taken together. Furthermore, lower levels are ontologically basic; they sustain higher levels in existence. Higher levels emerge upon and are determined by the entities and patterns of interaction at lower levels. If some story is true at a higher level, then some story must be true at a lower level but not vice versa.[3] In general, some physical (e.g., neurophysiological) state or other is necessary for a higher level (e.g., mental) state to exist, and when some specific physical state obtains, that is sufficient for the occurrence of the supervening (e.g., mental) state.

Closely related to this is the causal relationship between levels. Note first that events are what do the causing in the natural world; only events cause other events to occur. Second, a question arises about the causal efficacy of higher levels of description, most importantly, the mental level. Complementarians face a certain dilemma. On the one hand, they seem committed to treating higher levels of description as causally impotent epiphenomena that supervene upon lower level systems because each lowest level physical state is complete at its own level of description and sufficient for the emergence of the higher level state. On the other hand, complementarians allow that when higher level entities emerge, events at that level can cause events to occur at lower levels through feedback mechanisms and event-event (or state-state) causation. Unfortunately, as philosophers Kathleen Lennon and David Charles argue, the only way to accept a psychological level of causal descriptions and also hold "that physical explanation is complete, i.e. that all physically characterizable events are susceptible to explanation in terms of physically sufficient causes . . . is to accept [the] reduction [of the psychological to the physical]."[4]

The complementarity view eschews libertarian freedom and agency in favor of compatibilism. In the next section I shall examine more fully libertarian and compatibilist models of freedom, but for now it will suffice if we consider the act of raising a hand to vote. At the various levels of natural science, a complete account of such an act could be given in terms of biological systems, brain states and so forth. These levels of description would exclude the psychological level, since they would be what they are with or without the presence of the higher psychological level and would contain no reference to mental entities. But a complete, noninteracting account of the act could be given at a psychological level by appealing to the individual's desire to vote, the belief that raising a hand would satisfy this desire, and the willingness to raise a hand. Personal agency and action fall completely outside natural science levels of description complementary to the psychological level.

If we set aside human history (especially salvation history), then a consistent picture of divine action in the natural world emerges. God is not to be seen as a direct causal factor in the sense of suspending or overriding the laws of nature and acting as a primary causal agent who creates a gap in the natural fabric by acting in it in a way other than normal, regular activity. Rather, God is constantly active in each and every event that happens. God sustains natural processes in existence and expresses freedom to act by employing natural processes mediately as secondary causes to accomplish God's purposes in the world.[5] God works "in and through" the natural causal fabric, unfolding its potentialities according to deterministic or probabilistic laws of nature. God does this without leaving any causal gaps in lower level physical processes. God is the ground and ultimate cause of all things. Moreover, God's acting in and through natural events can be understood as the meaning and purposive pattern that can be seen in the providential unfolding of those events. As Howard J. Van Till puts it, God has created the world with functional integrity: "By this term I mean to denote a created world that has no functional deficiencies, no gaps in its economy of the sort that would require God to act immediately, temporarily assuming the role of creature to perform functions within the economy of the created world that other creatures have not been equipped to perform."[6]

Advocates of the complementarity view disdain what is called a god-of-the-gaps argument. Many complementarians complain that this type of argument adopts an epistemically inappropriate strategy in which God acts only when there are gaps in nature, we appeal to God merely to fill gaps in our scientific knowledge of naturalistic mechanisms, these appeals to God are used in apologetic arguments to support Christian theism, and God is manifest and proved only by the miraculous, by that which defies natural scientific explanation. Complementarians describe two problems with this god-of-the-gaps strategy. First, the success of natural science in reducing the number of gaps diminishes the need to believe in God. Second, this strategy assumes a faulty understanding of the integration of science and theology and the proper model of human and divine action as depicted in the complementarity model. Specifically, it fails because there simply are no such gaps in the natural world, given the views already presented in this section.

Two features of the complementarian attitude deserve comment. First, no advocate of theistic science with whom I am familiar claims that God only acts in the "gaps." God is constantly active in sustaining the world, in concurring with natural processes and the like. Advocates of theistic science simply believe that there is a scientifically and epistemically relevant distinction between primary and secondary causal acts of God and that both types of actions are relevant to the task of integrating science and theology. Second, belief in gaps should not be based on ignorance of a natural causal mechanism, but on positive theological, philosophical or scientific arguments that would lead one to expect such a gap. While most advocates of theistic science do use such a strategy for positive apologetic purposes, this need not be the case. And if apologetic purposes are part of our employment of theistic science, we need not hold that the *entire* ground for justifying belief in God is the explanatory power of "the God hypothesis" vis-à-vis gaps. Most critical discussions of god-of-the-gaps issues generate far more heat than light precisely because they represent a gross caricature of those who actually employ this strategy. The real question is, If God acts as a primary causal agent distinct from God's action as a secondary cause, does it follow that there will be miraculous gaps in the natural causal fabric that could, in principle, be relevant to scientific methodology? I believe the answer is yes. To see why, let us turn to the difference between libertarian and compatibilist views of freedom and agency.

Libertarian and Compatibilist Models of Agency

All Christians agree that we have free will, but there are major differences about what free will is. We can define determinism as the view that for every event that happens, there are conditions such that, given them, nothing else could have happened. For every event that happens, its happening was caused or necessitated by prior factors such that, given these prior factors, the event in question had to occur. Libertarians affirm free will and hold that determinism is incompatible with it. Compatibilists claim that freedom and determinism are compatible; thus determinism does not eliminate freedom. As we shall see, compatibilists have a different understanding of free will from the one embraced by libertarians and hard determinists.

1. *Compatibilism.* The central idea behind compatibilism is this. If determinism is true, then every human action is causally necessitated by events that obtained prior to the action, including events that existed before the agent's birth. That is, human actions are mere *happenings;* they are parts of causal chains of events that lead up to them in a deterministic fashion. But freedom, properly understood, is compatible with determinism.

2. *Libertarianism.* Libertarians claim that the freedom necessary for responsible action is not compatible with determinism. Real freedom requires a type of control over our actions—and, more important, over our will—such that, given a choice to do *A* (raise a hand and vote) or to do *B* (leave the room), nothing determines which choice is made. Rather, agents themselves simply exercise their own *causal powers* and will (or have the power to refrain from willing) to do one or the other. When agents will *A*, they could have also willed *B* without anything else being

different inside or outside of their being. They are the absolute originators of their own actions. When agents acts freely, they are a *first* or
unmoved mover; no event causes them to act. Their desires, beliefs or
what have you may influence their choice, but free acts are not caused
by prior states in the agent.

Suppose some person P freely performed some act e, say raising an
arm in order to vote. A more precise characterization of rational libertarian freedom and agency is this:

1. P is a substance that had the power to bring about e.
2. P exerted its power as a first mover (an initiator of change) to bring
about e.
3. P had the ability to refrain from exerting its power to bring about e.
4. P brought about e for the sake of some reason R.

We can see deeper differences between compatibilist and libertarian
accounts of freedom by looking at four areas central to an adequate
theory of free will.

1. *The ability condition.* Most philosophers agree that in order to have
the freedom necessary for responsible agency, an agent must have the
ability to choose differently from the way the agent actually does. A free
choice, then, is one where a person "can" will to do otherwise. Most
compatibilists and libertarians agree about this. They differ about what
it means to say that free acts are those in which persons "can" act other
than how they do act. According to compatibilists, the ability necessary
for freedom should be expressed as a hypothetical ability. Roughly, this
means that the agent would have done otherwise had some other
condition obtained, for example, had the agent desired to do so. We are
free if we can will whatever we desire even if our desires are themselves
determined. Freedom is willing to act on your strongest preference.

Libertarians claim that this notion of ability is really a sleight of hand
and not adequate for the freedom needed for responsible agency. For
libertarians, the real issue is not whether we are free to do what we want,
but whether we are free to want in the first place. A free act is one in
which the agent is the ultimate originating source of the act. Freedom
requires that we have the categorical ability to act, or at least to will to
act. This means that if we freely do (or will to do) A, we could have
refrained from doing (or willing to do) A, or we could have done (or
willed to have done) B without any conditions whatever being different.
No description of our desires, beliefs, character or other aspects of our
makeup and no description of the universe prior to and at the moment

of our choice to do *A* is sufficient to entail that we did *A*. It was not necessary that anything be different for us to do *B* instead. This implies that there will be a gap in the universe just prior to and just after a free act due to the causal activity of the agent as first mover.

The libertarian notion of categorical ability includes a dual ability: if we have the ability to exert our power to do (or will to do) *A*, we also have the ability to refrain from exerting our power to do (or will to do) *A*. By contrast, the compatibilist notion of hypothetical ability is not a dual ability. Given a description of a person's circumstances and internal states at time *t*, only one choice could obtain, and the ability to refrain is not there; the ability to refrain depends on the hypothetical condition that the person had a desire (namely, to refrain from acting) that was not actually present. There is no causal gap just prior to and just after the act of a substantial agent contributing causal power as a first mover into the natural causal chain of events because this view of agency is rejected by compatibilists.

2. *The control condition.* Suppose Jones raises a hand to vote. Compatibilists and libertarians agree that a necessary condition for the freedom of this act is that Jones must be in control of the act itself. But they differ radically as to what control is. In order to understand compatibilist views of the control condition, recall that compatibilists agree that determinism is consistent with freedom and that cause and effect is to be characterized as a series of events making up causal chains with earlier events together with the laws of nature (either deterministic or probabilistic) causing later events. The universe is what it is at the present moment because of the state of the universe at the moment before the present, together with the correct causal laws describing the universe. A crude example of such a causal chain would be a series of one hundred dominos falling in sequence from the first domino on until domino one hundred falls. Suppose all the dominos are black except numbers forty through fifty, which are green. Here we have a causal chain of events that progresses from domino one to one hundred, a chain that "runs through" the green dominos.

According to compatibilism, an act is free only if it is under the agent's own control. And it is under the agent's own control only if the causal chain of events—which extends back in time to events realized before the agent was even born—that caused the act (Jones's hand being raised) "runs through" the agent in the correct way. But what does it mean to say that the causal chain "runs through the agent in the correct way"?

Here compatibilists differ from each other. But the basic idea is that an agent is in control of an act just in case the act is caused in the right way by prior states of the agent (for example, by the agent's own character, beliefs, desires and values). This idea is sometimes called a causal theory of action.

Libertarians reject the causal theory of action and the compatibilist notion of control and claim that a different sense of control is needed for freedom to exist. Consider a case where a staff moves a stone but is itself moved by a hand that is moved by a person. In *Summa Contra Gentiles* 1.8, Thomas Aquinas states a principle about causal chains that is relevant to this example and, more generally, the type of control necessary for freedom according to libertarians:

> In an ordered series of movers and things moved [to move is to change in some way], it is necessarily the fact that, when the first mover is removed or ceases to move, no other mover will move [another] or be [itself] moved. For the first mover is the cause of motion for all the others. But, if there are movers and things moved following an order to infinity, there will be no first mover, but all would be as *intermediate movers*. . . . [Now] that which moves [another] as an instrumental cause cannot [so] move unless there be a principal moving cause [a first cause, an unmoved mover].

Suppose we have nine stationary cars lined up bumper to bumper and a tenth car runs into the first car, causing each to move the next vehicle until finally car nine is moved. Suppose further that all the cars are black except cars five to eight, which are green. What caused the ninth car to move? According to Aquinas, cars two to eight are not the real cause of motion for car nine. Why? Because they are only *instrumental causes;* each of these cars passively receives motion and transfers that motion to the next car in the series. The car that bumped into car one is the real cause, since it is the first mover of the series. It is the source of motion for all the others. Only first movers are the sources of action, not instrumental movers that merely receive motion passively and pass it on to the next member in a causal chain.

In our earlier example, neither the staff nor the hand is the controlling cause of the stone's motion, since each is an intermediate cause. Rather, the person is the first, unmoved mover and as such is the cause of action. For libertarians, it is only if agents are first causes, unmoved movers, that they have the control necessary for freedom. Agents must be the absolute, originating source of their own actions to be in control. If, as compatibilists picture it, agents are just a theater through which a chain of instrumental causes passes, then there is no real control. Further, the control that unmoved movers exercise in libertarian free action is a dual control—it is the power to exercise their own ability to act or to refrain from exercising their own ability to act.

3. *The rationality condition.* The rationality condition requires that agents have personal reasons for acting before intentional acts count as free. Consider again the case of Jones raising a hand to vote. In order to understand the difference between compatibilists and libertarians about how to handle this case in light of the rationality condition, we need to draw a distinction between an *efficient* and a *final cause.* An efficient cause is *that by means of which* an effect is produced. One ball moving another is an example of efficient causality. By contrast, a final cause is *that for the sake of which* an effect is produced. Final causes are teleological goals, ends or purposes for which an event is done; the event is a means to the end that is the final cause.

A compatibilist will explain Jones's voting in terms of efficient and not final causes. Jones had a desire to vote and a belief that raising a hand would satisfy this desire, and this state of affairs (the *belief/desire set* composed of the two items just mentioned) caused the state of affairs of a hand going up. In general, whenever some person S does A (raises a hand) in order to B (vote), we can restate this as S does A (raises a hand) because of a desire to B (vote) and a belief that by A-ing (raising a hand) desire B would be satisfied. On this view, a reason for acting turns out to be a certain type of state in the agent, a belief-desire state, that is the real efficient cause of the action taking place. Persons as substances do not act; rather, states within persons cause latter states to occur. The compatibilist, in possession of a clear way to explain cases where S does A in order to B, challenges the libertarian to come up with an alternative explanation.

Many libertarians respond by saying that our reasons for acting are final and not efficient causes. Jones raises a hand *in order to* vote, or perhaps in order to satisfy a desire to vote. Here the person acts as an unmoved mover simply by exercising power in raising an arm spontaneously. Beliefs and desires do not cause the arm to go up; the person does. But various reasons serve as final causes for the sake of which actions are done. Thus, compatibilists embrace a belief/desire psychology (states of beliefs and desires in the agent cause the action to take place), while many libertarians reject it and see a different role for beliefs and desires in free acts.

4. *Causation.* Suppose a brick breaks a glass. For the compatibilist, the only type of causation is event-event causation: an event of kind K (the moving brick touching the glass) in circumstances of kind C (the glass being in a solid state) occurring to an entity of kind E (the glass itself) causes an event of kind Q (the breaking of the glass) to occur. Here, all causes and effects in the chain are events standing to each other in either deterministic or probabilistic causal relations. If we say that a desire to vote caused Jones to raise an arm, we are wrong. Strictly speaking, a desiring to vote caused a raising of the arm inside of Jones.

Libertarians agree that event-event causation is the correct account of normal events in the natural world (events like bricks breaking glass). But when it comes to the free acts of persons, the persons themselves as substantial agents directly produce the effect.[7] Persons are agents and, as such, are first causes, unmoved movers who simply have the power to act as the ultimate originators of their actions. It is the self that acts, not a state in the self causing a moving of some kind. Libertarians claim that their view makes sense of the difference between actions (expressed by the active voice, in such statements as "Jones raised a hand to vote") and mere happenings (expressed by the passive voice, in such statements as "A raising of the hand was caused by a desiring to vote, which was caused by X, which was caused by Y, and so on").

Before we turn to the last section of the chapter, we are in a position to evaluate the claim made by Antony Flew and others to the effect that there is a dilemma between the theistic requirement of strong laws of nature (since in some sense they express the immutable divine will) and the admission of real exceptions to those laws (miracles). Since Richard Purtill addresses in chapter three the fact that miracles should not be construed as "exceptions" to the laws of nature, I will reserve my comments to the alleged dilemma itself. From what we have seen, advocates of libertarian agency have metaphysical and epistemological grounds for claiming that so-called strong laws of nature only govern event-event causality and are irrelevant for libertarian acts. And if primary causal miracles are a distinct type of libertarian act by God, then there is no dilemma here. There is just a difference between event causation and libertarian action.

Miracles, Agent Gaps and Science

Complementarian A. R. Peacocke has said that the "problem of the human sense of being an agent . . . acting in this physical causal nexus, is of the same ilk as the relationship of God to the world."[8] I agree. But whereas Peacocke uses this point to support the complementarian view and to place miracles outside the bounds of science, I claim that the analogy between human and divine action actually supports theistic science and the possibility of treating miraculous acts as part of science. The difference between us is this: Peacocke, and complementarians in general, adopt compatibilist models of divine or human action (at least for causality outside of salvation history) with the result that no gaps exist in the causal fabric. I see both divine and human action in terms of libertarian agency and believe that free acts leave *scientifically detectable gaps* in the natural world.

To see why complementarian compatibilists forbid gaps, consider the following statements by naturalist philosophers. John Searle has said that "our conception of physical reality simply does not allow for radical [libertarian] freedom."[9] The reason for this is that once you claim that the physical level of description is both basic and complete, you rule out the possibility of top-down feedback. As naturalist David Papineau has argued:

> I take it that physics, unlike the other special sciences, is *complete*, in the sense that all physical events are determined, or have their chances determined, by prior *physical* events according to *physical* laws. In other words, we never need to look beyond the realm of the physical in order to identify a set of antecedents which fixes the chances of subsequent physical occurrence. A purely physical specification, plus physical laws, will always suffice to tell us what is physically going to happen, insofar as that can be foretold at all.[10]

The reason for the remarks by Searle and Papineau is this. In every alleged case of where there is a description of top-down causation (for example, where a state of intending to raise my arm causes the raising of the arm), there will be a corresponding description of a causal sequence of events that run along the bottom level (for example, there will be a physical state "associated with" the mental state of intending to raise one's arm and a physical state "associated with" each moment of the arm's being raised). Moreover, the suggestion that the physical is the bottom level means not only that each upper level event has some lower level event or another correlated with it, but also that the description of the bottom level sequence of events is complete without any gaps. For example, at each moment during the process in which I desire to vote, believe that raising my arm will satisfy that desire, deliberate as to whether to vote, will to raise my arm, and raise it throughout a time of a few seconds, there will be a physical state in my brain and nervous system that is sufficient to produce the next physical state, and there is no room for feedback. Remember, the physical level description is complete and basic. Furthermore, each alleged description of a top-down causal connection will have a description that runs the other way and that is more consistent with the view that the physical level is at the bottom. And, in any case, even if one allows for top-down mental-to-physical feedback, this type of causality will still be event-event causation with no room for libertarian agency.

By contrast, in cases of libertarian action, say, just before one acts to raise an arm and during the raising of it, the description of the brain and central nervous system just prior to acting will not be sufficient to entail or causally account for the physical description resulting from the agent's own (first mover) exercise of causal power. Of course, at each moment there will be some physical state or another, but the events at the physical level will not form a continuous chain of causal events. Instead there will be a causal gap due to the action of the agent. This is why some have objected to libertarian acts because they violate the first law of the conservation of energy. I think such acts do indeed violate the first law, and, in fact, this is part of what it means for an agent to be in the image of God—he or she is capable of genuine creativity and novelty. Moreover, Robert Larmer argues that we must distinguish two forms of the First Law. A strong form states that energy can be neither created nor destroyed. A weak form states that in a causally closed system the total amount of energy remains constant. Libertarian agency is inconsistent with the strong but not the weak form, says Larmer, because the human body is not a causally closed physical system.[11] Larmer correctly sees that libertarian acts leave gaps in the natural causal fabric.

If we assume for a moment that libertarian agency is the correct model of divine action for primary causal miracles, then whenever God acts in this way, *there will be a gap in the natural world that could figure into scientific practice in at least three ways.* First, scientific methodology includes the psychology of discovery—roughly, the psychological processes scientists go through to come up with theories to guide their research. It is a known fact that in the history of science a hypothesis frequently has suggested itself to a scientist from the scientist's theological or metaphysical beliefs. Now if someone held that various things in the natural world were the result of a libertarian, miraculous act of God (for example, the beginning of the universe, the direct creation of first life and the various kinds of life, the direct creation of human beings in the Middle East, the flood of Noah), then such a belief could guide a scientist in postulating that there will be no natural explanation for the occurrence of these things. This could, in turn, lead him or her to try to discover evidence for these events (the flood of Noah, a Middle Eastern origin for human beings), or to try to falsify the suggestion that they were the result of miraculous acts by trying to discover natural mechanisms for their occurrence that he or she believes are not there.

Second, in a number of areas of science (forensic science, SETI, archaeology, psychology), scientific explanations for a phenomenon appeal to the desires, beliefs, intentions and actions of personal agents. Thus, for example, if we discovered that living systems are discontinuous with nonliving systems in such a way that living systems bear certain features that usually result from personal agency (for example, information in DNA, different kinds of design such as beauty or order), and if we have positive grounds for thinking that it is improbable that a naturalistic mechanism will be found to account for this, then one could legitimately see the origin of life as a gap in the history of the universe due to a primary causal act of God and appeal to divine action, intentions and so forth as part of *scientific* explanation.

Third, these features of living systems could, in turn, lend some confirmation to the hypothesis that life was indeed the result of a miraculous act of God. Such claims would be defeasible (that is, they would be subject to falsification in light of more data), but this is irrelevant since the defeasibility of virtually all scientific theories does not preclude rational acceptance of them. In these three ways—scientific discovery, scientific explanation that is a form of personal explanation, and scientific confirmation—gaps in the causal fabric predicted by theological models of primary causal divine agency regarding some natural phenomenon could enter into scientific methodology.

Some claim that we can never conclude that an event is a miracle because science may find a natural cause for the event in the future and this principle (that science ought only to search for natural causes) is the very foundation of scientific advance. I have already shown some reasons why I think methodological naturalism is not required for doing science, so I will not rehearse those reasons here. Moreover, I think that this position is a question-begging, science-of-the-gaps argument to the effect that since natural causes have been found for a number of phenomena, then natural causes will be found for all of them. I see no reason, however, to accept this argument and the attitude toward miracles that it exemplifies. If we have good theological, philosophical or scientific grounds for suspecting that some phenomenon is the result of a primary causal act of God (theistic scientists do not appeal to primary causes willy-nilly), then I do not see why we cannot do research in light of this conviction and, in principle, obtain confirmation for it in a specific case like the origin of life. In fact, if the kalam cosmological argument is reasonable (roughly, the argument for the claim that the universe had a beginning due to the primary causal agency of a personal being), and if there are grounds for believing in a designer from general features of the universe, then before we even begin to investigate the details of the natural world we already have justification for bringing *to* that investigation a prior belief in nonnatural libertarian agency.[12] And if we have grounds for thinking that finite human beings exercise that type of agency, this would contribute to the rational justification for accepting a primary causal explanation for some natural phenomenon and not holding out for a natural event cause come what may, since we already know (1) that libertarian acts do, in fact, exist, (2) something about what they are like, and (3) naturalism as a worldview is false since it cannot allow for the reality of libertarian action and the type of agents that perform it.

Conclusion

In concluding this chapter, I want to respond briefly to two well-known critics of theistic science—Richard Bube and Howard J. Van Till—in light of what we have learned. Bube claims that a scientific description is a deterministic one if it can predict a future state from a present one and an expression of chance if it can only predict the probability of a future state.[13] Moreover, scientific descriptions must be one or the other. Now Bube thinks that these observations raise a paradox about human responsibility. Such responsibility is hard to square with determinism (how can I be responsible if determined?), yet it also seems to require determinism (how can a responsible choice exist without being described in a definite cause [the basis of the choice] and effect [the result of the choice] sequence?). On the other hand, responsibility is hard to harmonize with chance, which seems to be required for responsible action, yet chance is utterly random. Bube's solution to the problem is simply to assert, without adequate justification, that scientific descriptions of determinism or chance do not entail determinism or meaninglessness as worldviews and that the two types of descriptions can be complementary. But if these scientific descriptions are true, then anything else we would say at a different level of description could not contradict what is said at the scientific level. Moreover, Bube fails to see that the real issue is the nature of agency and that libertarian freedom is a third (and more adequate) option that renders his dilemma incomplete.

When it comes to miraculous actions performed by God, Bube admits that no scientific descriptions can be given of such acts.[14] Now this would seem to require a libertarian view of such acts; otherwise, they would have complementary scientific descriptions. Yet Bube claims that such miraculous acts cannot figure into scientific practice. Why? Because in such acts there is no scientific mechanism available for scientific description, and therefore primary causal miracles are not susceptible to scientific investigation. It should now be obvious what is wrong with this claim: scientific investigation does not limit itself to *descriptions,* and a primary causal act of God could figure into scientific methodology in the three ways mentioned above, even though such acts themselves cannot be given a scientific description.

According to Howard J. Van Till, the functional integrity of creation implies that even "stubbornly persistent gaps" in human understanding should not be taken as evidence of a real gap to be bridged by a "special act of God," but rather as an invitation to discover a remarkably interesting mechanism lurking behind our veil of ignorance.[15] Van Till claims that one of the reasons advocates of theistic science treat gaps differently is that they fail to distinguish narrow naturalism (the mere idea that the physical behavior of some particular material system can be described in terms of the "natural" capacities of its interacting components and the interaction of the system with its physical environment) from broad naturalism (roughly, physicalism as a broad worldview). Apparently, Van Till thinks that critics of methodological naturalism fail to see that the former is different from and, in fact, does not give support to the latter.

It should now be clear, however, that advocates of theistic science are not guilty of this confusion. They simply believe that theistic science is a legitimate enterprise, that Scripture, divine libertarian agency and primary causality, and certain scientific evidences are best understood in light of gaps and "special acts of God," to use Van Till's phrase. For them, certain gaps are stubbornly persistent because they are both real and are to be expected given a widely held view of divine agency in the miraculous. Moreover, Van Till's characterization of narrow naturalism either is question-begging or represents a misunderstanding of divine action in the areas of investigation listed throughout this chapter (for example, the origin of first life). It is question-begging because advocates of theistic science do not view the origin of life, various kinds of life and so forth as involving solely natural capacities and physical interactions, and they see no sufficient evidence to change their minds. Alternatively, it is a misunderstanding because Van Till incorrectly locates a main intellectual drive toward theistic science in the conflation between two sorts of naturalism and not, as we have seen, where it should be. It is up to him to show clear examples of how this confusion on the part of advocates of theistic science figures essentially into their position.

In this chapter I have not had the space to defend libertarian agency for human or divine (primary causal) action, though I obviously think such a defense is possible. Instead I have tried to show that the claim that miracles are in principle outside the bounds of science is one that is embedded in an attitude that includes a complementarian, methodological naturalist view of science and reality, along with a compatibilist view of human and divine action in the natural world (outside salvation history). This, in turn, has led many to reject the presence of gaps requiring theistic explanation because, among other things, the backdrop just mentioned denies that such gaps exist. By contrast, while I would not limit the use of theistic science to the employment of direct, primary causal acts of God, it seems to me that if such acts have occurred in certain cases, and if libertarian agency is a good model for characterizing such acts, then there will, in fact, be gaps in the causal fabric that are irreducibly nonnatural and must be recognized as such within scientific practice. Whether or not miracles are outside the bounds of science, then, turns in part on our model of divine agency, which in turn can be understood on the basis of an analogy with human action. Complementarians may reject libertarian agency, but even if they do it should be clear why some of us who accept the libertarian model believe that the recognition of miracles can be part of *scientific* practice.

NINE

GOD'S EXISTENCE

W. DAVID BECK

T HE PROBLEM OF MIRACLES IS CLOSELY ASSOCIATED WITH THE QUES-
tion of God's existence. Miracles have even been used to argue for the
existence of God. As Douglas Geivett explains in chapter eleven, one
type of argument for miracles depends in part on first developing a
successful argument for God's existence. This chapter presents an approach to arguing for the existence of God in a way that sets the stage
for arguing that miracles are possible, perhaps even probable. What is
needed is an argument powerful enough not only to justify belief in the
existence of God but also to establish at least three things about the
nature of God:

1. God is a being powerful enough to produce events in space/time.
2. God is an intelligence with a capacity to frame the convergence of
events in space/time.
3. God is a personality with the moral concern to act in history.

As it happens, these three propositions are the conclusions of three
traditional arguments, often used independently to justify belief in the
reality of God. The cosmological argument concludes that there is a
being that is the cause of all existence in space/time, the teleological (or
design) argument that there is an intelligent designer of the universe,
and the moral argument that objective moral judgments are supported

by the will of a transcendent and authoritative moral personality. Since these three arguments differ with respect to the precise formulation of the conclusion reached, they can in combination exhibit the rationality of believing in the existence of a moral personality with sufficient power, intelligence and motive to act miraculously within the world, which owes its existence to that same personality.

Often these arguments are construed along lines that fit the pattern of inference to the best explanation:

1. Identify some prominent feature of reality that is puzzling and requires explanation.

2. Illustrate the inadequacy of available naturalistic explanations for this feature.

3. Infer the existence and activity of a supernatural being as the best explanation.

Arguments that follow this pattern do not "prove" the existence of God in the sense that the conclusion follows necessarily from obviously true premises. But nothing that ambitious is really needed. If a theistic hypothesis is the best explanation for a sufficiently wide range of puzzling phenomena, then it will be most reasonable to accept that hypothesis.[1]

The Cosmological Argument

There is no single argument that might be designated *the* cosmological argument. Rather, there are numerous categories of cosmological arguments, with individual versions of each.[2] Many cosmological arguments have in common, however, the inference to an ultimate cause from the contingency or dependency of things. I will present one version of the argument and then respond to common objections. I conclude that this type of argument is able to withstand attacks and that we are entitled to hold that there is a Being with the capacity to cause events in space/time, thus providing the *first component* of a theistic basis for affirming the reality of miracles.

Premise 1: Every physical object we observe to exist is contingent. This argument begins with a simple observation concerning the things[3] we see and know about in the physical world around us. It is not a statement about everything in the universe, let alone every possible entity, but only about those things we actually observe (or sense perceive either directly or indirectly). The key element in this first premise is the notion of "contingency." Just what is that? Possibly Paul implies a form of this argument in Romans 1:19-20: "What may be known about God is plain to them, because God has made it plain to them. For since the creation of the world God's invisible qualities—his eternal power and divine nature—have been clearly seen, being understood from what has been made, so that men are without excuse" (NIV). In this passage the phrase "since the creation" has not only a temporal but a causative sense that reinforces the "what has been made" clause. The point here is that everyone can see that certain things owe their existence to other things. Nothing we know of exists without being caused by something else in the universe; and these causes are themselves effects of other causes.

Patterson Brown has described this characteristic of some causal relations as transitivity,[4] that is, A is caused by B, but only as B is caused by C. Electrons and galaxies only pass on or transfer whatever they have received as effects of other causes. Every physical object we know of possesses this sort of contingency: it exists and functions only as it is caused by other objects in the chain and, if Einstein is right, by every other factor in the whole cosmic network of these causal chains.

Premise 2: The sequence of causally related contingent objects cannot be infinite. The first premise describes the universe as a system or network of causal chains. The point of the second premise is to indicate that this system, regardless of how complex and interconnected, and regardless of how extensive it may be, is nevertheless finite. In support of this conclusion, most cosmological arguments involve an appeal to analogies. For example, Thomas Aquinas uses the picture of a hand moving a stick moving a ball. But perhaps most frequently used and discussed is the train analogy.

Imagine that you are introducing some alien from Alpha Centauri to the marvels of planet Earth. In a forest clearing in front of you is a boxcar moving on the tracks. Baffled, your alien buddy asks you why it is moving. You reply that it is pulled by a boxcar in front of it but hidden by the trees. "And how does that boxcar move?" the alien asks. "It is pulled by another boxcar," you say. And so on.

This story invites us to imagine analogies for the various naturalistic scenarios that describe how it is that things exist in the real world. "The cosmos is a great circle of being," proposes the naturalist. But, returning to our story, stringing boxcars all the way around the earth until the last one hooks up to the first cannot explain the motion of the first boxcar. The naturalist persists: "The cosmos is an intricately evolved ecosystem in which everything is related causally to everything else." So boxcars clutter the world in an unimaginably complex system of railroading enterprise such that in some way every other boxcar is pulling the first one. We still have no accounting, however, for the motion of that first one.

It is tempting to settle the problem of ultimate causal explanation by noting that each boxcar is being pulled by the one in front of it. But this is where transitivity becomes crucial. It may well be true that boxcar A is pulled by boxcar B. But B can pull A only because B is being pulled by C. The pulling action of B is transitive. It occurs only because B is, in turn, pulled by C. And so it is also true that A is being pulled by C. And C, and therefore A, is pulled by D, and so on.

The naturalist may imagine yet another alternative. Suppose there are infinitely many boxcars. Or, speaking of the universe, suppose the naturalist says, "The causal explanation of objects in the universe is absorbed in infinite complexity." But now something important becomes obvious. An infinity of boxcars will still leave unsolved the problem of explaining why the first boxcar is moving and hence why any are. The problem is not with the arrangement of boxcars, nor is it a matter of the number of boxcars. The problem is that no boxcar in the chain has the capacity to generate or initiate its own motion. It can pass on the pulling, but it does not initiate it.

Likewise, the problem with everything we know of in the universe is its contingency. The supposition that the causal nexus is constituted by infinitely many contingent objects fails to be an ultimate explanation for the existence of any individual object in the nexus. There has been no full accounting for the existence of even the first item of the sequence currently under observation. As Thomas Aquinas summarizes: "But if in efficient causes it is possible to go on to infinity, there will be no first efficient cause, neither will there be an effect nor any intermediate efficient causes; all of which is plainly false."[5]

Conclusion: There must be a first cause of the system of contingent objects in causal sequence. Where does this argument lead? The appropriate conclusion may be inferred without effort. If the causal sequence is finite, as it must be, then there is a first cause. If there are finitely many boxcars in motion, then there is a first (or last depending on which way you look at it). Perhaps it is not obvious that the first cause must be God. The apostle Paul, however, observes that we know both the "eternal power" and the "divine nature" of God. Thomas Aquinas simply concludes that "it is necessary to admit a first efficient cause to which everyone gives the name of God."[6] But can we conclude that the first cause is God?

The concept of "first cause" has two implications. To say that it is the *first* cause is to say that it neither requires nor has a cause itself. First is first! Thus it is fundamentally different from every other cause *inside* the system: it is not contingent. It depends on, is limited by or exists because of absolutely nothing else. This first cause does not merely pass on causality in a transitive relation; rather, it literally initiates the causality. The apostle's phrase "divine nature" is literally "God-ness," which conveys the idea of nondependence.

To say of the conclusion that it is the first *cause* is to define its relation to everything else in the sequence, namely, that it is their cause. It is the cause of all things in the sequence in that it initiates all of the causal activity in the sequence, without forbidding that each cause is, in fact, the cause of the next one in the sequence. The only explanation for the imagined moving line of boxcars is that somewhere there is a locomotive powerful enough to pull the whole train, an engine that does not itself need to be pulled. This seems to be included in Paul's notion of eternal (all-there-ever-is) power. And so the concept of a first cause is richer than it might at first appear. It is the actual cause of the existence of everything in the universe, and it itself exists without any cause or dependency whatsoever. This we may indeed call "God."

Objections Considered

We can clarify the conclusion just reached by dealing with some major objections to this argument. One of the most frequent is that the conclusion of the argument still does not look much like God. Certainly it is not the triune God of the Bible, who seeks our relationship and worship. Walter Kaufmann, for example, concludes his discussion of Thomas Aquinas's arguments by remarking, "Clearly, the God of Aquinas' theology is not the God of Job, Moses, or Jesus."[7] How are we to derive God's personhood, love, holiness, uniqueness or otherness from the meager conclusion of the above argument? "God" appears in the cosmological argument merely as a nondescript causal power behind the universe.

Arguably, the cosmological argument does not yield a full concept of God. But the argument is sufficient to show that the naturalist judgment that the physical universe is all there is is clearly wrong.[8] There is at least one thing in the causal network that is not another contingent object and on which everything else depends. We should also note that the cosmological argument has sometimes been extended by drawing out the implications of the idea of an uncaused cause.[9] I have not attempted this here since my project is to elucidate a concept of God sufficient for establishing the possibility, perhaps even the probability, of miracles. This project begins with a cosmological argument that shows that there is a nonnatural agency *capable* of producing events in space/time.

Another criticism simply rejects all arguments against an infinite sequence by noting that an infinite mathematical series is logically possible. "One wonders why, if there can be infinite sequences in mathematics, there could not be one in causality," says Michael Martin.[10] But Martin's inference is unfounded. First, supposing the actual existence of infinitely many numbers does not affect the above argument for a necessarily finite causal nexus, for, presumably, the relation between elements in the number series is not causal. Furthermore, we should not confuse logical possibilities with actual realities. While it is perhaps conceivable that there are infinitely many causes in the chain of objects constituting the physical universe, the mere conceivability of this does nothing to recommend it to us for belief. Not everything that can be conceived should be believed, otherwise one would be obliged to believe two contradictory propositions just so long as both are conceivable. When faced with the choice of believing one or another of two contradictory propositions, both of which are conceivable, one should believe the proposition with the greater explanatory power.

Paul Edwards, another atheist, argues that what we encounter in the real world are complete causes such that there is no reason for thinking that the system of causes must be finite. That is, knowing that A is caused by B is enough to explain A, and we are not required to ask questions about C. The real world is more like a string of locomotives, he thinks.[11] Here there is a failure to appreciate the real nature of contingency and how this relates to causality in the actual world. No physical object we know of is like a locomotive; that is, nothing explains its own existence. This is the point of calling each individual physical object we observe "contingent." Nothing fully explains the existence of anything else by itself. Our universe is less like a sequence of locomotives than a sequence of boxcars.[12]

In his highly acclaimed book *A Brief History of Time,* Stephen W. Hawking suggests that space/time may be closed, "self-contained, having no boundary or edge," and that this would eliminate any need for a creator.[13] But this is just to assert that a circle of boxcars could explain the motion of any one of them. Robin Le Poidevin points out that whether linear or circular, the system cannot account for itself.[14] The problem, again, is the contingency of every object in the system, not the specific arrangement of the contingent causes.

Other criticisms are directed at the principle of causality, a principle common to all cosmological arguments. The complaint is that the argument either explicitly or tacitly *assumes* the principle that existence needs an explanation. But the force of the term *needs* has been variously understood. In some forms of the cosmological argument (Leibniz's is the famous example), the principle is construed as logically necessary. But it has often been argued that no such principle can or could be established as a point of logic.[15] The principle is at the very least, however, an empirical, scientific generalization about the facts of the physical world, a principle whose unexceptionable character we rely on in the practice of science. While the success of the principle in scientific practice provides a weaker basis for accepting the principle than would be the case if it was an a priori deliverance of reason, this principle does effectively govern rational decision-making. It would be a form of special pleading, then, to prohibit appeal to the principle of causality in our cosmological argument for the existence of God.

There are other lesser objections to this argument that do not, as far as I can tell, endanger it. Here, then, is a strong argument for the conclusion that there is a first cause of objects constitutive of the physical universe. This is the first point needed in affirming the action of God in history by means of a miracle.

The Teleological Argument

This argument is probably the oldest, simplest, shortest and easiest to understand of all the theistic arguments. It is based on the common perception that the universe, taken either as a whole or as some part of it, has features that are too complex to have occurred by chance. They must, therefore, have an intelligent source. Richard Swinburne points out that there is no question about the validity of the logic of this argument.[16] It is based on an analogy between the natural universe and machines. The most famous example of this type of analogy comes from William Paley's classic work *Natural Theology*.[17] Suppose, walking along, we discover a shiny object on the ground. We observe first the precise and regular motion of the hands and then discover inside the object an incredible array of gears, springs and levers, all working together to tell the exact time of day.

What should we conclude? Should we be amazed at what the elements can produce by chance? Surely not. We infer that a device with such intricate design, which carries out such precise means to an end, cannot simply have occurred without the aid of a designer. Paley draws a parallel between the watch example and the universe: "Every indication of contrivance, every manifestation of design which existed in the watch, exists in the works of nature, with the difference on the side of nature being greater and more, and that in a degree which exceeds all computation."[18] The teleological or design argument notes the intelligent design of tools and machines evident in their purposiveness and functionality and infers a similar intelligent design to explain similarity of purposiveness and functioning in the natural order.

Premise 1: The universe has features that exhibit functional and purposive structure. It is a simple observation that the natural universe includes elements that in their complex structure are means to an end. These complexities often lend themselves very nicely to a quantitative approach. In particular, the probability of these complexities may be measured statistically, and this avoids the pitfall of circularity.

The formulation of the design argument sketched here avoids certain problems associated with arguments about the universe as a whole. There are two problems here, both pointed out long ago by David Hume,[19] and both of which, though they can be overcome, only invite unnecessary difficulty. One problem is that we know too little about the universe as a whole to make any comparisons between it and machines. Moreover, since we know of only one universe, our basis for comparison is too small. The other problem is that the universe is full of examples of evil, chaos, disorder and apparently useless things (like the panda's thumb) that would also have to be explained as part of a universal analogy. We will return to these concerns shortly.

Premise 2: Features of the universe exhibiting functional and purposive structure cannot be explained by chance. Since we can calculate the probability of an event's occurrence, we can attach specific values to natural phenomena to indicate whether they might occur as a result of the normal randomness permitted by the laws of physics, that is, by chance. A few examples of the kinds of probabilities involved are needed here to indicate just how strong this argument is.

Fine-tuning. A great deal has been learned in recent years about the adaptedness of the universe to human life. Despite the innumerable possibilities of getting it wrong and the incalculable complexities of systems needed to make human life work, the cosmos got everything right. Hugh Ross, in a recent collection of evidence relevant to the teleological argument, lists fifty-seven examples of such "fine-tuning," each of which by themselves would be enough to suggest intelligent design. The probability of their accidentally occurring together is infinitesimally small. Here are a few examples of conditions that had to be met in order for life to arise on our planet.[20]

1. Mass density of the universe

If larger: too much deuterium from big bang, hence stars burn too rapidly

If smaller: insufficient helium from big bang, hence too few heavy elements forming

2. Polarity of the water molecule

If greater: heat of fusion and vaporization would be too great for life to exist

If smaller: heat of fusion and vaporization would be too small for life's existence; liquid water would become too inferior a solvent for life chemistry to proceed; ice would not float, leading to a runaway freeze-up

3. Oxygen quantity in atmosphere

If greater: plants and hydrocarbons would burn up too easily

If less: advanced animals would have too little to breathe

We must stress that these precise conditions themselves do not exist in isolation. They are all related to one another and dependent on the laws of physics in general. Not only did the universe get everything right when the slightest deviation at innumerable points would have eliminated the possibility of life, but the universe appears to have been preadapted for life.

DNA. The investigation of DNA is another rich source of evidence of design. Physicists Fred Hoyle and Chandra Wickramasinghe, commenting on just one phase of the development of DNA, concluded in 1981:

The trouble is that there are about two thousand enzymes, and the chance of obtaining them all in a random trial is only one part in $(10^{20})^{2000} = 10^{40,000}$, an outrageously small probability that could not be faced even if the whole universe consisted of organic soup. If one is not prejudiced . . . that life originated on the Earth, this simple calculation wipes the idea entirely out of court.[21]

The crucial thing about DNA is that it has to exist before there are intelligent creatures, and yet it has the character of encoded information which can only be produced by an intelligence.[22] Thus, it too demands that there be an intelligence external to any developing system.

Conclusion: There is an intelligent source of the functional and purposive structures in the universe. Let us be clear about the conclusion. Again, it must be obvious that our conclusion falls short of the God of the Bible. Many of David Hume's criticisms of the design argument make this very point. The argument does not entail that there is only one God, let alone that God is unqualifiedly good or unlimited. It is best to acknowledge these limitations of the argument and assimilate the argument into a total cumulative case for the existence of God. All that really follows from the design argument sketched here is that certain features of the universe could not have been produced by chance processes internal to the universe and that the actual source must have an intelligence beyond anything we can imitate or even imagine. That is all that we need in order to satisfy the second point required as a rational basis for affirming the reality of miracles. And the argument from design to this somewhat modest conclusion is further strengthened by the background evidence for the existence of the first cause referred to in the cosmological argument.

Objections considered. Analogical arguments can be perfectly good arguments; we use them all the time, many times a day. My choice of each word on this page as I write involves comparing contexts and situations in the past with my present needs, and this involves the making of analogies. Some of these choices will be better than others. Some will be just right, but some will be inappropriate, based on bad or insufficient evidence. This suggests the two fundamental ways that analogies may be weakened or discredited as inductive inferences. They may rest either on biased, selective or partial evidence, or else on inconclusive or insufficient data. The objections addressed below fit these two categories.

Some objections to the design argument stem from the presence of evil in the world alongside features of "design." This is not the place for a full-scale response to the notorious "problem of evil." Notice, however, that the presence of evil in the universe is irrelevant to the specific conclusion drawn in the above use of the design argument. The argument says nothing about the goodness of God; it only infers an intelligent source of design in the universe. Even if there were only one thing in the universe that manifested a high degree of complexity, and everything else was chaotic, meaningless, even evil, then there would still be enough evidence to support our conclusion that there is an intelligent designer.

Another frequent objection is that no matter how great the complexity of the structure may be, a finite number of microchanges may be all that is needed to yield that complexity; thus a completely random process of evolution remains an option. Richard Swinburne, however, has argued cogently that a series of small evolutionary changes only *describes* how the simple became complex; it does not *explain* it. In fact, he argues, evolution only intensifies the need for God. For it would take even more intelligence to produce a universe that develops in intricate patterns into functional complexity than it would simply to create a complex universe outright. An evolved universe would require the design of both means and ends, and not of ends alone.[23]

A common current objection appeals to the multiple-worlds hypothesis. John Leslie, for example, acknowledges the evidence for fine-tuning, but then argues that developments in quantum theory imply the existence of innumerable distinct universes of immense size within the larger universe. There are, as it were, enough "experiments" at universe production to have simultaneously produced any universe, even this very complex, finely tuned one, so that this is just one among many universes.[24]

Hugh Ross has done an excellent job of showing that the multiple-worlds hypothesis, in its various current forms, is not supported by physics.[25] Still, since the existence of many worlds is a logical possibility, the objection deserves a fuller response.

The hypothesis is really just a fancy form of the old given-enough-time-anything-can-happen argument. Leslie, for example, actually resorts to the analogy of a typing monkey that will eventually produce a transcript of a bit of Shakespearean literature if there is no limit to the opportunities to do so. But if the improbability of an event is so high that it cannot reasonably be expected to occur apart from outside input by an intelligent agent, then we should infer the existence of an outside intelligence to explain the occurrence of that event, regardless of how much time is available. If the monkey at the typewriter is not an agent with some intelligence, then there is nothing about an indefinite length of time at the typewriter that ensures that eventually the monkey would produce a Shakepearean sonnet. This is true even if it is *possible* that such monkeying around would reproduce one of Shakespeare's 154 sonnets. Furthermore, it is doubtful that the monkey would recognize the excellence of its own artifact. So there is the added difficulty of accounting for the existence of intelligences within this world of physical complexity, not merely the physical complexity itself.

Leslie's argument commits a form of the "gambler's fallacy." The gambler acts as if the odds of getting double sixes get better with each role of two dice. But, of course, the odds are one in thirty-six every time the gambler rolls the dice, regardless of how often they are thrown or what has come up during previous throws, or, analogous to the state of affairs described by Leslie, how many pairs are thrown at the same time. We are left, then, with the plausible conclusion that there is an intelligent source of design in the universe, an agent with the ability to direct means to an end. This is the second requirement in providing a basis for miracles as set out at the beginning of this chapter.

The Moral Argument

Of all of the arguments for God's existence, this one has received the least attention in the twentieth century, due primarily to the first premise. The argument begins by observing that there are objective moral absolutes, an idea that has been thoroughly controverted in contemporary philosophy. Nevertheless, C. S. Lewis's moral argument[26] offers a unique analysis of moral behavior from an empirical, observational standpoint that is, I am convinced, essentially correct. The version outlined here draws heavily on it.

Premise 1: Morality is an objective feature of our universe. Certainly, this point is difficult to prove. Lewis's argument is based on the character of human moral language. It is simply impossible, he reasons, for the larger context of social discourse to occur without making statements about what is right or wrong or without assuming that they are true or false. I agree with J. L. Mackie, an atheist, that our basis for this premise is observational.[27] Hence, it is logically possible that we are misled about all this even though it seems undeniably true. What I mean is that we simply must affirm objective moral values in order to make sense of our lives. That Adolf Hitler and Joseph Stalin were not really morally wrong, that we cannot judge a society to be truly guilty if it practices genocide or if it causes needless environmental damage are such repugnant proposals that we find it impossible to believe that they could be true.

Are the moral judgments we make every day about ourselves and about others emotive outbursts or conditioned patterns of behavior?[28] While we often hear this judgment expressed, it is doubtful that reasonable people really believe it. That the brutal slaughter of children is revolting, horrifying and antisocial but not immoral or wrong is nonsense. To assert that those who pass judgment on the slaughter of the innocent are just being intolerant is ridiculous. The claim is even self-defeating, for tolerance is itself assumed to be an objective, unexceptionable moral value.

Premise 2: Naturalistic "explanations" of the objectivity of morality are inadequate. This point is not especially controversial. Most naturalists concede it. Since any form of naturalistic evolution denies human freedom, it must deny responsibility, and hence it cannot be that my actions have any value.[29] For B. F. Skinner, all that remains is a "technology of behavior." Our values are arbitrary judgments. They are decisions that we make. Only persons who have the freedom to select views and actions can have the requisite insight to make moral choice possible and to actually decide on moral values or actions for themselves.

Social explanations of moral objectivity do not account for moral value. While it is often asserted that values derive from our society, culture, religion, parents, school and friends, at least two arguments show this to be wrong. First, we often think it plausible to make evaluative moral judgments about our own peers, as well as other societies. We could not, for example, evaluate Hitler's Germany if this were not so. Second, the fact that as free persons we are all equal makes it impossible for any one finite person to determine value for any other person. No other human person has the moral authority to make decisions about right or wrong for me.[30] This, however, leads to a dilemma. Only persons can be the source of values, yet no finite and socially conditioned person is in a position to determine authoritatively the values appropriate for other persons. So, if there really are objective values, there must be some "ultimate" person who has the moral authority to set the standards of right and wrong. We are thus driven to the following conclusion.

Conclusion: There must be a universal personal authority that is the source of morality. What is crucial about this argument is its implication that the source of this feature of the universe is a personality, at least in the sense required by the capacity to understand value and make free moral judgments. There is, of course, more to the concept of "person," but this is enough to show that there is a transcendent agent capable of moral concerns, decisions and actions that is the third component in providing a basis for miracles as indicated above.

Objections Considered

I have dealt with standard objections to the moral argument in the process of spelling it out. We can summarize them by saying that the current naturalistic orientation to philosophy, and our culture in general, makes it difficult to deal adequately with any of the principal concepts: value, person, freedom, choice, even right and wrong. All are alien to a naturalistic worldview. In the end, however, this says more about the poverty of this worldview than it does about the soundness of the moral argument. It is highly unlikely that our experience that lies behind these concepts is empty. Thus the moral argument seems quite secure.

Conclusion

We are, then, entitled to assurance that God exists and in particular that there is a God who can act intelligently and with moral concern within human history. The design argument and the moral argument each adds to our understanding of the nature of God, as given in the cosmological argument. If God is the cause of *all* contingent existence, then God is the cause of all properties of contingent objects as well. Thus we have a cumulative case for God's existence and a methodology for filling out our understanding of God's nature.[31]

Of course, the argument developed here does not give us a complete concept of God. But if God is infinite, then no argument or combination of arguments could give us a full concept. As William Alston observes, "It is the common teaching of all the higher religions that God is of a radically different order of being from finite substances and, therefore, that we cannot expect to attain the grasp of His nature and His doings that we have of worldly objects."[32] Nevertheless, we do have a concept of God sufficiently rich to meet the three requirements established at the beginning of this chapter.

The piece that is still missing, however, is knowing that God has in fact entered space/time and thus has acted in human history. How this is to be understood, as well as how such miracles have occurred, is discussed in ensuing chapters.

TEN

GOD'S ACTIONS

STEPHEN T. DAVIS

ONE OF THE CENTRAL CLAIMS OF CHRISTIAN THOUGHT IS THAT GOD acts in history. At least some of the events that occur in history—particularly (but not exclusively) miraculous events—occur because God brings them about. God, then, is an agent in human history and in human lives. God is a God who acts. Thus the God of Christianity is not the God of deism. Deism was a loosely defined philosophical and religious movement that thrived in Europe in the seventeenth and eighteenth centuries and in America in the eighteenth. For the deists, religion was limited to a few rationally demonstrable truths about God, the creation and morality. These truths included the existence of God, who created the universe, along with its immutable natural laws. But one crucial point where the deists differed from traditional Christian thought is that they rejected all robust notions of divine agency in the world. Indeed, they denied as superstitious all claims of direct interaction between God and the created world. Miracles, revelations, epiphanies and incarnations were all ruled out. Later deists suggested that God is like someone who winds a clock and then lets it run on its own without interference.

Here are three traditional Christian propositions about God:

1. God is immaterial.

2. God is a person.

3. God created the world and acts in history.

Proposition (1) means that God is nonphysical or incorporeal. We human beings are, in some strong sense, material objects. We are or possess physical bodies that take up space, deflect light, occupy a certain location, and have a certain color, mass and height. But God is not a material object in any of these senses. As Jesus said, "God is spirit" (Jn 4:24). God is invisible, incorporeal, disembodied; God has no mass, height, weight or physical location.

Proposition (2) is not explicitly stated in Scripture, but is an inference that Christians draw from what the Scriptures do say about God together with our concept of a person. *Person* is one of those words that probably cannot be defined rigorously. Nevertheless, let us loosely define the term as "a conscious purposive agent." *Conscious* means that persons are things that engage in "mental" or "conscious" acts like thinking, feeling, desiring, willing, believing and knowing. *Purposive* means that persons are things that have certain desires, intentions or aims, and set out to achieve them. *Agent* means that persons are things that have the ability to act, to do or to achieve things in the world. Obviously, there are limitations on what human agents can achieve. No matter how badly I might want to leap over a tall building, I could not do it. But if I wanted to walk to the library or telephone my wife, I almost certainly could do those things.

There are perhaps other notions that are constitutive of our concept of persons. For example, a person can be harmed or benefited; a person is able to make moral judgments; a person is a member of a linguistic community; and a person is able to formulate second-order desires or wants (that is, wants about wants, like the desire to cease desiring cigarettes). Accordingly, let us say that a person is a conscious, purposive agent that possesses a significant number of the properties just mentioned. To claim that God is a person is not to claim that God is a human person. It is to say that God, like human persons, is a conscious purposive agent. In fact, Christians hold that we are persons in virtue of the fact that God is a person and God created us in the divine image.

Proposition (3) is also an essential aspect of what Christians want to say about God. That God is the world's Creator is claimed in Genesis 1—2, is affirmed or presupposed throughout the Bible, and is the conclusion of any successful cosmological argument for the existence of God. The world is a contingent thing; it exists only because God brought it into existence and sustains it in existence. The claim that God acts in history, attempting to influence human beings and to bring God's purposes to fruition, is a universal presupposition of the entire Bible.

A Basic Model of Divine Action

Let me now explain the basic model of divine action that I want to defend in this chapter. It has a respected contemporary defender, William P. Alston of Syracuse University.[1] Let us say that God relates to the world, or acts on or in the world, in four main ways: (1) God brings the world into existence; (2) God sustains or upholds the world in existence; (3) God acts through natural causes in the world; and (4) God acts miraculously or outside of natural causes in the world. I will not discuss the first and second of these modes of divine action any further; let me concentrate on the third and the fourth.

The third category, which we might call *God's natural actions,* includes all those ways in which God acts in the world through natural laws, causes and events. Such actions do not involve any suspension or violation of natural laws or interference with the natural order. They are often classified under the rubric of divine providence or divine providential care. Christians believe that this is the most common form of divine activity in the world; this is how God usually works.

An example might be God's guiding or strengthening or enlightening someone. This might happen through thoughts or feelings that God causes the person to have, perhaps through the words or actions of some other human being or through some other natural event. It might even involve God's directly causing a person to have a certain thought or feeling (perhaps analogous to the way mind-body dualists say the human mind influences the body). It is quite possible that the person influenced by God in some such way as this will feel moved to say, "God has spoken to me." And that statement may well be correct.[2] Other examples would be God's acting through natural causes to bring it about that someone recovers from a serious disease, survives a dangerous accident or happens to be in just the right place at just the right time for something important to occur. (See, for example, the personal anecdote introducing Richard Purtill's chapter in this volume.) The point is that what God wants to occur in the world is indeed what occurs, and it occurs because God brings it about that it occurs, but it occurs via natural, lawlike means. Rather than intervening in the natural order, God acts by directing causes and forces and influences that are already there.[3]

The fourth category, *God's supernatural actions,* is the category of miracles. These are unusual events whereby God intervenes in the natural order to bring about an event that would not and could not otherwise have occurred. Many philosophers describe such events as *setting aside* or *bypassing* natural laws.[4] God does not bring about miraculous events through natural causes, influences and events; rather, God simply and directly *wills* that they occur. Accordingly, such events cannot be explained in terms of natural causes, influences or events. Any adequate explanation of them must mention God.

An example would be Jesus' turning water into wine at the marriage in Cana (Jn 2:1-11).[5] If this event occurred as described (and I believe that it did), there does not appear to be any adequate scientific or natural explanation of it; it was a direct act of God in the world. Other such events would be the biblical healings, nature miracles, epiphanies, voices from heaven, and the incarnation and resurrection of Jesus Christ.

Contemporary philosophers and theologians have located several difficulties in the Christian notion that God acts in the world. I will explain and discuss some of them in each of the following four sections. They can be formulated as questions. First, is the concept of an immaterial thing coherent? Second, is the concept of an immaterial person or agent coherent? Third, is the concept of an immaterial person or agent who is also timeless coherent? Fourth, is the category of miracle believable for modern people?

Is the Concept of an Immaterial Thing Coherent?
Some philosophers have argued that the very notion of an immaterial thing is incoherent, and thus that the concept of God, who is said to be an immaterial being, is incoherent. An incoherent concept is a concept that does not make sense or cannot possibly be instantiated or realized, like the concept of a square circle. The problem here is not that no square circles happen to exist—for logical reasons there *cannot* be any such thing. This is to be contrasted with coherent but noninstantiated concepts like unicorns. Such an animal—a horselike creature with one long horn protruding from its forehead—*could* exist but happens not to exist.

How might it be argued, then, that the very concept of an *immaterial thing* is incoherent? There is an argument to this effect in the influential book *Individuals* by P. F. Strawson.[6] Strawson argues that for any concept of an individual thing to be coherent, we must be able uniquely to identify or refer to that thing. That is, we must be able to pick it out among all other existing or even possible things so that there is no confusion about which thing we are referring to. With physical objects, reference is normally made to their physical properties—"that big gray rock over there," "the man in the blue suit" or "the sixth planet from the sun." But with immaterial objects no such reference in terms of physical properties can be made. When we try to speak of immaterial objects, then, we can never be sure what we are talking about, whether we are talking about the same thing when we try at different times to refer to it, or even whether two of us who are having a conversation about it are talking about the same thing. The very notion of an immaterial thing is accordingly incoherent.

Mind-body dualists usually claim that the immaterial thing called the soul or mind can be identified in terms of mental states like memories, beliefs and feelings. Possibly, then, God could be identified and thus successfully referred to in terms of God's mental states. But the problem with this proposal is that the mental states of other human persons are not directly accessible to us. We only know that a friend is angry because of that person's bodily behavior. And with God, who is supposed to be transcendent, the situation is even more difficult. How can we identify God in terms of God's mental states since we do not know God's mental states directly, and God (unlike humans) exhibits no bodily behavior from which we might infer God's mental states? Thus when we try to speak about God, we have no way of knowing what we are talking about, how many members of this class or type there are, or how to pick out one member of this class as opposed to others. In short, the very concept of an immaterial thing is unusable and incoherent.

Strawson is certainly correct in arguing that a concept, in order to be coherent, must be such that we can refer uniquely to the thing that instantiates it. It must have a clear and identifiable referent. But the rest of the argument—the point that no immaterial object can be uniquely referred to—is unconvincing. What about the number six? It is surely an immaterial object—the number six does not weigh anything or reside anywhere or take up space. But whether you think the number six is a separately existing thing or just an idea in our minds, the concept of it is obviously a coherent concept and can be uniquely referred to. Take the words "the only composite number between four and eight." Won't that description refer uniquely to the number six?

"But God is not like a number," a critic might say at this point, and that would certainly be true. Still, why can't God be uniquely referred to in terms of God's acts, for example, "the one who created the heavens and the earth" or "the one who raised Jesus from the dead"? Either such descriptions succeed in referring uniquely (if the God thus described actually exists), or they do not refer at all (if no God, or no one God who did the deeds mentioned, exists). Of course, the bare concept of "the one who created the heavens and the earth" may not tell us everything we might want to know about God, but the kind of reference-confusion behind Strawson's worry will not obtain here. The concept of "the one who created the heavens and the earth" is perfectly coherent.

As Thomas F. Tracy argues, it is possible to identify God in terms of a unique relationship that God has with some identifiable physical object, such as "the creator of the Milky Way galaxy" or "the one who caused the apostle Paul to regain his sight" (these are my examples, not Tracy's). Such references will typically involve what Tracy calls "telling a story" that creates a pattern within which we can understand a certain event as fitting what we understand to be God's purposive activity.

In general, we will be able to ascribe properties to God, and thus identify God, only if we can locate enduring patterns in the intentional activity of God. Tracy says, "Identification of God as a unique subject of speech involves a whole network of claims about the nature of God, the openness of human history and nature to God's influence, God's dealings with us in the past and his purposes for our future, and so on. The effect of this theistic story is to superimpose a pattern of divine intention on the events of human history."[7] Within the pattern of the theistic story, God will be identifiable; reference to God will successfully individuate God among all other possible or actual things. A causal relationship between X and Y can be a sufficient condition for identifying X ("the woman who hired me"; "the man who built this house"), as long as there is good reason to believe that the effects in question are the effects of an agent.

Is the Concept of an Immaterial Agent Coherent?

The concept of an immaterial *thing* may be coherent, but what about the concept of an immaterial thing that is also supposed to be an *agent*? Some thinkers have argued that such a notion is incoherent because what we might call "agent words" (for example, *loving, cruel, honorable, just, aggressive, forgiving*) lose whatever meaning they have *in the absence of a body*. Without loving or cruel or honorable bodily behavior to observe, the very attempt to attribute these properties to a thing will lack meaning.

Thus, speaking of the kinds of properties Christians usually attribute to God, Paul Edwards says:

> All these words lose their meaning if we are told that God does not possess a body. . . . For what would it be like to be, say, just without a body? To be just, a person has to *act* justly—he has to behave in certain ways. This is not reductive materialism. It is a simple empirical truth about what we mean by "just." But how is it possible to perform these acts, to behave in the required ways without a body? Similar remarks apply to the other divine attributes.[8]

Ergo, the concept of an immaterial agent is incoherent.

Again, it is quite correct to claim that secure reference to any agent, disembodied or not, must make use of descriptions that uniquely refer to or identify that agent. So if we are to speak coherently about God as a disembodied agent, we must be able uniquely to refer to God. But, as William Abraham asks, why should we allow the further point that having a body is part of the very concept of agency, that it is impossible to conceive of action without a body?[9] This seems a simple bit of dogmatic bluster on Edwards's part.

It is simply not true that agent words must lose their meaning in the absence of a body. What is true is that in the absence of a body the *normal signs we use to detect* the presence of, say, kindness or cruelty are missing. But there is no reason why a disembodied thing cannot behave kindly or cruelly (that is, be an agent); whether we could ever know this or be in a position to attribute kindness or cruelty to a disembodied agent is another question. But we can conceive of situations where we would be in such a position. Suppose we believe that a very powerful disembodied thing, X, exists. Suppose further that we believe that X is quite likely to be loving to human beings in a certain condition, C, and cruel to them in another condition, D. Suppose further that we notice certain human beings in condition C in apparent blissful happiness, and certain other human beings in condition D enduring terrible suffering. Suppose finally that we are completely unable to explain the happiness of the one group and the suffering of the other by ordinary or natural means. Then, I conclude, we would be within our intellectual rights in attributing these events to X. We might well call X (in the appropriate circumstances) kind or cruel.

The critic is arguing that agent words have no application to immaterial beings. It is part of the meaning of the sentence "John speaks to Mary" that John uses John's vocal cords in the relevant ways. But it is easily seen that this cannot be true. There are children who understand the sentence "John speaks to Mary" perfectly well without having any idea what vocal cords are. I suspect that most atheists understand the sentence "God spoke to Moses," even though they think it is false. Using one's vocal cords is of course the normal way that one person speaks to another, but those who insist that what can legitimately be called speaking cannot happen in any other way and that sentences like "God [an immaterial thing] spoke to Moses" are meaningless are caught in an overly rigid view of language.

But what if the critic argues that the problem is not precisely the question whether an immaterial thing can be an agent but whether an immaterial thing can be an agent in the material world? The critic would argue that *the only sorts of things that can cause physical events to occur are other physical events or things.* Thus the questions the critic would ask would be, How can an immaterial thing create the material world? How can an immaterial thing intervene in the material world and cause certain physical events to occur?

A possible counterexample to the critical claim above concerns psychokinesis. This phenomenon is defined as the movement of a physical object by purely mental effort, that is, without any direct or indirect physical contact with that object. An example would be making dice fall into a certain position simply by "willing" it to be so. I have no idea (nor even any firm opinion) whether psychokinesis actually occurs, but I am quite sure that it is conceivable—that the notion of psychokinesis is coherent. And if it is conceivable, it seems a short step to hold similarly that an immaterial thing can conceivably cause physical events to occur— to act as an agent. Of course, there are different senses of the word *conceive,* so I do not wish to place great emphasis on this argument. Still, it seems that in order to be an agent, we must be able to order our own activity purposefully and influence the world external to ourselves by that activity. It has yet to be shown that an immaterial thing cannot satisfy these conditions.

It does not seem that anyone is in a position to insist dogmatically that no event in the physical world can be brought about by an immaterial thing. After all, it is a crucial tenet of mind-body dualism that this sort of thing commonly occurs. That is, certain physical events (for example, my walking down the hall) are caused by certain mental events (for example, my deciding to check my mailbox); and certain mental events (for example, my being in a state of fear) are caused by certain physical events (for example, my facing an angry dog). Mind-body dualism is often criticized; there may be no theory that is more frequently attacked by contemporary philosophers of mind. Still, mind-body dualism has never been refuted, and many intelligent philosophers defend it.[10] It may well be true that some physical events are caused by certain sorts of nonphysical events.

Perhaps (as I say) no one is in a position dogmatically to insist that immaterial things cannot cause physical events to occur. But Michael Martin offers a probability argument for this very conclusion. Let me quote Martin's own version of it:

1. In terms of our experience, all created entities of the kinds that we have so far examined are created by one or more beings with bodies. [Empirical evidence]

2. The universe is a created entity. [Supposition]

2a. If the universe is a created entity, *then it is of the same kind as the created entities we have so far examined.* [Empirical evidence] [Probably]

3. The universe was created by one or more beings with bodies. [From (1), (2) and (2a) by predictive inference]

4. If the theistic God exists, then the universe was not created by a being with a body. [Analytic truth]

5. Therefore, the theistic God does not exist. [From (3) and (4) by *modus tollens*][11]

Let me raise two criticisms of this argument. First, I am not at all willing to concede to Martin's premise (1); indeed, I hold that every creature was created by something without a body, namely, God. Martin would reply to this point by insisting that premise (1) only means that *as far as we can tell from our experience,* all created entities were created by embodied beings. That is, in all cases where we are in a position to know who or what created some material object, it was created by another material object. (Perhaps Martin means situations where we happen to know, because we have seen, that a given desk was created by a certain carpenter, that a given watch was created by a certain watchmaker or that a given painting was created by a certain artist.) Then Martin adds, "We know of no cases where an entity is created by one or more beings without bodies. . . . No matter what kinds of things known to be created we have examined, none of them is known to be created by a disembodied entity."[12] And here I must demur: I believe I know of many such cases—all human beings, for example, were created by a being without a body, namely, God. So was the universe itself.

Second, the derivation of (3) from the premises above it is problematical. Even if the universe is a created entity, it seems to be quite different from (not of the same kind as) other created entities we have examined. Thus the degree of probability possessed by (3) will be too low to be convincing. It has this difference: while all the other created things of which we know were brought into existence by other created things, the universe (by which we mean the sum total of created things) could not have been. In other words, even if it is true (as I am unwilling to grant) that there is nothing that is known to have been created by an immaterial thing, it does not follow *even as a matter of probability* (or probability high enough to be significant) that nothing was created by an immaterial thing. It is quite possible for events unlike any we have ever knowingly experienced to occur.

Is the Concept of a Timeless Agent Coherent?

Christian philosophers and theologians disagree about God's relation to time. Some hold that God is temporally eternal and others hold that God is timelessly eternal. To say that God is temporally eternal (or everlasting) is to say that (1) God is eternal in the sense that there is no moment in time when God does not exist and (2) God is temporal in the sense that God exists "in" time (God has both temporal location and temporal extension). It makes sense, on this view, to speak about God existing *before* World War II or to say that God's act of bringing about the Second Coming of Christ is *in the future*. This is the view of God's relation to time that I have defended elsewhere[13] and have been presupposing thus far in this chapter.

A more difficult problem exists for those who hold that God is timelessly eternal or outside of time. To say that something is timeless is to say that it has no temporal location or temporal extension. Something has no temporal location if it makes no literal sense, for example, to say that it existed yesterday or will exist in exactly fifty years. Something has no temporal extension if it makes no literal sense, for example, to say that it lives for seventy years or that its life span lasted from 1442 until 1506. Thus the philosopher Boethius (c. 480-524) defined timelessness as "the complete possession all at once of illimitable life."[14] If God is timeless, then it seems that temporal terms (terms like *before, after, at the same time as, past, present, future, simultaneous with, always, forever, next year, at 4:00 p.m.*) cannot be predicated of God. Even a sentence like "God is *always* holy" makes no literal sense.

If God is an agent, then God does certain actions. And if God does an action in the world, it follows that we can coherently ask *when* God does that action. But how then can a timeless thing, defined as we have defined it, be an agent? That is, how can it act in time, as the God of the Bible is supposed to do? How can God punish someone, for surely a punishment is a sanction meted out to a person *after* a sin or crime has been committed? How can God warn someone, for surely to warn is to alert someone to some actual or possible *future* event? How can God forgive, for surely to forgive is to release someone of some *past* guilt? How can God bring something temporal into existence, for if God creates a temporal thing that comes into existence in 1955, doesn't it follow that God must have done the act of creation (and thus existed) *in* 1955?

A defender of timelessness will reply that an action (for example, the bringing of something, *X*, into existence) can be outside of time and its effect (the coming into existence of *X* in 1955) can be temporal. Why must the temporality of the effect require that the cause be temporal? What follows from God's creating a being that comes into existence in 1955 is not: *God, in 1955, brings X into existence,* but simply: *God timelessly brings X into existence, and X first exists in 1955.* That is, there is no incoherence in the notion of a timeless God timelessly willing that a certain event occur at a certain point in time. (Similarly, there is no incoherence in the notion of a spaceless or immaterial God causing a certain event to occur at some spatial point.)

A defender of timelessness need not hold that time is unreal or even that for God there is no time. The idea is, rather, that God created time (just as God created space) for creatures to exist in. And as an omniscient being, God knows time perfectly. But God's own being is not in time, and so the inner life of God is unrelated to time, change and the passage of time. The normal requirement in causality that a cause occur *first* and *then* its effect has no relation to a timeless being.[15]

Is the Category of Miracle Believable for Modern People?

The fourth objection to the basic notion of divine action that I will discuss concerns the arguments of certain twentieth-century revisionist theologians. Several of them have argued strenuously against the concept of divine miraculous acts in the world. For example, in a famous passage, German theologian and biblical scholar Rudolf Bultmann says,

It is impossible to use the electric light and the wireless and to avail ourselves of modern medical and surgical discoveries, and at the same time to believe in the New Testament world of spirits and miracles. We may think we can manage it in our own lives, but to expect others to do so is to make the Christian faith unintelligible and unacceptable to the modern world.[16]

Interpreting Bultmann's remark, theologian Van Austin Harvey says,

He meant that the act of turning a switch, speaking over a microphone, visiting a doctor or a psychiatrist is a *practical* commitment to a host of beliefs foreign to those of the New Testament. It is to say that the world of modern theory—be it electrical, atomic, biological, even psychological—is a part of the furniture of our minds and that we assume this in our reading of the newspapers, in our debates over foreign policy, in our law courts, and . . . in our writing of history. In other words, our daily intercourse reveals that we, in fact, *do not* believe in a three-story universe or in the possession of the mind by either angelic or demonic beings.[17]

The point that Bultmann and Harvey make is that the world of the New Testament—a world of miracles, spirits, demon possession and angels—is a world that is alien to and inconsistent with our complex and technological modern world. The way that we live today shows that we must reject the New Testament world as mythological and outmoded. The implication seems to be that the people of New Testament times were much more backward and superstitious than we are; that is why they were prepared to believe in miracles at the drop of a hat. They just didn't have the great benefit of our advanced scientific knowledge and reasoning power.

But surely this is misleading. If belief in miracles was so commonplace during ignorant times like the first century, why were such biblical miracles as Jesus' turning water into wine or Jesus' being raised from the dead taken to be so significant? It seems that the idea of water being turned into wine or of a dead man living again was no less intellectually scandalous to first-century folk than it is to us. (Note the reaction of the apostle Thomas to talk of the resurrection of Jesus in John 20, or of the Stoic and Epicurean philosophers to that same sort of talk in Acts 17.)

As to Bultmann's claim about the wireless (that is, the radio), exactly why is it impossible for a modern person who uses the wireless to believe that miracles occur? Surely there are very many people who both use the wireless and believe in miracles. (I am one of them.) Do our modern scientific beliefs require us to reject the notion that God occasionally acts miraculously in the world? I do not see why. And while it is in general true that rational people are committed to giving "natural" explanations of events whenever possible (and so were rational people in the first century), J. P. Moreland, in chapter eight in this volume, has offered a sophisticated account of how miracles might be recognized as part of the practice of science. At any rate, I fail to see any reason, either from Bultmann or Harvey, why a contemporary person cannot hold that miracles occur.[18]

Theologian Langdon Gilkey says:

Both the biblical and orthodox understanding of theological language was univocal. That is, when God was said to have "acted," it was believed that he had performed an observable act in space and time so that he functioned as does any secondary cause; and when he was said to have "spoken," it was believed that an audible voice was heard by the person addressed. In other words, the words "act" and "speak" were used in the same sense of God as of men. We deny this univocal understanding of theological words. To us, theological verbs such as "to act," "to work," "to do," "to speak," "to reveal," etc., have no longer the literal meaning of observable actions in space and time or of voices in the air.[19]

Gilkey argues that modern people simply do not allow that there are any miraculous acts of God in the world; there are no "wonders and voices." Christians once thought that the word *acts* was being used unequivocally in both "Bill Jones acts" and "God acts." The idea was that God acts in empirically observable ways, just as humans like Bill Jones do. But—so Gilkey reasons—it is not possible for us moderns to accept such a notion, and we have no analogous understanding of the word *acts* in "God acts" to replace it with. The only kind of divine activity in the world that is accordingly acceptable is my second category, God's natural actions.

But it is unclear to me precisely what it is that forbids us late-twentieth-century folk from holding that God can and does occasionally act miraculously in the world. One wishes that Gilkey, Bultmann and Harvey had spelled out just what they take the argument to be. Alston argues convincingly that all natural laws have built-in provisions for exceptions due to outside forces. What we call the law of gravity may well entail something like this: *Things that are heavier than air, when left unsupported near the vicinity of the earth, tend to fall toward the center of the earth*. But the existence of things like hummingbirds and helicopters does not destroy the law. Thus, Alston says, "Since the laws we have reason to accept make provision for interference by outside forces unanticipated by the law, it can hardly be claimed that such a law will be violated if a divine outside force intervenes; and hence it can hardly be claimed that such laws imply that God does not intervene, much less imply that this is impossible."[20]

Nor does it follow that the word *acts* is being used unequivocally in both "Bill Jones acts" and "God acts." At the very least, Gilkey has not shown that this cannot be the case. His point surely does not follow merely from the fact that Bill's acts are normally observable and God's are not. What about Bill's mental actions? Aren't they unobservable? And contrary to what Gilkey claims, it is possible to supply concrete and specifiable content to words like *acts* when applied to God. That is what I have been attempting to do in this discussion.

Other theologians argue that the very concept of "miracle" is out-moded, mythological and discredited. It is embedded in a worldview that is not ours. It is inconsistent with the modern view of science and history, since both disciplines presuppose that all events can in principle be explained in scientific terms. Some even suggest that given our modern understanding of nature and history, the very notion of an "act of God" is unintelligible, inconceivable and unacceptable. A finitely uncaused event is not an event.[21]

Alston responds to this sort of argument rather tersely:

I am afraid I do not find any of this very impressive as an argument for denying that divine interventions do, and can, occur. Let it be granted that the belief in such interventions runs counter to various features of the contemporary mind-set. But unless we have reason to think that our age is distinguished from all others in being free of intellectual fads and fancies, of attachments to assumptions, para-digms, and models that far outstrip the available evidence, of believing things because one finds one's associates believing them, and so on, this is hardly of any probative value.[22]

Conclusion

Something about the nature of reality follows from all of this. What is at the center of the universe? According to Christianity, it is not atoms in motion or a karmic cycle or an infinite void or even an omnipotent despot. *What is at the center of the universe is a personal relationship*, that is, a loving relationship among persons.[23] At its deepest level, this startling fact points to the loving, interpenetrating relationships among the trinitarian persons—the Father, the Son and the Holy Spirit. But it also means that we human beings were created out of the dynamics of that relationship and for the sake of that relationship.

Cosmically, the relationship between God and human beings was severed by the entrance of sin into the world. Personally, it is broken whenever we separate ourselves from God by sin. All of God's actions in history are expressions of the personal relationship that is at the center of reality. God is attempting redemptively to restore human beings to the splendor of that relationship. Christians affirm that the relationship is fully restored through the action of God in the world and preeminently through God's action in Jesus Christ. Its essence is summed up sublimely by the prophet Jeremiah: "I will be your God, and you shall be my people" (Jer 7:23). At the center of the universe is a personal relationship and a God who acts on its behalf.

I conclude that none of the four objections to the notion of divine activity in the world discussed here renders the notion incoherent or even mildly dubious. The traditional Christian notion that God acts in the world, both through natural causes and outside of them, seems eminently defensible. Accordingly, the real question is not whether God logically *could* be a "conscious purposive agent" in the world but whether there is any evidence that God *has been* such an agent. While answering that question is beyond the scope of this chapter, it is addressed in considerable detail in the final section of this volume.

ELEVEN

THE
EVIDENTIAL
VALUE OF
MIRACLES

R. DOUGLAS GEIVETT

H. D. LEWIS WROTE, "FEW TOPICS HAVE IN FACT BEEN MORE MISUN-derstood or mishandled than miracles; and this has often brought discredit on religion and made the way of its defenders hard."[1] Certainly, the relationship between the Christian belief in miracles and Christianity's general credibility is complex. We may refer to the nest of issues involved in this relationship by speaking of the "evidential value" of miracles. While the usefulness of this label is limited by its ambiguity, the very ambiguity of the label is a virtue. It is a virtue because the phrase effectively ranges over a set of concerns, all having to do with miracles and the task of justifying Christian religious belief. It is helpful, however, to organize these concerns into two general categories. The first category relates to concerns about whether it is reasonable to think that miracles have occurred. The second category of concern about miracles focuses on the role that miracles might play in supporting other religious beliefs. Herein lies the ambiguity of the phrase "the evidential value of miracles": the two types of concerns just distinguished refer, respectively, to the evidential *basis* of miracles and the evidential *use* of miracles.

In dealing with the evidential value of miracles, then, we are faced with two separable projects: (1) the project of exhibiting the evidential basis of miracles and (2) the project of indicating the evidential use of miracles. Let us call these the "basis project" and the "use project," respectively. We may speak collectively of these two subsidiary projects as aspects of the more general task of delineating the evidential *value* of miracles. Call this more general task the "value project."

I have spoken of the two subsidiary projects (the basis project and the use project) as "separable," and I wish to clarify what I mean by that. These projects can be distinguished; I do not mean that the basis project and the use project can each be fully executed separately. Actually, even this clarification is not quite precise enough for my purposes. For not only can we distinguish between the basis project and the use project, but we can distinguish at least *two ways of executing these projects in relation to one another*. This difference between ways of executing the basis project and the use project in relation to one another defines two very different ways of delineating the evidential value of miracles more generally (that is, of executing the value project).

One way is a top-down approach, and the other is a bottom-up approach. Both approaches allow that the basis project and the use project need to be executed "together," but they differ in their respective conceptions of the integral relationship between the basis project and the use project. Moreover, they express fundamentally different conceptions of both the evidential basis and the evidential use of miracles (and therefore of both the basis project and the use project as well).[2] Let us consider each in turn, beginning with the bottom-up approach.

The Ascent-to-God-from-Miracles Approach

One way of conceiving the relationship between the basis project and the use project is illustrated by the pattern of arguing for the existence of God from miracles: "One first establishes the existence of an anomalous fact [a religiously significant violation of natural law] . . . and then tries to show that it should be explained by the activity of an intelligent agent."[3] On this approach, the evidential *use* of miracles is tied to their value in showing that God exists. This aspect of the approach is fairly straightforward. It is the other aspect of this bottom-up approach, that aspect having to do with its conception of the evidential *basis* of miracles, that is more difficult to characterize and leads to a fair amount of misunderstanding.

What makes it tricky to formulate the argument in its strongest form is *the difficulty in knowing when precisely and explicitly to invoke the notion*

of miracle for its power to explain the occurrence of an unusual event.
According to this argument, what requires explanation, precisely, is an
event for which there is presently no known naturalistic (or scientific)
explanation. Identifying a suitable explanation for such an event is made
more difficult if it appears that the event has little chance of ever being
explained naturalistically (assuming a naturalistic prejudice does not
enter into the calculation of the odds). In that case it would be tempting
but disingenuous to insist on calling the event an "anomaly."

What is an anomaly? It is an event that cannot as yet be subsumed
under the explanatory principles of a particular paradigm endorsed by
an intellectual community. A paradigm is an integrated set of scientific
and metaphysical beliefs in terms of which investigatable entities are to
be identified, understood and explained. The anomalous character of an
event is normally thought to be paradigm relative. That is, the event in
question violates (or seems to violate) the understanding of the operation
of natural laws *within the framework of a ruling paradigm,* where a ruling
paradigm is one that enjoys the greatest support among intellectual
representatives within a field of study (such as biology, physics, the
philosophy of mind, theology, history, etc.).

One option for dealing with anomalies is to explore or develop the
finer features of the ruling paradigm so that the anomalous event comes
to be understood within its framework. Occasionally, the only satisfactory response to a really stubborn anomaly, however, is to overhaul the
ruling paradigm, which is, in effect, to exchange it for another paradigm.
In any case, the judgment that an event is anomalous is not to be taken
literally. It is simply "a-nomalous," or contrary to natural law, relative to
our current understanding of natural law. A literally anomalous event
would be an event for which no (realistic) understanding of the laws of
nature would play any role in the occurrence of the event. Such an event
would surely be a candidate for being called a miracle. On the other hand,
an event that descriptively conforms to the operation of the actual laws
of nature might still be a miracle as long as the correct explanation of
the event is to be given in terms of God's direct intervention and that
intervention only coincidentally and not essentially fits the pattern of
natural law. Left to our own devices, it would be difficult to identify such
an event as miraculous.[4]

Characteristically, to label an event an "anomaly" is to express the
expectation that that event will eventually come to be explained in an
entirely adequate fashion in terms of a fuller understanding of the laws

of nature, either in terms of the reigning paradigm or in terms of some new and more adequate paradigm. Since many events that once appeared to be quite mysterious to investigators have subsequently come to be understood in terms of the normal operation of natural laws, the concept of an anomaly is important for the practice of science. Nevertheless, this concept has sometimes been badly abused. It is abused, for example, when it is stretched to the point of excluding in principle the occurrence of phenomena that could never be explained in terms of even the fullest understanding of natural law. Phenomena of this kind would be literally a-nomalous, with no prospects of being explained naturalistically. And there is nothing inherent in the concept of an anomaly or in the proper practice of science to forbid the possible identification and correct explanation of an event of this kind. Such an event would simply have to be identified and explained nonnaturalistically.

Apart from withholding judgment on the matter, there are only two alternatives to assigning a naturalistic cause for an event of the kind in question (where a naturalistic cause is ruled out *ex hypothesi*): the event may have no causal explanation (that is, it may have occurred purely by chance) or it may (like certain other events familiar within human experience) have a nonnaturalistic explanation. Since no event has ever been definitively identified as a chance event, it would seem appropriate to assign a nonnaturalistic power or agent as the cause of the event we are now considering in the abstract. Furthermore, it must be assumed that the nonnatural power or agent responsible for the event must have the degree of power, ingenuity and magnanimity to cause the event in question. And it is at least possible to describe an event that would seem to require an agent-cause with properties characteristically associated with the Judeo-Christian concept of God. Finally, we cannot rule out the possibility of actually identifying an event with these properties should the event be performed in our presence. And all of this would be true even if we did not have much in the way of independent evidence for the existence of a supernatural power.

Perhaps this is an adequate representation of the argument to God's existence "from miracles." This argument is construed as an inference to the best explanation for certain anomalous states of affairs. Notice that it does not first argue *to* miracles and then *from* miracles to God. Rather, it reasons to miracles in the very act of reasoning to God. *For it is not until we notice that the agent responsible for the event must be (or probably is) God that we are in a position to call the event a miracle.* In this sort of situation, the evidential *basis* of miracles is brought to light in the process of *using* events that we later come to regard as miracles to infer the existence of God. What we consciously appeal to in this argument for the existence of God is our sense of the limitations of natural causes to account for the event and our awareness of the availability of a nonnatural explanation for the event. We are not at the outset of the reasoning process *aware* of the miraculous status of the event, though, of course, it will have been a miraculous event all along. That it is a miracle is something we find out as a result of carrying the argument through. In light of this, it might be helpful to point out how misleading it can be to refer to this argument for the existence of God as an *argument from miracles*. (But then, what are the chances of breaking with such an entrenched tradition?[5])

Evaluation of the Argument
Before turning to the next type of account of the relationship between the basis project and the use project, we need to consider some difficulties that might be raised for this bottom-up approach. First, the bottom-up approach faces the very real difficulty involved in determining which events that cannot as yet be explained naturalistically are merely anomalous and which are not and are therefore plausible candidates for being miraculous. Some would complain that "punting" to miracles in the absence of a naturalistic explanation is not an explanation of another kind, but a willful refusal to seek an explanation. As Thomas Kuhn might say in this regard, "You cannot predict the next scientific discovery."[6] Better to resist closure on the issue until a naturalistic explanation emerges.

In response, we need to keep in mind the notion of a *recalcitrant* experience, first described by Harvard philosopher W. V. O. Quine. A recalcitrant experience is one that stubbornly resists explanation within the framework of a given paradigm or web of beliefs.[7] Now if an experience or observation can resist explanation within the parameters of a particular paradigm of explanation to the point where a new paradigm seems required, why should it not be possible for some experience or observation to prove so recalcitrant that it would seem to resist scientific (that is, naturalistic) explanation altogether? The insistence that no experience *could* have this effect will seem ad hoc and question-begging in the extreme.[8] Furthermore, in the face of recalcitrant experiences, theorists have posited the existence of unobservable entities (for example, electrons, magnetic fields and black holes) to handle relevant explanatory difficulties. Perhaps this is all theists are doing when they infer the existence of God in order best to explain religiously significant recalcitrant experiences.

It is noteworthy that the critical literature on miracles going back even further than David Hume is especially preoccupied with the Christian belief in the resurrection of Jesus from the dead. This probably is not simply because philosophers have decided to isolate their discussion to miracle claims within more familiar traditions. A better explanation of this preoccupation with the resurrection, I think, is that what we have in the case of the resurrection is a recalcitrant experience of the highest order. As a friend of mine once remarked, it is a truly "bodacious" miracle. If the resurrection doesn't count as a violation of presumed natural law, then nothing does.

At any rate, given a choice between treating the alleged event of the resurrection as an anomaly that will eventually be explained by science and repudiating the historicity of New Testament reports concerning the resurrection, today's naturalist will generally opt for the latter. This presumably is because of the recalcitrant character of the event in question. In other words, the tendency to treat reports about the resurrection as fictitious, as fabrications, is evidence that such an event would be considered eminently recalcitrant for naturalism by naturalists themselves. They would sooner describe the alleged "event" as a nonevent than be forced to come up with a plausible explanation that is compatible with naturalism.

Second, it seems possible that even a bona fide miracle might conform to our present understanding of the pattern of natural law, even though a naturalistic explanation would be mistaken since the event is actually a miracle, directly caused by God. Or it might be that God's "special acts" are accomplished through the natural order, as William Alston has suggested (though they must still be extraordinary).[9] The above method of picking out miracles offers no clear way of identifying such events as miraculous.[10]

This is not a very serious difficulty since it will be other miracles— those that are more readily identifiable as such—that will occupy center stage in the argument from miracles to the existence of God. It might be possible at a later stage in an apologist's or theologian's program to develop an account of how more inconspicuous miracles are to be identified. While such miracles may not be important for specifically evidential purposes, they may have great religious importance in other respects.

Third, since the argument is made to carry so much of the burden of establishing the existence of God (so that the theistic character of the universe remains an open question apart from this argument), skeptics may prefer to think that any unexplained event occurring within the physical universe is at least in principle capable of naturalistic explanation. Response? Suppose that we could never decisively eliminate the possibility that the occurrence of a most extraordinary event was actually due to the operation of natural laws. This does not resolve the practical problem of making a rational decision about what to believe. Failure to eliminate the possibility of a naturalistic explanation does not entail that a naturalistic explanation currently exists or is close at hand. Nor would the availability of a naturalistic explanation entail that the correct explanation is a naturalistic one. It may be that a nonnatural explanation is more plausible even when a naturalistic explanation is in some remote sense "available." Certainly, in the complete absence of a plausible naturalistic explanation, it would not be at all reasonable to suppose that the event has no explanation.[11]

Fourth, it might seem odd that the theistic hypothesis could be sustained only by appeal to the power of that hypothesis to explain particular events as actions of a supernatural agent. Then the case for God's existence would be available only to those familiar with miracles. Moreover, the theistic hypothesis might seem to be a hypothesis with inherently greater potential for confirmation by means of other types of evidence besides miracles. In other words, if miracles point to the existence of God, is it not likely that there would also be other types of evidence for the existence of God? Would not an agent who performed identifiably miraculous events be manifest in other ways as well, through the created order, for example, or in private religious experience? The obvious response to this sort of worry is that the objection does not imply that the argument from miracles fails to justify belief in God for some thoughtful people. But it might be objected further that *if all anyone had to go on was miracles,* then it probably would not be possible to generate a case for the rich sort of theism embraced by the Christian.[12]

Two things may be said in response to this elaboration of the objection. First, if the miracles in question justify inference to the existence of God, they presumably also provide justification for belief in the divine authority of any message that accompanies those miracles.

Whatever else may be known about God will then be available in the details of that revelation. So miracles, at least indirectly, support a more richly developed theism. Second, an advocate of the argument from miracles may hold that this argument plays only a limited role in a larger cumulative case for theism. The only real question here, as for any piece of evidence included within cumulative-case arguments for the existence of God, is what is (uniquely) contributed by the argument from miracles to the total case for theism. Does it raise the degree of epistemic justification one has for belief in theism? Does it extend the knowledge of God that we have from other sources of evidence?

Advocates of the argument from miracles need to consider whether the argument is (1) both necessary and sufficient for justified belief in God, (2) necessary but not sufficient, (3) sufficient but not necessary, or (4) neither necessary nor sufficient, but still useful, say, as part of a cumulative case. It is perhaps not very difficult to think of particular advocates of positions (3) and (4). I know of no proponents of options (1) and (2). Nevertheless, the argument from miracles, as I have characterized it in this essay, requires that it is at the very least a *sufficient* condition for justified belief in God.

Fifth, in the case of Christianity, our awareness of events traditionally deemed miraculous usually is not based on firsthand observation, but on the testimony of alleged eyewitnesses. To make matters worse, this testimony speaks to us from the remote past. It does not seem reasonable to base belief in God on an assessment of the power of the theistic hypothesis to explain extraordinary events when these events are alleged to have happened centuries ago.[13] Often the Christian apologist will answer this objection by suggesting that if one takes the historian's own criteria for assessing the historicity of ancient events, the resurrection passes muster as a historically well-attested event of the ancient world.[14] Now we can imagine a critic responding as follows.

It may be that the New Testament reports concerning miracles enjoy the same measure of support for historical purposes as the best-attested reports of other ancient events (such as Caesar's crossing of the Rubicon in 49 B.C.) that we do not hesitate to accept. But no consensus has been reached among historians about the criteria that must be satisfied before the testimony of a *miraculous* event can be accepted as genuinely historical. Indeed, the tendency is in the other direction: to assume that, at best, eyewitnesses reached the conclusion that they had witnessed a miracle, but that the event that occasioned this conclusion probably was not being described accurately by that label. The historian can perhaps determine what first-hand observers *thought* they had observed; he cannot judge that they were right in their verdict regarding the nature of the event.

The attempt by Christian apologists to draw parallels between, say, the historicity of reports about Caesar's crossing the Rubicon and the historicity of reports about Jesus' resurrection from the dead is laudable. The critic will claim, however, that this effort completely misses the point. Historians simply have no means of testing the authenticity of reports of alleged miracles. While Caesar's crossing of the Rubicon is an event of the type historians routinely examine, the resurrection is not. This disanalogy between ordinary events and miracles pinpoints the central problem with the historical identification of miracles. Miracles are sui generis, and the principles of historical investigation have not been developed to handle them. The critic need not, on one level, dispute the apparent historical authenticity of a report of an alleged miracle, such as the resurrection. He may simply point out the irrelevance of this result by noting the incommensurability, for historians, of miracles and ordinary events.[15]

In response to this objection I have two modest suggestions to offer. First, setting aside its miraculous quality, it is unlikely that an alleged event like the resurrection would otherwise enjoy such historical authentication according to the highest standards of historical inquiry if the tomb was not in fact empty and Jesus was not observed alive again following his crucifixion and burial. Christian apologists need not insist that it is the judgment of history per se that a resurrection miracle took place some two thousand years ago. They may simply point out that numerous observations of the relatively innocent facts of the empty tomb and the living Jesus appearing at various times after his crucifixion and burial are supremely well attested historically. On the face of it, the phenomena of an empty tomb and the recognition of the physical presence of a familiar person are perfectly natural facts (Gary Habermas has called them "this-worldly phenomena"). There is no compelling reason to dispute their historicity. There is nothing particularly extraordinary about an empty tomb (the tomb was presumably empty before Jesus' body was laid to rest there). And people who believe they have spoken with a person of long and close acquaintance are generally given the benefit of the doubt when they report that they have seen the person again recently. In asserting that the tomb was observed to be empty, or that Jesus was seen alive on such and such a day, no miracle is explicitly affirmed. That a miracle occurred is inferred from these facts, facts as well attested historically as the crucifixion itself (which is not seriously disputed by historians of the New Testament, as far as I know).[16]

Second, the historian with a prejudice against miracles should be reluctant to infer, even, that first-century believers sincerely *thought* they had been eyewitnesses either of the empty tomb or of the resurrected Jesus in the flesh. For then the historian is faced with the problem of producing a plausible naturalistic explanation for this sort of conviction on the part of first-century eyewitnesses. And it would be part of the historian's task as a historian to investigate the possible explanations of this sort of phenomenon. To say that first-century believers were mistaken in their belief is not to offer an explanation for their belief. And to forbid the possibility that Jesus had literally risen from the dead is to exclude, in an ad hoc manner inappropriate to sober scholarship, what may be the best explanation for first-century belief in the resurrection.

None of these objections to the argument from miracles to the existence of God is conclusive. The argument begins with some particular event or set of events occurring on the level of human experience and ascends to the existence and agency of God as the best explanation of that event or set of events. The strength of this argument will depend on the possibility of identifying an actual event that cannot plausibly be explained naturalistically. Perhaps the best candidate for an event of that type is the alleged resurrection of Jesus from the dead. As the Christian Scriptures affirm, Jesus Christ "was declared with power to be the Son of God by the resurrection from the dead" (Rom 1:4 NASB; cf. Acts 2:22-24).

The Descent-from-God-to-Miracles Approach

The other approach to the relation between the basis project and the use project might be called "the descent-from-God-to-miracles approach," or "the top-down approach." It is described very concisely by Richard Purtill when he writes, "One traditional way of providing a rational basis for religious belief begins with arguments for the existence of God and goes on to argue that a certain body of religious beliefs can be known to be a revelation from God because miracles have been worked in support of those religious beliefs."[17] Here again we need to consider how each of our two subsidiary projects, the basis project and the use project, is to be understood, first generally and then in relation to each other.

According to this approach, the basis project and the use project are executed in two stages, beginning with the basis project. How the basis project is to be carried out in detail depends on who one asks. Let us consider two contemporary advocates of this approach to the value project, Richard Purtill and Richard Swinburne, noting a few differences between them.

Richard Purtill: The conditional probability of miracles. Richard Purtill seeks to exhibit the evidential basis of miracles by combining two considerations. First, he asserts the *possibility* of miracles on the grounds that God exists. God's existence is independently supported by such traditional theistic arguments as the cosmological argument and the design argument. Purtill then reasons that there is strong historical evidence that miracles have *actually* occurred. The individual whom he calls a rationalistic believer "bases his assent to particular doctrines on authority, his acceptance of authority on the evidence of miracles, and his acceptance of miracles on philosophical arguments for God and historical arguments for the actual occurrence of miracles."[18] Later in the same essay Purtill writes, "The argument for miracles consists of two stages—an argument for the general possibility of miracles, and an argument for the historical actuality of certain miracles."[19]

Of special interest for our purposes is Purtill's precise use of arguments for·the existence of God to exhibit the evidential basis of miracles. As he says, "If God exists, miracles are not impossible."[20] In other words, the demonstrable existence of God creates a certain logical space for miracles to occur. They can no longer be ruled out a priori. As H. D. Lewis puts it, "A world created by God . . . has room for a miracle in it."[21]

It might seem that one could jump directly from the possibility of miracles to the historical evidence to confirm their actual occurrence. But Purtill is more careful than this, and for good reason. While evidence for the existence of God supports the possibility of miracles, it does not follow that any event that looks like a violation of natural laws must be an actual miracle or that we should conclude that it is a miracle.[22] With apparent sensitivity to this point, Purtill makes three additional suggestions that smooth the path for the historical part of his program. First, he notes that there are no good arguments that miracles are improbable.[23] Second, he observes that God may wish to indicate by means of a miracle that some religious message has divine authority behind it.[24] And third, he remarks that it is possible to describe "circumstances in which miracles are to be expected."[25] In these ways, Purtill clears away "metaphysical objections" to miracles and opens the door to the possibility of finding that miracle is the best explanation of particular historical phenomena.

Consider each of Purtill's three points. First, he says there are no good arguments that miracles are improbable. We have direct reference here to probability. What we do not have is a discussion of the *relative* probability of miracles on theism. Does theism make it at all likely that miracles would happen? Purtill does not say. To point out that we have no *argument* for the improbability of miracles is not to show that miracles are more probable than not on theism. Still, it is significant that theism makes the notion of a miracle intelligible and available for explanatory use if necessary. Furthermore, even if the evidence of natural theology [26] does not indicate that miracles are probable, since it does indicate that miracles are possible (because it implies the existence of God), we may appeal to other types of evidence (for example, historical evidence) to assess the probability that God has acted in history.

Purtill's proposal is attractive, for it provides a stronger execution of the basis project than the bottom-up argument. This is because in the bottom-up argument the existence of a divine agent is posited in order to explain a phenomenologically peculiar sort of event that we observe to take place within the spatiotemporal world. Of course, part of what makes it reasonable to do so is that we first have the notion of agency (that is, agent-as-cause) available to us through our familiarity with our own agency as humans. But perhaps a nonhuman agency that is also not quite divine would adequately explain the violation of natural law. This is one objection to the bottom-up approach that I did not try to answer earlier, and that is because I can think of no satisfactory answer to it. Within Purtill's strategy, however, the notion of *divine* agency becomes available before we contemplate the need to explain phenomenologically weird events. Divine agency is not a posit for Purtill, but the result of a carefully developed series of arguments for God's existence.

With respect to Purtill's second point, two observations are in order. First, he observes that we can think of a *suitable* motive for God to perform miracles, namely, to confirm the production of a fuller divine revelation. This relates directly to Purtill's execution of the use project. The evidential use of miracles is tied to God's intentions in performing miracles. Among the intentions God may be acting on in performing miracles is God's intention to confirm divine sponsorship of propositional revelation, such as the witness of the Hebrew prophets or the preaching of Jesus (see Heb 2:3-4). Second, Purtill couches this motive in terms of possibility. As he says, God *may* have a desire to use miracles as confirmation of a revelation. While it might seem that the best we can do is speculate about God's actual intentions with regard to providing a revelation accompanied by miracles, and we cannot be sure that God has the relevant motives for producing a revelation, at least we have background evidence that God is an agent who could be motivated to produce a revelation.

What about Purtill's third point? Here he indicates that circumstances can be described "in which miracles are to be expected." With this suggestion we seem finally to go beyond the mere possibility of miracles and to enter the realm of probability. But what this development amounts to depends on the *sort* of circumstances that Purtill thinks will make it probable that a miracle has occurred. For him, the circumstances that make the occurrence of a miracle probable are *historical:* the actual promulgation of a revelation on the part of the historical Jesus. The idea goes something like this: Jesus appears on the stage of human history with a claim to being the revelation of God par excellence—the very incarnation of the God of heaven. Given the background knowledge or justified belief (1) that God exists, (2) that miracles therefore are not improbable and (3) that God might well have a motive to perform a miracle, we must ask, Does the behavior of Jesus conform overall to what we would expect if he was what he claimed to be? Purtill thinks it does and includes miraculous acts among the indications that we should look for to achieve such confirmation.

This does seem plausible. But why? Because miracles may function like a divine signature or like the emblem on God's signet ring, confirming God's actual sponsorship of a particular revelation claim. An action of God that would be an unequivocal indication of divine action would be an event with properties that could have no more reasonable explanation than that it was performed by God. It would be a characteristically divine act—a miracle, if you will.

In summary, Purtill's proposal is that the existence of God establishes the possibility of miracles and that *if* God had a desire to produce a revelation, actual identifiable miracles would provide the needed confirmation that God had actually produced a revelation. Thus, we have an existential claim and a conditional claim: God exists, and miracles are probable (only) *on the condition* that God intends to produce a revelation. The hypothesis that God intends to produce a revelation is tested by an appeal to history. If there is strong historical evidence that a miracle has occurred, then, given the possibility of miracles grounded in the actual (demonstrable) existence of God, that God does intend to produce a revelation is confirmed to some degree.

Of course, it remains possible that God has not produced a revelation and that God lacks a motive to do so. Perhaps God is not especially interested in the human condition; maybe the various religions are just so many attempts by struggling humans to satisfy themselves that God does care. If God cannot have sponsored all the events and so-called truths attributed to him—as is evident by inveterate doctrinal conflicts between religious perspectives—then it is evident that humans can get themselves to believe in the reality of supposed supernatural events that God has nothing to do with. Perhaps every religious believer who affirms miracles is merely engaging in just this sort of wishful thinking.

To transcend this particular difficulty, we need to ask, Is it possible, perhaps through an elaboration of the evidence provided by general revelation[27] and exploited in traditional arguments for the existence of God, to establish a prior probability that God intends to provide further special revelation and to confirm it with the production of one or more identifiable miracles? Alternatively, does it make sense to believe that the God revealed in natural theology has no interest in the human situation and therefore cannot be expected to provide an identifiable remedy or revelation that would address the particular contours of the human situation?

Richard Swinburne: The prior probability of miracles. As we have seen, Richard Purtill describes circumstances that he concludes make it probable that God has acted miraculously in history. Miracles would be probable if God had an interest in communicating with men and women and if God desired that they be able to recognize some message as his own. But notice, even if these circumstances obtain and miracles are therefore probable, we are in no position to *assess* the probability that a miracle has occurred if we cannot assess the probability that God has the relevant intentions to produce a revelation. If God does have the relevant intentions, and if having the relevant intentions makes it likely that God will act in history, then it is perhaps also likely that we would be able to access God's intentions even before we encountered a historically situated special revelation claim accompanied by miracles.

When it comes to discerning God's intentions, all we have to go on is the evidence of natural theology (regarding God's existence and nature) and phenomena historically associated with the lives of great religious figures. While Purtill emphasizes natural theology in order to establish the possibility of miracles, he requires historical evidence in order to generate any probability that God intends to act miraculously. For Purtill, the probability that God has the relevant intentions is entirely a function of the historical evidence that a miracle tradition and its associated revelation claim is true.

There are reasons for wanting a more complete account of the probability of miracles than what Purtill has developed. If we should decide to look for a revelation from God, without a reasonable basis for doing so,[28] it would be difficult to adjudicate between competing revelation claims. Without the support of natural theology for the expectation of a revelation, there would be no extrahistorical criteria for judging any particular revelation claim to be actually sponsored by God (and this would be true even if there was only one revelation claim extant in the world). The best we could hope for would be that a genuine revelation be accompanied by historically well-attested "miracles." This surely places a greater burden on historical evidence than would be required if there was a prior probability that God would produce a revelation and that this revelation would be accompanied by one or more miracles.

If, however, the evidence of natural theology is rich enough to invite the expectation of revelation, then it might also provide a few clues about what would be included in such a revelation. Should there be more than one candidate revelation to choose from, then, criteria for making a rational choice may be partly satisfied by an inspection of the actual content of competing revelation claims and the aptness or fitness between those revelation claims and their associated miracle traditions.

One may even suppose that if God wanted to produce a revelation that would be recognized as such by some or all of his human subjects, then God might consider posting signs that we should be on the lookout for such a revelation and might even offer clues concerning the form that the revelation might take. This would seem particularly prudent on God's part if it should happen that humans are so desirous of receiving a "word from God" that they might easily be misled by counterfeit revelations or fall prey to an inclination to manufacture counterfeits.[29]

Suppose God intends to produce a revelation and desires that humans be able to identify a candidate revelation as genuinely divine. Then, as Purtill suggests, it is also likely that a revelation from God would be accompanied by signs confirming its divine origin. For this seems to be the best way humans could recognize that God had indeed produced a revelation. Humans would be in an even better position to identify a genuine revelation from God *if they knew in advance to expect a revelation from God and what, in general outline, to expect such a revelation to include.*

Richard Swinburne's contribution to the top-down approach to the value project is twofold. First, he probes the resources of natural theology in order to establish the prior probability that God would produce a revelation, which might in turn be confirmed as authentic by means of an appropriate miracle, itself judged to be actual on the basis of historical research. Within the framework of a well-developed natural theology, and prior to any consideration of historical evidence, it is possible, he thinks, to infer that God would likely produce a revelation. This is what Swinburne means when he writes, "Given that there is good evidence that there is a God, there is some reason *a priori* to expect that there will be a revelation."[30]

The considerations that support the expectation of revelation include information, gleaned from general revelation, about what sort of agent God is, as well as a realistic appraisal of human cognitive and moral limitations with respect to God's purposes for human persons. In particular, Swinburne stresses the goodness of God and thus God's disposition to remedy undesirable features of the human condition that we cannot adequately deal with on our own. Consider the following:

1. If we are duty-bound to worship God in the most appropriate fashion, we have an interest in understanding the conditions for satisfactory worship.

2. We aspire to organize our lives in a meaningful, goal-directed way that is fitting given the larger structure of reality.

3. We want to know if there is an afterlife, as we naturally tend to hope, and, if there is an afterlife, how we can best prepare for it.

4. We strain to arrest pervasive moral confusion within human society, and we lack a realistic diagnosis of the moral recalcitrance of the human heart.

5. We desire to make sense of the suffering of sentient creatures, both human and animal.

These concerns and others constitute a human need for divine revelation, a need that we can expect a good God to address.[31]

Second, Swinburne distinguishes between internal and external evidence that God has actually produced a revelation answering to the needs of the human condition.[32] The *external* evidence that God has sponsored a particular revelation tradition takes the form of peculiar events surrounding the production of that tradition, events that we would be inclined to call miraculous because of their special character. (It is this sort of evidence that Purtill takes account of in assessing the probability that God intends to produce a revelation.) The *internal* evidence would be the content or internal features of that revelation itself. There are two things to notice about the significance of this internal evidence. First, the internal features of a revelation function as evidence that it is truly from God only because the expectation (generated by natural theology) that God would produce a revelation is not empty or purely speculative. That is, included among the data of general revelation are clues that God's interest in producing a revelation run along particular lines. Thus, that we are right to expect a revelation with certain features is partially confirmed by the presence of precisely those features within a candidate for revelation. Second, if it should happen that a plurality of mutually exclusive religious perspectives include miracle traditions of their own, one way to adjudicate between them is in terms of the internal features of their respective revelation claims and the fitness between those features and the miracles alleged to accompany their supposed revelations.

In sum, Swinburne detects within the framework of natural theology itself enough evidence to make it likely not only that God exists but also that God intends to produce a revelation that would be confirmed to us by miracles. When a candidate revelation fulfills expectations regarding the specific content of an antecedently likely revelation and that candidate revelation is accompanied by a historically well-attested event that it seems only God could produce, then we may accept that revelation claim as authentic. It is easy to see how one who accepted this framework for assessing the evidence concerning religious truth claims might conclude that the Christian revelation claim—with its diagnosis and proposed remedy for the human condition, together with its historically well-attested account of the resurrection of Jesus—is God's own revelation of himself in response to the human situation.

Conclusion

Among the various ways of construing the evidential value of miracles, Swinburne's approach is most promising. As it happens, it is an approach with a long and venerable history. William Paley's *A View of the Evidences of Christianity* (1794) and Joseph Butler's *The Analogy of Religion* (1736) both followed the same approach in its general outline. John Locke (1632-1704), too, endorsed this method in his writings on religion.[33] It is somewhat ironic that even David Hume, the religious skeptic and noted debunker of miracles, expressed sympathy with a central intuition of this perspective when, with the voice of Philo in the *Dialogues Concerning Natural Religion* (published posthumously), he concluded his appraisal of the evidence for God's existence with these words:

> The most natural sentiment, which a well-disposed mind will feel on this occasion, is a longing desire and expectation, that Heaven would be pleased to dissipate, at least alleviate, this profound ignorance, by affording some more particular revelation to mankind, and making discoveries of the nature, attributes, and operations of the divine object of our Faith.[34]

If there is any basis in the expectation alluded to here, it is unfortunate that Hume forbade appeal to the one device at God's disposal that could confirm the fulfillment of that expectation: an event that is (1) situated in space-time history, (2) supported by ample historical evidence, (3) eminently recalcitrant to any attempt at thoroughly naturalistic explanation and (4) closely linked to the most realistic diagnosis of the human condition, namely, the resurrection of Jesus Christ some two thousand years ago.[35]

PART 4
CHRISTIAN MIRACLES— CASE STUDIES

TWELVE
MIRACLES
IN THE WORLD
RELIGIONS

DAVID K. CLARK

Large letters on the side of a smoke-belching vehicle proclaimed, "Miracles happen every day!" Was a popular televangelist now advertising on a Saint Paul bus? The fine print told a different story—the sign promoted a New Age religion. If Christian televangelists and New Age cultists both appeal to miracles in support of their religions, do these conflicting claims cancel each other out? How can miracles provide evidence for one faith when another religion uses different miracles to bolster its case?

David Hume's Fourth Principle
Who hit whom first, Billy or Johnny? Each boy accuses the other. Without more information, their mother cannot decide which boy to believe. She may decide to discipline both children because the boys' claims seem to cancel each other. Similarly, the miracle claims of competing religions seem to neutralize each other. David Hume makes this point in part two of his famous essay "Of Miracles" (see chapter one of this volume). "All the prodigies of different religions are to be regarded as contrary facts, and the evidences of these prodigies, whether weak or strong, as opposite

to each other."[1] Hume then illustrates this principle with a courtroom analogy. Suppose a judge, after considering testimony that a defendant committed a crime, then hears that the defendant was in another state at the time of the crime. Hume says the "credit" of the earlier testimony is "destroyed" by the later testimony.[2]

But surely this is a hasty conclusion. When courts hear conflicting testimony, lawyers on both sides grill their opponents' witnesses. Each side looks for loopholes or inconsistencies in the testimony and for hidden motivations or character flaws in the witnesses. More specifically, lawyers try to give reasons to overpower their opponents' testimony. These reasons are called *rebutting defeaters;* they give additional facts that override or rebut previous testimony. Attorneys also seek to raise doubts to sabotage their rivals' evidence. These doubts are called *undercutting defeaters;* they undermine or dissolve the warrant for believing earlier testimony. Both sorts of defeaters are relevant in assessing miracle claims of competing traditions.

Imagine that Victim died violently. Defendant is tried for murder. The defense attorney argues that Victim committed suicide, pointing to the murder weapon covered with Victim's fingerprints to prove it. But suppose the prosecution produces Witness who claims, contrary to the lab evidence, that she actually saw Defendant murder Victim. Witness's testimony is a *rebutting defeater* to the theory, drawn from lab evidence, that Victim committed suicide.

Now suppose the defense proves, under cross-examination, that Witness was vacationing five thousand miles away in Hawaii at the time of Victim's death. This revelation is an *undercutting defeater* that erodes Witness's testimony. This revelation undermines or dissolves Witness's testimony *completely;* the testimony no longer negates the force of the lab evidence. Thus it might seem initially that Witness's testimony cancels the lab evidence. But when the undercutting defeater is introduced, then Witness's testimony is completely invalidated, leaving the lab evidence unscathed.

Hume's argument amounts to this: if one uses a miracle to confirm a religion, the many miracles reported in other religions act as *rebutting defeaters* that override any warrant the miracle of the one tradition could provide. But we should not conclude too quickly that various stories rebut each other. Rather, like the lawyers, we should seek to distinguish those miracle reports that are well authenticated from those that are discredited by *undercutting defeaters.* All miracle reports are not epistemically equal; rarely, if ever, is there a perfectly balanced evidential standoff between two well-documented miracle claims. Rather, the evidence supporting religious miracle accounts varies greatly in quality, and many reports are subject to a variety of defeaters. Thus, evaluating conflicting miracle accounts demands that we painstakingly examine the details of evidence.[3]

Before tackling our subject, we must address a preliminary issue. Different religions report many marvels or prodigies—a broad category including miracles and other extraordinary, miraclelike events. But even if marvels really occurred, we still have to decide what caused them. Some are mere tricks. Others are supernormal but natural events. For instance, a guru who learns to reduce his heart rate dramatically is not performing a miracle, but using an unusual mastery of natural principles to do a supernormal act. We will assume that naturally caused events do not provide evidence for a particular religion, since all religious views can account for them.

But unlike tricks or natural events, some marvelous events might be caused by spiritual forces. These are sometimes called magic. As traditionally understood, magic involves harnessing spiritual beings or powers through incantations and other arts. In the ancient Mediterranean world, for example, magicians used recipes or performed rituals to help their clients and to damage their clients' enemies. Scholars have quite different views on the distinction between miracle and magic. In the ancient world, the word *magic* acquired negative connotations because some magicians earned reputations as cheats. Thus, according to some interpreters, religious apologists scornfully labeled their opponents "magicians," reserving the term *miracle* for their own wonders. These scholars claim that name-calling, motivated by partisan loyalty, is the major or even the only difference between "miracle" and "magic."[4]

But Jesus' works (including especially his encounters with demonic spirits) are unlike magic in that he performed miracles by his own power and authority.[5] In biblical miracles, God graciously responded to requests for supernatural help. By contrast, magic generally involves manipulation of spiritual, perhaps demonic, forces. From a Christian viewpoint, it is best to interpret demonic acts as supernormal but natural events, since demons are part of the natural order that God created. We will assume, therefore, that miracles and magic are conceptually distinct.[6]

Our question in this chapter is not whether a miracle story can legitimately provide evidence for a religious viewpoint. Rather, the point is to answer Hume's charge that because there are too many stories of marvelous events, the claims emerging from mutually incompatible religious traditions defeat each other like two conflicting witnesses in court. In responding to this charge, we should evaluate particular miracle reports by addressing at least three categories of considerations. First, is the religion associated with this miracle story really open to the supernatural? Next, are the naturalistic arguments that people use to account for the rise of spurious miracle stories rightly applied to this particular miracle account? Finally, is this specific miracle claim historically well authenticated?

The Concept of Miracle in Various Religions

First, we should ask whether the religion associated with a miracle story we are evaluating is really open to the supernatural. This has two parts. (1) Some stories of marvels are associated with religions that have no logical place for the supernatural in their belief structures. (2) Other supposed miracles emerge in religions that have a founder or an early history that depreciates miracle claims. Miracles are alien to the thought and history of some religions.

1. Since *miracle* is partly defined as an act of a supernatural personal being(s) (see Richard Purtill's discussion in chapter three), any religion that lacks the idea of such a being(s) in its belief structure has no conceptual place for miracle. One could hardly defend the belief structure of such a religion by appealing to stories about events requiring the action of a supernatural being.

Consider original Buddhism. The Buddha, Siddhartha Gautama (c. 563-c. 483 B.C.), remained agnostic about an unchanging God or Absolute. He taught that impermanence characterizes everything we see. Those who are unaware that everything is impermanent are condemned to endless craving for something permanent. This craving, since it can never be fulfilled, leads to frustration and suffering. Thus bondage to selfish craving is the root of all human misery. According to the Buddha, relief comes through an ethical life that leads to a realization of impermanence—enlightenment—and release from craving and suffering.[7] Since the Buddha is clearly not committed to the existence of a permanent divine being, he could hardly appeal to a miraculous act of a god as evidence for the truth of his teaching.

As time passed, accounts of the Buddha's great powers did emerge. In one story, when Gautama returned home after his own enlightenment, he rose into the air, shooting out flames and streams of water from his body and walking in the sky.[8] But because Gautama's own teaching implies the impossibility of supernatural events, we should very likely explain the rise of these stories naturalistically.[9]

Although original Buddhist teaching excludes the supernatural, later Buddhism, like Hinduism, tolerates wide doctrinal variety. Both Hinduism and Buddhism developed many schools, some philosophical and some popular. Speaking generally, many philosophical schools of both Hinduism and Buddhism (as well as many New Age cults emerging today) assume a pantheistic worldview, a view that identifies "God" as an impersonal Ultimate Reality. Pantheism has no category labeled "free act by a divine person." So miracles are as alien to all forms of pantheism as they are to atheism. A miracle, an act of a personal God, could hardly support the truth of a worldview that denies the existence of a personal God.

In Hinduism, the pantheistic schools tend to discount and discourage popular polytheism. But polytheism and animism do have a theoretical place for supernatural works performed by divine beings. Given this, we cannot automatically discount stories of supernatural events that arise in polytheistic contexts. We must check these accounts in other ways.

2. Many religious founders, including Gautama, Confucius (c. 551-479? B.C.) and Lao Tzu (c. 604-c. 531 B.C.),[10] discouraged marvels. Gautama advised his disciples not to perform wonders even though many people in his day believed that the meditation leading to enlightenment also produced wonder-working power. In one story, the Buddha encountered a man who spent twenty years of fasting and penance learning to cross a river by walking on water. Gautama told the man his effort was wasted because he could cross on a ferry for a small coin.[11] The Buddha thought that such wonder-working actually hinders enlightenment because liberation from all desires should include overcoming even the craving for magical power. Further, marvelous events gave Buddhism no apologetic advantage, since representatives of many Hindu schools could (and still do) perform similar feats.[12]

Islam certainly has a conceptual place for the supernatural. Yet Muhammad (A.D. 570?-632) refused to buttress his religious authority with wondrous signs: "Signs are with Allah only, and I am only a plain warner" (Surah 29:50; cf. 13:27-31). Muhammad acknowledged that Moses performed miracles to confirm his message. The miracles even persuaded Pharaoh's magicians to trust God (Surah 7:103-26). Yet when challenged to perform a sign as Moses did, Muhammad said, "Glory to my Lord! am I aught but a moral messenger?" (Surah 17:90-93). For many Muslims, "the performance of miracles is a sign that a person's intention is still directed toward worldly approval, not exclusively toward God."[13]

Despite Muhammad's reluctance, however, some Muslims believe that Muhammad did perform miracles. Many believe he split the moon in two in order to convert unbelievers. Islamic traditions *(hadith)* ascribe many miracles both to Muhammad and to various saints. These personages supposedly predicted the future, walked on water and in the air, and miraculously produced food, clothing and other necessities. Followers of folk Islam continue even today to create new miracle stories. The Turkish press reported that when American (read *Christian*) astronaut Neil Armstrong stepped on the moon, he distinctly heard a strange sound that he only later recognized as the Muslim call to prayer. Some Turks count this as important evidence for Islam and against Christianity.[14]

There are problems with such beliefs, however. The splitting of the moon is based on a controversial understanding of a Qur'anic text (54:1). Outside the *hadith,* there are no reported sightings of the moon dividing, even though many ancient peoples carefully watched the sky. The traditions, which number about three hundred thousand, are controversial, and even Muslim scholars acknowledge that the vast majority are inauthentic.[15]

The most important miracle (and for many Muslims the only miracle) is the production of the Qur'an itself. Many support the miraculous origin of the Qur'an by pointing primarily to its sublime style.[16] One Muslim scholar says, "Muslims do not claim any miracles for Muhammad. In their view, what proves Muhammad's prophethood is the sublime beauty and greatness of the revelation itself, the Holy Qur'an, not any inexplicable breaches of natural law which confound human reason."[17]

When reports of miracles arise in religions where the early history depreciates miracles, this raises prima facie doubts about the historicity of those stories. Still, we should investigate these accounts in other ways. For example, we should certainly evaluate the quality of the historical documents reporting the alleged events. Further, we should judge whether the events in question are really miraculous instead of merely supernormal. Finally, we might look for arguments that show that the religion may have good reason to develop a tradition of miracles later in its history despite earlier resistance to miracles.

In sum, anyone interested in the evidential value of a particular miracle account in one of the world religions must ask whether the concept of miracle is at home, either conceptually or historically, in that particular religion. When a miracle report arises in a religion that denies a supernatural sphere or where the early history depreciates miracles, we have prima facie reason to expect a naturalistic explanation of that story.

Alternative Explanations for Miracle Stories

Next we should examine whether the naturalistic arguments that skeptics use to account for the rise of spurious miracle stories are rightly applied to a particular miracle claim we are examining. Skeptical interpreters offer four major sorts of hypotheses to explain the rise of spurious miracle stories. (1) Miracle stories are invented and gain credence due to a common human thirst for dramatic, unusual or surprising events. (2) Magicians concoct miracle stories or perform marvelous acts in order to attract attention to themselves. (3) Religious believers borrow miracle stories from other contemporary religions, perhaps using temporal, mythological language as a way to point to inexpressible, transcendent truths. (4) Apologists for religious causes or doctrines create miracle stories to manufacture evidence for their perspectives. When they legitimately apply, these points constitute undercutting defeaters in that they explain how miracle stories could develop even if no real miracle occurred.

1. Some argue that miracle stories develop when the human lust for the sensational causes miracle stories to evolve quickly and root themselves firmly in the minds of believers. Hume himself stresses this point:

> The passion of *surprise* and *wonder,* arising from miracles, being an agreeable emotion, gives a sensible tendency towards the belief of those events, from which it is derived. . . . With what greediness are the miraculous accounts of travelers received, their descriptions of sea and land monsters, their relations of wonderful adventures, strange men, and uncouth manners?[18]

While Hume's hypothesis contains some truth, we must apply it cautiously. For if, on examination, we find that some miracle tales are fanciful, this in no way nullifies other miracle claims for which we may find positive confirmation of authenticity. The fact that humans lust for miracle stories and often gullibly believe them shows only that we must exercise care in evaluating the evidential status of miracle claims. The

National Enquirer may print some absurd stories, but this does not mean we should automatically doubt serious reports in the *St. Paul Pioneer Press*. The lust for the sensational does not entail the falsehood, or even the improbability, of any particular miracle narrative. It merely represents a *potential* undercutting defeater for any particular miracle claim and invites us to exercise special caution in assessing that claim.

2. Some explain the rise of miracle stories by saying that magicians concoct miracle tales or perform marvelous acts in order to attract attention to themselves. Like the previous hypothesis, this principle contains some truth. Charlatans often feed off the prestige of a respected religion. When religious enthusiasts believe miracles are possible and begin to trust someone who claims to speak reliably for their religious tradition, they are susceptible to chicanery.[19]

Parenthetically, this type of explanation for the rise of some miracle traditions does not fit the case of Jesus. Jesus neither catered to his audience nor lusted for the attention of the crowds (see Jn 6:60-71). He differed from Simon the Magician, whom the apostles strongly condemned for trying to buy Holy Spirit power in order to perform flashier tricks (Acts 8:9-24). Similarly, several other religions also warn against using marvels simply to attract attention.

But again, a critic of spurious miracle stories must not exaggerate. Charlatanism, though detestable, does not in any way count against any genuine miracles we might find. Trickery and self-aggrandizement do not disprove *every* account of miracle, nor do they preclude the possibility of authenticating genuine miracles. They entail only the need to evaluate carefully the evidential status of all miracle claims. Religious counterfeits do not discredit genuine, supernatural phenomena any more than counterfeit dollar bills somehow invalidate real ones.

3. Some claim that miracle reports arise when religious believers borrow miracle stories from other contemporary religions, perhaps using temporal, mythological language as a way to point to inexpressible, transcendent truths. This judgment is probably correct in some instances. Yet again, we should avoid overgeneralizing; we should not infer that the fact of borrowing discredits all miracle stories. If two accounts of a miracle are similar in superficial ways, this does not entail that one story really depends on the other. Further, even if we knew that one religion adapted a miracle account from another, this would not show that the earlier report is spurious. Similarities between stories do not demonstrate cause and effect connections between those reports, nor do

they show that all miracle stories are false.

Consider, as an important example, the miracles of Jesus. The first-century Mediterranean world produced many accounts of miracles allegedly performed by Jewish holy men, various magicians and Hellenistic "divine men." Some scholars, especially of the history of religions school, portray Jesus as a representative of one of these groups. They emphasize parallels between stories about Jesus' miracles and accounts in non-Christian sources. For example, the Babylonian Talmud mentions a Jewish holy man named Honi who ended a drought when he drew a circle on the ground, stepped inside the circle, and told God he would not leave until rain came. According to the Talmud, God relented and sent the rain.[20] Josephus tells about one Eleazar who exorcised demons by putting a root up to a person's nose and drawing the demon out through the nostrils.[21] Some classify Jesus as one of these Jewish holy men.[22] Others see Jesus as a magician because he believed in demons and performed exorcisms.[23] Still others place Jesus in a loosely defined group of Hellenistic holy men.[24] The member of this group most often compared to Jesus is Apollonius of Tyana (died c. A.D. 98). Apollonius allegedly exorcised demons and raised a girl from the dead.[25]

Despite superficial similarities, however, Jesus is quite distinct from all these. As a Jew, Jesus obviously shared much with Jewish holy men. But the stories of Jesus' life do not borrow directly from accounts of Jewish holy men. For one thing, Jesus corrected the teachings of his contemporaries (see Mt 5—7). He connected with the Old Testament, but he resisted the official Judaism of his day. Further, the written sources that describe the Jewish holy men were written after the completion of the New Testament. Additionally, the New Testament reports about Jesus' miracles are far more reliable than accounts of the Jewish holy men.[26] It is most unlikely these stories shaped the narratives of Jesus' miracles.[27]

Similarly, Jesus was no mere magician. That he believed in demons and performed exorcisms is an insufficient basis for classing him as a magician. For one thing, magicians usually used objects or materials (like spittle) in their work. Though Jesus occasionally used spittle, he typically healed simply by speaking.[28] Further, Jesus did not rely on magical incantations and spells. (Incantations are scripted speech, full of odd or nonsense syllables, repeated word for word in a whisper or unusual voice. Their power supposedly lay in the precise repetition of coded words.) In contrast, Jesus simply commanded the demons by his own authority.[29]

Most important, Jesus rejected the usual view that demons fight against each other. Rather, he showed originality by teaching that all demons are united in opposing God and by interpreting his exorcisms as the first stage of a final victory of God over the demons.[30]

The suggested connection of Jesus to Hellenistic holy men like Apollonius is strained as well. Jesus' teaching is steeped in the Old Testament, not in Hellenism. Further, exorcisms were rare among the Hellenists, but more common for Jesus. Finally, the Hellenists characteristically emphasized predictions of the future, whereas Jesus did not.[31]

Despite some parallels, there are good reasons to distinguish Jesus from these ancient characters. Superficial similarities between Jesus and other ancient persons do not show that the major miracles surrounding the life and ministry of Jesus arose as Christians adapted other ancient stories. While we may uncover some cases where one religion likely appropriates material from another,[32] we should not conclude too quickly that superficial similarities between miracle stories demonstrates borrowing. Further, even where some adapting has occurred, this would not defeat any well-documented miracle accounts from which other religions may have borrowed.

4. Some argue that apologists fabricate miracle stories in order to provide evidence for religious causes or doctrines. If we had good reason *on other grounds* to believe that a specific alleged miracle did not occur, then we might account for the origin of a legend by saying that someone made it up simply to bolster an apologetic case. But if someone uses a miracle story for apologetic purposes, this does not show the story has no historical basis. History alone speaks to that point. If a miracle really happened, of course apologists would be right to use it as evidence!

Along with the other three interpretations considered in this section, the fourth hypothesis might seem to show that miracle stories are spurious in that it explains how miracle reports might arise. But these four explanations do not really prove that no miracle ever occurred. Suppose we grant these statements:

(a) *Some* miracle stories are invented due to the human thirst for the sensational.

(b) *Some* miracle stories are designed to attract attention.

(c) *Some* religions borrow miracle stories from other religions.

(d) *Some* miracle stories are created for apologetic purposes.

These statements do not show that no miracles have ever occurred. The occurrence of a genuine miracle and warranted belief that miracles have occurred—that God has actually acted in history—are compatible with acknowledging (a), (b), (c) and (d) as true.

These four explanations for the rise of miracle stories are compatible with *both* of these statements:

(e) No miracles ever occur; all miracle stories are nonhistorical.

(f) Some genuine miracles have occurred; many miracle stories are nonhistorical.

Since the four alternative explanations are compatible with (f), they cannot show that it is irrational to believe (f).

In sum, as naturalistic explanations for the emergence of miracle stories, these four hypotheses warrant consideration primarily when *good positive reasons* show that a particular miracle account is probably not genuinely historical. The four hypotheses can help us account for dubious miracle claims, but they do not *by themselves* constitute effective undercutting defeaters for any well-authenticated miracle stories we might find.

Historical Evidence for Miracle Claims

Finally, all this leads us to a centrally important issue: the *quality* of the evidence for any miracle claim. This issue assumes we have resolved some background issues, like whether we could recognize historical evidence for a miracle (see chapters five and six), or whether we have good antecedent reasons to expect that miracles might have occurred (see chapter eleven). But the next step is the patient, if tedious, investigation of actual historical evidence. To do this, investigators may ask three questions of any miracle claim: (1) What is the character of any alleged miracle? (2) What is the quality or general reliability of any documents reporting miracle events? (3) What corroborating evidence might support these miracle stories?

1. What is the character of a particular alleged miracle? Many reported marvels have natural causes. Some apparent miracles are simply illusions. A well-known example is the rope trick of India. An illusionist sits down and begins talking rapidly. Then he throws a rope into the air. It stiffens, allowing a small boy to climb up and vanish. Knife in hand, the illusionist follows him up. He dismembers the boy with the knife, then comes down and piles the body parts under a blanket. After proper incantations, the boy crawls out from under the blanket in one piece. The key to explaining the rope trick is that foreigners see no dismemberment. Unable to understand the local language, foreigners miss the hypnotic Hindustani

patter that apparently creates the illusion.[33]

Unlike the rope trick, yogic powers are apparently real. Yogis acquire extraordinary body control—enduring extreme temperatures or going without food for long periods. But the mastery of body functions is not supernatural. Over time, disciplined meditation enables an accomplished yogi to gain unusual skills, much as an Olympic-caliber archer develops, with sufficient practice, an amazing ability to hit the bull's-eye. Yogis can perform feats at will. By mastering certain higher laws of nature, they perform supernormal acts. Thus the yogi's marvels are not miraculous. "It would take away from his self-esteem if they were."[34]

Alleged miracles of healing may in some cases be natural events. Recognizing this possibility is important since most miracle claims in Christian history are purported cures. Many people apparently experience real biological symptoms of illness stemming from emotional causes. Various conditions (including the power of suggestion) can naturally alleviate such illnesses without miraculous intervention. So we cannot show that an unusual healing is a miracle until we rule out psychosomatic or naturalistic explanations of that healing.

We should recognize, further, the distinction between functional disorders (like back pain) and organic injury or diseases (like pancreatic cancer). Because healings of functional disorders do often occur naturally, it is difficult to show that they are miraculous. We might suppose that real organic cures are miraculous, but proving a miracle requires competent diagnosis of a preexisting organic disease.[35] Since the faith-healing business attracts many quacks, verifying alleged miraculous healing requires more than a smiling patient.

All this means that a Christian should not deny well-authenticated marvelous events associated with other religions. If evidence suggests that a marvel may have happened in another religion, a Christian could look for reasons that might suggest it is a trick or a natural event. Given the Christian view of spiritual beings, magical events caused by demonic spirits are possible, although it is best to see these as supernormal, not supernatural, since the agents in this case are creatures and not God. Indeed, a Christian might even acknowledge that God may have chosen to work miraculously outside the Judeo-Christian context. Since Christian theology can account for such events within its worldview, they do not constitute successful rebutting defeaters to the miracle claims that are central to Christian teaching.

2. What about the quality and general reliability of any documents

reporting miracle events?[36] One issue is dating. Virtually all ancient miracle stories outside the Bible are described in texts written long after the events they report. But we read the stories of Jesus' works in documents composed within a generation of his life,[37] by people who claimed to see the events, and in a context where friends and foes alike could either confirm or dispute the stories (see Acts 2:22; 26:26). By contrast, the story about the Buddha flying and shooting sparks, for example, is from *Mahāvastu* 3.115, a Mahāyāna-influenced text dating many centuries after the Buddha's life.[38]

Other considerations of quality are important. Consider Apollonius. Serious errors damage Philostratus's biography of this figure. He has Apollonius trekking to Babylon and to a splendid Nineveh, and speaking at length with their kings. But these cities were in ruins long before the time of Apollonius. Additionally, Philostratus's patron, Julia Domna, the wife of a Roman emperor, probably commissioned this biography as a propagandistic "counterblast to Jesus."[39] These circumstances betray the nonhistorical, and therefore untrustworthy, character of Philostratus's work.[40]

By contrast, the historical reliability of the New Testament documents enjoys powerful support. In addition to their early date, the Gospels possess solid confirmation based on both internal and external considerations. Internally, the Gospels are consistent without being identical. They have many characteristics of eyewitness accounts. If, for instance, the authors were fabricating legend or myth to support the claim that Jesus is God's anointed Messiah, it is very unlikely that they would have put in Jesus' mouth the words "My God, my God, why have you forsaken me?" (Mt 27:46). Externally, the Gospels enjoy confirmation from other ancient documents and archaeological finds. They faithfully reflect the cultural conditions of first-century Palestine and correctly identify many people and places of that era. Among ancient documents, the New Testament accounts of Jesus' life are uniquely reliable.[41]

3. What corroborating evidence might support these miracle stories? The stories about Jesus enjoy some corroboration when his opponents allude to his activities. For example, the Babylonian Talmud speaks of one "Yeshu" who "practised sorcery and enticed Israel to apostasy."[42] This use of "sorcery" admits that Jesus worked marvels but interprets his works as Satanic. Theoretically, Jesus' opponents could have made a stronger claim, denying that he performed apparent miracles. Yet prac-

tically, they could not deny the events. In choosing instead to reinterpret them, they indirectly lent credence to the miracles as having a historical basis. "Surely if Jesus had been a simple teacher whose self-understanding was greatly distorted by Christians of subsequent generations, some recollection of this fact would have remained for those opposed to Christianity to exploit."[43]

Other miracle traditions lack external confirmation of this sort. Take the Book of Mormon (BOM). According to the official story, Joseph Smith found golden tablets buried in the Hill Cumorah in western New York. Unable to read the tablets, Smith allegedly used two miraculous stones set into spectacles to translate the golden tablets, thus producing the BOM. Initially, the story of miraculous translation seems far-fetched. But we must examine it carefully by looking for confirming or disconfirming evidence. Since our only documenting source for this alleged translation miracle is the say-so of Joseph Smith, other forms of corroborating evidence—archaeology, for instance—would help.[44]

The BOM tells the story of a Nephite civilization in the New World. This civilization once covered North America and built thirty-seven cities, producing buildings, ships, coins and weapons. In their final defeat, 230,000 Nephites died on or around Cumorah. Civilizations and battles leave remnants. It is overwhelmingly probable that if the BOM were truly historical, a civilization of this magnitude would have left behind in North America and at Cumorah many artifacts for archaeologists to find.

But no archaeological evidence supports either the onetime existence of a Nephite civilization in North America or a huge battle in New York. To resolve the issue, one Mormon apologist argues that the Cumorah of the BOM is an unknown place in Central America, not the Cumorah in New York.[45] Evaluating this move requires a judgment about whether the Central American thesis plausibly fits Joseph Smith's story. If Smith meant that the Cumorah of the Nephites is the Cumorah in New York (as seems likely), then the utter absence of artifacts in New York is a serious undercutting defeater to the claim that the BOM was translated by miraculous means.[46]

In sum, like any historical research, investigation of an assertion that a miracle has actually occurred must explore the nature of the alleged event, the character of the documentary evidence for the event and the availability of corroborating evidence for that event. Any historian regularly uses considerations like these to evaluate nonmiraculous events.

Conclusion

A careful evaluation of the thousands of miracle stories from every religion would obviously require far more than a brief chapter. Our goal has been first to sketch a strategy we could use to assess conflicting religious miracle claims and then to sample briefly the results of applying that procedure. This has been a rapid survey of the principles, affording an examination of only a few sample miracle stories. But given the evidence explored here, David Hume's judgment that miracle claims from various religions successfully rebut each other is unconvincing.

We conclude that acknowledging the mere existence of conflicting miracle stories does not close the case on Christian miracle claims. Before conceding Hume's point, a good investigator must examine the evidence for miracle reports. Such analyses will show that accounts of alleged miracles connected with most religions are themselves subject to significant undercutting defeaters. But unsubstantiated stories do not overpower well-authenticated miracles evidentially. Thus we should conclude that Hume was hasty in claiming that miracles stories from various contrary religions count as rebutting defeaters that actually nullify each other evidentially. Hume's fourth point "cannot be used to pronounce on the historicity of any particular miracle." It only warns us to examine miracle stories thoroughly and with caution.[47]

This study suggests that the number of credible religious miracle accounts is probably quite small. In contrast to most stories within other religious traditions, several key miracle accounts surrounding the life of Jesus are well supported. The next few chapters of this book will move the argument forward by considering the evidence for and the value of such Christian miracle claims as fulfilled biblical prophecy, the incarnation and the resurrection of Jesus Christ.

THIRTEEN
FULFILLED
PROPHECY
AS MIRACLE

ROBERT C. NEWMAN

GEORGE FREDERICK HANDEL'S ORATORIO *MESSIAH* HAS TOUCHED millions in the two and a half centuries since it was first performed. Each Christmas portions of it are sung by thousands of choirs throughout the world, often in places where its message is no longer believed. For the message of Handel's *Messiah* is the message of the Bible—God has intervened in history to rescue people from sin and futility through Jesus his Messiah, and this was predicted far in advance by prophets sent to his people Israel.

Attempts to Avoid Miraculous Fulfillment

In churches that follow critical scholarship, the idea that God would send prophets to make successful predictions is treated as a quaint and outmoded concept that modern persons cannot accept. Such miracles simply do not happen. In these circles, therefore, the Bible is radically reinterpreted in order to explain away the need for literal fulfillment. Various techniques are used for this purpose.

First, radical critics often redate large portions of the Old Testament prophetic literature so as to have them written after the events they predict rather than before (as the Bible itself claims). For instance, parts of Isaiah (especially chapters 40—66) are ascribed to later authors to avoid both predicting the Babylonian exile and naming the king who would allow the Jews to return from it.[1] Daniel's prophecy of events leading up to the Maccabean revolt is so detailed that the whole book is removed from the traditional time of the prophet (sixth century B.C.) to the revolt some four centuries later.[2] Prophetic allusions to a siege against Tyre fulfilled in the time of Alexander (c. 330 B.C.) must mean that Zechariah 9—14 was written centuries later than Zechariah's time.[3] Conservative responses to such claims[4] are typically dismissed as special pleading, even though the conservative view matches the Bible's own representation of the matter. It also makes better sense of why anyone at the time would think these prophets were actually messengers from God, and it avoids having to charge half the writers (or editors) of the Old Testament with fraud or fiction.

Second, critical scholars frequently argue that the Hebrew prophets never meant for any elements of their preaching to refer to events beyond their own horizon.[5] Thus anything mentioned by a prophet that appears to be fulfilled centuries later was probably something the prophet expected to happen in his own day. The event predicted may have happened earlier, but we do not know enough about the prophet's time to identify the event. Or perhaps the prophet was mistaken in thinking it would happen then.[6] But again, this critical technique ignores the Bible's own claim that God knows the future and communicates some such information to his prophets.[7]

Other techniques are occasionally used to deny the literal fulfillment of prophecy—a later writer invented the fulfillment for an earlier prophecy,[8] someone staged the fulfillment of an earlier prediction,[9] or "fulfillment" is also common in pagan prophecy.[10] When all else fails, one can claim the prophetic utterance was vague or the fulfillment a mere coincidence. But suppose we really want to know whether or not miracles occur. Fulfilled predictions are one type of miracle[11] that can be tested centuries after the event took place. All we need is good evidence[12] (1) that the text clearly envisions the sort of event alleged to be the fulfillment, (2) that the prophecy was made well in advance of the event predicted, (3) that the prediction actually came true and (4) that the event predicted could not have been staged by anyone but God. The strength of this evidence is greatly enhanced if (5) the event itself is so unusual that the apparent fulfillment cannot be plausibly explained as a good guess.

Let us examine several prophecies in terms of these criteria. We will consider first some predictions about the nation Israel, then others about various city-states of the ancient world and, finally, several related to Israel's promised Messiah.

Israel: Hosea's Historical Parable

Not all of the Old Testament prophetic messages were entirely verbal; sometimes the prophets acted out their teachings in the form of object lessons. One of the most striking of these is the marriage of the prophet Hosea to the prostitute Gomer. According to Hosea 1:2, God instructed the prophet to take "an adulterous wife and children of unfaithfulness, because the land is guilty of the vilest adultery in departing from the LORD." Several children of uncertain paternity are born to Gomer, each functioning as a vivid object lesson illustrating the relationship between God and Israel. In chapter 2, Gomer abandons Hosea for her lovers, just as Israel abandoned God for the worship of the Canaanite storm god Baal and his consorts. In chapter 3, God instructs Hosea to take Gomer back, but apparently into some sort of restricted relationship rather than full marital intimacy. The significance of this action is explained as follows: "For the Israelites will live many days without king or prince, without sacrifice or sacred stones, without ephod or idol. Afterward the Israelites will return and seek the LORD their God and David their king. They will come trembling to the LORD and to his blessings in the last days" (Hos 3:4-5).

Here is a prediction of the enduring status of Israel: the people will lack certain specific items for "many days." It is astonishing that this brief description accurately portrays the condition of the Jewish people for nearly two thousand years, from the time of Jesus until the present. Israel has indeed gone without its own king descended from David since about 587 B.C. (a century after Hosea's own day), when the Babylonian king Nebuchadnezzar destroyed Jerusalem, deposed the Jewish king Zedekiah, and carried away most of the people to captivity in Babylon. During subsequent centuries the nation briefly had kings who were descendants of the Maccabees (around 100 B.C.) and then two kings of the Herod family (the last dying in A.D. 44). These puppet kings lacked the full regal splendor to which Israel had been accustomed in Hosea's day.

The Hebrew term in Hosea that is translated "prince" in English Bibles has a broader sense in Hebrew than it does in English usage; it signifies any ruler or government official.[13] Israel has been without its own government officials in Palestine from A.D. 70, when the Romans took Jerusalem, until the establishment of the modern state of Israel in 1948. Even if the exilic patriarch and *nasi'* are counted as "princes" in Hosea's sense, the period during which Israel had none of these officials is still substantial, from about 1100 to 1948.[14]

It is significant that Israel has been without a sacrificial cultus since the Romans destroyed the Jerusalem temple in A.D. 70. The "sacred stones" (literally "pillars") of Hosea's prophecy probably refer to the Canaanite pillars involved in Baal worship; Israel has been without these since the Babylonian exile began in 587 B.C. The ephod referred to by Hosea is a sort of vest, according to those passages in the Old Testament where its meaning can be made out.[15] Most occurrences of the word *ephod* in the Hebrew Scriptures refer to a garment worn by the Israelite priests. Israel has had no priests, and no use for priests, since the destruction of the temple by the Romans in A.D. 70. Nevertheless, the Israelites have generally been free from idolatry since the Babylonian exile in the sixth century B.C. These phenomena have characterized Israel for a long period of time, especially from A.D. 70 to the present. (Of course, the book of Hosea was written long before A.D. 70, having been translated into Greek by about 200 B.C.)

These six features (without king or government official, without sacrifice or sacred pillar, without priest or idol) involve a whole nation for many centuries, so it was certainly beyond the power of humans to stage their fulfillment. The six features are also most unusual. Israel had serious problems with idolatry for most of its history up to the time of Hosea, yet the prophet predicts that the Israelites will be free of idolatry for many days. Even more astonishing is his prediction that the nation Israel will at the same time be without features central to the system that God established for them in their sacred Scriptures: they will have no king, in spite of the covenant God made with David; they will lack sacrifice, despite its crucial place in the whole temple service. Here, indeed, is a striking picture of Israel—existing in a strange sort of limbo for almost two thousand years now—aptly pictured as a wife who is no longer running around, but neither does she have full marital intimacy with her husband!

The Nations: Twin City Prophecies
In addition to predictions regarding the nation of Israel, the Bible records numerous prophecies about the Gentiles, particularly Israel's

immediate neighbors. These predictions generally concern the destruction (and occasionally the restoration) of various cities and groups of people. Those who doubt that biblical prophets could actually predict the future typically dismiss these instances of prophecy with the comment that such "prophecies" can hardly fail to be fulfilled in the long run, since nearly every city will be destroyed eventually.

John Bloom has suggested an approach that circumvents this objection.[16] He notes that in scientific research, the effectiveness of a new medicine is tested by giving the new drug to one group while giving a tablet containing only inactive ingredients to a control group. If there is a statistically significant difference between the responses of the two groups, then probably the medicine is making the difference; if there is no such difference, it is judged to have no therapeutic value. Just as individuals in the control group typically are chosen to match individuals in the group taking the medicine, so Bloom proposes that a comparison be made between "twin cities" about which biblical prophecies are made. The test, then, is this: if we could interchange the names of the two cities without affecting their fulfillment, then the phenomenon of apparent fulfillment is not evidence. On the other hand, if a real difference results, then this is concrete evidence of fulfilled prediction. The strength of this sort of evidence will vary depending on whether the details predicted are common or unusual.

Of the many cities in the Bible about which predictions are made, Bloom has so far investigated four pairs that are sufficiently similar to be "twins": the Phoenician city-states Tyre and Sidon, the imperial capitals Babylon and Nineveh, the ancient Egyptian capitals Memphis and Thebes, and the Philistine cities Ekron and Ashkelon.

Tyre and Sidon. An elaborate prediction about the fate of Tyre is given in Ezekiel 26:3-14. We are told that "many nations" will come against it and tear down its walls; its rubble will be scraped away and it will become a bare rock. "Out in the sea she will become a place to spread fishnets. . . . You [Tyre] will never be rebuilt." Of Sidon fewer details are presented: God will "inflict punishment on her . . . send a plague upon her and make blood flow in her streets. The slain will fall within her, with the sword against her on every side" (Ezek 28:22-23).

The powerful seaport city-state of Tyre was besieged for thirteen years by Nebuchadnezzar, who took the city in 573 B.C. In the course of this extended siege, however, the inhabitants relocated the city to an island about one-half mile offshore, and Nebuchadnezzar's troops had to settle for very little plunder. Nearly 250 years later, in 332 B.C., Alexander the Great attacked the island city of "new Tyre." Having no navy, he used the rubble from the old mainland city and slave labor from the surrounding nations to build a causeway out to the island to capture the city. To obtain enough material for the causeway, the mainland site was scraped clean. Though the island city later recovered, a substantial village now occupying the northern part of the former island, the mainland site has never been restored. Moreover, parts of the former island are used even today for spreading fishnets.[17]

The Phoenician seaport city of Sidon was considered Tyre's twin even in antiquity. Like most ancient cities that survive to the present, Sidon has seen its share of disaster and bloodshed. It is surely a candidate for the literal fulfillment of Ezekiel's prediction. But if the names of Tyre and Sidon were reversed in these passages, the prophecies would not have been fulfilled. For Sidon has been rebuilt; mainland Tyre has not. Tyre has been scraped bare and its rubble cast into the sea; Sidon has not. Out in the sea, Tyre has become a place to spread fishnets; Sidon has not. The specifications about Tyre are sufficiently unusual to make coincidence unlikely. They were fulfilled by such actors over such a time span as to rule out the plausibility of intentional human fulfillment.

Babylon and Nineveh. These two cities were capitals of the powerful Babylonian and Assyrian empires, respectively. Of Babylon, Isaiah says, "Babylon, the jewel of kingdoms, the glory of the Babylonians' pride, will be overthrown by God like Sodom and Gomorrah. She will never be inhabited or lived in through all *generations;* no Arab will pitch his tent there, *no shepherd will rest his flocks there.* But desert creatures will lie there, jackals will fill her houses; there the owls will dwell, and there the wild goats will leap about. Hyenas will howl in her strongholds, jackals in her luxurious palaces" (Is 13:19-22).[18] Jeremiah adds, " 'No rock will be taken from you for a cornerstone, nor any stone for a foundation, for you will be desolate forever,' declares the LORD" (Jer 51:26).

The prophet Zephaniah gives a striking picture of Nineveh's desolation:

> He will stretch out his hand against the north and destroy Assyria, leaving Nineveh utterly desolate and dry as the desert. *Flocks and herds will lie down there, creatures of every kind.* The desert owl and the screech owl will roost on her columns. Their calls will echo through the windows, rubble will be in the doorways, the beams of cedar will be exposed. This is the carefree city that lived in safety. She said to

herself, "I am, and there is none besides me." What a ruin she has become, a lair for wild beasts! All who pass by her will scoff and shake their fists. (Zeph 2:13-15)

As predicted, both cities were destroyed—Nineveh immediately in the fall of its empire (612 B.C.), Babylon gradually some centuries after its fall to the Persians (539 B.C.) as Alexander's successors fought for pieces of his empire and the river Euphrates shifted its bed to leave the site of Babylon dry. Both became desolate for centuries. Even today, Arabs are afraid to live at the site of Babylon, and its soil is too poor to provide grass for grazing. Even more amazing is the fact that Babylon is quarried for its brick but not for its stone, which is burned to lime to make mortar.[19] By contrast, the site of Nineveh, which could not even be identified for many centuries, was used for grazing sheep.[20]

Once more, if the names were traded the prophecies would not have been fulfilled. In spite of its greatness and strategic location, Babylon has never been restored as a city. In contrast, Nineveh is now in the suburbs of the city of Mosul. Both were left dry, but only Nineveh has been used for grazing sheep.

Memphis and Thebes. Not much is said about Memphis and Thebes. In Ezekiel 30 we are told, "I will destroy the idols and put an end to the images in Memphis" (Ezek 30:13), and "I will . . . inflict punishment on Thebes . . . and cut off the hordes of Thebes" (Ezek 30:14-15). But in both cases, what was foretold was what happened.

Memphis was capital of Egypt during the Old Kingdom (c. 2500 B.C.) and again in the Hellenistic period (c. 200 B.C.). At the time of Jesus, the Greek historian Strabo described it as still a large, flourishing city with many temples.[21] But when Islam spread through Egypt six centuries later, its leaders did not want their soldiers to own property or settle in such prosperous pagan lands. So the invaders remained in their siege encampment a few miles down the Nile River north of Memphis. Eventually the camp became the city of Cairo. As the people of Memphis were drawn to this new location, the old city of Memphis became a stone quarry used to build Cairo. As a result the pagan idols of Memphis were recycled to become building materials. Only a handful of statues have been found on or near the modern site.

Thebes was also the capital of Egypt during the Middle and New Kingdoms (c. 1900-1000 B.C.) and intermittently thereafter. It succumbed to a three-year siege in 92 B.C., and was later destroyed during the reign of Caesar Augustus (c. 30 B.C.). It never recovered its population, and today only a few insignificant villages occupy the area. By contrast with Memphis, however, Thebes has "the greatest assemblage of monumental ruins in the world," including an enormous number of idols and statues that have survived intact.[22]

The biblical predictions for Memphis and Thebes, though brief, match what eventually happened. If we were to interchange the names of the cities, however, they would not even be possible matches. Thebes has lost its hordes but retains its idols. Memphis has lost its idols but is a suburb of Egypt's largest city, Cairo.

Ekron and Ashkelon. These were two of the five cities of the ancient Philistines, located in the coastal plain on the southwest border of Israel. The prophet Zephaniah says of them:

Gaza will be abandoned and Ashkelon left in ruins. At midday Ashdod will be emptied and *Ekron uprooted.* Woe to you who live by the sea, O Kerethite people; the word of the LORD is against you, O Canaan, land of the Philistines. *"I will destroy you, and none will be left."* The land by the sea, where the Kerethites dwell, will be a place for shepherds and sheep pens. *It will belong to the remnant of the house of Judah; there they will find pasture. In the evening they will lie down in the houses of Ashkelon.* The LORD their God will care for them; he will restore their fortunes. (Zeph 2:4-7)

The term *Kerethites* appears to be more or less synonymous with Philistines, and it may refer to their Cretan origin. The Philistine people have now vanished from history, as predicted above. Ashkelon was a coastal city and seaport, while Ekron was located some ten miles inland. Both cities continued to exist into the Crusader period (c. A.D. 1100), but were then destroyed. Ashkelon's harbor was filled with stones to keep it from being used in another Crusader invasion. As a result, the area had no value as a seaport, and it became a rural sheep-herding area. Ekron was not rebuilt, and even its location is uncertain. Ashkelon was rebuilt in modern times and became a Jewish city, as predicted. Again, if the names Ekron and Ashkelon were reversed, the prophecies would be falsified.

Thus for each of these four pairs of "twin cities," such specific predictions were made that if the names were reversed, the prophecies would be invalidated.

Israel's Messiah

A final category of fulfilled prophecy is messianic prophecy fulfilled in the historical figure of Jesus of Nazareth. While there are numerous candidate prophecies of this type, some of them more clearly messianic than others, and some more obviously fulfilled in the person of Jesus than others, I will briefly describe only two particularly interesting examples.

A light to the nations. Isaiah 40—56 forms the so-called servant section of this prophecy. A prominent theme in these chapters is the "servant of the LORD." Sometimes this figure seems to be the nation of Israel, sometimes an individual.[23] In one passage we are told:

> Here is my servant, whom I uphold, my chosen one in whom I delight; I will put my Spirit on him and he will bring justice to the nations. . . . I, the LORD, have called you in righteousness; I will take hold of your hand. I will keep you and will make you to be a covenant for the people and a light for the Gentiles, to open eyes that are blind, to free captives from prison and to release from the dungeon those who sit in darkness. (Is 42:1, 6-7)

A few chapters later this theme is resumed:

> Listen to me, you islands; hear this, you distant nations: Before I was born the LORD called me; from my birth he has made mention of my name. He made my mouth like a sharpened sword, in the shadow of his hand he hid me; he made me into a polished arrow and concealed me in his quiver. He said to me, "You are my servant, Israel, in whom I will display my splendor." But I said, "I have labored to no purpose; I have spent my strength in vain and for nothing. Yet what is due me is in the LORD's hand, and my reward is with my God." And now the LORD says—he who formed me in the womb to be his servant to bring Jacob back to him and gather Israel to himself, for I am honored in the eyes of the LORD and my God has been my strength—he says: "It is too small a thing for you to be my servant to restore the tribes of Jacob and bring back those of Israel I have kept. I will also make you a light for the Gentiles, that you may bring my salvation to the ends of the earth." This is what the LORD says—the Redeemer and Holy One of Israel—to him who was despised and abhorred by the nation, to the servant of rulers: "Kings will see you and rise up, princes will see and bow down, because of the LORD, who is faithful, the Holy One of Israel, who has chosen you." (Is 49:1-7)

While the servant is here called "Israel," this figure is also distinguished from Israel as the one who will bring the nation Israel back to God. The servant is a mysterious but glorious figure, abhorred by the nation and seemingly unsuccessful, but ultimately vindicated and honored even by rulers. This figure is to become a "light to the Gentiles" and bring God's "salvation to the ends of the earth." In the rabbinic literature, these passages are sometimes ascribed to the Messiah.[24] The New Testament recognizes their fulfillment in Jesus.[25]

Certainly this prophetic utterance of Isaiah occurred long before the beginning of the Christian era, no matter how many authors one thinks were involved in composing the text of the book of Isaiah. By New Testament times, the complete text was available both in the original Hebrew language and in a Greek translation, and probably also in an Aramaic paraphrase. Furthermore, when the New Testament writers apply these passages to Jesus, they are making this claim long before Christianity had become very successful. This was not a safe gambit on their part if we assume that they were merely guessing.

What is the evidence that Jesus Christ is the literal fulfillment of Isaiah's prophecy concerning the servant? Initially, Jesus is the founder of the largest religion in the world, numbering some 1.4 billion adherents.[26] He is also the only person claiming to be the Jewish Messiah who has founded a world religion among Gentiles. This accomplishment would have been very difficult to stage.

Furthermore, the prophecy envisions quite an unusual event. Here is a figure who is to be a light to Gentiles, but is abhorred by the nation Israel. Who would ever have expected that the Jewish Messiah would be generally rejected by Jews but widely accepted by Gentiles?

The time of the Messiah. As a final example, let us consider a passage that appears to predict the time of the coming of the Messiah. That some such prophecy was thought to have expired in the first century A.D. is suggested by remarks to this effect by the Jewish historian Josephus[27] and by the Roman historians Tacitus[28] and Suetonius.[29] For the sake of brevity, we quote only the first of these:

> But what more than all else incited them [the Jews] to the war [revolt against Rome, A.D. 66-73] was an ambiguous oracle, *likewise found in their sacred scriptures,* to the effect that *at that time* one from their country would become ruler of the world. This they understood to mean someone of their own race, and many of their own wise men went astray in their interpretation of it. The oracle, however, in reality signified the sovereignty of Vespasian, who was proclaimed [Roman] Emperor on Jewish soil.

If we search the Old Testament for a passage that gives some timed prophecy of this sort, the only good candidate is found in Daniel 9:24-26:

> Seventy "sevens" are decreed for your people and your holy city to finish transgression, to put an end to sin, to atone for wickedness, to bring in everlasting righteousness, to seal up vision and prophecy and to anoint the most holy.
>
> Know and understand this: From the issuing of the decree to restore and rebuild Jerusalem until the Anointed One, the ruler, comes, there will be seven "sevens" and sixty-two "sevens." It will be rebuilt with streets and a trench, but in times of trouble. After the sixty-two "sevens," the Anointed One will be cut off and will have nothing. The people of the ruler who will come will destroy the city and the sanctuary. The end will come like a flood: War will continue until the end, and desolations have been decreed.

There has been considerable argument about the interpretation of this passage.[30] A very reasonable interpretation, however, notes the significance of a decree issued by the Persian king Artaxerxes I during his twentieth year (445 B.C.). This edict officially approved Nehemiah's return to Jerusalem to rebuild its walls (Neh 2:1-9). The "sevens" of Daniel 9 (often translated "weeks") most likely refer to the recurring seven-year sabbatical cycle for land use,[31] since sixty-nine weeks of days would have run out before Daniel's prophecy could even have been circulated, and these weeks of years were an established institution in Israel. Using these cycles as units of measurement, the sixty-ninth such cycle (7 + 62), measured from the starting point of 445 B.C., spans the years A.D. 28-35. One cannot help but note with interest that on this analysis the "Anointed One" is "cut off " precisely when Jesus is crucified![32]

So the only Jew claiming to be Messiah who has inaugurated a world religion of predominantly Gentile adherents was cut off precisely when Daniel predicted! And the significance Christians ascribe to Jesus' death is given by Daniel—"to finish transgression, to put an end to sin, to atone for wickedness, to bring in everlasting righteousness." As it happens, Jesus Christ is also one of the most significant figures in world history, as even secular historians acknowledge.

Conclusion

More could be said about fulfilled prophecy in the Bible, and especially messianic prophecy fulfilled in Jesus of Nazareth.[33] Even when critical scholarship has done its best to redate Old Testament texts so as to avoid fulfilled prophecy, the constraints provided by the translation of the Old Testament into Greek (250-150 B.C.) and the rise of the Christian church leave a substantial residue of clear examples, several of which I have sketched here. Is this all a coincidence, or do miracles happen and biblical prophecies come true? A fair-minded reading of the biblical text and of the events of history should encourage us to pay more attention to the lyrics of Handel's *Messiah*.

FOURTEEN
THE INCARNATION OF JESUS CHRIST

JOHN S. FEINBERG

IF YOU WERE GOD, HOW WOULD YOU MAKE A CIRCULAR SQUARE? Before you thought about *how*, wouldn't you first have to decide *whether* it could be done? Some things can be done, though we might not know how, but others seem impossible because their very idea contains a logical contradiction. If one defines divine omnipotence so as to limit God's activities to the logically consistent, then even God cannot do some things, like make a circular square or a married bachelor.

I begin this way because many make similar claims about Jesus' virgin birth in relation to the incarnation. In Jesus we have a double miracle. Jesus Christ himself is a miracle because in him are united two distinct natures, one human and one divine. In addition, Christians claim that Jesus came into the world by means of a miracle, a virgin conception. Before asking if virgin births are possible and whether there is evidence that Jesus Christ was virgin born, we must ask if it is even possible for Jesus Christ to be the God-man, regardless of how he came to live among us. Many think it is impossible for God to become incarnate in the way orthodox Christian theology asserts because the idea of a God-man is as self-contradictory as that of a circular square or a married bachelor. So in Jesus' case, there can be no legitimate *how* question (virgin conceived or otherwise) because the answer to *whether* God could become incarnate is no.

The following argument is an example of the kind of logical problems allegedly inherent in the doctrine of the incarnation.

1. God is the Creator.
2. Christ is God.
3. Christ is man. (Christ is a man.)
4. Man is created. (Whatever is a man is created.)
5. The Creator is not created. (Whatever is the Creator is not created.)
6. Thus Christ is the Creator (1, 2).
7. Thus Christ is not created (5, 6).
8. Thus Christ is created (3, 4).
9. Thus Christ is created and not created (7, 8).[1]

Michael Martin goes even further. He argues that the doctrine of the incarnation is beclouded by both factual and conceptual problems. Even if one can solve the conceptual problems, there are still factual questions about whether there is any evidence that Jesus was the Son of God. But Martin doubts that any theist can solve the conceptual problems. In particular, four conceptual problems challenge the logical consistency of the doctrine. The first is reflected in the argument cited above that Christ was both created and uncreated. The second is that as God, Jesus must be omniscient—and necessarily so. As human, he is not omniscient. But then the *person* Jesus is both omniscient and not omniscient, a contradiction. A third problem arises from the second. Even if Jesus somehow can be omniscient, the Jesus of the Gospels does not appear to be omniscient. A final problem stems from God's moral perfection. As morally perfect, God can do no wrong. If one cannot fall to temptation (sin), how can one even be tempted to do so? If Jesus is God's Son, he must be morally perfect, incapable of falling into sin. But then it must also be impossible to tempt him. Of course, that contradicts scriptural teaching that he was tempted.[2]

Michael Goulder believes the problem is deeper than mere logical inconsistency. He distinguishes between *paradox* and *mystification*. A *paradox* is a statement that seems contradictory and may even be contradictory. Whether or not it actually is contradictory, with a genuine paradox the allegedly contradictory propositions are clear. We understand what they mean. On the other hand, a *mystification*, a pseudoparadox, appears to be a contradiction but is actually nonsense. This is so because the proposition asserted is in some sense radically unclear "and

upon probing is found not to be capable of being stated at all."[3] Goulder
believes that the doctrine of the incarnation is not just apparently
contradictory; it is apparent nonsense. We cannot even make sense of it.[4]

This is indeed a strong claim. John Hick also thinks there are problems
of meaning with the traditional orthodox doctrine, but he does not
conclude that it is therefore nonsense. Hick explains that the church
adopted the hypothesis of the two natures in Christ, and at various points
in church history tried to explain it. Despite various attempts, however,
no one has been able to give an "accepted account of what it means for
an individual to have two natures, one human and the other divine."[5]
According to Hick, this inability stems from understanding the doctrine
literally. Hick states, "That Jesus was God the Son incarnate is not literally
true, since it has no literal meaning."[6] Rather than look for another
explanation according to which the doctrine makes literal sense, Hick
suggests that we understand the doctrine metaphorically.[7] It is a metaphor that functions as a religious myth, and hence "it is a category
mistake to try to specify it as an hypothesis of theological science."[8]
Although the Councils of Nicaea and Chalcedon intended their claims
about Jesus as divine and human to be taken literally, today it makes sense
to speak of Jesus only as human.

Ground Rules and Strategies

What shall we say to all of this? My contention is that the orthodox
Christian doctrine of the incarnation is to be taken literally and that it is
not logically incoherent. I intend to show why and how that is so. Before
turning to my explanation, I must clarify some ground rules and strategies central to this discussion.

First, I must distinguish the doctrine's logical coherence from its
truth. As Martin rightly notes, even if the doctrine *is* logically consistent,
that provides no evidence that Jesus of Nazareth was in fact God
incarnate. A case can be made that Jesus was God incarnate, but that is
not this chapter's goal. Nor is the goal to marshal evidence that Jesus
was virgin born. My purpose is more modest, though it is foundational
to any factual discussion about whether Jesus was God incarnate or virgin
born. Before we discuss *how* Jesus came to earth and what evidence
suggests that he is the God-man, we must first ascertain *whether* the very
idea of a God-man is self-contradictory. The issue for this chapter is
whether the incarnation doctrine is logically coherent. Since there is a
distinction between the questions of the doctrine's truth and of its

coherence, it will not do to reject a defense of the doctrine's logical coherence as inadequate because it offers no evidence that Jesus really was the Son of God. Likewise, evidence that Jesus really was the God-man will not explain how this is logically possible.

A second matter stems from the first. What does it mean to say that a proposition or a concept is self-contradictory? In logic a contradiction is the affirmation and denial of one and the same proposition at the same time. To level the charge of contradiction is not to claim simply that two ideas do not appear to fit together. Nor does it mean that though they fit together, we do not yet see how, though we may later. It does not even mean that God knows how they fit together, though we do not. It means that *there is no possible way for anyone ever to explain how the ideas can all be true and yet not contradict one another.*

Given the nature of this charge as it relates to the incarnation, there are at least two ways to meet it. One could produce evidence that Jesus actually is God incarnate (that is, he is both human and divine) and then argue that since there is an *actual* case of incarnation, of course an incarnation is *possible*. The other way to answer the charge of no *possible* way to harmonize the ideas is to offer a *possible* way. Proponents of the incarnation, following this strategy, would not need to prove that their explanation is the actual way or even a plausible way to fit the ideas together; only that it is a possible way for all the claims about Christ to be true. I have chosen the second strategy for several reasons. Most of the evidence one would employ in the first strategy would appeal to biblical claims. But this would likely shift the discussion to a defense of believers' interpretation of Scripture and of Scripture's reliability. Moreover, even if theists succeed in convincing skeptics about Scripture, skeptics will still demand an explanation of *how* the claims about Christ as God and man can be true without contradiction. Hence I have chosen the second strategy, which in effect says to skeptics, "You have asked for a possible way that all these claims about Christ's person can be true. I will show you a way to harmonize them that removes the apparent contradictions."

Lest readers fear that I plan to offer any sort of explanation, even an outrageous one, just so it removes the formal contradiction, I must add that I intend to give an explanation that not only removes the apparent contradiction but is also plausible (though offering evidence for its plausibility is not the point of this chapter). Moreover, while the apparent logical problems could be removed by appealing to a kenotic Christology, I accept the task of offering an account that removes apparent contradictions without sacrificing the orthodox doctrine of the incarnation. The kenotic view solves the problems by claiming that in becoming incarnate Christ divested himself of all divine attributes.[9] While this removes apparent logical inconsistencies, it does so at too high a price.

The Orthodox Doctrine

It is always possible that a contradiction will be found in the Incarnation doctrine because it has been delineated incorrectly. For example, if one holds that the incarnation means that God literally changed into a man (leaving his deity behind), or if one believes that in becoming a man Christ's divine nature was humanized or his human nature deified, there will be problems of logical coherence with such ideas. Hence, we must begin with a clear understanding of the doctrine.

In Philippians 2:5-11 the apostle Paul presents the doctrine clearly. In verse 6 he says that prior to the incarnation Jesus existed *en morphē theou* ("in the form of God"). Though *morphē* often refers to what is outward, commentators agree that in this context the word refers to Christ's internal nature or essence.[10] Hence the phrase says in effect that Jesus Christ is God. Despite Christ's deity, however, Paul says (v. 7) that Christ "emptied himself" *(heauton ekenōsen)*. The rest of the verse contains two participial phrases that explain how he emptied himself. Jesus emptied himself *morphēn doulou labōn* ("by taking on the form or nature of a bondservant") and *en homoiōmati anthrōpōn genomenos* ("by being made in the likeness of men"). The first phrase means that he took on the essential nature of a bondservant. Lest we think this did not involve his taking on a real human nature, Paul removes all doubt with the second phrase. The word *homoiōmati* is especially significant. Paul is saying that Jesus Christ took on the basic building blocks of human nature (an immaterial substance and a material one). Were those "building blocks" of the same nature and structured together as they are in human beings? The words *en homoiōmati anthrōpōn* assure us that the material and immaterial substances that Christ took on are like those of human beings, and they were conjoined in Christ as they are in other humans. Christ was a real human being. He did not just appear to be human.

Notice that Christ's emptying did not involve giving up his divine nature, but rather taking on a complete human nature. Notice also that in verses 9-11 Paul speaks of Christ's exaltation. Nothing in those verses even slightly hints that this exaltation involved a return of a divine nature that somehow departed at the incarnation.

If Christ's emptying involved taking on a complete human nature, of what did he empty himself? The answer most consistent with biblical teaching about the incarnate Christ is that while maintaining his divine nature, he gave up the full and constant exercise of his divine powers and the continual display of the glory that are his as God. That is, he ceded the privileges of being God without relinquishing the position of being God.[11]

The portrait of the incarnate Christ is clear. He is fully God and fully man. Taking on a human nature did not involve mixing divine attributes with human, nor converting one nature to the other. In the words of the Council of Chalcedon (A.D. 451), Jesus Christ was "truly God, and the same truly man," one Lord "manifested in two natures, without confusion, without conversion, indivisibly, inseparably. The distinction of the natures being by no means abolished by the union, but rather the property of each preserved and combined into one person and one hypostasis, not one severed or divided into two persons, but one and the same Son and Only-begotten, viz., God, Logos, and the Lord Jesus Christ."[12]

Thomas Morris's Proposal

Although there are various ways to explain the doctrine so as to defend its rational coherence,[13] we want an explanation that upholds the orthodox notion while being as plausible as possible. While my task in this chapter is only to show that the doctrine is logically coherent, at some point the theist will want to argue that what is logically possible is also likely true. And at that point in the comprehensive apologetic task that includes establishing the truth of the incarnation, it will make a difference that theists choose an explanation of the doctrine's logical coherence that is also plausible. Thomas V. Morris's *The Logic of God Incarnate* offers the most extensive recent defense of the doctrine's coherence, and his basic strategy seems correct. Hence I shall sketch the main elements of his proposal.

Three distinctions. Morris's proposal centers on three basic distinctions and a theory about the mind and will of Christ. First, he differentiates between an *individual essence* and a *kind-essence*. An individual essence is "the whole set of properties individually necessary and jointly sufficient for being numerically identical with *that individual.*"[14] If this is the sense in which we use the term *nature* or *essence,* no one could have more than one individual essence. Each person's individual essence would include all the properties true of that person.[15] In Christ's case all his divine and human properties taken together would make up his individual essence.

But there is another sense of the term *nature* or *essence.* Scientists and metaphysicians (and sometimes ordinary people) commonly divide things in the world into different kinds of entities. As Morris explains, "A natural kind can be understood as constituted by a shareable set of properties individually necessary and jointly sufficient for membership in that kind. Such a set of properties can be characterized as a kind-essence, or a kind-nature."[16]

Morris believes that this distinction between a kind-essence and an individual essence is necessary for making sense of the claim that Jesus was one person with two natures. If the only notion of nature we use is that of individual essence, then Jesus, having only one individual essence, must have only one set of properties, and it is hard to see how they could be a combination of human and divine properties. Something will be lost from either his humanity or his deity. On the other hand, if we invoke the notion of kind-essence, it is possible to explain the composition of Christ's person. Being fully human, he belongs to the natural kind of humanity, as all humans do. Being divine, he also belongs to the natural kind of divinity. Thus, the *person* Jesus Christ is a combination of a fully divine kind-essence and a fully human kind-essence. All properties of each nature remain what they are, despite the union of the two natures in one person. The *individual essence* of the person Jesus Christ contains all the divine and human properties he has *in virtue of* his having two natures and exemplifying two *kind-natures.*

It is also in virtue of the kind-essence concept that we can make sense of the identity claim that Jesus (the man who lived on earth for some thirty-three or so years) is God the Son (the eternally existing second member of the Godhead). If the identity claim means that there is only one kind-nature in Christ, then the identity claim expresses a logical impossibility, for it is impossible for a natural kind to have both divine and human properties. One person can, however, have both human and divine properties, if that person exemplifies two separate kind-essences, one human and one divine.

Even granting the distinction between an individual essence and a kind-essence, there still seems to be a problem with the incarnation. It is one thing to say that Jesus exemplifies the human kind-essence, but another to see his humanity as complete humanity, just as ours is. After all, Jesus was not conceived by a human father and mother. Wouldn't that be necessary for him to qualify as a real human being? Questions like these lead to a second distinction, that between *common properties* and *essential properties*. Common properties are the characteristics that many or most individuals of a given kind-essence will have. Essential properties are qualities an individual must have in order to exemplify at all the kind-essence in question. Someone could be human without having *all* properties *common* to human beings, but one could not be human and lack a quality that is part and parcel of the very essence of human beings. For example, it is hard to see how someone lacking a body or the ability to reason (never had these and never will) could qualify as a human. But there might be a being who qualified as a real human being, even though she was born with only four toes on her right foot. Absence of common properties does not mean absence of the natural kind; absence of essential properties does.

With this distinction in hand, Morris raises the crucial question: "Once we acknowledge a clear distinction between commonality and essence, what forces the Christian to count as essential any common *human* properties which would preclude a literal divine incarnation?"[17] I think this is correct. There are human properties that most of us have, such as properties associated with our origin (we came into the world by natural reproduction involving a human father and a human mother), that Jesus does not have. Why should those properties be the defining properties for being human? There is no obvious reason why this must be so.[18] What critics of the incarnation must do (and have not done) is show that Jesus' humanity lacks any of the proper ties that are essential to being a human.

Some may grant that Jesus has whatever properties are essential to being human, but still complain that because he has other properties in virtue of being the Son of God that are neither essential to being human nor common to any other humans, it is hard to believe that he is a real human being just like the rest of us. In reply, Morris introduces a third distinction between being *fully human* and being *merely human*. To be fully human one must have all properties essential to human beings, and Jesus does. But he also has such properties of deity as existing from eternity. How can this be true of anyone who is fully human? Morris answers that it can be true because Jesus, while fully human is not merely human. Being merely human is to have all properties essential to being fully human. But the Christian doctrine of the incarnation holds that in order to be fully human, one need not be merely human! Jesus has every essential property possessed by everyone who is merely human (thus he is fully human); but as fully divine as well, he is not *merely* human. Once we understand that Christ's nonhuman properties are not properties of his human nature but of his divine nature, we can see how a *person* who is fully human could have properties that no one who is *merely* human could have.[19]

The two-minds hypothesis. This may seem a promising way to understand the incarnation, but Morris knows the real test comes when trying to make sense of how Jesus can exemplify very human qualities at the same time that he has similar divine attributes that *contradict* those human qualities.[20] In particular, Jesus as divine is omniscient, but as human he has limited knowledge. Hence the properties of omniscience and of limited knowledge are both predicated of one and the same *person*, and that is a contradiction. Moreover, one wonders whether at any moment of his earthly life the *person* Jesus knew everything or only some things. If everything, then how can Scripture say (Lk 2:52) that he grew in wisdom and knowledge?

Morris answers that in Christ there were two minds (two distinct ranges of consciousness), one divine and one human. Christ possessed the eternal mind of God the Son, which knows all things. But he also possessed a "distinctly earthly consciousness that came into existence and grew and developed as the boy Jesus grew and developed."[21] The relation between the two minds was asymmetrical. That is, the divine mind knew and had access to everything the human mind knew, but the human mind had access to the divine only when the divine mind allowed it access. What Jesus knew through his human mind alone and apart from any access it had to his divine mind was only what was available to any other human living at that time. But since he was not merely human, Jesus had access to information that no mere human could know apart from divine revelation.[22]

If this sounds strange, Morris thinks some analogies help. For example, sometimes a person has a dream with himself in it. But at the same time, "the dreamer 'as sleeper' is somehow aware, in what could be called an overarching level of consciousness, that it is just a dream that is going on, in which he is playing a role as one of the characters."[23] These two levels of consciousness operating at once in the same person are analogous to what Morris means with his two-minds theory of Christ.

Another analogy comes from modern depth psychology. Psychologists say an ordinary human has an unconscious or subconscious mind, as well as a conscious mind. It stands in an asymmetric accessing relation to the conscious mind in a way parallel to the accessing relation of the divine mind and the earthly consciousness of Jesus. From what Morris says about Jesus, he sees the divine mind as parallel to the human unconscious, for he says that Jesus' range of mentality would have an extra depth in virtue of his divinity.[24]

A final analogy appeals to people who have multiple personalities—two or more distinct ranges of consciousness. Such cases make the idea of Jesus as one person with two levels of consciousness more plausible.[25]

The two-wills hypothesis and temptation. Morris also addresses the problem of Christ's sinlessness. As God, Christ has the property of necessary goodness, so he cannot even be tempted, let alone sin (Jas 1:13). But as fully human, Christ must have the capacity to be tempted and to sin. Indeed, Hebrews 4:15 says he was tempted in all points like us, but he did not sin. The apparent contradiction is twofold: (a) as divine, Jesus cannot be tempted, but Scripture says he was (presumably, as human); (b) as divine, Jesus could not sin, but as human, he had to be able to sin; otherwise he could not even be tempted.[26]

How should the defender of Chalcedonian orthodoxy respond? Morris argues that we should not grant that the *person* Jesus Christ could sin. Since Jesus is divine, and since an essential property of deity is necessary goodness (which precludes sin), we cannot hold that Jesus could sin. Of course, if being able to sin is an essential property of human nature, then Jesus' individual essence apparently has the essential properties of being unable to sin and being able to sin. Morris reasons that while being able to sin is a *common* human property, there is no reason to think it an *essential* human property. Christians hold that even some *mere* humans cannot sin (for example, those in the womb or those in the glorified state of eternity). Thus the ability to sin must not be essential to being human. Hence no property *essential* to being human conflicts with Christ's essential divine property of necessary goodness.[27]

Although this explains how Jesus can be necessarily good (though fully human), it also necessitates that he cannot sin, and that makes it hard to see how he can even be tempted. At this point Morris offers another distinction and argues that we must realize that Christ had two wills—one divine and one human. How does this solve the problem? Let me explain.

We can see how Jesus could be necessarily good and still be tempted if we understand the difference between a *logical possibility* and an *epistemic possibility*. That which is logically possible can be done in the sense that doing it does not actualize a contradiction. Because Christ has the property of necessary goodness (that is, metaphysically he is necessarily good), he cannot sin. Hence for him to sin would be to actualize a contradiction (do what he cannot do), and, of course, that is impossible. Logic tells us that it is impossible, for logic tells us that one cannot actualize a contradiction. On the other hand, something is an epistemic possibility if one *thinks* one can do it, even though metaphysically one cannot (that is, even if one's nature is such that it is logically impossible to do the act).[28] Hence Jesus could be tempted to sin if he thought he could sin and did not know he could not sin. This could be true of Jesus if his *human* belief-set did not contain the information that he was necessarily good (or that necessary goodness entails the metaphysical impossibility of sinning).

This is a remarkable view. Morris is saying that even though it was metaphysically (and hence logically) impossible for Jesus to sin (because of his necessary goodness), his human mind would not know that unless his divine mind gave his human mind that information. But Jesus' divine mind never divulged that fact (and his human mind apparently never figured it out, regardless of how many times Jesus resisted temptation), so Jesus' earthly mind did not know he could not sin. Hence he could be tempted to do what metaphysically he could not do, namely, sin.[29]

None of this matters, of course, if Jesus' divine will is the only will he has, or if his divine will controls his human will. Morris replies that we should reject the monothelite heresy of only one will in Christ. Christ had both a human will and a divine will. Thus it is possible that his human will, following what his human mind knew, could be tempted. Still, if his divine will controlled his human will to the point of causally determining him not to sin, then his human will did not resist temptation freely. Moreover, if his divine will made it impossible for his human will to fall to temptation, many would find it hard to see how his human will could genuinely be tempted to sin. Of course, if Jesus' temptations were only a sham, then Scripture is wrong when it says he was tempted in all points like us. Morris answers that neither the divine mind nor the divine will controlled the human mind or human will in Jesus.[30] He was "free" to be tempted, and he resisted freely. By freedom, Morris means libertarian free will.[31]

Morris illustrates how this might work. Suppose someone enters a room freely. Unknown to him, electrodes have been implanted in his brain which, when activated, will prevent him from deciding or trying to leave the room before he has been there for two hours. He considers leaving before the two-hour mark, but decides against it. Thus he never even comes close to activating the electrodes that would prevent him from leaving. When the two hours end, however, he decides to leave and does. Did he act freely in staying for two hours and then leaving? Morris says yes.

Morris sees this as analogous to Christ's case. The electrodes made it impossible for the man to leave, but they never causally played any part in his decision to stay or leave. Similarly, Christ's necessary goodness made it impossible for him to sin, but that attribute never caused him to reject sin. This is because in his earthly consciousness he did not know he had this property. And it always turned out that when confronted with temptation, Jesus freely resisted, so his necessary goodness never intervened to prevent him from sinning, any more than the electrodes stopped the man from leaving the room early.[32]

Interacting with Morris

The central issue of this chapter is whether it is logically coherent for Jesus to be both fully human and fully divine at the same time. So the critical question about Morris's proposal is not whether it is plausible but whether it offers a possible way to unite in one person a divine and a human nature. Though I do not agree with all he says, I believe the major points in Morris's proposal present a possible way. I want to explain why this is so.

Morris's main distinctions. I begin with the idea of a kind-essence. Nothing about this idea is self-contradictory. Moreover, there is no apparent reason why one person could not exemplify two kind-essences, unless those essences could not fit together. To show that Christ's kind-essences can fit together, I must say more about his being.

Initially, we must clarify what it means to be both fully human *and* fully divine. To be fully human, one must be a combination of a material substance (a body) and an immaterial substance (the entity that performs all acts of cognition).[33] To be fully divine, according to orthodox Christianity, one must be an immaterial substance with unlimited cognitive powers. The orthodox notions of God and man demand that mind be immaterial. If mind is material (for instance, if the mind just is the physical brain), then the incarnation doctrine is in trouble. Christ's one body could contain one brain (mind, on a strictly materialist theory), but it is not clear how Christ's one body could contain two brains, one identified with the divine mind and the other with the human mind. So if the incarnation is to be possible, mind must be immaterial.[34]

But if mind is immaterial, one cannot object that there cannot be two minds in Christ on the grounds that there is not enough space in that body for two. Immaterial substances do not take up space, so there is no more problem of finding "enough room" for two of them in one body than there is for finding room for one in one body.[35] But if this is so, then so far we see no impossibility of Christ having both a human and a divine nature, given the properties of both of those natures.

Perhaps there is a different problem with uniting these two natures in Christ. Although there is enough "room" in Christ for a human and a divine nature, maybe the properties of each nature are so disparate that there is no way to unite them.[36] In reply, we might conclude this if we were talking about uniting a frog and a prince in one hypostasis. The physical qualities of a frog and of a prince are so different and their mental capacities are so different that it is hard to see how such a union could occur. But that is not the case with a God-man. Man is said to be the image of God. As image, he shares to some degree qualities that God has. Orthodox theologians debate the exact constituents of the *imago Dei,* but they generally agree that regardless of whatever else constitutes the *imago,* it at least includes reason, emotion and will plus some sort of spiritual capacity. If these capacities in humans were totally different from God's faculties, there might be a major problem in uniting a human and a divine mind in one person. But both God and human beings have the capacity to reason, will and feel. God has those capacities to an infinite degree while man has them to a finite degree. There seems to be no reason to believe that divine cognitive powers are *qualitatively* so different from human powers that a union of a divine and a human mind could not possibly occur.

There is something more to this objection as John Hick raises it. If the objection is that something antecedently human subsequently acquires divine properties (Christ's human mind is omniscient—at times Hick speaks as though this is what he means),[37] that would be a problem. But Chalcedon never claimed that Christ's divine nature took on human qualities or that his human nature took on divine properties. Moreover, when Christ did exhibit knowledge beyond that of mere humans, he did not possess in his human mind all knowledge possessed by the divine mind, but only some. So why it would be impossible to contain this extra information in a human brain (to use Hick's words) is unexplainable.

Maybe there is a problem with a divine mind functioning through a human body and brain. But if it is possible to unite a human immaterial substance with a human body, why is it impossible to unite a divine immaterial substance with a human body? If a reasoning, willing, feeling, *human* immaterial substance can function and express itself through a human brain and body, why can't a *divine* immaterial substance that performs the same activities do so as well? In answering this question, one must be careful not to beg it by saying that it is just impossible for something infinite to unite with and work through something finite. That is precisely what is at issue in this study.

What shall we say about Morris's three main distinctions? The idea of a kind-essence is not self-contradictory, and we have seen several respects in which a human kind-essence and a divine kind-essence could unite in one person. It is also hard to see how the idea of an individual essence is self-contradictory. Nor do those two concepts contradict one another. Moreover, the notions of common and essential properties are not self-contradictory, nor do they contradict one another. And Morris's ideas of being merely human and of being fully human are not self-contradictory, nor do they contradict one another. As Morris uses these distinctions, they do explain consistently how one person can have two distinct natures.

A plausible two-minds theory. If there are problems with Morris's proposal, they most likely involve his two-minds and two-wills theories and his handling of the problems of Christ's knowledge and his sinlessness. As to the two-minds theory, I have a slight problem with Morris's version of it, but not a problem that destroys it. In fact, from what I have said about a *complete* human and a *complete* divine nature, I do not see how Christ could be fully human and fully divine and not have two minds. If he lacks either mind, he is either not fully human or not fully divine.[38]

My main concern is with Morris's analogies of two levels of consciousness in dreams, the conscious and unconscious mind, and multiple personalities. Though analogies are not identities, analogies should compare items that are truly similar, at least in regard to the matter for which the comparison was made in the first place. The problem with Morris's analogies is that each one involves different levels or kinds of consciousness, but those levels of consciousness belong in each case to *numerically one and the same mind.* But in Christ there are not just two separate levels of consciousness. There are, numerically speaking, two distinct immaterial substances (minds).

Does this destroy the two-minds theory? Not unless there must be an apt naturalistic analogy for it to be believable. Morris never puts this stipulation on the theory, nor would I. We do not normally invoke this rule with other concepts to ensure their intelligibility, so why require it here? Moreover, I cannot see how there could be a naturalistic analogy to the two-minds theory because it is hard to think of any natural being that literally possesses two minds. Anyway, inability to offer an apt analogy shows nothing about the logical coherence of the view.

Some will respond that there still is a problem, for it is impossible for two minds to function together in one person. Of course, this would be impossible if it is impossible for immaterial minds to causally interact with one another or with bodies. But the very idea of such causal interaction is not self-contradictory per se. Of course, this two-minds view presupposes an immaterial notion of mind, and if such a view can be established on other grounds, then my position moves beyond being possible to being plausible (likely to be true).[39]

In sum, if an immaterial substance such as a mind can causally interact with such a different kind of thing as a physical body, there seems to be no logical incoherence in the notion of one immaterial substance causally interacting with another, especially since they are the same kind of substance. And there seems to be no contradiction in thinking that two immaterial substances can communicate with one another. Those who think that God has in times past communicated with humankind will have additional reasons for accepting this idea.

What is the relevance of this to Christ? Even as there is no impossibility of Christ's divine mind interacting with his material body, it is hard to see any logical impossibility about his human and divine minds communicating with and causally interacting with one another. On occasion, his divine mind would give his human mind information it could not have known otherwise (for example, Jn 4:16-29). That would happen as a function of immaterial substances being able to communicate and causally interact with one another.

But if Christ's divine mind was always functional in the historical Jesus, wouldn't he always necessarily be aware of the contents of that mind? Not necessarily, if the relation between his two minds was asymmetric. If the usual level of consciousness running through Christ's mind was his human stream of consciousness, and if his human mind had access to the contents of his divine mind only when the divine mind gave access, there is no reason why the contents of his divine mind would be present to his human mind unless his divine mind allowed access to them. Many psychologists tell us that the human mind is not always consciously aware of everything it knows. If ordinary humans are not continuously aware of everything their one mind knows, why should we think that Christ's human mind always knew the contents of his divine mind? Although Christ's natures (and thus minds) were united, they were still distinct, so there is no reason this union would mandate that the contents of each mind would transfer to the other.[40] If that were mandated, then both minds in Christ would be omniscient, and that obviously was not the case. Hence the two-minds theory seems the best way to think of Christ's intellectual capacities, and it explains how Jesus as divine would be omniscient, but as human would not be.[41]

Tempting the impeccable God-man. What about the matter of tempting God? It is here that Morris's views most need modifying. Morris opts for dyothelitism against monothelitism, and in this I fully agree. If Christ has a fully human and a fully divine nature, he must be everything God and man are. But how could there be either a divine mind or a human mind without each having the capacity to will? So of necessity we must hold to two wills in Christ.

I have a problem, however, with Morris's claim that Jesus did not know he was necessarily good. This might have been true very early in Jesus' life, but not by the time he reached manhood. Morris affirms the orthodox biblical understanding of Christ. But in the Gospels Jesus is portrayed as thinking of himself as God. How could he think he was God and not think he was necessarily good? As a Jew raised in orthodox Judaism, Jesus would have found it unthinkable that God could sin. And if Jesus understood himself to be divine, he would know that he could not sin, even if he never thought, *I have the modal property of necessary goodness.*

Since Morris affirms the biblical view of Christ, he should not solve the problem of Christ's temptation by denying that Christ knew he was impeccable. To deny that Christ knew he was necessarily good removes the apparent contradiction with his temptation being genuine, but since Scripture shows that Christ claimed to be God, it is hard to see how he could be ignorant of his own impeccability.

The point is so obvious that there must be a reason why Morris denies that Jesus knew he was necessarily good. And there is. The reason is Morris's notion of free will. If Christ knew he was necessarily good, he could not resist temptation freely, according to Morris. In fact, he could not even be tempted. But what kind of freedom is this? It is libertarian or contra-causal free will. According to this view of freedom, often called incompatibilism, genuine free human action is incompatible with causal conditions that decisively incline the will one way or another. If Jesus had this kind of freedom and also knew he was necessarily good, he could not resist temptation freely. His knowledge would be one of the factors causally determining him to refrain from sin. It would guarantee resisting temptation (or not even being tempted), but with libertarian free will there can be no such guarantees. Agents with libertarian freedom must always be able to do otherwise than they do, if they are acting freely. Thus in order to safeguard libertarian free will, ensure that Christ's temptation was genuine and ensure that he resisted it freely, Morris holds that Jesus was ignorant of his necessary goodness.

Although Morris's move is understandable, it leads to this claim about Christ's self-knowledge that is hard to square with Scripture. I am not suggesting that incompatibilism is self-contradictory. Nor am I saying that anyone who holds to incompatibilism must explain how Christ could freely resist temptation by denying that he knew he was impeccable. My point is that Morris's particular handling of this issue creates the problems with scriptural teaching I have mentioned.

Although incompatibilists might handle these issues in some other way than Morris does, there is yet another option for theists, and it is the way I would handle Christ's temptations. It involves a different view of free will known as compatibilism. Elsewhere I have explained and defended this deterministic notion of freedom.[42] According to compatibilism, genuinely free human action is compatible with causes that decisively incline the will without constraining it. To act under constraint is to act against one's wishes. To act without constraint is to act in accord with one's desires. Given this view of freedom, Jesus could know that he was necessarily good, and this information would likely be a factor that inclined him to do good. Resisting temptation, however, would be unfree only if this factor (or others) constrained him to resist temptation against his wishes. But there is no reason to think Jesus resisted temptation because he was forced to do so against his desires. Let me explain.

Jesus' knowledge of his necessary goodness would be one factor that would lead him to do good, but it was not the only factor. Those who know Christ as Savior know that the more one resists temptation, the easier it becomes to do so the next time. Likewise, the more one falls to temptation, the more comfortable one becomes with sin, and the easier it is to fall the next time. But if humans can make progress in resisting temptation, why could not Christ in his humanity do so as well? In fact, Scripture says he did, for he learned obedience through the things he suffered so as to be prepared to be our Savior (Heb 5:8-9). In addition, Scripture teaches that as one remains in fellowship with the Holy Spirit, there is added strength and power to resist temptation (cf. Rom 8). Jesus also lived in fellowship with the Holy Spirit and relied on his power.

All of these factors help us resist sin and love righteousness. Do they make us resist sin unfreely (against our wishes)? Of course not. God's work in us is evident by the fact that our desires gradually become more and more attuned to righteousness. If this is so for us, it is hard to see why this was not so for Christ in accord with his humanity. His acts of righteousness and resisting temptation were causally determined, but not contrary to his wishes, and not solely in terms of his knowledge that he could not sin.

Some will say this still is not freedom because Christ's good actions were causally determined. But this amounts to a typical complaint some indeterminists level at compatibilists, namely, "Yours is not legitimate or real freedom." Of course, this is question-begging, for both libertarian and compatibilistic free will are logically possible kinds of freedom. Neither view can win the debate by defining its opponent out of existence! So compatibilism is not logically self-contradictory, nor is my explanation logically inconsistent by incorporating it. And it is a way to solve the problem of how Christ could resist temptation freely while knowing that he is necessarily good.

Some will think this still misses the main point. Even if, given compatibilism, Jesus does good freely, knowing he cannot sin means he cannot even be tempted to sin. I think this is a more serious issue than the freedom question, but it is answerable. As humans walk in the Spirit, it becomes easier for them to fight sin. But that does not mean they cannot be genuinely tempted to sin. Some sins tempt more than others, but there is some attraction to do wrong in each case.

Just as this is true for us, so it was for Christ. Some temptations undoubtedly were not very attractive to him. When Satan offered Christ all the kingdoms of the world if Christ would worship him, I doubt that this tempted Jesus very much because he likely knew de jure that they were already his and that someday de facto he would possess them. On the other hand, when Jesus was tempted to turn stones into bread, this probably posed a greater temptation if only because at that moment he was hungry. But in neither case did Jesus reply that he could not obey Satan because, as necessarily good, he could not even try to sin if he wanted to. Rather, he answered Satan by quoting Scripture (not a bad practice for anyone). His responses show that apart from what he knew about his inability to sin, he really did not want to sin. He resisted (compatibilistically) freely.

But one temptation, the temptation to forgo the cross, was a major struggle for Jesus. We see him in the garden of Gethsemane asking the Father to allow this cup to pass from him, if possible. Yet he prays that the Father's will be done. This is no prayer of unwilling resignation, but rather a willing acceptance of what must be done. Clearly, Jesus did this of his own free will, for he said that no one could make him lay down his life; he would do so of his own accord (Jn 10:17-18).

Some may think that even this temptation was not genuine because Jesus knew he would not disobey. Moreover, he knew he would rise in three days, so there should have been no fear of the death experience. None of this would tempt him. I thoroughly disagree. Scripture says that he sweat drops as of blood over this issue. Knowing he would rise from the dead in three days did not render the nails painless, nor the beatings, nor the crown of thorns, nor hanging on a cross for all those hours. Jesus had surely seen enough crucifixions to know that this would not be a pleasant experience, regardless of the final outcome. There had to be temptation to forgo it, especially when he knew he could avoid it all.

An analogy to Christ's temptations is the matter of whether a genuine Christian can apostatize. Many evangelical Christians believe that once a person accepts Christ as Savior, salvation cannot be lost. The believer is sealed with the Holy Spirit (Eph 1:13; 4:30) and is protected by the power of God working through his faith (1 Pet 1:5) to keep him true to the Lord. Those who believe in the eternal security of the believer, however, still know they can be tempted to turn from Christ. Believers have at times been tempted to doubt Christianity. Moreover, in the midst of intense affliction the temptation to turn from God can be very strong. So the fact that one cannot lose salvation does not make it impossible to be genuinely tempted to apostatize.

But is the temptation resisted freely? Does God's protection of believers' salvation make them resist temptation to apostatize against their wishes? No. On the contrary, many people resist temptation to fall away not because they know they cannot actually fall away and thus they resign themselves to being a Christian (even though they wish to fall away), but because they love God and his Word too much to turn away. They really are tempted to fall away, but various factors of their life with God lead them *in accord with their wishes* (and thus freely) to maintain faith and a Christian walk.

If this is true of eternally secure believers, why couldn't Christ, despite his necessary goodness, freely resist sin though genuinely tempted? I think some believe this to be impossible partly because they think that unless people actually fall into sin, it is not clear that they really have been tempted. James 1:13-15 shows that it is possible to be tempted without sin.[43] And our own experience shows that there can be real temptation, even if it is impossible for us to sin (as in the case of apostasy). Is my example of apostasy truly analogous to the case of Christ? I think so, since in both cases something makes it impossible to commit a particular sin. But in neither case does that impossibility make it impossible to be tempted to sin, nor does it make resistance unfree. An impeccable Savior is no more untemptable than an invincible army is unattackable.[44]

A final question. One problem remains. How does this understanding of Christ explain how the *person* Jesus Christ performed any action? Humans as complete persons do various activities in virtue of a particular part of their being; the same is true for Christ. If I kick a football, it is not my liver, kidneys or emotions that kick it, but it is still proper to attribute the action to me, the agent. I do it by virtue of my foot, which is able to kick. The same is true for any other mental or physical activity. The act is attributed to the whole person, even though the person does it in virtue of that aspect of his being that can perform the activity. The same is true for Christ. Thus it is proper to say that the person Jesus Christ died in virtue of his human nature that could experience death. And it is correct to say that Jesus cast out demons in virtue of the power available to him through his divine nature.

Conclusion

If God were to become incarnate, how would he do so? As noted at the outset of this chapter, before answering the *how* question, one must answer *whether* it could be done. In light of Thomas Morris's proposal, along with my amplifications and changes, I conclude that it is possible for God to become incarnate and also possible to give an account of the incarnation that is internally coherent. This chapter presents a *possible* way that all the main beliefs about Christ can be true. Careful reflection on my explanation shows as well that it answers Martin's four main problems with the coherence of the doctrine.[45] I also believe a case can be made for the truth of this explanation, but all that is needed to meet the charge of contradiction is to explain a *possible* way the incarnation *could be* true. In this chapter I have done so.

FIFTEEN
THE EMPTY
TOMB OF JESUS

WILLIAM LANE CRAIG

ACCORDING TO JOHN DOMINIC CROSSAN, THE COCHAIR OF THE highly publicized Jesus Seminar, after the crucifixion Jesus' corpse was probably laid in a shallow grave, barely covered with dirt and subsequently eaten by wild dogs; the story of Jesus' entombment and resurrection was the result of "wishful thinking."[1]

Crossan presents no specific evidence, much less probative evidence, for this allegation; rather it is just his hunch as to what happened to the body of Jesus based on customary Jewish practices. Since he does not accept the historicity of the discovery of the empty tomb (not to speak of the resurrection), Crossan surmises that Jesus' corpse was laid in the graveyard normally reserved for executed criminals, but he offers no specific evidence for this surmise, nor does he directly engage the evidence that prompts most scholars to accept the historicity of Jesus' entombment.

This omission is important, since the historicity of the burial of Jesus in the tomb and the discovery of his empty tomb tend to stand or fall together. On the one hand, if the burial story can be shown to be false (that is, legendary or fictitious) at its core, then obviously the story of Jesus' tomb being found empty must be false as well. On the other hand, if the burial story is fundamentally reliable, then those who deny the empty tomb must face the very difficult question of how the belief in Jesus' resurrection could originate or be sustained in the face of a tomb containing his corpse. Thus any discussion of the historicity of Jesus' empty tomb must begin with a consideration of what happened to the body of Jesus after the crucifixion.

The Fact of Jesus' Burial

Typically, crucified bodies were allowed to remain on the cross until their flesh was devoured by birds of prey or by wild animals, or, due to Jewish sensibilities, they were buried in a common dirt graveyard reserved for criminals. Sometimes the corpses would be given to family members for proper burial, though this was not done in cases of criminals executed for treason, as Jesus was. In the absence of any evidence to the contrary, then, one would surmise, like Crossan, that Jesus' corpse was buried in the common plot along with those of the two thieves crucified with him.

But there is evidence to the contrary. The evidence indicates that something quite different happened to the body of Jesus—indeed, the very novelty of the gospel account bespeaks its historicity: Jesus is said to have been buried in a tomb by a Jewish Sanhedrist, a member of the very court that had condemned him. A number of facts have led the large majority of New Testament critics to accept the fundamental historicity of the burial account of Jesus.

1. *Jesus' burial in the tomb is attested by multiple early sources.* The story of Jesus' burial is found in all four Gospels. Although Matthew's and Luke's deviations from Mark's account might be seen as editorial changes made to Mark's material, the sporadic and uneven nature of their verbal agreements with each other over against Mark suggest that while Matthew and Luke shared the same stream of tradition as Mark, Mark's account was not their (only) source. In any case, John's narrative is probably literarily independent of the other three Gospels and thus serves to confirm the main outline of the story.

As to the age of these traditions, the burial story was doubtless part of Mark's source material for the story of Jesus' passion. The burial story served to close Jesus' passion as well as to create anticipation of his coming resurrection. Since Mark is the earliest of our Gospels, having been written prior to A.D. 70, the pre-Markan passion story must be even older. In fact, according to the German commentator Rudolf Pesch, this source is incredibly old.[2] For Paul's Last Supper tradition (1 Cor

11:23-25) presupposes the pre-Markan passion account; hence, the latter must have originated in the first years of existence of the Jerusalem fellowship. Confirmation of this is found in the fact that the pre-Markan passion story speaks of the "high priest" without using his name (Mk 14:53, 54, 60, 61, 63). This implies that Caiaphas was still the high priest when the pre-Markan passion story was being told, since there would then be no need to mention his name. Since Caiaphas was high priest from A.D. 18 to 37, the latest date for the origin of the tradition is A.D. 37.

Moreover, Paul gives independent and early confirmation of Jesus' burial in the traditions handed on by him to the church he founded in Corinth. It is now generally recognized that in 1 Corinthians 15:3-5 Paul is passing on a primitive Christian tradition summarizing the central elements of Christian belief and preaching:

> For I handed on to you as of first importance what I in turn had received: that Christ died for our sins in accordance with the scriptures, and that he was buried, and that he was raised on the third day in accordance with the scriptures, and that he appeared to Cephas, then to the twelve.

The grammatically unnecessary threefold "and that" (often omitted in English translations), as well as the succession of the events, makes it highly probable that the tradition's mention of the burial is not meant merely to underscore the death but refers to a distinct event, the burial of Jesus. But was that event Jesus' burial in the tomb? The answer to that question may be found by comparing this traditional summary to the Gospel accounts on the one hand and to the apostolic sermons in the book of Acts (particularly Acts 13:29-30) on the other. What we discover is a perfect concordance between the four lines of the summary and the stories of Jesus' crucifixion, entombment, resurrection and appearances. This makes it very clear that the second line of the tradition handed on by Paul summarized the story of Joseph's laying the body of Jesus in the tomb.

As to the age of this tradition, we know that in A.D. 36, just three years after his conversion, Paul spent two weeks on a fact-finding mission in Jerusalem with Cephas and James (Gal 1:18), the two individuals mentioned in 1 Corinthians 15:5-6, and he probably received the tradition at that time, if not earlier in Damascus. That means that this tradition goes back to within the first five years after Jesus' death in A.D. 30. Thus we have in Paul's tradition and in the pre-Markan passion source extremely early, multiple attestation of the fact of Jesus' burial in the tomb. (Given the age of this information, it cannot be dismissed as legendary, since the time span available was far too short for legendary tendencies to erase the hard historical core of the tradition.)

2. *The person of Joseph of Arimathea is probably historical.* Even skeptical scholars agree that it is unlikely that Joseph, as a member of the Sanhedrin, could have been a Christian invention. Raymond Brown, one of the greatest New Testament scholars of our day, explains that Joseph's being responsible for burying Jesus is "very probable," since a Christian fictional creation of a Jewish Sanhedrist who does what is right for Jesus would be "almost inexplicable," given the hostility in early Christian writings toward the Jewish leaders responsible for Jesus' death.[3] In particular, it is unlikely that Mark invented Joseph in view of his statements that the whole Sanhedrin voted for Jesus' condemnation (14:55, 64; 15:1). Brown notes that the thesis of Joseph's invention is rendered even more implausible in light of his identification with Arimathea, a town of no importance and having no scriptural symbolism. To this may be added the fact that the Gospels' descriptions of Joseph receive unintentional confirmation from incidental details; for example, his being rich from the type and location of the tomb. The consistent descriptions of the tomb as an acrosolia, or bench tomb, and archaeological discoveries that such tombs were used by notables during Jesus' day make it plausible that Jesus was placed in such a tomb. The incidental details that the tomb was unused and belonged to Joseph are quite probable, since Joseph could not lay the body of a criminal in just any tomb, especially since this would defile the bodies of any family members also reposing there.

Joseph's being at least a sympathizer of Jesus not only is independently attested by Matthew and John, but seems likely in view of Mark's description of his special treatment of Jesus' body as opposed to those of the thieves, whose bodies were presumably dispatched in the customary way. We can only speculate about how Joseph managed to obtain Jesus' corpse from the Roman authorities. His status as a Sanhedrist would undoubtedly have helped, and Mark admits that Joseph needed courage to approach Pilate with his request. That Pilate granted his request perhaps confirms the Gospels' conviction that Pilate really believed Jesus to be innocent.

3. *The burial story itself is simple and in its basic elements lacks theological reflection or apologetic development.* Most scholars would concur with Rudolf Bultmann's judgment to this effect.[4] We appear to

have here a primitive tradition recounting Joseph's begging the body of Jesus and his laying it, wrapped in linen, in a tomb, a tradition that has not been significantly overlaid with either theology or apologetics.

4. *The burial story is credible in light of Jewish preservation of the graves of holy men.* During Jesus' time there was an extraordinary interest in the graves of Jewish martyrs and holy men, and these were scrupulously cared for and honored. This suggests that the grave of Jesus would also have been noted so that it too might become such a holy site. The disciples had no inkling of any resurrection prior to the general resurrection at the end of the world, and they would probably therefore not have allowed the burial site of the Teacher to go unnoted. This interest makes very plausible the women's lingering to watch the burial and their subsequent intention to anoint Jesus' body with spices and perfumes (Lk 23:55-56).

5. *No other burial tradition exists.* If the burial of Jesus in the tomb by Joseph of Arimathea is legendary, then it is very strange that conflicting traditions nowhere appear, even in Jewish polemic. That no remnant of the true story, or even a conflicting false one, should remain is hard to explain unless the Gospel account is a substantially correct account.[5]

Taken together, these five considerations make the historical credibility of the burial account quite high, a fact recognized by the majority of New Testament critics. According to German scholar Wolfgang Trilling, "It appears unfounded to doubt the fact of Jesus' honorable burial—even historically considered."[6]

The Fact of the Empty Tomb

If Jesus was in fact buried in Joseph's tomb, then (barring his resurrection) either the story of the discovery of his empty tomb is legendary or fictitious, or else there is some natural explanation for his tomb's being vacant. During the first half of the twentieth century, the empty-tomb story was widely regarded among scholars as a late legend. But a remarkable turnabout has taken place during the second half of the twentieth century, such that one can speak of a reversal of scholarship on this issue. Several lines of historical evidence provide good grounds for affirming the historicity of Jesus' empty tomb.

1. *The credibility of the burial story supports the fact of the empty tomb.* If the burial story is fundamentally accurate, the site of Jesus' tomb would have been known to Jews (through Joseph) and Christians (through the women) alike. But in that case it would have been impossible for the

resurrection faith to survive in the face of a tomb containing the corpse of Jesus. The disciples could not have adhered to the resurrection, and scarcely anyone else would have believed them if they had. Their Jewish opponents could have exposed the whole affair by pointing to the occupied tomb, or perhaps even exhuming the body of Jesus, as the medieval Jewish polemic *Toledoth Yeshu* portrays them doing. Thus, if we accept the historicity of the burial account, then it is a short and reasonable inference to the historicity of the empty tomb as well.

Against this first line of evidence in support of the empty tomb, Karl Martin Fischer lodges two objections. (1) The argument presupposes that the Christian concept of resurrection was like the Jewish concept, that *this* flesh and *these* bones are constitutive of the resurrection body. But Paul precludes any such understanding in his doctrine of the resurrection body. Fischer's point is apparently that the Christian concept of resurrection would permit the disciples' affirmation of Jesus' resurrection even given general knowledge of the place where his body still lay interred. (2) The argument presupposes that Christians appealed to the empty tomb in their preaching, which is false.[7]

As for objection (1), 1 Corinthians 15:35-50 shows that Paul held that the mortal body had to be raised and transformed into the resurrection body: "it is sown a physical body, it is raised a spiritual body" (v. 44). Regardless of how one construes "spiritual body," it is clear that for Paul the resurrection body is historically continuous and numerically identical with the earthly body, that is, they are not two distinct entities. Moreover, Fischer admits that Jewish people believed this; why think that the original disciples were an exception? In any case, nothing is said to explain how belief in Jesus' resurrection could flourish in Jerusalem in the face of Jewish convictions and opposition. Objection (2) is puzzling, since this first line of evidence says nothing about the place of the empty tomb in the apostolic preaching. Even if Christians did not appeal to the empty tomb (itself a moot point in light of Acts 2:29-32; 13:29-30), the fact remains that given the reliability of the burial account, Jesus' tomb would have been known and so must have been empty in order for resurrection faith to flourish. Whether the Christian preachers drew this inference themselves or used it apologetically is simply irrelevant.

2. *Paul's testimony implies the fact of the empty tomb.* Some scholars have taken the empty tomb story to be legendary because Paul never explicitly refers to Jesus' empty tomb. Bultmann, for example, declared, "The stories of the empty tomb are legends, of which Paul does not yet

know."[8] Bultmann's argument from silence, however, fails to reckon with the occasional nature of Paul's letters. Were some Corinthians not abusing the Lord's Supper, for example, we should have no reference in Paul's letters to the Christian practice of Communion. Doubtless some scholars would then have said that Pauline churches did not observe the Lord's Supper. Absence of evidence is not necessarily evidence of absence. With respect to the empty tomb, there can be little doubt that Paul accepted not only the burial but also the empty tomb of Jesus, as is evident (1) from the sequence in 1 Corinthians 15:3-5: "died—was buried—was raised," (2) from the concept of resurrection itself, (3) from Paul's Pharisaic background and language, (4) from the expression "on the third day," (5) from the phrase "from the dead" (Rom 4:24), (6) from Paul's doctrine of resurrection and transformation of the body and (7) from his belief in the personal return of Christ (1 Thess 4:14-17).[9] All these imply a physical resurrection and therefore an empty tomb. It seems nearly certain, then, that Paul believed in the empty tomb.

Anton Vögtle and Rudolf Pesch, Lorenz Oberlinner and others are willing to concede that Paul believed in the empty tomb, but they protest that this does not imply that the tomb was actually empty.[10] But the question surely presses: How is it historically conceivable for the apostle Paul to have believed in the empty tomb of Jesus if in fact the tomb was not empty? Paul was in Jerusalem six years after the events themselves. The tomb must have been empty by then. But more than that, Cephas, James and the other Christians in Jerusalem with whom Paul spoke must also have believed that the tomb was empty and had been empty from the moment of the resurrection. If this were not so, Pauline theology would have taken an entirely different route, trying to explain how resurrection could still be possible, though the body remained in the grave. But neither Christian theology nor apologetics ever had to face such a problem. It seems unintelligible how Pauline theology could have taken the direction that it did had the tomb not been empty from the start.

Furthermore, there is good reason to think that Paul was familiar with the empty-tomb tradition. The third line in the tradition handed on by Paul corresponds to the empty-tomb story in the Gospels, the clause "he was raised" mirroring "he has risen" (Mk 16:6 NIV). This makes it likely that the empty-tomb tradition stands behind the third line of the formula, just as the burial tradition stands behind the second. Two conclusions follow. First, the tradition that the tomb was found empty must in all probability be reliable. (Time would have been insufficient for an empty-tomb legend to replace the historical memory of the fate of Jesus' corpse.) Second, given his knowledge of the context of the traditions that he delivered (so evident in his knowledge of Jesus' betrayal in his recounting the Last Supper), Paul no doubt knew the tradition of the empty tomb summarized in the formula he quotes in 1 Corinthians 15. If the discovery of the empty tomb is not historical, then it seems virtually inexplicable how both Paul and the early formulators of the tradition could have accepted it.

3. *The presence of the empty-tomb narrative in the pre-Markan passion story supports that narrative's historical credibility.* That the empty tomb story (Mk 16:1-8) was part of the pre-Markan passion story is evident from these facts: (1) the empty-tomb story is bound up with the immediate context of the burial account and the passion story; (2) verbal and syntactical similarities bind the empty-tomb story to the burial narrative; (3) the passion story would probably not have been circulated without victory at its end; and (4) the correspondence between the events of the passion and the formula of 1 Corinthians 15:3-5 confirms the inclusion of the empty-tomb account in the pre-Markan passion story. From the nature of the events themselves, such a conclusion makes good sense: there was no continuous, running account of the appearances because the appearances themselves were unexpected, sporadic, witnessed by people at various locations and occasions, whereas the empty-tomb story related a fact that was, so to speak, "common property" of the early Christian fellowship.

If this is the case, it seems futile to attempt to construe the empty tomb account as an unhistorical legend. It seems astounding that Pesch himself can try to convince us that the pre-Markan empty-tomb story is an unhistorical fusion of three literary forms from the history of religions: door-opening miracles, epiphany stories, and stories of seeking but not finding persons who have been translated into heaven.[11] Make no mistake: given the age of the pre-Markan passion story (even if not as old as Pesch argues) and its origin in Jerusalem, it seems very unlikely that the account could, at its core, be an unhistorical legend.

4. *The nature of the empty-tomb narrative itself is theologically unadorned and nonapologetic.* The resurrection is not described, and later theological motifs that a late legend might be expected to incorporate are wholly lacking. Comparison of Mark's account with those in later apocryphal Gospels like the *Gospel of Peter* underlines the simplicity of

the Markan story. The *Gospel of Peter* inserts, between Jesus' being sealed in the tomb and the visit of Mary Magdalene early Sunday morning, an account of the resurrection itself. According to this account, the tomb is surrounded not only by Roman guards but also by the Jewish Pharisees and elders, as well as a multitude from the surrounding countryside. Suddenly in the night there rings out a loud voice in heaven, and two men descend from heaven to the tomb. The stone over the door rolls back by itself, and they go into the tomb. Then three men come out of the tomb, two of them holding up the third man. The heads of the two men reach up into the clouds, but the head of the third man reaches up beyond the clouds. Then a cross comes out of the tomb, and a voice from heaven asks, "Have you preached to them that sleep?" And the cross answers, "Yes."

This is how legends look: they are colored by theological and other developments. By contrast, Mark's account of the discovery of the empty tomb is simple and seems to be pretty much a straightforward report of what happened. This suggests that the account is primitive and factual, even if dramatization should occur in the role of the angel.

Michael Goulder disagrees, claiming that the Markan narrative is thoroughly theologically determined, being a Christian midrash.[12] He attempts to show the presence of Old Testament motifs in the narrative (for example, Josh 10:16-27). But Goulder's methodology is no better than the old *religionsgeschichtliche Methode,* which found parallels scattered everywhere without showing any genealogical link between them. It is ironic that Goulder's article in *Theology* is followed by a piece entitled "The Use of Evidence in New Testament Studies," in which the author complains that too many scholars think it sufficient to show that the evidence *can* be interpreted in accordance with their hypothesis rather than that their interpretation is *required* by the evidence.[13] This is certainly Goulder's failing, and following his method would bring chaos to historical studies.

Against his view of the empty-tomb story stands the fact that the most significant elements of the Joshua story are conspicuously missing from the Markan story: the guard at the tomb (this is, of course, Matthean, which complicates Goulder's thesis by requiring that the other Evangelists are also writing midrash), reflection on Jesus as the king, description of Jesus coming out of the tomb, and declaration of Jesus' conquering his enemies. Such minor similarities as the stone over the entrance and taking down the bodies before nightfall are established Jewish practice.

For other details of the Markan story, Goulder searches hither and yon: the stone and its sealing come from the lion's den (Dan 6:17), Joseph of Arimathea from Joseph the Old Testament patriarch (Gen 50), Mary as a witness from Miriam the sister of Moses (Ex 15:21, in connection with Ps 38:11-14), Salome from King Solomon, and so forth. After a while such a methodology suffers self-refutation by *reductio ad absurdum*. The fact is that the Markan narrative appears to transmit a primitive tradition with little or no theological reflection, and this counts in favor of its historical reliability.

Crossan rejoins that Mark's simplicity is deceptive and does not bespeak the primitiveness of the tradition of the empty tomb.[14] According to Crossan, Mark's tradition actually included a colorful account of the resurrection of Jesus, but Mark suppressed it for theological reasons. Crossan thinks that Mark's theological perspective was that the resurrection of Jesus was to be followed by his imminent return in glory, with no appearances in between. So Mark excised the resurrection appearance from his tradition and retrojected it back into his Gospel as the transfiguration, where it serves as a foretaste of Jesus' Second Coming. Thus the simplicity of the empty-tomb story is misleading, actually being the result of theological reflection.

Crossan's hypothesis hinges crucially on the widely rejected idea that Mark implies no resurrection appearances, but only Jesus' appearance at his return (Mk 13:26; 14:62). Clearly Jesus' predictions of his glorious return do not preclude resurrection appearances after his predicted resurrection from the dead (Mk 8:31; 9:9, 31; 10:34). And in Mark 14:28 and 16:7 we are clearly to understand that such resurrection appearances will take place. Jesus' going before the disciples to Galilee and the restricted circle of the witnesses make it clear that Mark is not envisioning Jesus' Second Coming in Galilee (not to mention the problem that Mark knows that such did not occur). But if Mark contemplates resurrection appearances, then no reason remains for him not to preserve a resurrection narrative akin to the *Gospel of Peter*'s if he had it. As for the transfiguration, most critics regard this narrative as so firmly embedded in its context that it is not plausibly thought of as a retrojected resurrection narrative. In any case, Mark 16:1-8 lacks any theological reflection on Jesus' glorious return, as well as other theological motifs, like his descent into hell, victory over his enemies and so forth. This bespeaks its primitiveness.

5. *The discovery of the empty tomb by women is highly probable.* Given

the low status of women in Jewish society and their lack of qualification to serve as legal witnesses, the most plausible explanation, in light of the Gospels' conviction that the disciples were in Jerusalem over the weekend, why women and not the male disciples were made discoverers of the empty tomb is that the women were in fact the ones who made this discovery. This conclusion receives confirmation from the fact that there seems to be no reason why the later Christian church should wish to humiliate its leaders by portraying them as cowards hiding in Jerusalem while the women boldly carry out their last devotions to Jesus' body, unless this were in fact the truth. Their motive of anointing the body by pouring oils over it is entirely plausible in light of contemporary custom; indeed, its apparent conflict with Mark 14:8 makes it unlikely that the Gospel writer invented this intention. Furthermore, the listing of the women's names weighs against unhistorical legend at the story's core, for these persons were known in the early Christian fellowship and so could not be easily associated with a false account.

Oberlinner objects to this consideration because the women are not being used as witnesses to the empty tomb but merely to relay the angel's message to the disciples. Since the women were at the crucifixion, they are the most obvious candidates for the job.[15] But why, we may ask, have the message relayed at all? Why is it not given directly to the disciples? Why not have the male disciples at the cross as well? The careful recounting of the women's presence at the cross, then at the burial, then at the empty tomb shows that their role as historical witnesses of those events is being recalled.

Vögtle and Pesch, on the other hand, object that this consideration presupposes the accuracy of the burial story. The fact that the male disciples do not discover the empty tomb is just one more proof that the tomb was not found empty![16] But I fail to see how the narrative's failure to cast male disciples in the role of discoverers of the empty tomb presupposes the credibility of the burial account (itself a pretty safe presupposition in any case). On the objectors' view, the empty tomb story is a legend and therefore does not entail that the burial account is accurate. Suppose, then, that Jesus was buried in the common plot for criminals. Why do we have a legend arising about women discovering his empty tomb rather than one describing the male disciples making this discovery? Vögtle and Pesch offer nothing to deal with this anomaly. The most plausible explanation of the women's role is surely that they were in fact the ones who found Jesus' tomb empty.

6. *The earliest Jewish polemic presupposes the empty tomb.* From information incidentally furnished by Matthew (28:15), we know that Jewish opponents of the Christian Way did not deny that Jesus' tomb was empty. Instead they charged that the disciples had stolen Jesus' body. From here the controversy over the guard at the tomb sprang up. Notice the response of the earliest Jewish polemic to the disciples' proclamation "He has been raised from the dead" (Mt 27:64). Did the Jewish antagonists respond with "His body is still in the tomb in the garden," or "Jesus was thrown into the criminals' graveyard and eaten by dogs"? No. They responded, "His disciples came by night and stole him away" (Mt 28:11-14). The earliest Jewish polemic was an attempt to explain away the empty tomb. The fact that the Jewish polemic never denied that Jesus' tomb was empty, but only tried to explain it away, is persuasive evidence that the tomb was in fact empty.

Peter Carnley attempts to turn back the force of this consideration by claiming that the Jewish polemic presupposes only that the location of the tomb was lost or forgotten.[17] What Carnley fails to appreciate is that the allegation of body snatching made by the polemic actually *implies* (not merely *fails to deny*) the empty tomb. The polemic did not assert, as Carnley claims, that "the emptiness of a grave . . . would not prove anything more than that the body had been stolen." Rather, it asserted that the body had been stolen, which implies the factuality of the empty tomb.

Fischer objects that because the Jewish polemic occurred after A.D. 70, it was impossible for anyone to check on the truth of the guard story or the empty-tomb report. Matthew's account shows only that the Jews knew the *story* of the empty tomb.[18] But Fischer fails to reckon with the fact that there is an obvious tradition history behind the debate into which Matthew enters and with the fact that pre-Matthean traditions are evident in the story itself.[19] And in any case, even on Fischer's hypothesis it remains inexplicable why Jews in the period after A.D. 70, first encountering the legend of the empty tomb, would respond, not by denouncing the fiction but by agreeing with it and trying to explain it away!

Taken together, these six considerations furnish good evidence that the tomb of Jesus was actually found empty by a small group of his women followers. As a plain historical fact this seems to be amply attested. As D. H. Van Daalen has remarked, it is extremely difficult to object to the fact of the empty tomb on historical grounds; most objectors do so on the basis of theological or philosophical considerations.[20] But these cannot, of course, change empirical facts. And interestingly, New Testament scholars increasingly recognize this. According to Jacob Kremer, "By far, most exegetes hold firmly . . . to the reliability of the biblical statements about the empty tomb," and he lists twenty-eight prominent scholars in support.[21]

Explaining the Empty Tomb

If the tomb of Jesus was found empty, the question becomes, How does one most plausibly explain this fact? Although the empty tomb may have proved at first ambiguous and puzzling to the disciples, today we know that most alternative explanations for the empty tomb are simply incredible (for example, the disciples' stealing the body, Jesus' not being dead or the women's going to the wrong tomb). The old rationalistic explanations have thoroughly failed to provide plausible historical explanations that fit the facts without bruising them.[22] Naturalistic explanations are not plausible with respect to our background information (for example, medical knowledge of the pathology of crucifixion makes the apparent death theory intrinsically improbable). Nor do they render probable the specific evidence (for example, the disciples' evident sincerity and willingness to be martyred for their faith is quite improbable on the assumption of the conspiracy theory).

To my knowledge, the only naturalistic explanation of the empty tomb that deserves any consideration is the suggestion that some third party stole the body.[23] The famous Nazareth inscription seems to imply that tomb robbery was a widespread problem in first-century Palestine. It could be that some unknown person or persons broke into the tomb and absconded with the body. There is no positive evidence for this hypothesis, so to that extent it is a mere assertion. Moreover, there are positive considerations against it.

First, we know of no third party with a motive for stealing the body. Robbers had no reason to break into the tomb, since nothing of value was interred with the body, nor would they have carted away the dead man's body. Enemies or persons bitterly disappointed in Jesus might conceivably desecrate the grave, but again, it would be pointless to carry off the corpse and hide it.

Second, apparently no one but Joseph, those with him and the women initially knew exactly where the tomb was. Joseph probably surprised his fellow Sanhedrists by placing the body in his own tomb instead of having it buried in the criminals' graveyard. Hence it is difficult to see how some third party could have taken the body, not having been present at the burial.

Third, since the women probably found the tomb empty on Sunday morning,[24] the would-be thieves must have hatched their conspiracy, stolen the body and disposed of it sometime between Friday night and Sunday morning. Given the tumultuous confusion at Jesus' public trial and execution—and during Passover time no less—this sort of derring-do strains credulity.

Fourth, the presence of the grave clothes in the tomb, which so struck John (Jn 20:6-7), seems to preclude theft of the body. The fact that the grave clothes were left in the tomb is vouched for by the witness of the Beloved Disciple and by the tradition embodied in Luke 24:12.[25]

Fifth, conspiracies of the suggested type tend to come to light eventually, either through discovery or disclosure or at least rumor. It is hard to believe that when the disciples began to preach that Jesus had been raised from the dead, the malefactors could have kept their secret long. Jewish authorities would certainly have been glad to have any such information. But the tradition contains no trace of this.

Finally, perhaps the most serious objection to this hypothesis is that it seeks to explain only half of the evidence (namely, the empty tomb) and completely ignores the other half (that is, the appearances). A second hypothesis to explain the appearances must be added. But if explanatory scope is a criterion for preferring one hypothesis to another, then the resurrection as an overarching explanation for empty tomb and appearances is to be preferred to separate hypotheses for the same facts.

So it seems that no plausible naturalistic explanation is yet available for the fact of the empty tomb. On the hypothesis of an actual resurrection, however, the evidence is just as we might expect it to be. Before we can infer that the resurrection of Jesus is therefore the best explanation of the evidence, we need to ask whether it, like traditional naturalistic explanations, is not grossly implausible with respect to our background information. It might be said that the resurrection itself is so intrinsically improbable that it is even *more* implausible than some admittedly implausible naturalistic explanation and so is not to be preferred.

But such an objection simply takes us back to the traditional problem of miracles. The plausibility of miracles has been addressed thoroughly, and from several angles, in the second and third sections of this volume. In light of these discussions, the hypothesis that God raised Jesus from the dead cannot be said to be intrinsically implausible.

If the resurrection is no more implausible relative to our background knowledge than are naturalistic hypotheses, and if the resurrection renders more probable the specific evidence concerning the empty tomb than do naturalistic hypotheses, then the resurrection of Jesus is to be preferred as the best explanation. The case of the empty tomb of Jesus should not, however, be considered in isolation from other relevant evidence concerning the resurrection of Jesus, such as his postmortem appearances. We must seek the best explanation not only for the empty tomb but also for the postresurrection appearances. Therefore, a consideration of the historical credibility of the appearance traditions must be the next order of business.

SIXTEEN

THE RESURRECTION APPEARANCES OF JESUS

GARY R. HABERMAS

THIS CHAPTER FOCUSES ON A SINGLE, CRUCIAL ASPECT OF THE NEW Testament report concerning the life of Jesus. We will concentrate on some of the grounds for the assertion that after his death Jesus appeared alive to his followers.

Critical studies have sometimes attempted to cover too much territory when dealing with the topic of Jesus' resurrection. However, rather than highlight what many contemporary scholars think *cannot* be known about the New Testament testimony, I want to concentrate on the evidence that we *do* have. It is my contention that, arguing from an approach that emphasizes the minimal, best-established facts surrounding the appearances, we still have ample evidence to determine what really happened after Jesus' death.

Probably a majority of contemporary critical scholars are impressed by the evidence that first-century Christians genuinely believed they had seen Jesus after his crucifixion. For example, after introducing the subject of Jesus' resurrection, Reginald Fuller boldly asserts, "That within a few weeks after the crucifixion Jesus' disciples came to believe this is one of the indisputable facts of history."[1] But what caused the disciples to believe? From earliest times it was claimed that Jesus appeared to his followers. Fuller concludes, "That the *experiences* did occur, even if they are explained in purely natural terms, is a fact upon which both believer and unbeliever may agree."[2] In other words, while Fuller remains skeptical about many facets of the New Testament reports, he allows that the early followers of Jesus had some sort of actual experiences that they took to be grounds for their belief in Jesus' resurrection. James D. G. Dunn is even more forceful. He thinks that "it is almost impossible to dispute" that the first Christians had "visionary experiences" that cannot be explained as less than the disciples' belief that they had experienced actual appearances of the risen Jesus.[3]

What is the basis for these comments? Why have the majority of contemporary critical scholars taken so seriously the New Testament assertion that Jesus' followers claimed to have seen him alive after his death by crucifixion? Can these experiences be better explained by some naturalistic means? In this chapter I will begin by describing some background material. Then I will turn directly to a subject that is too seldom highlighted—the evidential basis for believing that Jesus actually appeared to his followers after his death. I propose a consideration of two main topics: the evidence that the earliest disciples' experiences were visual in nature, and the feasibility of a naturalistic explanation for these experiences. In keeping with the major emphasis in contemporary thought, the testimony of the apostle Paul will be our chief source, but we will also note the corroboration of his testimony at every point by non-Pauline material.

The Earliest Christian Report: Some Background

It is not the purpose of this chapter to present in detail all of the relevant general background evidence for the conclusions reached here. Much of this material is available in specialized resurrection studies and elsewhere. I have set forth more fully my own conclusions on these matters in other publications,[4] and numerous critical studies are in general agreement with me concerning the main outline of the relevant data.[5] The material presented more concisely in this section is well evidenced, which largely accounts for its acceptance across a wide theological spectrum. Further, while the framework sketched here is certainly important, the repudiation of it would by no means entail that the main thesis of this chapter is specious, since there is more than one way to support that thesis. But space limitations alone require that we bypass the details of important background material in order to concentrate on the topic set for this chapter.

I begin by stating a handful of important conclusions reached by a majority of researchers. This is not meant to suggest that the conclusions of this chapter are based merely on the fact of this contemporary consensus. Many of the sources cited here provide an indication of the necessary argumentation for those who are interested.

1. There is little doubt, even in critical circles, that the apostle Paul is the author of the book of 1 Corinthians. Rarely is this conclusion questioned.[6]

2. For at least a few decades, the focus of critical attention in relation to Jesus' resurrection appearances has been the text in 1 Corinthians 15:3ff. Virtually all scholars agree that in this text Paul recorded an ancient tradition(s) about the origins of the Christian gospel. Numerous evidences indicate that this report is much earlier than the date of the book in which it appears.[7]

3. The vast majority of critical scholars concur on an extremely early origin for this report.[8] Most frequently, it is declared that Paul received the formula between two and eight years after the crucifixion, around A.D. 32-38.[9]

4. Researchers usually conclude that Paul received this material shortly after his conversion during his stay in Jerusalem with Peter and James (Gal 1:18-19), who are both included in Paul's list of individuals to whom Jesus appeared (1 Cor 15:5, 7).[10]

These preliminary conclusions are exceptionally important for our task in this chapter: to examine the basis for Jesus' postdeath appearances to his followers. In the pre-Pauline formula of 1 Corinthians 15:3ff. alone we have an extraordinarily early tradition, arising within a very short time after the events themselves, reported by an apostle, who could very well have received it from other apostles who followed Jesus during his earthly ministry. Here, as I hope to show, is a significant pointer to the nature of those early experiences.

Contemporary scholars recognize the importance of 1 Corinthians 15:3ff. Historian Hans von Campenhausen writes of this text, "This account meets all the demands of historical reliability that could possibly be made of such a text."[11] A. M. Hunter repeats this assessment.[12] After discussing this ancient tradition, C. H. Dodd emphatically declares, "The date, therefore, at which Paul received the fundamentals of the Gospel cannot well be later than some seven years after the death of Jesus Christ. It may be earlier."[13]

Corroboration of Paul's Testimony

As already mentioned above, the majority of critical scholars (exemplified by Fuller and Dunn) rarely dispute the statement that the earliest Christians thought that Jesus had appeared to them after his death and resurrection. It is sometimes even said that this fact is as well established as any recorded in the New Testament. What data support such a conviction? We will begin by looking primarily at Paul's teachings, providing four arguments in favor of the early apostolic belief that Jesus appeared to his followers. Even for those who doubt portions of the background data, there is still an excellent foundation for the authoritative nature of Paul's report. At each of these points we will also see that Paul's testimony is corroborated by non-Pauline material. (See table 1 for all nine points, including four Pauline arguments and five lines of argument from non-Pauline sources corroborating Paul's testimony.)

1. Paul explains that he had received material that he, in turn, passed on to others, including a list of eyewitness appearances of Jesus to his disciples (1 Cor 15:3-7). If Paul received this data from Peter and James, as suggested above, this tradition is further corroborated by apostolic authority.

Another indication of this is provided by Paul's testimony in Galatians 1:18-20. Describing his personal and lengthy visit with Peter in Jerusalem shortly after his conversion, Paul uses the term *historeō*, most likely indicating an investigative inquiry. William Farmer argues that the word in this context signifies that Paul cross-examined Peter.[14] During this visit Paul also visited James (Gal 1:19). In any case, the immediate context suggests that the chief topic of conversation concerned the nature of the gospel (Gal 1:11-16), which included reference to Jesus' resurrection (1 Cor 15:1-4). As Dodd declares, a maximum of "seven years after the crucifixion" Paul "stayed with Peter for a fortnight, and we may presume they did not spend all the time talking about the weather."[15]

We have additional confirmation of a lesser contention. There are several indications that the material in 1 Corinthians 15:3ff. does not originate with Paul. Jewish New Testament scholar Pinchas Lapide lists eight linguistic considerations suggestive of non-Pauline origin, agreeing with the virtually unanimous opinion of critical scholarship.[16]

Our conclusions, then, do not rest exclusively on knowing the actual date and circumstances under which Paul received this tradition. That Paul learned it very early is assured, since the material minimally predates not only the writing of 1 Corinthians (about A.D. 55-57), but Paul's

initial trip to Corinth (about A.D. 51) when he first preached the facts of
the gospel (15:1-3) only about twenty years after Jesus' death. Further,
at the very least this report comes from a source that Paul considered to
be authoritative. Otherwise, as an apostle himself, it would be more
difficult to explain not only why Paul accepted it, but why he made it his
central proclamation.[17]

Paul's Testimony	Non-Pauline Corroboration
1. Paul claimed that he received this creedal material from others (1 Cor 15:3), probably from Peter and James in Jerusalem, c. A.D. 33 to 38 (Gal 1:18-20; especially 1:18: *historeō*).	1. *Literary Evidence from 1 Cor 15:3 ff.* (1) Technical terms *delivered* and *received* (2) Parallelism and stylized account (3) Proper names Cephas and James (4) Non-Pauline terms (5) Triple "and that" *(hoti)* clauses (6) Two references to Scripture being fulfilled (7) Possibly Aramaic original text ("Cephas," etc.)
2. Paul is himself an eyewitness to a resurrection appearance of Jesus (1 Cor 15:8; cf. 1 Cor 9:1; Gal 1:16).	2. *Three Accounts of the Appearance to Paul in Acts:* 9:1-9 22:1-11 26:9-19
3. Paul's gospel message was "checked out" by the Jerusalem apostles (Gal 2:1-10) and specifically approved (vv. 6-10).	3. *The Jerusalem Council* in Acts 15:1-31, whether the same or a different occasion from Gal 2:1-10, extends apostolic approval to Paul's gospel message.

4. Paul said the apostles were preaching the same message he was concerning the resurrection appearances of Jesus (1 Cor 15:11; cf. vv. 12, 14, 15).	4. *Corroborated by the Kerygmatic Creeds in Acts:*
	 1:21-22* 5:29-32*
	 2:22-36* 10:39-43*
	 3:13-16* 13:28-41*
	 4:8-10
	
	 * disciples are groups of witnesses
	 witnesses implied:
	                          10:41-41; 13:31
	
	 5. *Corroborated by Gospel Appearance Accounts:*
	     Mt 28
	     Lk 24
	     Jn 20—21

Table 1. Early Testimony to Jesus' Resurrection Appearances

Therefore, if critical scholars are correct that Paul received the creedal material in 1 Corinthians 15:3ff. from Peter and James in Jerusalem in the early 30s A.D., then we have strong evidence that the reported appearances of the risen Jesus came from the original apostles. But even if this scenario is rejected, we still know that the material predates Paul's initial trip to Corinth in A.D. 51, that it comes from a source that he considered to be authoritative, and that it was Paul's central proclamation. In short, this tradition is very early and appears to be a reliable indicator that certain witnesses claimed that Jesus appeared to them after his death.

2. Strictly speaking, Paul did not even have to rely on the testimony of others, including the original apostles. He also believed himself to be an eyewitness to an appearance of the resurrected Lord, as he notes at the end of the formula (1 Cor 15:8; cf. 9:1).

Additional corroboration of Jesus' appearance to Paul is contained in the three accounts of this event recorded in Acts (9:1-9; 22:1-11; 26:9-19). Although it cannot be pursued here, this event is strongly evidenced by a number of factors.[18]

3. Fourteen years following Paul's two weeks in Jerusalem with Peter, he returned to the city with the express goal of confirming the nature of the gospel he was preaching. While meeting with the apostolic leadership there (Peter, John and James the brother of Jesus), Paul was told that the content of his teaching was accurate (Gal 2:1-10).

According to Acts 15:1-35, a similar discussion took place about the nature of Paul's gospel proclamation. Once again Peter and James the brother of Jesus were both involved; and once again the apostolic verdict was that Paul's gospel preaching was accurate (vv. 7-21). Whether this is the same meeting described in Galatians 2 is debatable, but it makes little difference for our purposes. If it was the same meeting, then we have additional confirmation of Paul's account of that meeting. If these are different events, then we have two very similar situations that confirm the main point. The accuracy of Paul's gospel message was corroborated by the apostolic community.

4. After recounting the creed and listing key witnesses to the appearances of Jesus, Paul declared that all the other apostles were currently preaching the same message concerning Jesus' appearances (1 Cor 15:11-15). In other words, we have it on Paul's authority that these resurrection appearances were also being proclaimed by the original apostles.

Additional non-Pauline confirmation of this very point comes from more than one source. Early creedal material contained in the beginning of Acts enjoys strong textual support. A number of critical scholars note several features indicating that these passages accurately represent the early Christian message. While some disagree, Dodd discerns "a large element of Semitism" and "a high degree of probability" for an Aramaic original, plus an absence of negative signs denoting a later stratum.[19] Additionally, the messages are succinct and theologically unadorned, thereby evincing what many scholars think is an earlier layer of proclamation. These texts testify to several important details concerning Jesus' resurrection, including group appearances.[20] In almost every instance, a chief theme is that the disciples were "witnesses" to these sightings.[21]

Another indicator of the appearances to the original apostles is the Gospel accounts. Although these cannot be defended here, there are good reasons to trust these texts.[22] Even from a critical viewpoint, it can be shown that several of the appearance narratives report early tradition, as Dodd argues after a careful, analytical study. He contends that the appearance narratives in Matthew 28:8-10, 16-20 and John 20:19-21, and, to a lesser extent, Luke 24:36-49, are based on early material. The remaining Gospel accounts of Jesus' resurrection appearances are lacking in typical mythical tendencies and likewise merit careful consideration.[23]

Here we have nine indications that the apostles testified that Jesus appeared to them after his resurrection from the dead.[24] Our information comes from apostles (or individuals close to them) who were authoritative eyewitnesses. A few critics have resisted even this guarded conclusion. Donald Viney charges that there is no eyewitness testimony for Jesus' appearances except Paul's and that Paul nowhere states that what he saw was physical in nature.[25] But Viney has several hurdles to overcome.

On one level, if any of the following scenarios obtain, we would have additional eyewitness material beyond Paul: (1) if Paul received the creedal material in its present form from Peter, James or any other apostle (on this point alone, asserts Lapide, the data is strong enough that it "may be considered as a statement of eyewitnesses"[26]); (2) if the creedal passages of Acts accurately represent apostolic preaching of the gospel facts; and (3) if any of the individual appearance pericopes in the four Gospels came from eyewitnesses, especially if the particular book itself was actually written by an apostle or was significantly influenced by one.

An additional point should also be raised here. Regardless of whether the New Testament writings are authored by eyewitnesses, R. T. France argues that such an approach is actually unnecessary. Rather, we need to judge the texts by the same criteria as those used in ancient historiography, where researchers are more interested in having early sources that are supported by strong tradition.[27] As we have seen, this is certainly the case with the data for Jesus' resurrection appearances, such as we find in 1 Corinthians 15:3ff. a text that historian Hans von Campenhausen states "meets all the demands of historical reliability that could possibly be made."[28]

Further, Viney admits that we do have Paul's eyewitness report but downplays Paul's testimony because we do not have the apostle's description of any physical appearance. Later we will consider briefly the form of Jesus' appearances, but it must be emphasized here that establishing that Jesus appeared in a *physical form* is secondary to showing that he actually appeared in *some form*. So Viney must still account for Paul's own eyewitness testimony, which is a challenge in itself.

Finally, though the number of eyewitness descriptions is important, this is secondary to the truthfulness of the reports. Therefore, Viney would have to show not only that we lack eyewitness testimony (which he does not even deny), but that absolutely none of the nine evidences produced in this section is capable of providing any probable testimony for the resurrection appearances. In brief, he must disqualify all nine evidences in order to show that there are no credible historical arguments.

Michael Martin objects that we do not know how Paul received his information, that it comes too many years later, and that we have no reason to think that he or any other witness is trustworthy.[29] But I have already noted several strong reasons to think that Paul received his data from credible sources. At the least, the creedal material is early, is of central importance, and is presented on Paul's authority, a witness whose authenticity Martin acknowledges. That we do not, perhaps, know everything on the subject is no reason to denigrate what we do know. Martin is mistaken about our having insufficient details at this point. What we know must still be explained.

I have also pointed out that it is not even necessary to know the precise time and circumstances of this creedal information in order to make our case. Even if virtually all scholars who address this issue are mistaken, the date of Paul's trip to Corinth is only about twenty years after Jesus' death. This is early enough for the recall of important experiences, especially those as crucial as this. Paul's early recollection qualifies as credible evidence. In this regard, Martin is even more clearly incorrect.

Like Viney, Martin can only disregard the trustworthiness of the appearance testimony if he can disallow each of the above nine arguments for these events, since they explicitly deal with the element of reliability. To repeat, the primary issue is whether we have credible material, for whatever reasons. While critics often doubt the Gospel accounts, even the remainder of the material is very difficult to disregard. What are the chances that it is incorrect at every point? But while the individual evidences are strong, the cumulative force is still greater. This point is even more compelling because Martin also admits that Paul was an eyewitness to a postresurrection appearance, that he was sure that Jesus was risen, and that the early Christians also proclaimed this event.[30]

To conclude this section, four of the arguments for Jesus' resurrection appearances come from Paul: his early reception of the creedal account, the appearance to Paul himself, his testimony that his message was given the stamp of approval by other apostles, and his own confirmation of their appearance reports. In short, the Pauline data are strong. Seemingly few, if any, scholars hold that Paul was totally mistaken on all four counts. As Dodd summarizes, "Thus Paul's preaching represents a special stream of Christian tradition which was derived from the main stream at a point very near to its source." As a result, "Anyone who should maintain that the primitive Christian Gospel was fundamentally different from that which we have found in Paul must bear the burden of proof."[31]

Corroboration for each of these four Pauline arguments comes from the detailed literary evidence that 1 Corinthians 15:3ff. is pre-Pauline, the three Acts accounts of Paul's conversion, the apostolic confirmation of Paul's gospel message in Acts 15, and the primitive texts in Acts. In addition, we have the Gospel accounts, taken either as a whole or in the individual appearance narratives. Concerning the Acts creeds alone, Dodd concludes that we have the essential apostolic preaching of the gospel from the early Jerusalem church, including their attestation to Jesus' resurrection appearances.[32]

A Naturalistic Solution?
How can these nine assorted strands of information best be combined and explained? It is perhaps no wonder that most critical scholars think that the disciples' experiences were visual in nature. This is clearly what was claimed, and no other conclusion satisfies all of the data. Dunn

comments, "It is almost impossible to dispute that at the historical roots of Christianity lie some visionary experiences of the first Christians, who understood them as appearances of Jesus, raised by God from the dead."[33] At the very least, the apostles believed that they had seen the risen Jesus. Even Rudolf Bultmann asserted that historical criticism can confirm "the fact that the first disciples came to believe in the resurrection," with this faith being expressed in the form of appearances of the risen Lord.[34] To repeat Fuller's earlier comment: "That Jesus' disciples came to believe this is one of the indisputable facts of history . . . a fact upon which both believer and unbeliever may agree."[35]

It is not difficult to recognize widespread agreement on these points. Historian Michael Grant thinks that an examination can actually prove that the earliest witnesses were convinced that they had seen the risen Jesus.[36] As Carl Braaten contends, even skeptics conclude that the earliest believers thought the Easter appearances were real events in space and time.[37] Wolfhart Pannenberg concurs: "Few scholars, even few rather critical scholars, doubt that there had been visionary experiences."[38]

Subjective visions. So the next question is, Can naturalistic solutions adequately account for all the facts? Because of the strength of the appearance data, we will not here entertain any such proposal unless it is specifically directed at least to the disciples' belief that they had seen the risen Jesus. Actually, the majority of hypotheses are not directly concerned with this aspect.[39] The thesis that is most clearly aimed at providing a naturalistic explanation for the disciples' conviction that they had seen the risen Jesus is the hallucination (or subjective vision) theory. After conceding the disciples' belief in Jesus' resurrection and its expression in terms of appearances, Bultmann observed that some might explain these as subjective visions. Yet he concluded that historical interest in the discovery of a cause is misplaced.[40]

But can hallucinations (or other subjective phenomena) adequately explain the facts? Even a brief critique is sufficient to reveal some of the significant problems that have signaled the failure of these attempts. Hallucinations are private events.[41] However, I have already mentioned Jesus' appearances to groups of people.[42] Further, while a hallucination generally is rooted in one's own hopeful expectations, the disciples despaired after the death of Jesus and did not expect him to rise; they had to be convinced that he was raised. Another major problem for this suggestion is that Jesus showed himself to a variety of persons, both individually and in g oups, at several times, places, and in different circumstances. To think that all of those persons were automatically candidates for hallucinatory experiences multiplies the improbable, bordering on naiveté.[43]

Additionally, it is very unlikely that hallucinations could inspire the radical personal transformation of the disciples, even to the point of being willing to die for their faith. And what about the family skeptic, James the brother of Jesus, and Paul, the persecutor of Christians? Did these two unbelievers long to envision the risen Jesus? Nor do hallucinations explain the empty tomb, so some other theory is needed here.[44] Not surprisingly, numerous critical scholars of varied theological perspectives have voiced their displeasure with these hypotheses of subjective influence.[45] Pannenberg concludes that "these explanations have failed to date."[46]

Comparatively few scholars today pursue the naturalistic theories that were so prevalent a century ago. This point is emphasized, not to deny that one might be revived from time to time, but only to show that it is generally conceded that the known facts are sufficient to refute these alternative views. Dunn explains that "alternative explanations of the data fail to provide a more satisfactory explanation."[47] In fact, these attempts are frequently even castigated by scholars. Raymond Brown proclaims that "the criticism of today does not follow the paths taken by the criticism of the past. No longer respectable are the crude theories of fraud and error popular in the last century."[48]

Objective visions. Today critical scholars most often allow that Jesus actually appeared, but they propose that this appearance occurred in some nonphysical fashion. This view should be very carefully distinguished, however, from the hypotheses of subjective influence discussed in the previous section, for here Jesus is still thought to have been literally revealed in some real sense, though the exact form of this manifestation is often unspecified. The appearances are frequently said (at a minimum) to have included an experience of light phenomena plus an impartation of meaning and mission, where Jesus was understood to be translated to an eternal, eschatological realm.[49]

This view is not another naturalistic alternative, but an appeal beyond nature, usually in terms of the eternal or eschatological realm breaking into time. For example, Hans Grass concludes that the apostles actually saw Jesus. The quite literal (though noncorporeal) resurrection appearances were of divine origin, imparting the truth of the living Lord.[50] Interestingly, a major reason why scholars hold that these visions are objective is precisely because of the untenability of the hallucination hypothesis.[51]

Although we cannot critique the objective-vision view here in all the detail it deserves, even the limited material presented so far argues against it. For instance, it is difficult to think that Paul has a noncorporeal view in mind when he relates Jesus' appearance to the five hundred at one time (1 Cor 15:6), much less to other groups (15:5, 7). Further, one of the Acts creeds (10:35-43), which Dodd says makes the best case for an Aramaic original,[52] clearly discusses a group appearance where Jesus ate with his disciples. This is an unlikely practice for a disembodied vision! Moreover, the type of evidence we find in the Gospels, including individual, well-evidenced pericopes, strongly supports the bodily nature of Jesus' appearances.[53]

A more forceful argument for the literal physical resurrection and in-the-flesh appearances is that Paul's anthropology strongly favors a corporeal resurrection body. After an intricate and authoritative treatment of the subject, Robert Gundry has concluded that "the raising of Jesus from the dead was a raising of his physical body."[54] His own study of the same subject brought John A. T. Robinson to a similar conclusion concerning Jesus' resurrection body:

> All the appearances, in fact, depict the same phenomenon, of a body identical yet changed, transcending the limitations of the flesh yet capable of manifesting itself within the order of the flesh. We may describe this as a "spiritual" (1 Cor. 15:44) or "glorified" (cf. 1 Cor. 15:43; Phil. 3:21) body . . . so long as we do not import into these phrases any opposition to the physical as such.[55]

Finally, the empty tomb presents special problems for the noncorporeality thesis. The most obvious conclusion is that the same body that died had also been raised and had appeared to the early believers.[56] (See chapter fifteen by William Lane Craig for more about the significance of the empty tomb.) Although it is not possible to discuss further the exact nature of Jesus' resurrection body, enough has already been said to yield some insight into the matter. The same texts that argue for the appearances also indicate a bodily resurrection. But the chief purpose of this chapter has been to argue for the reality of Jesus' resurrection appearances as actual examples of New Testament miracles, rather than to characterize their exact nature.[57] As strange as it may seem, those who opt for objective visions agree that Jesus really did appear to his followers.

Accordingly, it is insufficient merely to speak in terms of popular slogans like "Something occurred to the disciples but we do not know what," or "Jesus lives on" only through his teachings. These and other related views fail to explain what happened to Jesus himself and are discredited by the historically ascertainable data. As Dunn reminds us:

> There is no justification for reducing the meaning of "the resurrection of Jesus" to something like "the continuing significance of Jesus" or "the disciples' realization that Jesus' message could not die." By "resurrection" they clearly meant that something had happened to Jesus himself. God had raised him, not merely reassured them. He was alive again.[58]

Most critical scholars think either that the resurrection can be accepted by faith as an actual occurrence or that some sort of appearances (abstract or bodily) must be postulated as the historical cause for the disciples' belief. While it is usually thought that Jesus actually appeared in some sense, the belief that Jesus rose in a physical body is a minority view.[59] Still, I have noted a few of the reasons one might have for holding that Jesus rose in a transformed but still physical body.

Conclusion

In the previous sections the focus has been, respectively, on the two complementary topics set forth at the outset. First, nine lines of historical argument (four Pauline and five non-Pauline) indicate that the earliest disciples actually had visual experiences that they concluded were appearances of the risen Jesus. At the very least, virtually all scholars have concluded from the data that this is their own testimony concerning what they believed had happened to them.

Second, the facts discredit naturalistic theories, which are inadequate explanations of the facts. Only hallucinations (or related theories of subjective influence) even directly address the multifaceted approach taken here.[60] Yet there are numerous roadblocks preventing this thesis from being a viable explanation of the apostles' experiences.

What happens when the apostles' visual experiences are juxtaposed with the failure of alternative accounts to explain the specific data?[61] Many resurrection studies concern cognate issues, distracting attention away from the central matters discussed in this chapter. But when we concentrate on just the two topics investigated here, we find that the disciples' testimony is best explained by their actually having witnessed appearances of the risen Jesus. No other explanation adequately accounts for all the facts.

This discussion has concentrated on the historical facts that can be verified by critical procedures.[62] The four arguments based on Paul's testimony are well supported by data and are rarely challenged by New Testament researchers. Moreover, of the five corroborative, non-Pauline considerations treated here, two are particularly impressive: the literary evidence for the resurrection creed in 1 Corinthians 15:3ff., and the creedal confessions from Acts. While the other non-Pauline contentions are not always as widely recognized, these six can even bear the weight of the argument and have yet to be discredited. The remaining three, however, must also be answered.

Critical scholars like to emphasize what we cannot know about the New Testament narratives. But it is illuminating to concentrate on what *can* be positively concluded from these sources. Questions concerning other portions of the New Testament should not be allowed to vitiate these conclusions.

It has been shown in this chapter that the disciples truly believed and taught that the risen Jesus appeared to them. Further, beyond our nine arguments, numerous additional evidences also indicate that there actually were such appearances. Examples of the latter have barely been mentioned in this chapter. They include the transformation of the earliest apostles, especially when they were willing to die specifically for the proclamation of the resurrection, the fact that this message was their central tenet and therefore subject to more intense scrutiny both by themselves and unbelievers, as well as the facts in favor of the empty tomb.[63] But on the other hand, naturalistic theories—such as the subjective-vision hypothesis—are discredited by the data.

The visual claims of the earliest eyewitnesses are therefore vindicated: the most likely explanation is that the same Jesus who had recently died had been raised from the dead and had actually appeared to his followers, both individually and in groups.[64] The data show that the disciples witnessed actual appearances of the risen Jesus, which they faithfully reported in a historically ascertainable fashion.

CONCLUSION

HAS GOD ACTED
IN HISTORY?

R. DOUGLAS GEIVETT
& GARY R. HABERMAS

HAS GOD ACTED IN HISTORY? THIS QUESTION HAS NO PEERS. THE very thought that God has personally and perceptibly entered into human history should excite the soul. Serious reflection about the possible reality of miracles should not be left to scholars. If there is evidence that God does act as an agent among men and women, then that evidence needs to be weighed by all who care about the significance of their own lives. If God has acted in human history, particularly in the Incarnation, earthly life and resurrection of Jesus Christ, then human beings clearly are a focus of God's interest and concern.

Of course, it should interest the general public to know that there are sober-minded scholars today who affirm the credibility of miracles. To the outsider, the academy can appear to be a monolith of naturalistic prejudice against all things spiritual. The truth is, theistic realism is thriving in the academy, particularly among philosophers. In this book we have assembled a group of intellectual representatives of the Christian tradition to make the case for miracles. Many others consider it reasonable to believe that miracles have happened.

In the mid-twentieth century, Ernst Troeltsch mocked belief in miracles and spoke of "the clumsy miracle apologetic."[1] While it is true that some appeals to miracles in defense of particular religious beliefs have been inelegant, misguided and grossly exaggerated, the hypothesis that God has acted in history is a reasonable explanation for certain historically well-attested events. But we need to consider what it means to say that belief in miracles is reasonable for our generation.

First, the evidence must indeed be strong before it can be reasonable to believe in miracles. As rational human beings, we naturally regard miracle claims with suspicion. After all, we understand what a miracle is by contrasting it with the regularities of our experience. There is a sense in which miracles are inherently improbable: they are, in the nature of the case, *infrequent.* Thus, the probability that several centuries ago a dead man returned to life is very low, given our regular experience of dead people remaining in that unfortunate condition. If it is reasonable to believe that Jesus was raised from the dead, then the evidence must be great enough to overcome the prima facie probability that he was not raised.

Second, our awareness of the improbability of miracles—understood as infrequent by definition—does not settle the question of whether it is reasonable to believe in miracles. For other circumstances could lead us to revise our initial assessment of the probability of miracles based on observed regularities. There may be strong evidence that God exists, that God is interested in providing a remedy for the human condition, that the accurate identification of God's remedy requires a sign of its divine sponsorship. In addition, there may be much evidence that the grave of one man—who announced the arrival of God's solution to the human condition—was somehow emptied of its corpse, and that appearances of the same man alive again were widely reported for a period of time by credible witnesses who knew him well. These conditions alter the probabilities considerably. The question is, do these conditions make it likely that the highly unusual event of a literal resurrection from the dead actually happened?

Third, one can responsibly believe in miracles without having *proof* that miracles have happened. The demand for proof as a condition for believing is unrealistically and unnecessarily high. Much of what we believe results from thinking about what makes the most sense in light of all the evidence at our disposal. That is a responsible way to believe. Of course, we may also change our minds when we encounter new evidence or when we come to see different relationships among the evidential data. One need not postpone belief in miracles if one has reason to believe that one has investigated an appropriate range of evidence for and against miracles. If one's evidence for miracles is much greater than one's evidence against miracles, then it is intellectually responsible for one to believe that miracles have happened.

Fourth, those who reflect on these matters must exercise personal responsibility in believing. One person cannot believe for another. But one person can help another person toward belief by presenting evidence. It is true that what is reasonable for one person to believe may not be reasonable for another person to believe. It may even be reasonable for person A to believe that person B is unreasonable for believing in miracles at the same time that it is actually reasonable for B to believe in miracles. And it may be reasonable for person A to deny miracles and yet believe that person B is reasonable in affirming miracles.

When strenuous arguments are made for and against the credibility of miracles, those watching the intellectual ping-pong match from the sidelines may well be confused. It is tempting to withhold belief when there are well-informed and intelligent people on both sides of the question. But we should withhold belief only if that is the most reasonable attitude to adopt. Remaining undecided may be most convenient, but that does not make it most reasonable.

There is a better response. When one encounters a question about which intelligent people disagree, one should not withdraw from the challenge of personal decision. Rather, one should consider what makes the most sense on the basis of one's own effort to collect, understand and weigh the evidence. Anyone who genuinely desires to believe what is true about miracles will probably increase the chances of doing that by seeking to believe what is most rational. We hope this book will assist in that effort.

Fifth, those who have not reflected on the evidence for miracles have no business insisting that it is unreasonable to believe in miracles. It is possible to cling to the denial of miracles as an article of faith without rational justification. Why would anyone do that? The belief that miracles have never happened and never will, that God does not exist, or that if God exists God is indifferent about human affairs may be a source of comfort to some. The picture of "an unencumbered will confronting an unmysterious world" is an interpretation of the human situation that has some appeal.[2] Certainly, as long as we entertain the possibility that there is a God with whom we have to do, that this God may have an interest in how we organize our lives, that God has taken the initiative to draw us to himself, and that God awaits our response—as long as these remain possibilities for us—we will be haunted with misgivings about the control we have over our own lives, about the point of our existence, and about our future destiny.

Sixth, on the other hand, some who have investigated the evidence for miracles have nevertheless denied the reality of miracles (some have denied the rationality of belief in miracles as well) and have presented objections to the case for miracles. Anyone who believes in miracles and desires to be intellectually responsible must address these objections openly and honestly. In an effort to acquaint our readers with recurring arguments against miracles, we have included essays by David Hume and Antony Flew. The sorts of arguments advanced by Hume, Flew and other critics of miracles are carefully examined by other contributors to this volume.[3]

Seventh, in this particular context, where we are called upon to make reasonable decisions about what to believe about miracles, the stakes are high. The apostle Paul wrote that if we believe in the resurrection of Jesus and he is not raised, we are of all people most miserable (see 1 Cor 15:13-19). But what misery awaits those who will not believe if it is both true and reasonable to believe? There are *practical* dimensions to the problem of rational belief about miracles. For one thing, we should be motivated to investigate thoroughly the evidence for miracles. Moreover, we should not set inordinately high standards for reasonable belief in miracles. Finally, if we consider the evidence for miracles to be strong, but we still find it hard to believe, we should meditate on the value of believing in miracles for the sake of eventually coming to believe. William James observed that "in the metaphysical and religious sphere, articulate reasons are cogent for us only when our inarticulate feelings of reality have already been impressed in favor of the same conclusion."[4]

So far we have considered our intellectual responsibilities relative to the evidence that God has acted in history. But the value of miracles is not limited to their role in confirming religious truths. If we seriously believe that God is a personal agent who acts in human history, we must allow that God may have other purposes for producing miracles. It may even be that the evidential value of miracles is secondary to the value they have in addressing the needs of human beings. For example, the New Testament maintains that the resurrection of Jesus represents victory over the grave, not only for Jesus but for all who believe in him (see Jn 11:25-26; 1 Cor 6:14; 15:20; Phil 3:21; 1 Pet 1:3-5). This is why

Jesus is represented as the "first fruits" of the resurrection (1 Cor 15:20).

In our view, the case for miracles is strong and needs to become better known outside the academy. It is not just a provocative rumor that God has acted in history, but a fact worthy of our intellectual conviction. The miracles of Christianity are not an embarrassment to the Christian worldview. Rather, they are testimony to the compassion of God for human beings benighted by sin and circumstance.

Notes

Introduction/Geivett and Habermas

[1]David Shatz, "The Overexamined Life Is Not Worth Living," in *God and the Philosophers: The Reconciliation of Faith and Reason,* ed. Thomas V. Morris (New York: Oxford University Press, 1994), p. 273.

[2]This is because removal of the miraculous eviscerates the Christian faith. So much of the strength and vigor of Christianity depends on the *factuality* of miracles. As the apostle Paul wrote, "If Christ has not been raised, then our preaching is vain, your faith also is vain. . . . If Christ has not been raised, your faith is worthless; you are still in your sins" (1 Cor 15:14, 17 NASB). At the very least, then, the apologist must answer the charge that the presence of miracles within the New Testament Gospels cancels their claim to historical reliability. This is the bare minimum, and with fulfillment of this task some have been satisfied.

[3]See H. D. Lewis, *Philosophy of Religion* (London: English Universities Press, 1965), p. 305.

[4]Examples are provided in Thomas Woolston's "A Defense of the Discourses on Miracles" (1729) and Anthony Collins's "A Discourse of Free Thinking" (1713), both contained in *Deism: An Anthology,* ed. Peter Gay (Princeton, N.J.: D. Van Nostrand, 1968), pp. 135-38, 81-84, respectively.

[5]Albert Schweitzer's classic discussion of both approaches is found in *The Quest of the Historical Jesus: A Critical Study of Its Progress from Reimarus to Wrede,* trans. W. Montgomery from the first German edition of 1906 (New York: Macmillan, 1968); see chapters 5-8, for example.

[6]Translated by Edwyn C. Hoskyns (London: Oxford University Press, 1933).

[7]For one early discussion of such matters, see Karl Barth, *The Resurrection of the Dead* (New York: Fleming H. Revell, 1933), pp. 130-45.

[8]Rudolf Bultmann, "New Testament and Mythology," in *Kerygma and Myth: A Theological Debate,* ed. Hans Werner Bartsch (New York: Harper and Row, 1961), pp. 3-8.

[9]Ibid., pp. 9-16; see also Rudolf Bultmann, *Jesus Christ and Mythology* (New York:

Scribner's, 1958), pp. 16-18.

[10]Representative studies include James M. Robinson, *A New Quest of the Historical Jesus,* Studies in Biblical Theology, First Series, 25 (London: SCM Press, 1959), and Günther Bornkamm, *Jesus of Nazareth,* trans. Irene and Fraser McLuskey with James M. Robinson (New York: Harper and Row, 1960).

[11]For the seminal work written by a group of theologians sometimes called the "Pannenberg circle," see Wolfhart Pannenberg, ed., *Revelation as History,* trans. David Granskou (London: Collier-Macmillan, 1968).

[12]Jürgen Moltmann, *Theology of Hope: On the Ground and the Implications of a Christian Eschatology,* trans. James W. Leitch (New York: Harper and Row, 1967).

[13]Some major works include Geza Vermes, *Jesus the Jew: A Historian's Reading of the Gospels* (New York: Macmillan, 1973); E. P. Sanders, *Jesus and Judaism* (Philadelphia: Fortress, 1985); James H. Charlesworth, *Jesus Within Judaism* (Garden City, N.Y.: Doubleday, 1988); John P. Meier, *A Marginal Jew: Rethinking the Historical Jesus* (Garden City, N.Y.: Doubleday, 1991); John P. Meier, *Mentor, Message, Miracle* (Garden City, N.Y.: Doubleday, 1994).

[14]Representative volumes include Robert W. Funk, Roy W. Hoover and the Jesus Seminar, *The Five Gospels: The Search for the Authentic Words of Jesus* (New York: Macmillan, 1993); John Dominic Crossan, *The Historical Jesus: The Life of a Mediterranean Jewish Peasant* (San Francisco: HarperCollins, 1991); Marcus J. Borg, *Jesus: A New Vision: Spirit, Culture and the Life of Discipleship* (San Francisco: HarperCollins, 1987).

[15]A. J. Ayer, *Language, Truth and Logic* (New York: Dover, 1946), p. 5.

[16]See the essays in *The Logic of God: Theology and Verification,* ed. Malcolm L. Diamond and Thomas V. Litzenburg Jr. (Indianapolis: Bobbs-Merrill, 1975).

[17]For further detail concerning some of the problems inherent in this once popular movement, see David Elton Trueblood, *Philosophy of Religion* (New York: Harper, 1957), pp. 195-202.

[18]See, for example, Roderick Chisholm, *Theory of Knowledge,* 3d ed. (Englewood Cliffs, N.J.: Prentice-Hall, 1989), pp. 75-76 (cf. pp. 58-60); William P. Alston, "A 'Doxastic Practice' Approach to Epistemology," in *Knowledge and Skepticism,* ed. Marjorie Clay and Keith Lehrer (Boulder, Colo.: Westview, 1989); Paul K. Moser, "Procedural Epistemic Rationality," in *Knowledge and Evidence* (Cambridge: Cambridge University Press, 1989); and Alvin I. Goldman, "Epistemics: The Regulative Theory of Cognition," in *Naturalizing Epistemology,* ed. Hilary Kornblith (Cambridge, Mass.: MIT Press, 1985), pp. 217-30.

[19]For an exceptional compilation of such defenses by a number of contemporary philosophers, see John Donnelly, ed., *Logical Analysis and Contemporary Theism* (New York: Fordham University Press, 1972). On the specific question of miracles, see especially Richard Swinburne, *The Concept of Miracle* (London: Macmillan, 1970).

[20]For a few early examples from the journal for the Society of Christian Philosophers, see Stephen T. Davis, "Is It Possible to Know That Jesus Was Raised from the Dead?" *Faith and Philosophy* 1 (April 1984): 147-59; Gary R. Habermas, "Knowing That Jesus' Resurrection Occurred: A Response to Davis," *Faith and Philosophy* 2 (July 1985): 295-302; and Stephen T. Davis, "Naturalism and the Resurrection: A Reply to Habermas," *Faith and Philosophy* 2 (July 1985): 303-8.

[21]It is interesting that Auguste Comte was not only a forerunner of philosophical

positivism, as mentioned above, but also one of the earliest influences on this historical movement.

[22]For excellent anthologies covering this historical debate, including contributions by Dilthey, Croce and Collingwood, see Hans Meyerhoff, ed., *The Philosophy of History in Our Time: An Anthology* (Garden City, N.Y.: Doubleday, 1959), primarily section 1. And see especially Patrick Gardiner, ed., *Theories of History* (New York: Macmillan, 1959), part 1 in particular.

[23]For the later dialogue, see especially the essays by Carl Becker, Charles Beard, Morton White, Ernest Nagel and W. H. Walsh in Meyerhoff, *The Philosophy of History in Our Time*, section 2; and the selections by Walsh, White, Isaiah Berlin, Christopher Blake and William Dray in Gardiner, *Theories of History*, part 2; cf. particularly the contributions by Walsh and J. A. Passmore in William H. Dray, ed., *Philosophical Analysis and History* (New York: Harper and Row, 1966).

[24]David Hume, *An Enquiry Concerning Human Understanding*, 3d ed., rev. P. H. Nidditch, with introduction and analytic index by L. A. Selby-Bigge (Oxford: Clarendon, 1975), p. 110. See p. 30 of this volume.

[25]C. S. Peirce, *Values in a Universe of Chance*, ed. P. P. Wiener (New York: Doubleday, 1958), pp. 292-93; cited by J. C. A. Gaskin, *Hume's Philosophy of Religion*, 2d ed. (Atlantic Heights, N.J.: Humanities, 1988), p. 158.

[26]Antony Flew has rightly warned about the possibility of misunderstanding Hume's argument in Section X of the *Enquiry* if it is taken out of context, and Flew does a fine job of providing some of that context in his own edited volume of Hume's *Writings on Religion* (LaSalle, Ill.: Open Court, 1992), pp. 58-62. The chapter by Flew in the present volume also clarifies Hume's effort, as do several chapters in part 2.

[27]The phrase is borrowed from Robin W. Winks, ed., *The Historian as Detective: Essays on Evidence* (New York: Harper and Row, 1968, 1969), p. xxiv.

[28]Stuart C. Hackett, *The Reconstruction of the Christian Revelation Claim: A Philosophical and Critical Apologetic* (Grand Rapids, Mich.: Baker, 1984), p. 326.

[29]Hackett argues that the *revelatory status* of predictive prophecy would not be compromised if it turned out that "a faculty of predictive insight is an intrinsic human potentiality which is actualized in certain aspects of the biblical revelation" (ibid.).

[30]See ibid., pp. 328-29.

[31]See R. E. Clements, "The Messianic Hope in the Old Testament," *Journal for the Study of the Old Testament* 43 (1989): 3-19.

Chapter 1/Hume

[1]This chapter is a reprint of the famous Section X of David Hume's *An Enquiry Concerning Human Understanding* (1777). The spelling in this eighteenth-century essay has been modernized and Americanized.

[2]Plutarch, *in vita* Catonis.

[3]No Indian, it is evident, could have experienced that water did not freeze in cold climates. This is placing nature in a situation quite unknown to him; and it is impossible for him to tell *a priori* what will result from it. It is making a new experiment, the consequence of which is always uncertain. One may sometimes conjecture from analogy what will follow; but still this is but conjecture. And it must be confessed, that, in the present case of freezing, the event follows contrary to the

rules of analogy, and is such as a rational Indian would not look for. The operations of cold upon water are not gradual, according to the degrees of cold; but whenever it comes to the freezing point, the water passes in a moment, from the utmost liquidity to perfect hardness. Such an event, therefore, may be denominated *extraordinary*, and requires a pretty strong testimony, to render it credible to people in a warm climate: But still it is not *miraculous*, nor contrary to uniform experience of the course of nature in cases where all the circumstances are the same. The inhabitants of Sumatra have always seen water fluid in their own climate, and the freezing of their rivers ought to be deemed a prodigy: But they never saw water in Muscovy during the winter; and therefore they cannot reasonably be positive what would there be the consequence.

[4]Sometimes an event may not, *in itself, seem* to be contrary to the laws of nature, and yet, if it were real, it might, by reason of some circumstances, be denominated a miracle; because, in *fact,* it is contrary to these laws. Thus if a person, claiming a divine authority, should command a sick person to be well, a healthful man to fall down dead, the clouds to pour rain, the winds to blow, in short, should order many natural events, which immediately follow upon his command; these might justly be esteemed miracles, because they are really, in this case, contrary to the laws of nature. For if any suspicion remain, that the event and command concurred by accident, there is no miracle and no transgression of the laws of nature. If this suspicion be removed, there is evidently a miracle, and a transgression of these laws; because nothing can be more contrary to nature than that the voice or command of a man should have such an influence. A miracle may be accurately defined, a *transgression of a law of nature by a particular volition of the Deity, or by the interposition of some invisible agent.* A miracle may either be discoverable by men or not. This alters not its nature and essence. The raising of a house or ship into the air is a visible miracle. The raising of a feather, when the wind wants ever so little of a force requisite for that purpose, is as real a miracle, though not so sensible with regard to us.

[5]*Hist.* lib. iv. cap. 81. Suetonius gives nearly the same account *in vita* Vesp.

[6]This book was written by Mons. Montgeron, counselor or judge of the parliament of Paris, a man of figure and character, who was also a martyr to the cause, and is now said to be somewhere in a dungeon on account of his book.

There is another book in three volumes (called *Recueil des Miracles de l'Abbé Paris*) giving an account of many of these miracles, and accompanied with prefatory discourses, which are very well written. There runs, however, through the whole of these a ridiculous comparison between the miracles of our Saviour and those of the Abbé; wherein it is asserted, that the evidence for the latter is equal to that for the former: As if the testimony of men could ever be put in the balance with that of God himself, who conducted the pen of inspired writers. If these writers, indeed, were to be considered merely as human testimony, the French author is very moderate in his comparison; since he might, with some appearance of reason, pretend, that the Jansenist miracles much surpass the other in evidence and authority. The following circumstances are drawn from authentic papers, inserted in the above-mentioned book.

Many of the miracles of Abbé Paris were proved immediately by witnesses before the officiality or bishop's court at Paris, under the eye of cardinal Noailles, whose character for integrity and capacity was never contested even by his enemies.

His successor in the archbishopric was an enemy to the Jansenists, and for that reason promoted to the see by the court. Yet 22 rectors or *curés* of Paris, with infinite earnestness, press him to examine those miracles, which they assert to be known to the whole world, and undisputably certain: But he wisely forbore.

The Molinist party had tried to discredit these miracles in one instance, that of Mademoiselle le Franc. But, besides that their proceedings were in many respects the most irregular in the world, particularly in citing only a few of the Jansenist witnesses, whom they tampered with: Besides this, I say, they soon found themselves overwhelmed by a cloud of new witnesses, one hundred and twenty in number, most of them persons of credit and substance in Paris, who gave oath for the miracle. This was accompanied with a solemn and earnest appeal to the parliament. But the parliament were forbidden by authority to meddle in the affair. It was at last observed, that where men are hated by zeal and enthusiasm, there is no degree of human testimony so strong as may not be procured for the greatest absurdity: And those who will be so silly as to examine the affair by that medium, and seek particular flaws in the testimony, are almost sure to be confounded. It must be a miserable imposture, indeed, that does not prevail in that contest.

All who have been in France about that time have heard of the reputation of Mons. Heraut, the *lieutenant de Police,* whose vigilance, penetration, activity, and extensive intelligence have been much talked of. This magistrate, who by the nature of his office is almost absolute, was invested with full powers, on purpose to suppress or discredit these miracles; and he frequently seized immediately, and examined the witnesses and subjects of them: But never could reach any thing satisfactory against them.

In the case of Mademoiselle Thibaut he sent the famous De Sylva to examine her; whose evidence is very curious. The physician declares, that it was impossible she could have been so ill as was proved by witnesses; because it was impossible she could, in so short a time, have recovered so perfectly as he found her. He reasoned, like a man of sense, from natural causes; but the opposite party told him, that the whole was a miracle, and that his evidence was the very best proof of it.

The Molinists were in a sad dilemma. They dared not assert the absolute insufficiency of human evidence, to prove a miracle. They were obliged to say, that these miracles were wrought by witchcraft and the devil. But they were told, that this was the resource of the Jews of old.

No Jansenist was ever embarrassed to account for the cessation of the miracles, when the church-yard was shut up by the king's edict. It was the touch of the tomb, which produced these extraordinary effects; and when no one could approach the tomb, no effects could be expected. God, indeed, could have thrown down the walls in a moment; but he is master of his own graces and works, and it belongs not to us to account for them. He did not throw down the walls of every city like those of Jericho, on the sounding of the rams horns, nor break up the prison of every apostle, like that of St. Paul.

No less a man, than the Duc de Chatillon, a duke and peer of France, of the highest rank and family, gives evidence of a miraculous cure, performed upon a servant of his, who had lived several years in his house with a visible and palpable infirmity.

I shall conclude with observing, that no clergy are more celebrated for strictness of life and manners than the secular clergy of France, particularly the rectors or *curés* of Paris, who bear testimony to these impostures.

The learning, genius, and probity of the gentlemen, and the austerity of the nuns of Port-Royal, have been much celebrated all over Europe. Yet they all give evidence for a miracle, wrought on the niece of the famous Pascal, whose sanctity of life, as well as extraordinary capacity, is well known. The famous Racine gives an account of this miracle in his famous history of Port-Royal, and fortifies it with all the proofs, which a multitude of nuns, priests, physicians, and men of the world, all of them of undoubted credit, could bestow upon it. Several men of letters, particularly the bishop of Tournay, thought this miracle so certain, as to employ it in the refutation of atheists and freethinkers. The queen-regent of France, who was extremely prejudiced against the Port-Royal, sent her own physician to examine the miracle, who returned an absolute convert. In short, the supernatural cure was so uncontestable, that it saved, for a time, that famous monastery from the ruin with which it was threatened by the Jesuits. Had it been a cheat, it had certainly been detected by such sagacious and powerful antagonists, and must have hastened the ruin of the contrivers. Our divines, who can build up a formidable castle from such despicable materials; what a prodigious fabric could they have reared from these and many other circumstances, which I have not mentioned! How often would the great names of Pascal, Racine, Arnaud, Nicole, have resounded in our ears? But if they be wise, they had better adopt the miracle, as being more worth, a thousand times, than all the rest of their collection. Besides, it may serve very much to their purpose. For that miracle was really performed by the touch of an authentic holy prickle of the holy thorn, which composed the holy crown, which, etc.

[7]Lucret.

[8]*Nov. Org.* lib. ii. aph. 29.

Chapter 2/Flew

[1]It is, I suggest, significant that there appears to be no such generally accepted program today. Certainly, when in the early sixties I was working on the book later republished as *God: A Critical Enquiry* (La Salle, Ill.: Open Court, 1984), "I did ask several Christian friends to name the work or works which they believed provided the most formidable advocacy." But "they found great difficulty in thinking of anything which seemed to them to be even halfway adequate, and there was almost no overlap between the different lists eventually provided" (p. x).

[2]See H. Denzinger, ed., *Enchiridion Symbolorum,* rev. ed. (Freiburg im Breisgau: Herder, 1953), p. 1806. Instead of the phrase "be known for certain" *(certo cognosci)*, an earlier draft read "be demonstrated" *(demonstrari)*.

[3]Ibid., p. 1813.

[4]*On the Truth of the Catholic Faith: Summa Contra Gentiles,* trans. Anton C. Pegis (Garden City, N.Y.: Doubleday/Image, 1955).

[5]Reprint; London: S.P.C.K., 1938, p. 51.

[6]First Corinthians 15:14 (KJV). In England today, and no doubt elsewhere also, it is impossible to overemphasize Paul's point, for we have numerous clerics who (while ever eager to present their conventionally left-wing politics as part if not the whole of the teachings of Christianity) are not, in any traditional understanding, Christians at all.

[7]Reprinted by the Liberty Press of Indianapolis in 1984.

[8]Pp. 404-5 in the standard Clarendon edition.

[9]The sneer quotes around the word *proved* are, of course, supplied by me rather than by Hume.

[10]It was, presumably, his memories of many such sermons that led Hume to introduce his provocative fiction of the resurrection of the great Queen Elizabeth.

[11]For a discussion of this argument see, for instance, my *An Introduction to Western Philosophy,* rev. ed. (London: Thames and Hudson, 1989), pp. 218-22, or my *God, Freedom and Immortality: A Critical Analysis* (Buffalo, N.Y.: Prometheus, 1984), pp. 61-68. Additionally, see "The Presumption of Atheism" in *Contemporary Perspectives on Religious Epistemology,* ed. R. Douglas Geivett and Brendan Sweetman (New York: Oxford University Press, 1991), and compare the section on Pascalian wagering in the same volume of essays.

[12]For an interpretation and discussion of this radical critique see, for instance, my *Hume's Philosophy of Belief* (London: Routledge and Kegan Paul, 1961), chap. 9.

[13]"Essay on the Miracles Recorded in Ecclesiastical History," in *The Ecclesiastical History of M. L'Abbe Fleury* (Oxford: J. H. Parker, 1842), 2.8.2.

[14]This quotation, as well as those that follow in the present paragraph, are drawn from Section XI of *An Enquiry Concerning Human Understanding;* see the third edition, revised by P. H. Nidditch (Oxford: Clarendon, 1975), pp. 139, 144 and 146.

[15]This awkwardly repetitious expression is employed in order to avoid the inappropriate application of the pronouns *he* or *she* or *it* to a Being defined as not only personal (and hence not an it) but also incorporeal (and hence lacking reproductive, or any other, organs).

[16]That their God could consistently and truly be said to ensure that human choices are freely made in the senses in which that God decides that they shall be made was contended by Aquinas as well as by Luther and Calvin, though their reactions to this insight were very different. See, for instance, passages quoted in Antony Flew and Godfrey Vesey, *Agency and Necessity* (Oxford: Blackwell, 1987), pp. 72-87.

[17]Joseph Butler, *Works,* ed. W. E. Gladstone (Oxford: Oxford University Press, 1896), 1:372 (2.10.2 of *The Analogy of Religion, Natural and Revealed, to the Constitution and Course of Nature* [1736]).

[18]Ibid., 1:162 (1.6 of *The Analogy*). I cannot recommend too strongly Sir Leslie Stephen's treatment of Butler in his classic study of *English Thought in the Eighteenth Century,* 3d ed. (1902; reprint, New York: P. Smith, 1949). Compare also Terence Penelhum, *Butler* (London: Routledge and Kegan Paul, 1985).

[19]For a further development of a counterapologetic of the kind indicated above, see my *Atheistic Humanism* (Buffalo, N.Y.: Prometheus, 1992), chaps. 1-4.

Chapter 3/Purtill

[1]C. S. Lewis, *Screwtape Letters* (New York: Macmillan, 1961), pp. 127-28.

[2]C. S. Lewis, *Miracles* (New York: Macmillan, 1966), p. 63.

[3]Thorleif Boman, *Hebrew Thought Compared with Greek* (New York: Norton, 1960), and C. F. Whitley, *The Genius of Ancient Israel* (Amsterdam: Philo, 1969).

[4]David Hume, *An Enquiry Concerning Human Understanding,* 3d ed., rev. P. H. Nidditch (Oxford: Clarendon, 1975), p. 115 (p. 33 of chap. 1 of this book).

[5]Antony Flew, *Hume's Theory of Belief* (London: Routledge and Kegan Paul, 1961), pp. 217-18.

[6]Alastair McKinnon, " 'Miracle' and 'Paradox,' " *American Philosophical Quarterly* 4 (1967): 309.

[7]I do not mean to imply, however, that McKinnon's other views about miracles are explicitly identified and treated by other authors of this volume. McKinnon's opposition to the concept of miracle advanced in this chapter bears a family resemblance to objections that others have raised. Hence, McKinnon's other specific criticisms of miracles as understood in this book will frequently be addressed only indirectly, as similar objections by others are treated more directly.

[8]See Richard Swinburne, *The Concept of Miracle* (London: Macmillan, 1970), p. 27 and elsewhere.

[9]Lewis, *Miracles,* p. 106.

Chapter 4/Geisler

[1]The discussion here follows the treatment in my *Miracles and the Modern Mind* (Grand Rapids, Mich.: Baker, 1992), chaps. 2-4.

[2]See chapters 5, 6, 12, 13, 15 and 16 of this volume for material relevant to the other arguments. Chapters 3, 6, 7, 8 and 11 have a bearing on the in-principle argument I address in this chapter.

[3]David Hume, *An Enquiry Concerning Human Understanding,* 3d ed., rev. P. H. Nidditch (Oxford: Clarendon, 1975), Section X, part 1; see chap. 1 of the present volume, p. 30.

[4]Ibid.; see chap. 1, pp. 30-33.

[5]Ibid.; see chap. 1, p. 33.

[6]Antony Flew, "Miracles," in *The Encyclopedia of Philosophy,* ed. Paul Edwards (New York: Macmillan, 1967), 5: 349-50.

[7]Ibid., p. 352.

[8]Ibid.

[9]Ibid., p. 350.

[10]Ibid., p. 352.

[11]Stanley Jaki, *Miracles and Physics* (Front Royal, Va.: Christendom, 1989), p. 23.

[12]C. S. Lewis, *Miracles* (New York: Macmillan, 1947), p. 105.

[13]Hume, *Enquiry,* 10.1.122; see chap. 1 of this volume, p. 33.

[14]Richard Whately, *Historical Doubts Concerning the Existence of Napoleon Bonaparte,* in *Famous Pamphlets,* ed. Henry Morley, 2d ed. (London: George Routledge and Sons, 1890), pp. 274, 290.

[15]Hume, *Enquiry,* 10.1.118; see chap. 1 of this volume, p. 30.

[16]David Hume, *An Abstract of a Treatise on Human Nature,* 1740 ed. (Cambridge: Cambridge University Press, 1938), pp. 14-16.

[17]See Geisler, *Miracles and the Modern Mind,* pp. 57-58.

[18]See Carl Sagan, *Broca's Brain* (New York: Random House, 1979), p. 275.

[19]This same distinction is the key to understanding the possibility of a supernatural intelligent Cause of origins in the scientific realm. See my *Origin Science* (Grand Rapids, Mich.: Baker, 1987), chaps. 5-6. See also chap. 8 in the present volume.

[20]See Geisler, *Miracles and the Modern Mind,* pp. 38-39.

[21]Antony Flew, "Theology and Falsification," in *The Existence of God,* ed. John Hick (New York: Macmillan, 1964), p. 227.

[22]Ibid.

[23]It will not do for the naturalist to insist that if God causes all natural events, then God causes evil too (e.g., earthquakes or tornadoes). First, this reasoning only shows at most that God is the cause of natural disaster; it does not establish that God does

not do miracles. Further, even if God is the cause of all natural calamities, it does not mean that God has no good purpose for doing so. Further, natural disasters may be the byproduct of good effects produced by God in the same way that sawdust is only a byproduct of a sawmill. Like natural disasters, sawdust can be utilized for good purposes. And whatever residual "waste" exists may be necessary for the greater good.

[24]See Norman L. Geisler and Winfried Corduan, *Philosophy of Religion*, 2d ed. (Grand Rapids, Mich.: Baker, 1988), chaps. 16-17; Norman L. Geisler, *The Roots of Evil* (Richardson, Tex.: Word, 1989); and R. Douglas Geivett, *Evil and the Evidence for God* (Philadelphia: Temple University Press, 1993).

[25]Jaki, *Miracles and Physics*, p. 100.

Chapter 5/Beckwith

[1]David Hume, *An Enquiry Concerning Human Understanding*, 3d ed., rev. P. H. Nidditch, with introduction and analytic index by L. A. Selby-Bigge (Oxford: Clarendon, 1975), p. 116. See p. 33 of chap. 1 in this volume.

[2]Other concerns about the objectivity of history, which space limitations prevent me from covering here, include whether historians' knowledge of the past is direct or indirect, whether historians' incomplete knowledge of the past supports relativism and whether it is possible to test for historical truth. See Carl Becker, "What Are Historical Facts?" in *The Philosophy of History*, ed. H. Meyerhoff (Garden City, N.Y.: Doubleday, 1959); Charles Beard, "The Noble Dream," in *Varieties of History*, ed. F. Stern (Cleveland, Ohio: World, Meridian, 1956); E. H. Carr, *What Is History?* (New York: Random House/Vintage, 1953); Norman L. Geisler, *Christian Apologetics* (Grand Rapids, Mich.: Baker, 1976), chap. 15; William Lane Craig, *Apologetics: An Introduction* (Chicago: Moody Press, 1984), pp. 126-50; and Ronald H Nash, *Christian Faith and Historical Understanding* (Grand Rapids, Mich.: Zondervan, 1984), pp. 77-109.

[3]This seems to be Van Harvey's point in his *The Historian and the Believer* (London: SCM Press, 1967), p. 109. Gary R. Habermas cites and critiques this objection in his *Ancient Evidence for the Life of Jesus: Historical Records of His Death and Resurrection* (Nashville: Thomas Nelson, 1984), pp. 25-27.

[4]For more on these and other historical facts entailed by the claim that Jesus rose from the dead, see Habermas, *Ancient Evidence*, and William Lane Craig, *Knowing the Truth About the Resurrection: Our Response to the Empty Tomb*, rev. ed. (Ann Arbor, Mich.: Servant Books, 1988).

[5]See, for example, Richard Swinburne, *The Concept of Miracle* (London: Macmillan, 1970), pp. 53-71; Gary R. Habermas, *The Resurrection of Jesus* (Lanham, Md.: University Press of America, 1984), pp. 12-90, 123-34; Craig, *Apologetics*, pp. 116-21; Norman L. Geisler, *Miracles and the Modern Mind: A Defense of Biblical Miracles*, rev. ed. (Grand Rapids, Mich.: Baker, 1992), pp. 55-65, 93-100, 111-26; Francis J. Beckwith, *David Hume's Argument Against Miracles: A Critical Analysis* (Lanham, Md.: University Press of America, 1989), pp. 54-64, 71-84; Ronald H. Nash, *Faith and Reason: Searching for a Rational Faith* (Grand Rapids, Mich.: Zondervan, 1988), pp. 225-40; Winfried Corduan, *Reasonable Faith: A Textbook of Christian Apologetics* (Nashville: Broadman and Holman, 1993), pp. 155-62; and Leon Pearl, "Miracles: The Case for Theism," *American Philosophical Quarterly* 25 (October 1988).

[6]See Becker, "What Are Historical Facts?" and Beard, "The Noble Dream."

[7]Becker, "What Are Historical Facts?" pp. 130-31.

[8]For more on this, see Ronald Nash's essay, chap. 7.

[9]Geisler, *Christian Apologetics*, p. 297.

[10]Nash, *Christian Faith*, pp. 87-88.

[11]Geisler, *Christian Apologetics*, p. 297.

[12]Ibid.

[13]Carr, *What Is History?* p. 8.

[14]Becker, "What Are Historical Facts?" p. 132.

[15]For example, John Warwick Montgomery writes, "But the issue here is a *miracle:* a resurrection. How much evidence should a reasonable human being require in order to establish such a fact? Could evidence ever justify accepting it?" (John Warwick Montgomery, *Human Rights and Human Dignity* [Grand Rapids, Mich.: Zondervan, 1986], p. 154). Montgomery responds to this problem by citing Thomas Sherlock's *The Tryal of the Witnesses* (1743) and stating that Sherlock "is essentially correct that a resurrection does not in principle create any insuperable evidential difficulty. . . . In Jesus' case, the sequential order is reversed [i.e., instead of the normal sequence of life followed by death, a resurrection entails death followed by life], but that has no epistemological bearing on the weight of evidence required to establish death or life"(pp. 154-55).

[16]Antony Flew, *David Hume: Philosopher of Moral Science* (Oxford: Blackwell, 1986), p. 81.

[17]Richard Blodgett, "Our Wild, Weird World of Coincidence," *Reader's Digest* 131 (September 1987): 127.

[18]Richard A. Epstein, *The Theory of Gambling and Statistical Logic* (New York: Academic Press, 1967), p. 222.

[19]Alvin Plantinga, "Is Theism Really a Miracle?" *Faith and Philosophy* 3 (April 1986): 113.

[20]J. C. A. Gaskin, *Hume's Philosophy of Religion* (London: Macmillan, 1978), p. 115.

[21]Ibid.

[22]Hume, *Enquiry*, p. 116; p. 33 of chap. 1 in this volume.

[23]As cited in John Warwick Montgomery, "Science, Theology and the Miraculous," in his *Faith Founded on Fact* (New York: Thomas Nelson, 1978), p. 55.

[24]See Swinburne, *The Concept of Miracle*, pp. 41-48. Montgomery explains that legal reasoning is an example of evidential criteria based on certain regularities. See John Warwick Montgomery, *The Law Above the Law* (Minneapolis: Bethany House, 1975), p. 86.

[25]Swinburne writes, "So then a claim that a formula L is a law of nature and a claim that testimony or trace of a certain type is reliable are established in basically the same way—by showing that certain formulae connect observed data in a simple coherent way" (*The Concept of Miracle*, p. 43). That simplicity and coherence are values which the scientist seeks in formulating any law or theory is defended by not a few philosophers of science. On this, see W. H. Newton-Smith, *The Rationality of Science* (London: Routledge and Kegan Paul, 1981), pp. 226-32.

[26]A fine example of naturalism-of-the-gaps is Hume's defense of maintaining naturalism in his fictional account of Queen Elizabeth's resurrection, which is discussed by Antony Flew in his chapter for this volume. See Hume, *Enquiry*, p. 128; p. 42 in chap. 1 of this volume.

[27]Ernst Troeltsch, "Historiography," in *Encyclopedia of Religion and Ethics* (New York: Scribner's, 1955), 6:718.

[28]Antony Flew, *God: A Critical Enquiry*, 2d ed. (La Salle, Ill.: Open Court, 1984), p. 140. William Lane Craig writes, "Flew's real objection is that in order to study history, one must assume the impossibility of miracles. This viewpoint is simply a restatement of . . . Troeltsch's principle of analogy" (*Apologetics*, pp. 123-24).

[29]Geisler, *Miracles and the Modern Mind*, pp. 79-80.

[30]For an evaluation of contemporary miracles, see Norman L. Geisler, *Signs and Wonders* (Wheaton, Ill.: Tyndale, 1988), chap. 9. Geisler, who believes that the miraculous "sign gifts" (1 Cor 12—14) are not for this age, nevertheless maintains that there is substantial evidence that God has directly performed numerous miracles in our contemporary world. For a critique of Geisler's view of the sign gifts, see Francis J. Beckwith, reviews of *Sign and Wonders* by Norman L. Geisler and *The Third Wave of the Holy Spirit* by C. Peter Wagner, *Journal of the Evangelical Theological Society* 33 (September 1990): 394-98.

[31]Special thanks are due to the editors of this volume for their valuable and thoughtful comments and suggestions.

Chapter 6/Corduan

[1]David Hume, *An Enquiry Concerning Human Understanding*, 3d ed., rev. P. H. Nidditch, with introduction and analytic index by L. A. Selby-Bigge (Oxford: Clarendon, 1975), Section X; see chap. 1 of this volume.

[2]Antony Flew, "Miracles," in *The Encyclopedia of Philosophy*, ed. Paul Edwards (New York: Macmillan, 1965), 5:348-49; see also Antony Flew, *God and Philosophy* (New York: Delta, 1966), pp. 140-58; and Flew's general remarks on miracles in *Did Jesus Rise from the Dead? The Resurrection Debate*, by Gary R. Habermas and Antony Flew, ed. Terry L. Miethe (San Francisco: Harper and Row, 1987), pp. 4-8.

[3]Flew, "Miracles," p. 348.

[4]Ibid., p. 352.

[5]Guy Robinson, "Miracles," *Ratio* 9 (1967): 155-66.

[6]Ibid., p. 163.

[7]The issue of the relationship between science and the miraculous receives further elaboration by J. P. Moreland in chapter 8 of this volume.

[8]Patrick Nowell-Smith, "Miracles," in *New Essays in Philosophical Theology*, ed. Antony Flew and Alasdair MacIntyre (London: SCM Press, 1955), pp. 243-53.

[9]Stephen J. Wykstra, "The Problem of Miracle in the Apologetic from History," *Journal of the American Scientific Affiliation* 30, no. 4 (December 1978): 154-63.

[10]Margaret A. Boden, "Miracles and Scientific Explanation," *Ratio* 11 (1969): 137-44.

[11]John Warwick Montgomery, "Science, Theology and the Miraculous," *Journal of the American Scientific Affiliation* 30, no. 4 (December 1978): 145-53.

[12]See, for example, George I. Mavrodes, "Miracles and the Laws of Nature," *Faith and Philosophy* 2 (October 1985): 333-46, and the reply by Joshua Hoffman, "Comments on 'Miracles and the Laws of Nature,' " *Faith and Philosophy* 2 (October 1985): 347-52.

[13]This issue is addressed in greater detail by Ronald Nash in chapter 7 of this volume.

[14]H. A. Ironside, *Addresses on Luke* (New York: Loizeaux Brothers, 1946), p. 135.

[15]Fritz Rienecker, *Das Evangelium des Lukas*, Wuppertaler Studienbibel (Wuppertal:

Brockhaus, 1959), p. 131.

[16]*The NIV Study Bible,* ed. Kenneth Barker (Grand Rapids, Mich.: Zondervan, 1985), p. 1545.

[17]R. F. Holland, "The Miraculous," *American Philosophical Quarterly* 2 (January 1965): 43-51.

[18]Norman L. Geisler, *Christian Apologetics* (Grand Rapids, Mich.: Baker, 1976), p. 77.

[19]Douglas K. Erlandson, "A New Look at Miracles," *Religious Studies* 13 (1977): 417-28.

[20]Robert Young, "Miracles and Epistemology," *Religious Studies* 8 (1972): 123. See also the ensuing exchange: Tan Tai Wei, "Mr. Young on Miracles," *Religious Studies* 10 (1974): 333-37, and Robert Young, "Miracles and Credibility," *Religious Studies* 16 (1980): 465-68.

[21]Colin Brown, *Miracles and the Critical Mind* (Grand Rapids, Mich.: Eerdmans, 1984), p. 19.

[22]Montgomery, "Science, Theology and the Miraculous," p. 145.

[23]Thomas Aquinas, *On the Truth of the Catholic Faith: Summa Contra Gentiles,* trans. Anton C. Pegis (Garden City, N.Y.: Doubleday/Image, 1955), p. 77.

[24]See Douglas Geivett's fuller discussion of the evidential value of miracles in chapter 11.

[25]C. S. Peirce, *Essays in the Philosophy of Science,* ed. Vincent Thomas (New York: Liberal Arts, 1957), pp. 126-43.

[26]Other cases of fulfilled predictive prophecy constitute an additional type of miracle claim; see Robert Newman's discussion of this specific type of miracle in chapter 13.

[27]Antony Flew, "Theology and Falsification," in *New Essays in Philosophical Theology,* ed. Flew and MacIntyre, p. 99.

[28]Habermas and Flew, *Did Jesus Rise from the Dead?* pp. 49-50.

[29]Nowell-Smith, "Miracles," p. 253.

[30]Compare the remarks by Frank Beckwith in chapter 5.

[31]See David Clark, chapter 12, for further discussion of miracles associated with competing religious traditions.

Chapter 7/Nash

[1]For a fuller discussion, see Ronald H. Nash, ed., *Process Theology* (Grand Rapids, Mich.: Baker, 1987), and Ronald H. Nash, *The Concept of God* (Grand Rapids, Mich.: Zondervan, 1983). Panentheism can be thought of as a position somewhere between theism's belief in a personal, almighty, all-knowing God and the impersonal god of pantheism that is identical in some way with nature or the world order. While the god of panentheism is not identical with the world, this god and the world necessarily coexist eternally. Another basic feature of panentheism is the denial of the view that God can act as an efficient cause, a belief that precludes any belief in either creation or such miracles as the incarnation and the resurrection.

[2]For a criticism of some recent attacks on the full deity and humanity of Jesus, see Ronald H. Nash, *Is Jesus the Only Savior?* (Grand Rapids, Mich.: Zondervan, 1994).

[3]For a defense of this claim, see Ronald H. Nash, *The Word of God and the Mind of Man* (Phillipsburg, N.J.: Presbyterian and Reformed, 1992).

[4]William J. Abraham, *An Introduction to the Philosophy of Religion* (Englewood Cliffs,

N.J.: Prentice-Hall, 1985), pp. 104-5.

[5]My discussion will focus on naturalists who are what we call physicalists, that is, people who insist that everything that exists can be reduced to physical or material entities. But there are also thinkers who reject physicalism (that is, who deny the physicalist's claim that all of reality can be reduced to physical or material entities) who are also naturalists because they deny the possibility of any divine intervention in the natural order. Certain kinds of Platonists are naturalists in this second sense. Because we live in a day when physicalists control the agenda, I will concentrate on the first type of naturalist.

[6]S. D. Gaede, *Where Gods May Dwell* (Grand Rapids, Mich.: Eerdmans, 1985), p. 35.

[7]C. S. Lewis, *Miracles* (New York: Macmillan, 1960), pp. 6-7.

[8]William H. Halverson, *A Concise Introduction to Philosophy*, 3d ed. (New York: Random House, 1976), p. 394.

[9]Stephen T. Davis, "Is It Possible to Know That Jesus Was Raised from the Dead?" *Faith and Philosophy* 1 (April 1984): 154.

[10]See note 5 above for an important qualification.

[11]I owe the point in the last half of this paragraph to Doug Geivett.

[12]For a response to this attitude, see J. P. Moreland's chapter 8 in this book.

[13]Some naturalists attempt to argue that the theist's understanding of reality alters the foundations of science so radically as to, in effect, make it impossible. Answering this important but badly mistaken objection at this point would introduce a very long interruption into the chapter. Interested readers will find a rebuttal in several sources, including Ronald H. Nash, *Faith and Reason: Searching for a Rational Faith* (Grand Rapids, Mich.: Zondervan, 1988), chap. 17; Jerry H. Gill, *Faith in Dialogue: A Christian Apologetic* (Waco, Tex.: Word, 1985), pp. 33-34; and Richard Bube, *The Human Quest* (Waco, Tex.: Word, 1971), pp. 115-16. Again, see chapter 8 in this book.

[14]This touches on another complex issue that I do not pursue in this essay, namely, whether miracles must be viewed as violations of the laws of nature. In another book I counsel against this position, although I recognize that many other Christian theists, including Richard Purtill in his chapter 3 of this volume, define miracles as exceptions to the laws of nature (see Nash, *Faith and Reason*, chap. 16-17).

[15]See also Nash, *Faith and Reason*, chap. 9.

[16]I discuss the criteria by which we should test worldviews in my books *Worldviews in Conflict* (Grand Rapids, Mich.: Zondervan, 1992) and *Faith and Reason*. The tests include reason or logical consistency, outer experience (conformity to what we know about the world around us), inner experience (conformity to what we know about our own nature) and practice (the claim that any worldview worthy of our respect ought to be a system we can live out in our everyday life). These tests are hardly original with me and are seldom challenged. For other discussions of such tests, see William J. Wainwright, *Philosophy of Religion* (Belmont, Calif.: Wadsworth, 1988), chap. 7, and Keith Yandell, "Religious Experience and Rational Appraisal," *Religious Studies* 10 (1974): 173-87.

[17]Lewis, *Miracles*, p. 12. C. S. Lewis enthusiasts will note that I am following his argument in the second edition of the book (published in 1960). The first edition included an argument against naturalism that Lewis came to see as fallacious.

[18]Ibid., p. 14.

[19]Ibid., p. 15.

[20]Ibid., pp. 14-15.

[21]The kind of argument Lewis rejects here is similar to the fallacious argument he himself had advanced (and later rejected) in the first edition of *Miracles.*

[22]For example, a person suffering from a particular disorder might believe something "heard" as an inner voice. We tend to judge such people as mad when their conclusions lack any justifying ground. The beliefs of the philosopher I describe may also have a cause, for example, something that happened in the philosopher's childhood. One would hope that a person aspiring to the title of philosopher would be able to produce grounds for his or her beliefs.

[23]Lewis, *Miracles,* p. 16.

[24]Ibid., p. 18.

[25]Ibid., p. 25.

[26]Richard Taylor, *Metaphysics,* 2d ed. (Englewood Cliffs, N.J.: Prentice-Hall, 1974), p. 115.

[27]Ibid., pp. 116-17.

[28]Ibid., p. 117.

[29]Ibid., pp. 117-18.

[30]Ibid., pp. 118-19.

[31]For a more recent exploration of a similar line of attack on metaphysical naturalism, see Alvin Plantinga, *Warrant and Proper Function* (New York: Oxford University Press, 1993), chaps. 11-12.

[32]Richard L. Purtill, *Reason to Believe* (Grand Rapids, Mich.: Eerdmans, 1974), p. 44.

[33]While I do not discuss the subject of ethics in detail here, moral principles seem to be in as much difficulty as logical principles in the worldview of metaphysical naturalists. Treating both adequately certainly seems to force us to recognize the existence of things that transcend the purely natural order, things that exist, in other words, outside the box.

[34]In Nash, *Faith and Reason,* chapters 16-17, I consider some other things metaphysical naturalists might say regarding miracles.

Chapter 8/Moreland

[1]Michael Ruse, *Darwinism Defended* (London: Addison-Wesley, 1982), p. 322.

[2]See J. P. Moreland, ed., *The Creation Hypothesis* (Downers Grove, Ill.: InterVarsity Press, 1994), chaps. 1 and 2; "Creation Science and Methodological Naturalism," in *Man and Creation,* ed. Michael Bauman (Hillsdale, Mich.: Hillsdale College Press, 1993), pp. 105-39; *Christianity and the Nature of Science* (Grand Rapids, Mich.: Baker, 1989), chaps. 1, 6; "Conceptual Problems and the Scientific Status of Creation Science," *Perspectives on Science and Christian Faith* 46 (March 1994): 2-13.

[3]D. M. Mackay, *Human Science and Human Dignity* (Downers Grove, Ill: InterVarsity Press, 1979), p. 28. Richard Bube has complained that my characterization of complementarity is confused and is actually a description of what he calls compartmentalization. See his *Putting It All Together* (Lanham, Md.: University Press of America, 1995), p. 168; cf. pp. 95-100, 167-87. For Bube, compartmentalization treats science and theology as different descriptions about different kinds of things with no common ground or possibility of conflict. Complementarity views

science and theology as different descriptions of the same reality. Unfortunately, Bube is simply wrong in this complaint about my position. What he calls compartmentalization is close to what I call the "two-realms" view of integration, and my description of complementarity is an accurate one. The source of Bube's confusion is revealing. I claim that the complementarity view eschews interaction between science and theology, and Bube says that it embraces such interaction. Bube, however, equivocates on what "interaction" means in this context. For me, it is "epistemic" interaction, roughly the same description of the same reality that can be in conflict or in harmony to varying degrees of strength. For Bube, interaction amounts to taking two different (noninteracting, in my sense) perspectives and forming them into a whole. For example, a completely scientific description of the origin of life in natural terms could be described in theological terms as God's activity in bringing life into being. It is clear that Bube's notion of interaction is not the one I deny in explicating complementarity. Moreover, my use of the notion of interaction is crucial in understanding the significance for scientific methodology of gaps in the natural causal fabric due to libertarian agency and primary causal activity on God's part.

[4]David Charles and Kathleen Lennon, eds., *Reduction, Explanation and Realism* (Oxford: Clarendon, 1992), pp. 3-4.

[5]I set aside debates about the exact nature of secondary causality (for example, disputes over occasionalism and alternative accounts), since the distinction between primary and secondary causality is functionally and epistemologically significant irrespective of the exact nature of the metaphysical account of the difference between them. Whatever else one wants to say here, secondary causality will be God's usual way of acting, and the laws of nature will be regular and normal here (regardless of whether they are deterministic or probabilistic). Primary causality will be God's unusual way of acting that could be epistemically detected due to the contrast in this type of action compared to the regular, usual sequences of events that constitute secondary causality.

[6]Howard J. Van Till, "When Faith and Reason Cooperate," *Christian Scholar's Review* 20 (September 1991): 42.

[7]Thus a necessary condition for libertarianism (but not for compatibilism) is that persons are substances rather than property-things (as complementarianism requires).

[8]Arthur Peacocke, *Creation and the World of Science* (Oxford: Clarendon, 1979), p. 132.

[9]John Searle, *Minds, Brains and Science* (Cambridge: Harvard University Press, 1984), p. 98.

[10]David Papineau, *Philosophical Naturalism* (Oxford: Blackwell, 1993), p. 16.

[11]Robert Larmer, "Mind-Body Interaction and the Conservation of Energy," *International Philosophical Quarterly* 26 (September 1986): 277-85. Thus, Papineau's so-called empirical argument is question-begging: (1) the history of science shows that whatever causes we discover for physical effects are themselves physical; (2) if we allow for real mental states that are not epiphenomenal, then such states leave unacceptable gaps in the natural world that violate the completeness of physics; and (3) therefore we should embrace some version of physicalism (token physicalism is his recommendation; see Papineau, *Philosophical Naturalism*, pp. 16-32). This argument begs the question because the completeness of physics is precisely at issue.

If libertarian agency is real, then the history of science confirms only the weak and not the strong form of the first law.

[12]See Moreland, *Creation Hypothesis*, pp. 18-33.

[13]Bube, *Putting It All Together*, pp. 22-26. It is clear from this definition that the notion of chance is epistemological for Bube, not metaphysical. This is why a description that is an expression of chance in Bube's sense is consistent with ontological determinism. In reality, determinism rules, though epistemologically we may not be able to predict future states in all cases.

[14]Ibid., pp. 25-26, 65-70.

[15]Howard J. Van Till, "Special Creationism in Designer's Clothing: A Response to *The Creation Hypothesis*," in *Perspectives on Science and Christian Faith* 47 (June 1995): 127.

Chapter 9/Beck

[1]On the standards that it is reasonable to expect a theistic argument to meet, see Alvin Plantinga, "Belief in God," in *Perspectives in Philosophy*, ed. Michael Boylan (Ft. Worth, Tex.: Harcourt Brace Jovanovich, 1993), p. 394; see also Plantinga's article on the epistemology of religious belief in *A Companion to Epistemology*, ed. Jonathan Dancy and Ernest Sosa (Oxford: Blackwell, 1992), pp. 438-39. For a thorough study of inference to the best explanation, see Peter Lipton, *Inference to the Best Explanation* (London: Routledge, 1991). For a shorter excellent introduction to this type of inference, discussed in connection with the design argument for the existence of God, see William J. Wainwright, *Philosophy of Religion* (Belmont, Calif.: Wadsworth, 1988), pp. 53-55.

[2]For a threefold taxonomy of cosmological arguments and a historical survey of each major type of cosmological argument, see William Lane Craig, *The Cosmological Argument from Plato to Leibniz* (London: Macmillan, 1980).

[3]I use the term *thing* in this context to refrain from commitment to any particular physics. Michael Martin in *Atheism: A Philosophical Justification* (Philadelphia: Temple University Press, 1990), chap. 4, and J. L. Mackie in *The Miracle of Theism* (Oxford: Clarendon, 1982), chap. 5, both think that the cosmological argument is dependent on ancient Greek physics.

[4]See Patterson Brown, "Infinite Causal Regression," *The Philosophical Review* 75 (October 1966): 510.

[5]Thomas Aquinas *Summa Theologica* 1.2.3.

[6]Ibid.

[7]Walter Kaufmann, *Critique of Religion and Philosophy* (Garden City, N.Y.: Anchor, 1961), p. 161.

[8]Take, for example, Carl Sagan's first line in *Cosmos* (New York: Random House 1980), p. 4: "The Cosmos is all that is or ever was or ever will be."

[9]For a good example of how this works in Thomas Aquinas, see Brian Davies, *The Thought of Thomas Aquinas* (Oxford: Clarendon, 1992), chap. 5; see also Norman Geisler and Winfried Corduan, *Philosophy of Religion*, 2d ed. (Grand Rapids, Mich.: Baker, 1988), chap. 9. For an alternative approach, see the interesting article by Thomas V. Morris, "Metaphysical Dependence, Independence and Perfection," in *Being and Goodness: The Concept of God in Metaphysics and Philosophical Theology*, ed. Scott MacDonald (Ithaca, N.Y.: Cornell University Press, 1991), pp. 278-97.

[10]Martin, *Atheism*, p. 97.

[11]Paul Edwards's essay "The Cosmological Argument" is reprinted in *Philosophy of Religion: Selected Readings,* ed. William L. Rowe and William J. Wainwright (New York: Harcourt Brace Jovanovich, 1973), pp. 136-48. A good discussion of this type of objection to the cosmological argument can be found in C. Stephen Evans, *Philosophy of Religion: Thinking About Faith* (Downers Grove, Ill.: InterVarsity Press, 1985), pp. 50-59.

[12]In his essay "Concerning Infinite Chains, Infinite Trains and Borrowing a Typewriter," *International Journal for Philosophy of Religion* 14 (1983): 71-86, David A. Conway discusses the use of these examples. But he ignores the transitivity of existential causality in the real world.

[13]Stephen W. Hawking, *A Brief History of Time: From the Big Bang to Black Holes* (Toronto: Bantam, 1988), pp. 140-41; cf. p. 136. Carl Sagan, in the introduction to Hawking's book, drew the explicit theological implication here attributed to Hawking:

This is also a book about God . . . or perhaps about the absence of God. The word God fills these pages. Hawking embarks on a quest to answer Einstein's famous question about whether God had any choice in creating the universe. Hawking is attempting, as he explicitly states, to understand the mind of God. And this makes all the more unexpected the conclusion of the effort, at least so far: a universe with no edge in space, no beginning or end in time, and nothing for a Creator to do. (p. x)

This assessment has to be considered in light of Hawking's own remarks:

[I]f something like the no-boundary proposal were correct . . . the laws of physics would hold even at the beginning of the universe, so God would not have had the freedom to choose the initial conditions [of the universe]. Of course, He would still have been free to choose the laws that the universe obeyed. However, this may not have been much of a choice. There may only be a small number of laws, which are self-consistent and which lead to complicated beings like ourselves who can ask the question: What is the nature of God? (Stephen W. Hawking, 1987 lecture titled "The Origin of the Universe," in *Black Holes and Baby Universes* [Toronto: Bantam, 1993], p. 98)

Notice that Hawking's remarks do not entail a strictly closed universe where God has no role at all to play. First, even if God's choices in setting the initial conditions of the universe were limited, God still had choices and may have had to exercise choice in order to produce this universe. Second, God's choices are thought to be (possibly) limited precisely in connection with the goal of producing a universe with "complicated beings" who can meaningfully entertain theological questions. This suggests that God may have had the choice of creating no world at all or of creating a world without creatures capable of theological curiosity. Even on Hawking's view, then, the actual universe may not be closed in the strict sense; its origin may have depended on God's interest in creating a particular sort of world and his power to act on his intentions to produce such a world. If Hawking's no-boundary proposal entails that the universe is closed, this is an entailment that Hawking himself either does not recognize or refuses to acknowledge publicly. Indeed, he stresses that "science cannot answer the question: Why does the universe bother to exist?" (Hawking, *Black Holes and Baby Universes,* p. 99; cf. Hawking, *A Brief History of Time,* pp. 140-41, 174-75); this suggests that for all Hawking knows (or claims to know) about the boundary conditions of the universe, God may be required to produce the universe. (See the discussion of this point by William Lane Craig, who construes Hawking as an advocate of one version of the cosmological argument made famous by G. W. Leibniz [1646-1716], in *Theism, Atheism and Big Bang Cosmology,* by William Lane Craig and Quentin Smith [Oxford: Clarendon, 1993], pp. 279-82.)

Of course, Hawking does say that while the laws of the universe "may have been ordained by God, . . . it seems that He does not intervene in the universe to break the laws" (*Black Holes and Baby Universes,* p. 98). But this does not imply that the universe is closed to God's establishment of initial conditions. Furthermore, Hawking is merely expressing his own acceptance of methodological naturalism, a view that is ably critiqued by J. P. Moreland in chapter 8 of this volume. (I owe all of these observations about the theological implications of Hawking's position to Doug Geivett.)

[14]Robin Le Poidevin, "Creation in a Closed Universe, or Have Physicists Disproved the Existence of God?" *Religious Studies* 27 (March 1991): 39-48.

[15]A good discussion of the issue can be found in Bruce Reichenbach, *The Cosmological Argument: A Reassessment* (Springfield, Ill.: Charles Thomas, 1972), chap. 3. See also Wainwright, *Philosophy of Religion,* pp. 44-47, and George N. Schlesinger, "A Pragmatic Version of the Principle of Sufficient Reason," *Philosophical Quarterly* 45 (October 1995): 439-59.

[16]Richard Swinburne, *The Existence of God,* rev. ed. (Oxford: Clarendon, 1991), chap. 8, and "The Argument from Design," reprinted in *Contemporary Perspectives on Religious Epistemology,* ed. R. Douglas Geivett and Brendan Sweetman (New York: Oxford University Press, 1992), pp. 201-11.

[17]The full title is *Natural Theology: Or, Evidences of the Existence and Attributes of the Deity, Collected from the Appearances of Nature* (1802). It is available as edited by Frederick Ferré (Indianapolis: Library of Liberal Arts, 1963).

[18]Ibid., p. 13.

[19]See his discussion in any edition of the *Dialogues Concerning Natural Religion* (1777). A good evaluation of these can be found in Evans, *Philosophy of Religion,* chap. 3.

[20]These examples are taken from two tables in Hugh Ross's essay "Astronomical Evidences for a Personal, Transcendent God," in *The Creation Hypothesis,* ed. J. P. Moreland (Downers Grove, Ill.: InterVarsity Press, 1994), esp. pp. 160-69.

[21]Fred Hoyle and Chandra Wickramasinghe, *Evolution from Space* (New York: Simon and Schuster, 1981), p. 24.

[22]For a good discussion of this example, see Walter Bradley and Charles Thaxton, "Information and the Origin of Life," in Moreland, *The Creation Hypothesis,* pp. 173-210.

[23]A brief version of this argument can be found in Richard Swinburne, *Evidence for God* (Oxford: Mowbrays, 1986), p. 9; cf. Dallas Willard, "The Three-Stage Argument for the Existence of God," in Geivett and Sweetman, *Contemporary Perspectives,* pp. 217-21.

[24]See John Leslie, "How to Draw Conclusions from a Fine-Tuned Cosmos," in *Physics, Philosophy and Theology: A Common Quest for Understanding,* ed. Robert Russell, William Stoeger and George Coyne (Notre Dame, Ill.: University of Notre Dame Press, 1988), pp. 297-311.

[15]Ross, "Astronomical Evidences," pp. 155-56.

[26]This argument was first published as *Broadcast Talks* in 1942 and is widely available today as *Mere Christianity* (New York: Macmillan, 1943).

[27]See Mackie, *Miracle of Theism*, chap. 6.

[28]This commonly expressed view can be found in B. F. Skinner, *Beyond Freedom and Dignity* (New York: Knopf, 1971).

[29]One of the best discussions of this point is by C. S. Lewis in *Mere Christianity*, chap. 2.

[30]See the excellent discussion in Ed Miller, *God and Reason* (New York: Macmillan, 1972), chap. 6.

[31]For helpful treatments of the idea of a cumulative case, see Basil Mitchell, *The Justification of Religious Belief* (New York: Seabury, 1973), chap. 3; and R. Douglas Geivett, *Evil and the Evidence for God* (Philadelphia: Temple University Press, 1993), pp. 90-95.

[32]William P. Alston, "Religious Experience and Religious Belief," in Geivett and Sweetman, *Contemporary Perspectives*, p. 302.

Chapter 10/Davis

[1]See especially his essays "Divine and Human Action" and "God's Action in the World," in *Divine Nature and Human Language: Essays in Philosophical Theology*, by William P. Alston (Ithaca, N.Y.: Cornell University Press, 1989), pp. 81-102 and 197-222 respectively. See also his "How to Think About Divine Action," in *Divine Action: Studies Inspired by the Philosophical Theology of Austin Farrer*, ed. Brian Hebblethwaite and Edward Henderson (Edinburgh: T & T Clark, 1990), pp. 51-70.

[2]Dallas Willard develops these ideas in much greater detail in his *In Search of Guidance: Developing a Conversational Relationship with God* (San Francisco: HarperCollins, 1993), especially pp. 92-107, 178-240.

[3]One subcategory of divine natural activity in the world is called "double agency." This is a complex topic, and I am not able to do it justice here. In a theological context, double agency is a situation where an event occurs that is simultaneously and fully caused both by God and by some human agent or agents. The human agent acts fully and is not merely a passive instrument of God, and God acts fully and is not merely passively "sustaining" what the human agent has freely chosen to do. An example would be liturgical pardon as understood in some confessions, where a member of the clergy declares to a repentant sinner or to a congregation, "You are forgiven"—an event that is at the same time a free and sovereign act of divine forgiveness. See Owen Thomas, "Recent Thought on Divine Agency," in Hebblethwaite and Henderson, *Divine Action*, pp. 46-49.

[4]Some Christian philosophers propose an alternative conception of miracles that does not speak in terms of violations of natural laws. This issue is addressed more fully in Richard Purtill's essay, chapter 3 in this volume.

[5]See my article "The Miracle at Cana: A Philosopher's Perspective," in *Gospel Perspectives*, vol. 6, *The Miracles of Jesus*, ed. David Wenham and Craig Blomberg (Sheffield: JSOT Press, 1986), pp. 419-42.

[6]P. F. Strawson, *Individuals* (Garden City, N.Y.: Anchor, 1959). Strawson was arguing more against the notion of an immaterial soul than against the concept of God; nevertheless, his argument can easily be adapted to apply to the notion of an immaterial God.

[7]Thomas F. Tracy, *God, Action and Embodiment* (Grand Rapids, Mich.: Eerdmans, 1984), p. 79.

[8]Paul Edwards, "Some Notes on Anthromorphic Theology," in *Religious Experience and Truth*, ed. Sidney Hook (New York: New York University Press, 1961), p. 243.

[9]William J. Abraham, *An Introduction to the Philosophy of Religion* (Englewood Cliffs, N.J.: Prentice-Hall, 1985), p. 57.

[10]See, for example, Richard Swinburne, *The Evolution of the Soul* (Oxford: Clarendon, 1986); and J. P. Moreland, "A Defense of a Substance Dualist View of the Soul," in *Christian Perspectives on Being Human*, ed. J. P. Moreland and David M. Ciocchi (Grand Rapids, Mich.: Baker, 1993), pp. 55-79.

[11]Michael Martin, "Atheistic Teleological Arguments," in *Contemporary Perspectives on Religious Epistemology*, ed. R. Douglas Geivett and Brendan Sweetman (New York: Oxford University Press, 1992), p. 47; italics Martin's.

[12]Ibid., pp. 48-49.

[13]See Stephen T. Davis, *Logic and the Nature of God* (London: Macmillan, 1983), pp. 8-24.

[14]Boethius, *The Theological Treatises and the Consolation of Philosophy*, Loeb Classical Library (London: William Heinemann, 1918), pp. 403-5. What I am calling "timelessness" Boethius called "eternity."

[15]Helpful discussions of divine timelessness are found in William Hasker, *God, Time and Knowledge* (Ithaca, N.Y.: Cornell University Press, 1989), pp. 144-85; and Paul Helm, *Eternal God: A Study of God Without Time* (Oxford: Clarendon, 1988).

[16]Rudolf Bultmann, "The New Testament and Mythology," in *Kerygma and Myth*, ed. Hans Werner Bartsch (New York: Harper and Row, 1961), p. 5.

[17]Van Austin Harvey, *The Historian and the Believer* (New York: Macmillan, 1966), pp. 114-15.

[18]For more on this and related points, see Stephen T. Davis, *Risen Indeed: Making Sense of the Resurrection* (Grand Rapids, Mich.: Eerdmans, 1993), pp. 34-42.

[19]Langdon Gilkey, "Cosmology, Ontology and the Travail of Biblical Language," in *God's Activity in the World: The Contemporary Problem*, ed. Owen C. Thomas (Chico, Calif.: Scholars Press, 1983), p. 32.

[20]Alston, "How to Think About Divine Action," p. 56.

[21]See Gordon Kaufman, "On the Meaning of 'Act of God,' " in *God the Problem* (Cambridge, Mass.: Harvard University Press, 1972), pp. 134-35.

[22]Alston, "God's Action in the World," p. 210.

[23]I owe this point to the Reverend Darrell Johnson.

Chapter 11/Geivett

[1]H. D. Lewis, *Philosophy of Religion* (London: English Universities Press, 1965), p. 307.

[2]If it should happen that these two methodologies are compatible, and even more so if they are complementary in some sense, then we will need a further distinction—between the thesis that one must at best choose between the two accounts of the evidential value of miracles and the thesis that these two accounts may be combined in some fashion. The latter thesis would then constitute a third conception of the general project of exhibiting the evidential value of miracles.

[3]William J. Wainwright, *Philosophy of Religion* (Belmont, Calif.: Wadsworth, 1988), pp. 61-62.

[4]William Alston considers the possibility that "God always acts through the natural order" and asks how the "special" acts of God might be identified as God's own on that assumption. The guidelines he provides for identifying special acts of God that are accomplished through the natural order may also have application when we seek to identify an act of God that might have been accomplished through the natural order even if it was not. See Alston, *Divine Nature and Human Language: Essays in Philosophical Theology* (Ithaca, N.Y.: Cornell University Press, 1989), pp. 213-17.

[5]For further discussion of the argument from miracles to the existence of God, see Brian Davies, *Thinking About God* (London: Geoffrey Chapman, 1985), pp. 50-58; Wainwright, *Philosophy of Religion,* pp. 58-62. Unfortunately, these authors do not stress the value of positive evidence that some miracle has or may have occurred. Most notably, Christian belief in the resurrection of Jesus is supported by historical evidence that the tomb of Jesus was found empty just days after he was confirmed dead and buried, and that following his death and burial Jesus appeared bodily alive to his disciples and others for a period of about forty days. That Jesus was raised from the dead is further confirmed by the improbable genesis of the Christian church within a few weeks after Jesus' ignominius death, and of a full-blown Christology within about twenty years. As Colin Brown writes, "The church itself constitutes a trace left by the event that Christians call the resurrection of Jesus" (*Miracles and the Critical Mind* [Grand Rapids, Mich.: Eerdmans, 1984], p. 96). See chapters 15 and 16 of the present volume, by William Lane Craig and by Gary Habermas, respectively, for a fuller development of these positive evidences.

[6]See Giovanna Borradori, *The American Philosopher: Conversations with Quine, Davidson, Putnam, Nozick, Danto, Rorty, Cavell, MacIntyre and Kuhn,* trans. Rosanna Crocitto (Chicago: University of Chicago Press, 1994), p. 167. As Michael Luntley has written, "The range of our [scientific] explanations is as broad as the range of our inquisitiveness. Wherever we have asked 'how? or 'why?,'' sooner or later, with perseverance, some good luck and occasional flashes of genius, we have come up with the answer" (*Reason, Truth and Self: The Postmodern Reconditioned* [London: Routledge, 1995], p. 46).

[7]See Willard Van Orman Quine, "Two Dogmas of Empiricism," in his *From a Logical Point of View,* 2d ed. (Cambridge, Mass.: Harvard University Press, 1961), and the book *The Web of Belief* by W. V. Quine and J. S. Ullian (New York: Random House, 1970).

[8]The reality of highly recalcitrant phenomena that strenuously resist naturalistic explanation has been acknowledged by authorities in various fields. For example, John Searle, a prominent philosopher of mind at the University of California at Berkeley, remarks that "ordinary human behavior has proven peculiarly recalcitrant to explanation by the methods of the natural sciences" (*Intentionality: An Essay in the Philosophy of Mind* [Cambridge: Cambridge University Press, 1983], p. x). And Stephen W. Hawking, an astrophysicist of undisputed sophistication, confesses, "Although science may solve the problem of how the universe began, it cannot answer the question: Why does the universe bother to exist? I don't know the answer to that" (*Black Holes and Baby Universes* [Toronto: Bantam, 1993], p. 99). The historian should be prepared to admit, when confronted with strong evidence for the resurrection, that history may not be able to explain the occurrence of the event, and to do so without declaring against the *possibility* of such an occurrence.

[9]See note 4 above.

[10]See William L. Rowe, *Philosophy of Religion: An Introduction,* 2d ed. (Belmont, Calif.: Wadsworth, 1993), p. 127 n. 12.

[11]See Wainwright, *Philosophy of Religion,* p. 60; Davies, *Thinking About God,* pp. 50-58. William Rowe, however, seems to think that it might be reasonable to acknowledge the violation of a law of nature by a particular event and still withhold any inference to God's existence as the explanation for that event (see Rowe, *Philosophy of Religion,* pp. 125-26). Richard Swinburne, on the other hand, sees value in the argument from miracles, although he evidently prefers to place the argument alongside other arguments in a cumulative case for the existence of God. See his *Faith and Reason* (Oxford: Clarendon, 1981), p. 180 n. 2; cf. his *The Concept of Miracle* (London: Macmillan, 1970), p. 74 n. 1, and "Miracles," *The Philosophical Quarterly* 18 (1968): 320-28.

[12]See Rowe, *Philosophy of Religion,* p. 126 and p. 127 n. 13; cf. Swinburne, "Miracles," esp. pp. 325-26.

[13]I do not here consider the potential evidential value of alleged contemporary miracles on behalf of Christianity. I have in mind, rather, such historical events as the resurrection of Jesus Christ, which Christians, along with the apostle Paul (1 Cor 15:12-19), have regarded as in some sense essential to Christianity.

[14]See William Lane Craig, "Did Jesus Rise from the Dead?" in *Jesus Under Fire: Modern Scholarship Reinvents the Historical Jesus,* ed. Michael J. Wilkins and J. P. Moreland (Grand Rapids, Mich.: Zondervan, 1995), pp. 141-76, and *Assessing the New Testament Evidence for the Historicity of the Resurrection of Jesus* (Lewiston, N.Y.: Edwin Mellen, 1989).

[15]See, for example, Peter Carnley, *The Structure of Resurrection Belief* (Oxford: Clarendon, 1987), pp. 89, 94, 185.

[16]Notice, furthermore, that the New Testament does not speak of figures witnessing the resurrection; what they witnessed were these other facts.

[17]Richard L. Purtill, *Thinking About Religion: A Philosophical Introduction to Religion* (Englewood Cliffs, N.J.: Prentice-Hall, 1978), p. 65.

[18]Ibid., p. 66.

[19]Ibid., p. 68.

[20]Ibid., p. 66.

[21]Lewis, *Philosophy of Religion,* p. 303.

[22]I have developed a related point in "The Interface of Theism and Christianity in a Two-Step Apologetic," *Ratio: Essays in Christian Thought* 1 (Autumn 1993): 211-30.

[23]Purtill, *Thinking About Religion,* p. 72.

[24]Ibid., p. 70.

[25]Ibid., p. 72.

[26]"Natural theology" is a label for the systematic formulation of reasons to believe that God exists, that God has a particular nature, and that God stands in relation to the world in certain definite ways. For my own attempt to sketch a plausible natural theology, see my *Evil and the Evidence for God* (Philadelphia: Temple University Press, 1993), chaps. 6-7.

[27]By "general revelation" I mean such sources of information about God and God's relationship to the world as we find in the entire realm of creation, human conscience, and the overall pattern of history. For an account of the differences between general revelation and special revelation, and of the particular value of

general revelation, see my essay "General Revelation and the God of the Bible," *Bible-Science News* 32, no. 4 (1994): 1-5.

[28]One may have any one of a number of independent reasons to look for a revelation from God. An expectation of revelation may be generated by the evidence of natural theology, as already suggested; one may simply have a compelling desire to be in touch with one's creator; or one may, on encountering religious traditions that acknowledge the existence of sacred texts, develop an interest in the question of authenticity regarding those texts.

[29]Furthermore, if we suppose that God desires to produce a revelation that has the best prospects for being understood, we might expect that revelation to be embodied in a set of propositions expressed—in the very act of revelation—by sentences in a natural language.

[30]Swinburne, *Faith and Reason,* p. 180; see also Swinburne's *Revelation: From Metaphor to Analogy* (Oxford: Clarendon, 1992), chap. 5.

[31]Ibid., chap. 5. I develop similar points in chapters contributed to two recent publications: Wilkins and Moreland, *Jesus Under Fire,* chap. 7; and *More Than One Way? Four Views on Salvation in a Pluralistic World,* ed. Dennis L. Okholm and Timothy R. Phillips (Grand Rapids, Mich.: Zondervan, 1995), chap. 4. See also my extensive discussion of the problem of evil, as it relates to the question of God's existence, in *Evil and the Evidence for God.*

[32]Swinburne, *Revelation,* chap. 6.

[33]See John Locke, *The Reasonableness of Christianity,* ed. I. T. Ramsey (Stanford, Calif.: Stanford University Press, 1958).

[34]David Hume, *Dialogues Concerning Natural Religion,* ed. Norman Kemp Smith (1779; Indianapolis: Bobbs-Merrill, 1947), p. 227.

[35]I wish to thank Howard Geivett, J. P. Moreland, Paul Moser, Wes Morriston, Brendan Sweetman and Daniel Yim for their valuable comments on earlier versions of this chapter.

Chapter 12/Clark

[1]David Hume, "Of Miracles," in *An Enquiry Concerning Human Understanding,* 3d ed., rev. P. H. Nidditch (1748; Oxford: Clarendon, 1975), Section X, part 2; see chap. 1, p. 38, in the present volume.

[2]Ibid.

[3]Joseph Houston, *Reported Miracles: A Critique of Hume* (Cambridge: Cambridge University Press, 1994), pp. 203-7.

[4]See Harold Remus, *Pagan-Christian Conflict over Miracle in the Second Century* (Cambridge, Mass.: Philadelphia Patristic Foundation, 1983), pp. 52-72. A. A. Barb argues that magic is a corruption of earlier religion rather than the primitive source from which religion evolved ("The Survival of Magical Arts," in *The Conflict Between Paganism and Christianity in the Fourth Century,* ed. Arnaldo Momigliano [Oxford: Clarendon, 1963], pp. 100-125). Scholars who conflate the terms *miracle* and *magic* may do so because they judge the miracle claims of all traditions to be spurious. But it is unfortunate to conflate these terms, for whatever reason, since they are conceptually distinguishable even if the concept of miracle is never exemplified.

[5]Graham H. Twelftree, *Jesus the Exorcist: A Contribution to the Study of the Historical Jesus* (Peabody, Mass.: Hendrickson, 1993), p. 173.

[6]Defining these two categories conceptually does not describe precisely how to distinguish actual miracles from magical events or demonic acts. See Winfried Corduan's chapter 6, "Recognizing a Miracle."

[7]For a good source on Eastern religions, see Stuart C. Hackett, *Oriental Philosophy: A Westerner's Guide to Eastern Thought* (Madison: University of Wisconsin Press, 1979), pp. 71-108.

[8]See discussion in Edward J. Thomas, *The Life of Buddha as Legend and History* (London: Routledge and Kegan Paul, 1949), pp. 211-48.

[9]"Naturalistic explanations" are interpretations of a miracle story which say that no miracle really occurred, since the stories are best explained as the result of nonmiraculous forces.

[10]Archie Bahm, *Tao Teh King*, 2d ed. (Albuquerque: World Books, 1986), p. 89, for example, discusses Taoism's negative attitude toward wonders.

[11]Reported in Geoffrey Ashe, *Miracles* (London: Routledge and Kegan Paul, 1978), p. 135.

[12]The same hesitation about powers *(siddhi)* pervades yoga. See Mircea Eliade, *Yoga: Immortality and Freedom,* 2d ed., trans. Willard R. Trask, Bollingen Series 56 (Princeton, N.J.: Princeton University Press, 1969), pp. 85-90.

[13]Annemarie Schimmel, *Mystical Dimensions of Islam* (Chapel Hill: University of North Carolina Press, 1975), p. 212.

[14]I have in my possession Turkish newspaper clippings to this effect. My purpose in telling this story is to illustrate the tendency of religious believers to create new stories.

[15]For example, Sayyid Ahmad Khan; see John L. Esposito, *Islam: The Straight Path,* 2d ed. (New York: Oxford University Press, 1991), pp. 134-35.

[16]Muslims cite the Qur'an's fulfilled prophecies, unity, scientific accuracy and mathematical structure. They say an illiterate Muhammad wrote a work that transforms lives. For response, see Norman L. Geisler and Abdul Saleeb, *Answering Islam: The Crescent in the Light of the Cross* (Grand Rapids, Mich.: Baker, 1993), pp. 100-106, 158-69.

[17]Isma'il Faruqi, *Islam* (Niles, Ill.: Argus, 1984), p. 20. Critics note that other works—those of Blaise Pascal or William Shakespeare—are sublime, but not necessarily miraculous. Other arguments (e.g., fulfilled prophecy) must be examined one by one.

[18]Hume, "Of Miracles," pt. 2; see chap. 1 of this volume, pp. 34-35.

[19]For an exposé of alleged Christian faith healer Peter Popoff, for example, see James Randi, *The Faith Healers* (Buffalo, N.Y.: Prometheus, 1987), pp. 139-81.

[20]*Ta'anit* 23a.

[21]Josephus *Antiquities of the Jews* 8.2.5.

[22]For example, Geza Vermes, *Jesus the Jew: A Historian's Reading of the Gospels* (New York: Macmillan, 1973).

[23]For example, Morton Smith, *Jesus the Magician* (San Francisco: Harper and Row, 1978); John Dominic Crossan, *The Historical Jesus: The Life of a Mediterranean Jewish Peasant* (San Francisco: HarperSanFrancisco, 1991). For a critique of Crossan, see Craig A. Evans, review of *The Historical Jesus* by John Dominic Crossan, *Trinity Journal* 13 (1992): 230-39.

[24]For example, Gerd Theissen, *The Miracle Stories of the Early Christian Tradition,* trans. Francis McDonagh (Philadelphia: Fortress, 1983), pp. 265-76.

[25]It is interesting that Philostratus, the biographer, raises serious doubts about whether the girl was really dead (see *Life of Apollonius* 4.45).

[26]See David Wenham and Craig Blomberg, eds., *Gospel Perspectives,* vol. 6, *The Miracles of Jesus* (Sheffield: JSOT Press, 1986).

[27]On the demise of the holy-man hypothesis, see Jack Dean Kingsbury, "The 'Divine Man' as the Key to Mark's Christology—The End of an Era?" *Interpretation* 35 (1981): 243-57.

[28]Some argue that the earliest documents show Jesus doing magic similar to that of first-century magicians and that later editors purged the similarities from their accounts. Thus Mark shows Jesus using spittle (7:33; 8:23), but Matthew and Luke edited out the reference. See John M. Hull, *Hellenistic Magic and the Synoptic Tradition,* Studies in Biblical Theology, 2d series, 28 (Naperville, Ill.: A. R. Allenson, 1974). For a contrary argument, see Jesus Seminar member John J. Rousseau, "Jesus, an Exorcist of a Kind," in *Society of Biblical Literature Seminar Papers 1993,* ed. Eugene H. Lovering Jr. (Atlanta: Scholars Press, 1993), pp. 129-53.

[29]Twelftree, *Jesus the Exorcist,* p. 173.

[30]Edwin Yamauchi, "Magic or Miracle? Diseases, Demons and Exorcisms," in *Gospel Perspectives,* vol. 6, *The Miracles of Jesus,* ed. David Wenham and Craig Blomberg (Sheffield: JSOT Press, 1986), pp. 128-49; Twelftree, *Jesus the Exorcist,* pp. 223-24.

[31]See Barry Blackburn, *Theios Aner and the Markan Miracle Traditions: A Critique of the "Theios Aner" Concept as an Interpretative Background of the Miracle Traditions Used by Mark* (Tübingen: J. C. B. Mohr, 1991).

[32]See Thomas, *Life of Buddha,* pp. 237-48.

[33]Ashe, *Miracles,* pp. 131-33.

[34]Ibid., p. 131. Martin Prozesky cites a chapter entitled "The Law of Miracles" in Paramhansa Yogananda, *Autobiography of a Yogi* (n.p. Rider, 1950). Prozesky comments that "there are Hindus who say that the power to produce these baffling feats is acquired by spiritually advanced people who have learnt how to overcome the limitations of the world of matter. If this is so, then the supposed causal link between miracles and God, as defined by Christianity, is significantly weakened" (Prozesky, *A New Guide to the Debate About God* [London: SCM Press, 1992], p. 113). Prozesky's claim that many marvelous events are really unusual applications of natural forces is well taken. But contrary to his last suggestion, that *some* marvels are caused by natural forces does not entail that *all* alleged miracles are merely natural events.

[35]The best-known claims to healing miracles are those at the Lourdes shrine. To rule out fraud, a medical bureau, open to any interested physician, examines hundreds of pilgrims before and after visiting the shrine. Without saying that the wonders at Lourdes are real miracles, I cite them as unusual because some effort is made to gain a prior and competent medical diagnosis. See Robert D. Smith, *Comparative Miracles* (St. Louis, Mo.: B. Herder, 1965), pp. 81-96.

[36]Of course, belief in contemporary miracles could be warranted not only by written documents but also by reliable eyewitnesses or oral testimony.

[37]Supporting an early date (before A.D. 70) for the Gospels is E. Earl Ellis, "Dating the New Testament," *New Testament Studies* 26 (1980): 487-502.

[38]See Thomas, *Life of Buddha,* pp. 211-48.

[39]James Ferguson, *The Religions of the Roman Empire* (Ithaca, N.Y.: Cornell University Press, 1970), p. 51; cf. Howard Clark Kee, *Miracle in the Early Christian World*

(New Haven, Conn.: Yale University Press, 1983), pp. 253-56.

[40]For examples of dating and documentary problems with non-Christian miracle claims, see Gary R. Habermas, "Resurrection Claims in Non-Christian Religions," *Religious Studies* 25 (1989): 167-77.

[41]See, for example, Craig Blomberg, *The Historical Reliability of the Gospels* (Downers Grove, Ill.: InterVarsity Press, 1987), sec. 4.

[42]*Sanhedrin* 43a. John P. Meier doubts that this reference represents an entirely independent tradition about Jesus (*A Marginal Jew: Rethinking the Historical Jesus*, vol. 1, *The Roots of the Problem and the Person*, Anchor Bible Reference Library [New York: Doubleday, 1991], pp. 96-97).

[43]Blomberg, *Historical Reliability*, p. 198.

[44]Mormon missionaries appeal to "new world archaeology" to validate the BOM, even claiming that archaeologists of the Smithsonian Institution and the National Geographic Society use the BOM as a field guide. These institutions regularly deny this claim, and some Mormons admit that no archaeologists who are not Mormons follow the BOM in their work. See Mormon apologist Paul R. Cheesman, *The World of the Book of Mormon* (Bountiful, Utah: Horizon, 1984), p. 15.

[45]Ibid., p. 86.

[46]For a readable critique of "new world archaeology," see Harry L. Ropp, *The Mormon Papers: Are the Mormon Scriptures Reliable?* (Downers Grove, Ill.: InterVarsity Press, 1977), pp. 47-54. For more information, see Jerald and Sandra Tanner, *Mormonism—Shadow or Reality?* 5th ed. (Salt Lake City, Utah: Utah Lighthouse Ministry, 1987), pp. 97-125J.

[47]See William Lane Craig, "The Problem of Miracles: A Historical and Philosophical Perspective," in *Gospel Perspectives*, vol. 6, *The Miracles of Jesus*, ed. David Wenham and Craig Blomberg (Sheffield: JSOT Press, 1986), p. 43.

Chapter 13/Newman

[1]See, for example, Otto Eissfeldt, *The Old Testament: An Introduction* (Oxford: Blackwell, 1965), pp. 303-46; Ernst Sellin and Georg Fohrer, *Introduction to the Old Testament* (Nashville: Abingdon, 1968), pp. 374-75; and Brevard Childs, *Introduction to the Old Testament as Scripture* (Philadelphia: Fortress, 1979), pp. 316-18. Scripture passages quoted in this chapter are from the New International Version.

[2]See Eissfeldt, *The Old Testament*, pp. 512-29; Sellin and Fohrer, *Introduction to the Old Testament*, pp. 477-78; and Childs, *Introduction to the Old Testament as Scripture*, pp. 611-13.

[3]See Eissfeldt, *The Old Testament*, pp. 429-40; Sellin and Fohrer, *Introduction to the Old Testament*, pp. 464-68; Childs, *Introduction to the Old Testament as Scripture*, pp. 474-76.

[4]See, for example, R. K. Harrison, *Introduction to the Old Testament* (Grand Rapids, Mich.: Eerdmans, 1969); Oswald T. Allis, *The Old Testament: Its Claims and Its Critics* (Nutley, N.J.: Presbyterian and Reformed, 1972); and Raymond B. Dillard and Tremper Longman III, *An Introduction to the Old Testament* (Grand Rapids, Mich.: Zondervan, 1994).

[5]See Dewey M. Beegle, *Prophecy and Prediction* (Ann Arbor, Mich.: Pryor Pettengill, 1978), pp. 67, 80.

[6]So Beegle sees the prophecies of Haggai and Zechariah as predicting that Zerub-

babel would be the Messiah (ibid., pp. 53-60).

[7]See Deuteronomy 18:20-22; Isaiah 44:24-28; 46:8-11.

[8]This strategy is often used to explain away the "fulfillment" of Psalm 22 by the soldiers who cast dice for Jesus' garments. See, for example, J. M. Creed, *The Gospel According to St. Luke* (London: Macmillan, 1957), p. 287.

[9]This is a common critical interpretation of Jesus' riding into Jerusalem on the donkey. See, for example, Hugh J. Schonfield, *The Passover Plot* (New York: Bernard Geis, 1965), p. 119.

[10]For a response, see Calvin E. Stowe, "Biblical Prophecy and Pagan Oracles," in *The Evidence of Prophecy*, ed. Robert C. Newman (Hatfield, Penn.: Interdisciplinary Biblical Research Institute, 1994), pp. 9-18.

[11]See Purtill, chapter 3, on the definition of a miracle.

[12]Indisputable evidence is not required, for one can always hold to David Hume's dictum with such tenacity that nothing but God can shake one loose from it. We should be trying to find out whether miracles occur or not, not trying to see if events that seem miraculous can be explained away by any possible device. In this chapter I strive for interpretations that fit a fair reading of the texts rather than seeking to rebut all alternative interpretations.

[13]See the relevant entries in Francis Brown, S. R. Driver and Charles A. Briggs, *A Hebrew and English Lexicon of the Old Testament* (Oxford: Clarendon, 1966), p. 978; and William L. Holladay, *A Concise Hebrew and Aramaic Lexicon of the Old Testament* (Grand Rapids, Mich.: Eerdmans, 1971), p. 354.

[14]See the more detailed discussion in John A. Bloom, "Hosea's Prophetic History of the Jews," in Newman, *The Evidence of Prophecy*, pp. 67-82.

[15]See G. Henton Davies, "Ephod," in *The Interpreter's Dictionary of the Bible* (Nashville: Abingdon, 1962), 2:118-19; G. L. Archer, "Ephod," in *The Zondervan Pictorial Encyclopedia of the Bible* (Grand Rapids, Mich.: Zondervan, 1975), 2:332-33; and R. K. Harrison, "Ephod," in *The International Standard Bible Encyclopedia* (Grand Rapids, Mich.: Eerdmans, 1979-88), 2:117-18.

[16]Much of the discussion in this section follows the treatment by John A. Bloom, "Truth via Prophecy," in *Evidence for Faith: Deciding the God Question*, ed. John Warwick Montgomery (Dallas: Probe/Word, 1991), pp. 173-92.

[17]In addition to the article by Bloom, "Truth via Prophecy," see Robert W. Manweiler, "The Destruction of Tyre," in Newman, *The Evidence of Prophecy*, pp. 21-30.

[18]The emphasis is added here and in other Scripture citations below for the purpose of contrasting significant items in the prediction.

[19]Bloom, "Truth via Prophecy," p. 185.

[20]Besides Bloom, "Truth via Prophecy," see Elaine A. Phillips, "The Fall of Nineveh," in Newman, *The Evidence of Prophecy*, pp. 41-51, on the destruction of Nineveh as predicted by the prophet Nahum.

[21]Strabo *Geography* 17.1.31-32; cf. Bloom, "Truth via Prophecy," p. 179.

[22]Francis L. Griffith, as cited in Bloom, "Truth via Prophecy," p. 181.

[23]A nice presentation of the structure and flow of Isaiah's servant section is provided by Allan A. MacRae in *The Gospel of Isaiah* (Hatfield, Penn.: Interdisciplinary Biblical Research Institute, 1992).

[24]For a treatment of this topic, including documentation, see the compilation in Alfred Edersheim, *The Life and Times of Jesus the Messiah* (Grand Rapids, Mich.: Eerdmans, 1967), 2:726.

[25]Isaiah 42:6 is alluded to in Luke 2:32 and Acts 26:3; Isaiah 49:6 in these two passages, as well as in John 8:12 and 9:5.

[26]See the statistical comparisons among world religions in David B. Barrett, ed., *World Christian Encyclopedia* (New York: Oxford, 1982), p. 4.

[27]Josephus *Jewish War* 6.5.4.

[28]Tacitus *Histories* 5.13.

[29]Suetonius *The Lives of the Caesars,* "The Deified Vespasian," 4.5.

[30]See discussions in J. Barton Payne, *Encyclopedia of Biblical Prophecy* (New York: Harper and Row, 1973), pp. 383-88; Gerard Van Groningen, *Messianic Revelation in the Old Testament* (Grand Rapids, Mich.: Baker, 1990), pp. 824-36; Paul Feinberg, "An Exegetical and Theological Study of Daniel 9:24-27," in *Tradition and Testament: Essays in Honor of Charles Lee Feinberg,* ed. Paul Feinberg and John Feinberg (Chicago: Moody Press, 1983).

[31]See, for example, Exodus 23:10-11; Leviticus 25:1-7.

[32]Details are given in Robert C. Newman, "Daniel's Seventy Weeks and the Old Testament Sabbath-Year Cycle," *Journal of the Evangelical Theological Society* 16 (1973): 229-34. This has been updated in "The Time of the Messiah," in Newman, *The Evidence of Prophecy,* pp. 111-18.

[33]See the recent items by Montgomery, Newman, Payne and Van Groningen in the above notes, plus the older classic works in the bibliography for this chapter.

Chapter 14/Feinberg

[1]Allan Bäck, "Aquinas on the Incarnation," *The New Scholasticism* 56 (Spring 1982): 128.

[2]Michael Martin, *The Case Against Christianity* (Philadelphia: Temple University Press, 1991), pp. 125-29.

[3]Michael Goulder, "Paradox and Mystification," in *Incarnation and Myth: The Debate Continued,* ed. Michael Goulder (Grand Rapids, Mich.: Eerdmans, 1979), p. 52.

[4]Ibid., pp. 51-54.

[5]John Hick, "Is There a Doctrine of the Incarnation?" in Goulder, *Incarnation and Myth,* p. 48.

[6]John Hick, "Jesus and the World Religions," in *The Myth of God Incarnate,* ed. John Hick (Philadelphia: Westminster, 1977), p. 178.

[7]Ibid., pp. 177-78. For Hick's own proposal regarding the meaning of the metaphor/myth of the incarnation, see Hick, "Jesus and the World Religions," p. 178.

[8]Hick, "Is There a Doctrine of the Incarnation?" p. 49.

[9]For further discussion of kenotic theologies see, for example, E. L. Mascall, "*Does God Change? Mutability and Incarnation:* A Review Discussion," *The Thomist* 50 (1986); and Thomas V. Morris, *The Logic of God Incarnate* (Ithaca, N.Y.: Cornell University Press, 1986), passim.

[10]In this chapter I use the terms *nature* and *essence* interchangeably to speak of all the qualities of a thing. Those properties make up the essence of the thing. As for Christ, he had both a divine essence and a human essence (each with its respective characteristics).

[11]This interpretation fits the context. At Philippi factions arose around certain Christians who held positions of influence in the church. Those factions threatened the unity of the church. In Philippians 2:1-4 Paul pleads for unity of thought and

love as well as for concern toward others. Paul does not ask them to give up their positions, but only urges them not to use their positions to push their will on others. In verses 5-11 Paul turns to Christ as the example. He, too, had a position. He never gave it up, but to serve us while on earth he willingly relinquished exercise of all the power and privilege that go with being God. Christ lost nothing by doing this, for God highly exalted him after the time of emptying. The application to the Philippian leaders is clear.

[12]"The Creed of Chalcedon," in *The Creeds of Christendom: With a History and Critical Notes,* ed. Philip Schaff (Grand Rapids, Mich.: Baker, 1931), 2:62-63. In this chapter the terms *hypostasis* and *suppositum* will be used synonymously. A *suppositum* is "an independently existing ultimate subject of characteristics" (Alfred Freddoso, "Human Nature, Potency and the Incarnation," *Faith and Philosophy* 3 [January 1986]: 28). As such, the *hypostasis* or *suppositum* is the bearer of properties (see Morris, *The Logic of God Incarnate,* p. 154).

[13]See Morris's discussion of several ways to defend this doctrine in *The Logic of God Incarnate,* pp. 24-32.

[14]Ibid., p. 38.

[15]In this chapter *person* means "just a suppositum with an intellectual nature, that is, a suppositum essentially endowed with intellect and free will" (Freddoso, "Human Nature, Potency and the Incarnation," p. 29). Since there is only one suppositum in Jesus Christ and since he has both intellect and free will, there is only one person Jesus Christ. His two natures (each with intellect and free will) do not entail that there are two persons in Christ. There would be two persons in Christ only if there were two hypostases in him that were never really united (this is the Nestorian heresy). But Chalcedon said there was a genuine union of the two natures in one hypostasis, the person Jesus Christ.

[16]Morris, *The Logic of God Incarnate,* p. 39.

[17]Ibid., p. 64 (italics mine). See also the preceding pages for an explanation of the distinction between common and essential properties.

[18]See Morris's further discussion about the matter of origins as it relates to essential human properties (ibid., pp. 68-70).

[19]See ibid., pp. 65-66, including Morris's helpful summary.

[20]Michael Martin makes precisely this objection (Martin, *The Case Against Christianity,* pp. 136-37).

[21]Morris, *The Logic of God Incarnate,* p. 103.

[22]Ibid.

[23]Ibid., pp. 104-5.

[24]Ibid., p. 105.

[25]Ibid., pp. 105-6.

[26]See ibid., pp. 138-46.

[27]See ibid., pp. 142-44.

[28]See ibid., p. 148.

[29]See ibid., pp. 148-49.

[30]Ibid., p. 150.

[31]See chapter 8 by J. P. Moreland for an in-depth discussion of this concept.

[32]See Morris, *The Logic of God Incarnate,* pp. 151-53.

[33]The trichotomist position demands two immaterial substances, but that need not detain us here.

[34]A nontheological case can be made for mind as immaterial (for example, it is hard to explain such things as intentionality on a strictly materialist theory of mind), but this is not the place to do so. My point is that this is an assumption the orthodox theist must bring to the incarnation debate. And of course, the question is whether all these views that are assumed and explained do remove the apparent contradiction in regard to Christ's being.

[35]Those who hold the trichotomist position will in no way protest, but neither should anyone who understands the nature of immaterial substances.

[36]John Hick raises this objection. See his review of Morris's position in "The Logic of God Incarnate," *Religious Studies* 25 (1989): 411-13. Michael Durrant ("The Logic of God Incarnate—Two Recent Metaphysical Principles Examined," *Religious Studies* 24 [1988]: 123-27) relatedly complains about Morris's fully human/merely human distinction. He complains that the contrasts are not contrasts within a grade, class or ontological level (a quantitative comparison) but contrasts between things in different grades (a qualitative contrast), a contrast between someone who has fully made it within a grade and someone who makes it in one grade but does not fail to make it in another as well. But why is this a problem? Durrant thinks the distinction makes no real contrast because both do not refer to beings in the same grade. But this is a real contrast, one between someone who makes it fully in one grade and someone who makes it fully in two grades or levels.

[37]See Hick, "The Logic of God Incarnate," p. 414.

[38]Despite my point about the necessity of two minds in Christ, some see other ways to uphold the orthodox doctrine of the incarnation. For an intriguing (though problematic) proposal that addresses this issue without invoking a two-minds theory see Thomas D. Senor, "God, Supernatural Kinds and the Incarnation," *Religious Studies* 27 (1991): 353-70.

[39]For evidence that mind is immaterial and that immaterial minds can interact with physical bodies (including brains), see Gary R. Habermas and J. P. Moreland, *Immortality* (Nashville: Thomas Nelson, 1992), chaps. 2-3, and Karl R. Popper and John C. Eccles, *The Self and Its Brain* (New York: Springer-Verlag, 1977).

[40]Hick complains that if Christ's human mind had access to his divine mind only when the divine mind gave access, this is the same relation any human mind has to God's knowledge. Does that mean God is incarnate in all of us? Morris anticipates the problem and responds. For Morris's answer and Hick's reaction see Morris, *The Logic of God Incarnate,* p. 162, and Hick, "The Logic of God Incarnate," pp. 421-22. I think the proper answer to Hick is that there is a fundamental difference between Christ's case and ours. Our having access to God's knowledge does not stem from our mind and body being ontologically united to God's mind. Our very being as individual persons does not include the very being of God. In Jesus' case, however, there is an ontological union of natures so that an ontological part of the hypostasis Jesus Christ *is* a divine nature. This ontological difference sufficiently distinguishes our access and Christ's access to the divine mind.

[41]Michael Martin complains that if there really are two minds in Christ, there must be two persons. Morris thinks Christ's is a special case, but Martin complains that Morris offers no evidence that Christ's case is special (see Martin, *The Case Against Christianity,* p. 138). This is a prime example of ignoring the "ground rules" of the problem, for it demands *proof* that the one-mind-equals-one-person rule does not apply to Christ. Since the charge against the incarnation is logical contradiction, all

Morris must show is that Christ is a possible exception to that rule and that, granting that exception, the incarnation is not incoherent. Morris need not prove that Jesus is the exception.

[42]See my "God Ordains All Things," in *Predestination and Free Will,* ed. Randall Basinger and David Basinger (Downers Grove, Ill.: InterVarsity Press, 1986).

[43]Michael Martin gives this impression. He says that to be tempted to sin means being attracted to or being led on by one's desire to do something immoral. But "it is absurd to suppose that a morally perfect being could be attracted to or led on by his desire to, for example, torture or murder" (Martin, *The Case Against Christianity,* p. 144). Surely Martin is right that some sins by their very nature will not likely tempt (let alone trap) a perfect being. But Martin assumes that if one had these desires even in the slightest one would have committed the sin. I reply that this is a deficient notion of temptation. As the epistle of James says, there is a point in the allurement process when sin is conceived; prior to that, there is temptation, but no sin (Jas 1:15). This is true for all sins, including the ones Martin mentions.

[44]W. G. T. Shedd, *Dogmatic Theology* (Grand Rapids, Mich.: Zondervan, 1969), 2: 336.

[45]Martin raises problems about whether the doctrine of the incarnation is likely true (see *The Case Against Christianity,* pp. 146-58), but those issues question the truth of the doctrine, not its logical coherence. That topic is beyond the purview of this chapter.

Chapter 15/Craig

[1]Richard N. Ostling, "Jesus Christ, Plain and Simple," *Time,* January 10, 1994, pp. 32-33. See John Dominic Crossan, *Jesus: A Revolutionary Biography* (San Francisco: HarperSanFrancisco, 1994).

[2]Rudolf Pesch, *Das Markusevangelium,* 2 vols., Herders Theologischer Kommentar zum Neuen Testament 2 (Freiburg: Herder, 1977), 2:21; cf. 2:364-77.

[3]Raymond E. Brown, *The Death of the Messiah: A Commentary on the Passion Narratives in the Four Gospels,* 2 vols., Anchor Bible Reference Library (New York: Doubleday, 1994), 2:1240.

[4]Rudolf Bultmann, a scholar so skeptical that he believed that all the information we have about the historical Jesus could be written on a four-by-six-inch index card, nevertheless called Mark's account of Jesus' burial "an historical report which makes no impression of being legendary, apart from the women who appear . . . as witnesses in v. 47 and vs. 44, 45" (Rudolf Bultmann, *Die Geschichte der synoptischen Tradition,* 2d ed., Forschungen zur Religion und Literatur des Alten und Neuen Testaments 12 [Göttingen: Vandenboeck und Ruprecht, 1970], p. 296. On the role of women, see my discussion later in the present chapter.

[5]Crossan attempts to discern other burial traditions in the *Epistula Apostolorum* (a Coptic document from the second century) and Lactantius *Divine Institute* 4.19 (from the early fourth century). That Crossan finds these late, derivative and sometimes fanciful sources to be more trustworthy purveyors of historical tradition than the New Testament documents is a comment on his methodology. In any case, these sources do not in fact offer alternatives to the burial account of the Gospels but paraphrased summaries of it that no more exclude burial by Joseph of Arimathea than does the Apostles' Creed. The desire to polemicize against the Jews leads Lactantius to include Joseph under the general rubric "the Jews." The same motive

governs Acts 13:27-29, to which Crossan also appeals. Finally, John 19:31 has to do only with a request to speed up the crucifixion process, not with actual burial.

[6]Wolfgang Trilling, *Fragen zur Geschichtlichkeit Jesu* (Düsseldorf: Patmos Verlag, 1966), p. 157.

[7]Karl Martin Fischer, *Das Ostergeschehen*, 2d ed. (Göttingen: Vandenhoeck und Ruprecht, 1980), pp. 63-64.

[8]Rudolf Bultmann, *Theologie des Neuen Testament*, ed. Otto Merk, 7th ed. (Tübingen: J. C. B. Mohr, 1961), p. 48.

[9]For a relevant discussion of these points, see my *Assessing the New Testament Evidence for the Historicity of the Resurrection of Jesus* (Lewiston, N.Y.: Edwin Mellen, 1989).

[10]Anton Vögtle and Rudolf Pesch, *Wie kam es zum Osterglauben?* (Düsseldorf: Patmos Verlag, 1975), p. 87; Lorenz Oberlinner, "Die Verkündigung der Auferweckung Jesu im geöffneten und leeren Grab," *Zeitschrift für die Neutestamentlichen Wissenschaft* 73 (1982): 168.

[11]Pesch, *Das Markusevangelium*, 2:522-36. Cf. Rudolf Pesch, "Zur Entstehung des Glaubens an die Auferstehung Jesu," *Theologische Quartalschrift* 153 (1973): 201-28, and "Stellungnahme zu den Diskussions-beiträgen," *Theologische Quartalschrift* 153 (1973): 270-83. Pesch thinks the account of the stone's being rolled away is the product of door-opening miracle stories. When it is pointed out that no such door opening is narrated in Mark, Pesch gives away his case by asserting that it is a "latent" door-opening miracle! The angelic appearance he attributes to epiphany appeals to a literary genre for seeking, but not finding, someone for the search for Jesus' body, adducing several largely irrelevant texts (e.g., 2 Kings 2:16-18; Ps 37:36; Ex 26:21) plus a spate of post-Christian or Christian-influenced sources (*Gospel of Nicodemus* 16:6; *Testament of Job* 39-40) and even question-begging texts from the New Testament itself. He does not come to grips with his own early dating and does not show how legend could supplant historical recollection.

[12]Michael Goulder, "The Empty Tomb," *Theology* 79 (1976): 206-14; Crossan makes rather similar claims concerning the origin of the burial story.

[13]J. M. Ross, "The Use of Evidence in New Testament Studies," *Theology* 19 (1976): 214-21.

[14]John Dominic Crossan, *The Historical Jesus* (Edinburgh: T & T Clark, 1991), p. 296.

[15]Oberlinner, "Die Verkündigung der Auferweckung," p. 177.

[16]Vögtle and Pesch, *Osterglauben*, p. 94.

[17]Peter Carnley, *The Structure of Resurrection Belief* (Oxford: Clarendon, 1987), pp. 55-56.

[18]Fischer, *Ostergeschehen*, pp. 63-64.

[19]See William Lane Craig, "The Guard at the Tomb," *New Testament Studies* 30 (1984): 273-81.

[20]D. H. Van Daalen, *The Real Resurrection* (London: Collins, 1970), p. 41; see also Gerald O'Collins, *The Easter Jesus*, 2d ed. (London: Darton, Longman & Todd, 1980), p. 91. The historian Michael Grant concludes:

> Even if the historian chooses to regard the youthful apparition as extra-historical, he cannot justifiably deny the empty tomb. True, this discovery, as so often, is differently described by the various Gospels—as critical pagans early pointed out. But if we apply the same sort of criteria that we would apply to any other ancient

literary sources, then the evidence is firm and plausible enough to necessitate the conclusion that the tomb was indeed found empty. (Michael Grant, *Jesus: An Historian's Review of the Gospels* [New York: Scribner's, 1977], p. 176)

[21] Jacob Kremer, *Die Osterevangelien—Geschichten um Geschichte* (Stuttgart: Katholisches Bibelwerk, 1977), pp. 49-50.

[22] See my *The Historical Argument for the Resurrection of Jesus* (Lewiston, N.Y.: Edwin Mellen, 1985).

[23] David Whittaker, "What Happened to the Body of Jesus? A Speculation," *Expository Times* 81 (1970): 307-10. Whittaker supposes the thieves to have been ordinary vandals. This hypothesis takes for granted that there was no guard at the tomb.

[24] Mark's dating of the women's visit on "the first day of the week" rather than "on the third day" shows how extremely primitive this tradition is, a fact confirmed by the Semitic flavor of the phrase.

[25] On the historical credibility of this tradition, see William Lane Craig, "The Disciples' Inspection of the Empty Tomb (Luke 24:12-24; John 20:1-10)," in *John and the Synoptics,* ed. A. Denaux, Bibliotheca Ephemeridum Theologicarum Lovaniensium 101 (Louvain: University Press, 1992), pp. 614-19.

Chapter 16/Habermas

[1] Reginald H. Fuller, *The Foundations of New Testament Christology* (New York: Scribner's, 1965), p. 142.

[2] Ibid., emphasis added.

[3] James D. G. Dunn, *The Evidence for Jesus* (Louisville, Ky.: Westminster, 1985), p. 75.

[4] For example, see Gary R. Habermas, *The Historical Jesus* (Joplin, Mo.: College Press, 1996); with Antony G. N. Flew, *Did Jesus Rise from the Dead? The Resurrection Debate,* ed. Terry Miethe (San Francisco: Harper and Row, 1987); "Jesus' Resurrection and Contemporary Criticism: An Apologetic," *Criswell Theological Review* 4, no. 1 (Fall 1989): 159-74 and 4, no. 2 (Spring 1990): 373-85.

[5] For just a few examples, see Reginald Fuller, *The Formation of the Resurrection Narratives* (New York: Macmillan, 1971); Raymond Brown, *The Virginal Conception and Bodily Resurrection of Jesus* (New York: Paulist, 1973); Ulrich Wilckens, *Resurrection,* trans. A. M. Stewart (Edinburgh: St. Andrew, 1978); Pinchas Lapide, *The Resurrection of Jesus: A Jewish Perspective* (Minneapolis: Augsburg, 1983); William Lane Craig, *Assessing the New Testament Evidence for the Historicity of the Resurrection of Jesus* (Lewiston, N.Y.: Edwin Mellen, 1989).

[6] Clarence Tucker Craig explains: "It is unnecessary to discuss the authenticity of the letter. . . . No letter has better external testimony than this one. . . . It is well established that a corpus of Pauline letters circulated widely by the first half of the second century and contained our letter." See Craig's "Introduction and Exegesis of 1 Corinthians," in *The Interpreter's Bible,* ed. George Arthur Buttrick (New York: Abingdon-Cokesbury, 1953), 10:13.

[7] For numerous details, see Fuller, *The Formation of the Resurrection Narratives,* pp. 9ff.; Lapide, *The Resurrection of Jesus,* pp. 97-99. For a list of some of the reasons for these conclusions, see Terry L. Miethe and Gary R. Habermas, *Why Believe? God Exists!* (Joplin, Mo.: College Press, 1993), p. 267. In addition to Fuller and Lapide, scholars who agree on the early date include Brown, *Virginal Conception and Bodily Resurrection,* pp. 81, 92; John A. T. Robinson, *Can We Trust the New Testament?*

(Grand Rapids, Mich.: Eerdmans, 1977), p. 125; Rudolf Bultmann, *Theology of the New Testament*, trans. Kendrick Grobel (New York: Scribner's, 1951, 1955), 1: 296; Paul Van Buren, *The Secular Meaning of the Gospel* (New York: Macmillan, 1963), pp. 126-27. Compare Marcus Borg, "Thinking About Easter," *Bible Review* 10, no. 2 (April 1994): 15; Willi Marxsen, *The Resurrection of Jesus of Nazareth*, trans. Margaret Kohl (Philadelphia: Fortress, 1970), p. 80; Günther Bornkamm, *Jesus of Nazareth*, trans. Irene and Fraser McLuskey with James M. Robinson (New York: Harper and Row, 1960), p. 182; Joachim Jeremias, "Easter· The Earliest Tradition and the Earliest Interpretation," in *New Testament Theology*, trans. J. Bowden (New York: Scribner's, 1971), p. 306.

[8]Joachim Jeremias declares that this confession is "the earliest tradition of all" (in "Easter: The Earliest Tradition and the Earliest Interpretation," p. 306). Wilckens asserts that it "indubitably goes back to the oldest phase of all in the history of primitive Christianity" (*Resurrection*, p. 2).

[9]Some of the many critical scholars who adopt such a date include Hans Grass, *Ostergeschehen und Osterberichte*, 2d ed. (Göttingen: Vandenhoeck und Ruprecht, 1962), p. 96; Oscar Cullmann, *The Early Church: Studies in Early Christian History and Theology*, ed. A. J. B. Higgins (Philadelphia: Westminster, 1966), pp. 65-66; Leonard Goppelt, "The Eastern Kerygma in the New Testament," in *The Easter Message Today* (New York: Thomas Nelson, 1964), p. 36; Wolfhart Pannenberg, *Jesus—God and Man*, trans. Lewis L. Wilkens and Duane Priebe (Philadelphia: Westminster, 1968), p. 90; Fuller, *The Formation of the Resurrection Narratives*, pp. 10, 14, 28, 48; C. H. Dodd, *The Apostolic Preaching and Its Developments* (Grand Rapids, Mich.: Baker, 1980), p. 16; A. M. Hunter, *Jesus: Lord and Saviour* (Grand Rapids, Mich.: Eerdmans, 1976), p. 100; Brown, *Virginal Conception and Bodily Resurrection*, p. 81; Thomas Sheehan, *First Coming: How the Kingdom of God Became Christianity* (New York: Random House, 1986), pp. 110, 118; G. E. Ladd, *I Believe in the Resurrection of Jesus* (Grand Rapids, Mich.: Eerdmans, 1975), p. 105. Hans Küng dates this traditional statement between A.D. 35 and 45 (*On Being a Christian* [Garden City, N.Y.: Doubleday, 1976], p. 348). Norman Perrin places the date at no later than A.D. 50, but he does not give a closer approximation in *The Resurrection According to Matthew, Mark and Luke* (Philadelphia: Fortress, 1977), p. 79. Gerald O'Collins is not aware of any scholar who places the date for Paul's reception of this material after the A.D. 40s (see *What Are They Saying About the Resurrection?* [New York: Paulist, 1978], p. 112). Crucially, our major conclusions would still follow even with a later date.

[10]For some of those scholars who generally favor this Jerusalem scenario, see the list in the previous note. Grass is an exception when he postulates that Paul received this tradition in Damascus, requiring an even earlier date (*Ostergeschehen und Osterberichte*, p. 96). Sheehan, Küng and Perrin do not appear to answer this question in their immediate contexts.

[11]Hans von Campenhausen, "The Events of Easter and the Empty Tomb," in *Tradition and Life in the Early Church*, (Philadelphia: Fortress, 1968), p. 44.

[12]Hunter, *Jesus: Lord and Saviour*, p. 100.

[13]Dodd, *The Apostolic Preaching*, p. 16.

[14]William R. Farmer, "Peter and Paul, and the Tradition Concerning 'The Lord's Supper' in 1 Cor. 11:23-25," *Criswell Theological Review* 2 (1987): esp. 122-30. On the Petrine nature of the gospel creed in 1 Corinthians 15:3ff., see pp. 135-38.

[15]Dodd, *The Apostolic Preaching*, p. 16.

[16]Lapide, *The Resurrection of Jesus*, pp. 97-99. Fuller agrees, citing similar data (*The Formation of the Resurrection Narratives*, pp. 9-14), as does Brown (*Virginal Conception and Bodily Resurrection*, pp. 81-84). For other details, including numerous additional scholars who hold such a position, see Miethe and Habermas, *Why Believe?* p. 267.

[17]We do not even need to venture into Paul's other New Testament writings in order to show that he considered this message to be his central proclamation. Such a conclusion is evident from the opening verses of this text, where Paul explains that the believer stands on this foundation (1 Cor 15:1) and that one's personal salvation comes from one's response to this material (15:2). But Paul also points out that there is really no such thing as the Christian faith, and that such belief is vain, unless the message of Jesus' resurrection is true (15:12-20).

[18]See Daniel P. Fuller, *Easter Faith and History* (Grand Rapids, Mich.: Eerdmans, 1965), chaps. 7-8; Gary R. Habermas and J. P. Moreland, *Immortality* (Nashville: Thomas Nelson, 1992), pp. 71, 245-46.

[19]Dodd's extended and influential discussion of these passages is found in *The Apostolic Preaching*, pp. 17-31. John Drane (*Introducing the New Testament* [San Francisco: Harper and Row, 1986], p. 99) asserts:

> The earliest evidence we have for the resurrection almost certainly goes back to the time immediately after the resurrection event is alleged to have taken place. This is the evidence contained in the early sermons in the Acts of the Apostles. . . . But there can be no doubt that in the first few chapters of Acts its author has preserved material from very early sources.

[20]For this theme, see the early confessions in Acts 2:22-33; 3:14-15, 26; 4:10; 5:30; 10:39-43; 13:27-37. All but the last is attributed to Peter. The last two texts strongly imply group appearances of Jesus.

[21]This theme occurs in Acts 2:32; 3:15; 5:32; 10:41; 13:31.

[22]See W. Craig, *Assessing the New Testament Evidence*, pp. 161-347; Grant Osborne, *The Resurrection Narratives: A Redactional Study* (Grand Rapids, Mich.: Baker, 1984), pp. 41-192.

[23]C. H. Dodd, "The Appearances of the Risen Christ: An Essay in Form-Criticism of the Gospels," in *More New Testament Studies* (Grand Rapids, Mich.: Eerdmans, 1968).

[24]This includes four Pauline and five non-Pauline arguments, counting the linguistic considerations in 1 Corinthians 15:3ff. in the latter category. Any evidence from the Gospel accounts could be further subdivided into separate points.

[25]Donald Wayne Viney, "Grave Doubts About the Resurrection," *Encounter* 50, no. 2 (Spring 1989): 128-31.

[26]Lapide, *The Resurrection of Jesus*, p. 99.

[27]R. T. France, *The Evidence for Jesus* (Downers Grove, Ill.: InterVarsity Press, 1987), pp. 122-25.

[28]von Campenhausen, "The Events of Easter and the Empty Tomb," p. 44.

[29]Michael Martin, *The Case Against Christianity* (Philadelphia: Temple University Press, 1991), pp. 81-84, 89.

[30]Ibid., pp. 81, 85, 90.

[31]Dodd, *The Apostolic Preaching*, p. 16.

[32]Ibid., pp. 21-23, 26, 31.

[33]Dunn, *The Evidence for Jesus,* p. 75.

[34]Rudolf Bultmann, "New Testament and Mythology," in *Kerygma and Myth,* ed. Hans Werner Bartsch, trans. Reginald H. Fuller (New York: Harper and Row, 1961), p. 42; cf. p. 39.

[35]Fuller, *The Foundations of New Testament Christology,* p. 142.

[36]Michael Grant, *Jesus: An Historian's Review of the Gospels* (New York: Macmillan, 1977), p. 176.

[37]Carl Braaten, *History and Hermeneutics* (Philadelphia: Westminster, 1966), p. 78.

[38]Wolfhart Pannenberg, "The Historicity of the Resurrection: The Identity of Christ," in *The Intellectuals Speak Out About God,* ed. Roy Varghese (Chicago: Regnery Gateway, 1984), p. 260.

[39]At the risk of oversimplification, we will very briefly entertain a few examples of such theses. Our purpose here is not so much to disprove completely these alternative attempts as it is to show that they do not even account for the appearance data alone. The charge that the disciples stole Jesus' dead body can hardly account for their being so convinced that they had actually seen the risen Jesus some time later, even less for their willingness to die for this belief! If someone else stole the body, this does not at all address the data for the appearances unless another thesis is employed. Besides all the exceptionally weighty (especially medical) problems in any supposition that Jesus did not die on the cross, the final refutation is that in his weakened, bloodied, limping condition, he could not have convinced his disciples that he had been raised in the first place, and certainly not in an eternal, glorified body! Thus, beyond all the other problems, a swoon hypothesis does not properly account for the quality of Jesus' appearances. Neither can legends and comparative mythology explain the more substantial testimony given by early eyewitnesses concerning the appearances, such as I have recounted above. These naturalistic options also run aground when they attempt to explain additional aspects of the resurrection evidence, such as the empty tomb, the radical transformation of the disciples, the centrality of the resurrection proclamation and the conversions of both Paul and James. For a more detailed consideration of such implausible naturalistic hypotheses, see Habermas and Moreland, *Immortality,* pp. 55-65; W. Craig, *Assessing the New Testament Evidence,* pp. 374-79, 397-404.

[40]Bultmann, "New Testament and Mythology," pp. 39-42. A more recent expression is Gerd Lüdemann, *The Resurrection of Jesus: History, Experience, Theology,* trans. John Bowden (London: SCM Press, 1994), pp. 54-59.

[41]Clinical psychologist Gary R. Collins explains (in personal correspondence dated February 21, 1977):

> Hallucinations are individual occurrences. By their very nature only one person can see a given hallucination at a time. They certainly are not something which can be seen by a group of people. Neither is it possible that one person could somehow induce an hallucination in somebody else. Since an hallucination exists only in this subjective, personal sense, it is obvious that others cannot witness it.

For some similar ideas, see J. P. Brady, "The Veridicality of Hypnotic, Visual Hallucinations," in *Origins and Mechanisms of Hallucinations,* ed. Wolfram Keup (New York: Plenum, 1970), p. 181; Weston La Barre, "Anthropological Perspectives on Hallucinations and Hallucinogens," in *Hallucinations: Behavior, Experience and Theory,* ed. R. K. Siegel and L. J. West (New York: John Wiley, 1975), pp. 9-10.

[42]To take examples from the early creedal statements alone, the pre-Pauline report

in 1 Corinthians 15 enumerates three group appearances ("to the twelve" [v. 4], to five hundred [v. 6], and "to all the apostles" [v. 7]), while at least two of the creedal statements in Acts also imply group appearances to the apostles (10:40-42; 13:30-31).

[43]Rarely, someone claims that more than one person can share the same hallucination. One effort to argue that collective hallucinations are possible (although without any reference to Jesus' resurrection) is made by Leonard Zusne and Warren H. Jones in *Anomalistic Psychology: A Study of Extraordinary Phenomena of Behavior and Experience* (Hillsdale, Mich.: Lawrence Erlbaum Associates, 1982), pp. 135-36. But this sort of claim falls short at many points, some of which will be mentioned briefly.

Their chief cases of "collective hallucinations" are references to Fatima-like religious experiences, since known instances of such shared phenomena are said to be basically religious in nature (ibid., p. 135). But this is problematic because it begs the very question of whether such experiences could possibly be objective ones. In other words, if the instances of such collective phenomena tend to be religious, why must it be assumed that they are subjective, nonveridical experiences? How do we know that they are hallucinations at all?

This position is strangely unfalsifiable—many purely natural, physical sightings by groups of people could be similarly dismissed without much fear of refutation. By this criterion, how could we ever distinguish between a hallucination and a normal, physical sighting?

Furthermore, much of the New Testament data not only differ from but contradict the necessary conditions for these "collective hallucinations." For example, Zusne and Jones explain that "expectation" and "emotional excitement" are "prerequisites" for such group sightings. Actually, the former "plays the coordinating role" (p. 135). But this does not apply to the witnesses of Jesus' resurrection appearances, who were confronted by the utter realism of the fresh and unexpected death of their dear friend, the one who had given meaning to their lives. This is *completely unlike* those in the examples above, who exuberantly gathered for the explicit purpose of seeing something.

Other distinctions also exist, further showing that Jesus' resurrection appearances are decisively dissimilar. The resurrection accounts occur over a greater variety of times, settings and circumstances, including the element of surprise. Besides Paul, James was another skeptic whose life was utterly transformed after meeting the risen Jesus. That the apostles were willing to give their lives specifically for this belief also separates them from the modern enthusiasts above. The empty tomb would still require another, independent explanation.

Then, even if it could be shown that individuals have hallucinated simultaneously, it does not at all follow that these experiences are collective. Since hallucinations are private events peculiar to individuals (see note 41 above), how could they share *exactly the same* subjective visual perception? It is far more likely that the collective phenomena in question are either perceptual misinterpretations of physical manifestations (as Zusne and Jones suggest on p. 136) or *individual* hallucinations experienced by some, while others present are not hallucinating.

One wonders if Zusne and Jones might not even agree with such a critique. They end their discussion with the startling admission that these "group hallucinations" have a "dubious status" because, after all, it is not even possible to be sure that these individuals were actually hallucinating (p. 136; cf. pp. 134-35)!

[44]For many more details on this theory, see Gary R. Habermas, *The Resurrection of Jesus: A Rational Inquiry* (Ann Arbor, Mich.: University Microfilms, 1976), pp. 127-45. A much briefer critique, including additional information, sources and objections, is found in Habermas and Moreland, *Immortality,* pp. 60-61.

[45]For examples, see Hans Grass, *Ostergeschehen und Osterberichte,* pp. 96, 242; Paul Tillich, *Systematic Theology* (Chicago: University of Chicago Press, 1971), 2:156; Karl Barth, *Church Dogmatics,* ed. G. W. Bromiley and T. F. Torrance (Edinburgh: T & T Clark, 1956), 4/1, p. 340; Raymond Brown, "The Resurrection and Biblical Criticism," *Commonweal* 87, no. 8 (November 1967): 233; Bornkamm, *Jesus of Nazareth,* p. 185; Lapide, *The Resurrection of Jesus,* pp. 124-26; Jeremias, "Easter: The Earliest Tradition and the Earliest Interpretation," p. 302; Fuller, *The Formation of the Resurrection Narratives,* pp. 46-49; Robinson, *Can We Trust the New Testament?* pp. 123-25; Pannenberg, *Jesus: God and Man,* pp. 94-97; A. M. Ramsay, *The Resurrection of Christ* (London: Collins, 1961), pp. 41, 49-50; Neville Clark, *Interpreting the Resurrection* (Philadelphia: Westminster, 1967), pp. 100-101.

[46]Pannenberg, *Jesus: God and Man,* p. 96.

[47]Dunn, *The Evidence for Jesus,* p. 76.

[48]Brown, "The Resurrection and Biblical Criticism," p. 233. Similarly, and also after listing a number of nonmiraculous options, Karl Barth exclaimed: "To-day we rightly turn up our nose at this." Then, after noting the presence of problems with such views, Barth notes that "these explanations . . . have now gone out of currency" (Barth, *Church Dogmatics,* 4/1, p. 340).

[49]Grass, *Ostergeschehen und Osterberichte,* p. 93; Fuller, *The Formation of the Resurrection Narratives,* pp. 46-49, 169-72, 181; Jeremias, "Easter: The Earliest Tradition and the Earliest Interpretation," pp. 308-9; Wilckens, *Resurrection,* pp. 116-25; Jürgen Moltmann, *Theology of Hope,* trans. James W. Leitch (New York: Harper and Row, 1967), pp. 172, 181, 188, 190, 197-98, 202. Compare the protest against disembodied luminosity in Gerald O'Collins, "Luminous Appearances of the Risen Christ," *The Catholic Biblical Quarterly* 46 (1984): 247-51, 254.

[50]Grass, *Ostergeschehen und Osterberichte,* pp. 231-32, 276-79.

[51]The original position, known as the "objective vision theory," is usually attributed to German scholar Theodor Keim (*Die Geschichte Jesu von Nazara,* vol. 3, 1872). Keim argues for his view only after his famous critique of Strauss's hallucination hypothesis. The more contemporary version was probably signaled in 1956 by Grass, who also disliked hallucination hypotheses (see *Ostergeschehen und Osterberichte,* pp. 96, 242, 279). On the differences between Keim's particular version and twentieth-century renditions, see Fuller, *The Formation of the Resurrection Narratives,* p. 33.

[52]Dodd, *The Apostolic Preaching,* p. 20.

[53]For a detailed account of the Gospels' testimony, see W. Craig, *Assessing the New Testament Evidence,* pp. 117-59, 391-97.

[54]For the fully developed case, see the massive evidence compiled in Robert H. Gundry, *Soma in Biblical Theology: With Emphasis on Pauline Anthropology* (Cambridge: Cambridge University Press, 1976; Grand Rapids, Mich.: Zondervan, 1987), p. 182. See chapters 1, 5-6, 12 and, especially, chapter 13: "The *Soma* in Death and Resurrection."

[55]John A. T. Robinson, "Resurrection in the NT," in *The Interpreter's Dictionary of the Bible,* ed. George Buttrick (Nashville: Abingdon, 1962), 4:48; cf. John A. T.

Robinson, *The Body* (Philadelphia: Westminster, 1952).

[56]For a number of additional considerations on the bodily nature of Jesus' resurrection body, see Gary R. Habermas, "The Early Christian Belief in the Resurrection of Jesus: A Response to Thomas Sheehan," *Michigan Theological Journal* 3, no. 2 (Fall 1992): 115-20.

[57]Concentrating, however, on the apologetic question of the factuality of the appearances does not exempt us from the crucial theological question of the nature of Jesus' resurrection body. For the contemporary evangelical debate on this point, compare Murray J. Harris, *Raised Immortal: Resurrection and Immortality in the New Testament* (Grand Rapids, Mich.: Eerdmans, 1983), and Norman L. Geisler, *The Battle for the Resurrection* (Nashville: Thomas Nelson, 1989). See also the review articles by Francis J. Beckwith, Gary R. Habermas and Scot McKnight in the *Journal of the Evangelical Theological Society* 33, no. 3 (September 1990).

[58]Dunn, *The Evidence for Jesus,* p. 75 (his emphasis).

[59]For a survey of five contemporary models for understanding the resurrection appearances, see Habermas, "Jesus' Resurrection and Contemporary Criticism: An Apologetic," pp. 160-72.

[60]Again, this is because the objective vision thesis is not a naturalistic theory. It still postulates actual (though nonphysical) appearances, and thus it does not preclude the resurrection or the supernatural. Lüdemann is an example of a critical scholar who agrees here *(The Resurrection of Jesus,* p. 59).

[61]As an irreducible minimum, even the apostles' belief in these appearances cannot be explained adequately by alternative hypotheses, in light of such data as have been presented here.

[62]Here we must be careful to emphasize that conclusions are not established because the critics agree, but because the facts indicate that the critical consensus is correct. This critical consensus is impressive, but the crucial consideration is that the data show that Jesus appeared to his disciples after his death.

[63]See Habermas and Moreland, *Immortality,* chap. 4, for a defense of each of these evidences, as well as other data favoring the resurrection appearances of Jesus.

[64]Evidence for God's existence renders this conclusion even more likely. As Antony Flew states, "Certainly given some beliefs about God, the occurrence of the resurrection does become enormously more likely" (see Habermas and Flew, *Did Jesus Rise from the Dead?* p. 39).

Conclusion/Geivett and Habermas

[1]Ernst Troeltsch, *Christian Thought: Its History and Application,* ed. with an introduction by Baron F. von Hügel (New York: Meridian Books, 1957), p. 43.

[2]See Basil Mitchell, *Morality: Religious and Secular* (Oxford: Clarendon, 1980), p. 105.

[3]Although Flew's position is well known from many earlier publications, not only is his chapter an original contribution to our volume, but none of the other contributors have seen it.

[4]William James, *The Varieties of Religious Experience: A Study in Human Nature* (New York: Longmans, Green, 1925), p. 74.

Bibliography

Note: Each entry in this bibliography is identified in terms of its approximate level of
difficulty: 1 indicates the most introductory level, 2 an intermediate level, and 3
the most advanced level.

Chapter 1/Hume
Burns, R. M. *The Great Debate on Miracles*. London and Toronto: Bucknell University
Press, 1981. [2]
Hume, David. *An Enquiry Concerning Human Understanding*. 3d ed. Revised by
P. H. Nidditch. Introduction and analytic index by L. A. Selby-Bigge. Oxford:
Clarendon, 1975. [2]
_____. *Of Miracles*. Edited by Antony Flew. La Salle, Ill.: Open Court, 1985. [2]
_____. *Writings on Religion*. Edited by Antony Flew. La Salle, Ill.: Open Court,
1992. [2]

Chapter 2/Flew
Bradley, F. H. "The Presuppositions of Critical History." In *Collected Essays*. Oxford:
Clarendon, 1935. 1:1-70. [2]
Broad, C. D. "Hume's Theory of the Credibility of Miracles." *Proceedings of the
Aristotelian Society* 17 (1916-1917): 77-94. [2]
Flew, Antony. *David Hume: Philosopher of Moral Science*. Oxford: Blackwell, 1986.
Chapter 5. [2]
_____. *Hume's Philosophy of Belief*. London: Routledge and Kegan Paul; New York:
Humanities Press, 1961. Chapter 13. [2]
Grant, R. M. *Miracle and Natural Law in Graeco-Roman and Early Christian
Thought*. Amsterdam: North Holland, 1952. [2]
Houston, Joseph. *Reported Miracles: A Critique of Hume*. Cambridge: Cambridge
University Press, 1994. [3]
Moule, C. F. D., ed. *Miracles*. London: Mowbrays, 1965. [2]
Swinburne, Richard, ed. *Miracles*. New York: Macmillan; London: Collier-Macmillan,
1989. [3]
Taylor, A. E. *David Hume and the Miraculous*. Cambridge: Cambridge University
Press, 1927. [2]

Whately, Richard. *Historic Doubts Concerning the Existence of Napoleon Bonaparte.* 2d ed. London: George Routledge & Sons, 1890. [1]

Chapter 3/Purtill

Alston, William P. "God's Action in the World." In *Divine and Human Language: Essays in Philosophical Theology.* Ithaca, N.Y.: Cornell University Press, 1989. [2]

Brown, Colin. *Miracles and the Critical Mind.* Grand Rapids, Mich.: Eerdmans, 1984. [2]

Colwell, Gary. "On Defining Away Miracles." *Philosophy* 57 (1982): 327-36. [2]

Fitzgerald, Paul. "Miracles." *Philosophical Forum* 18 (1985): 48-64. [2]

Flew, Antony. *David Hume: Philosopher of Moral Science.* Oxford: Blackwell, 1986. Chapter 5. [2]

Gaskin, J. C. A. "Miracles and Revelation." In *Hume's Philosophy of Religion.* 2d ed. Atlantic Heights, N.J.: Humanities Press, 1988. [2]

Locke, John. "A Discourse of Miracles." In *Works of John Locke.* Vol. 9. London, 1823. [2]

McKinnon, Alastair. "Miracle and Paradox." *American Philosophical Quarterly* 4 (1967): 308-14. [2]

Swinburne, Richard. *The Concept of Miracle.* New York: Macmillan, 1970. [2]

Chapter 4/Geisler

Broad, C. D. "Hume's Theory of the Credibility of Miracles." In *Human Understanding.* Edited by Alexander Sesonske and Noel Fleming. Belmont, Calif.: Wadsworth, 1965. First published in *Proceedings of the Aristotelian Society* 17 (1916-17): 77-94. [2]

Fitzgerald, Paul. "Miracles." *Philosophical Forum* 18 (1985): 48-64. [2]

Flew, Antony. "Miracles." In *The Encyclopedia of Philosophy.* Edited by Paul Edwards. New York: Macmillan/Free Press, 1967. 5:346-53. [2]

Geisler, Norman L. *Miracles and the Modern Mind.* Grand Rapids, Mich.: Baker, 1992. [1]

Rein, Andrew. "Repeatable Miracles?" *Analysis* 46 (1986): 109-12. [2]

Wallace, R. C. "Hume, Flew and the Miraculous." *Philosophical Quarterly* 20, no. 80 (July 1970): 230-43. [2]

Yandell, Keith E. *Hume's "Inexplicable Mystery": His Views on Religion.* Philadelphia: Temple University Press, 1990. Chapter 15. [3]

Chapter 5/Beckwith

Beckwith, Francis J. *David Hume's Argument Against Miracles: A Philosophical Analysis.* Lanham, Md.: University Press of America, 1989. [2]

_____. "Hume's Evidential/Testimonial Epistemology, Probability and Miracles." In *Faith in Theory and Practice: Essays on Justifying Religious Belief.* Edited by Elizabeth S. Radcliffe and Carol J. White. Chicago: Open Court, 1993. Pages 117-40. [3]

Brown, Colin. *Miracles and the Critical Mind.* Grand Rapids, Mich.: Eerdmans, 1984. [2]

Craig, William Lane. "The Problem of Historical Knowledge." In *Apologetics: An Introduction.* Chicago: Moody Press, 1984. [2]

Davis, Stephen T. "Is It Possible to Know That Jesus Was Raised from the Dead?" *Faith and Philosophy* 1 (April 1984): 147-59. [2]

Flew, Antony. *God: A Critical Enquiry.* 2d ed. La Salle, Ill.: Open Court, 1984. Pages 134-52. [3]

_____. "Miracles." In *The Encyclopedia of Philosophy.* Edited by Paul Edwards. New York: Macmillan, Free Press, 1967. 5:346-53. [2]

Geisler, Norman L. *Christian Apologetics.* Grand Rapids, Mich.: Baker, 1976. Chapter 15. [1]

Habermas, Gary. "Knowing That Jesus' Resurrection Occurred: A Response to Davis." *Faith and Philosophy* 2 (July 1985): 295-302. [2]

Montgomery, John Warwick. *The Shape of the Past: A Christian Response to Secular Philosophies of History.* Rev. ed. Minneapolis: Bethany House, 1975. [2]

Nash, Ronald H. *Christian Faith and Historical Understanding.* Grand Rapids, Mich.: Zondervan, 1984. [1]

Swinburne, Richard. *The Concept of Miracle.* New York: Macmillan, 1970. [2]

_____, ed. *Miracles.* New York: Macmillan, 1989. [3]

Chapter 6/Corduan

Boden, Margaret A. "Miracles and Scientific Explanation." *Ratio* 11 (1969): 137-44. [2]

Brown, Colin. *Miracles and the Critical Mind.* Grand Rapids, Mich.: Eerdmans, 1984. [2]

Erlandson, Douglas K. "A New Look at Miracles." *Religious Studies* 13 (1977): 417-28. [3]

Flew, Antony. *God and Philosophy.* New York: Delta, 1966. [2]

_____. "Miracles." In *The Encyclopedia of Philosophy.* Edited by Paul Edwards. New York: Macmillan/Free Press, 1967. 5:346-53. [2]

Geisler, Norman L. *Miracles and the Modern Mind.* Grand Rapids, Mich.: Baker, 1992. [1]

Holland, R. F. "The Miraculous." *American Philosophical Quarterly* 2 (January 1965): 43-51. [3]

Montgomery, John Warwick. "Science, Theology and the Miraculous." *Journal of the American Scientific Affiliation* 30 (1978): 145-53. [1]

Nowell-Smith, Patrick. "Miracles." In *New Essays in Philosophical Theology.* Edited by Antony Flew and Alasdair MacIntyre. London: SCM Press, 1955. [2]

Robinson, Guy. "Miracles." *Ratio* 9 (1967): 155-66. [3]

Wykstra, Stephen J. "The Problem of Miracle in the Apologetic from History." *Journal of the American Scientific Affiliation* 30 (1978): 154-63. [2]

Young, Robert. "Miracles and Epistemology." *Religious Studies* 8 (1972): 115-26. [3]

Chapter 7/Nash

Lewis, C. S. *Miracles.* New York: Macmillan, 1960. [1]

Nash, Ronald H. *Faith and Reason: Searching for a Rational Faith.* Grand Rapids, Mich.: Zondervan, 1988. [1]

_____. *Worldviews in Conflict.* Grand Rapids, Mich.: Zondervan, 1992. [1]

Plantinga, Alvin. *Warrant and Proper Function.* New York: Oxford University Press, 1993. Chapters 11-12. [3]

Purtill, Richard L. *Reason to Believe*. Grand Rapids, Mich.: Eerdmans, 1974. [1]
Wainwright, William J. "Is Theism the Best Explanation? Assessing World-Views."
    In *Philosophy of Religion*. Belmont, Calif.: Wadsworth, 1988. [2]
Yandell, Keith. "Religious Experience and Rational Appraisal." *Religious Studies* 10
    (1974): 173-87. [3]

Chapter 8/Moreland
The Complementarity View
Bube, Richard. *The Human Quest*. Waco, Tex.: Word, 1971. [1]
Connell, Richard J. *Substance and Modern Science*. Notre Dame, Ind.: University of
    Notre Dame Press, 1988. [2]
Mackay, Donald M. *Human Science and Human Dignity*. Downers Grove, Ill.:
    InterVarsity Press, 1979. [1]
Peacocke, A. R. *Creation and the World of Science*. Oxford: Clarendon, 1979. [2]
_____. *God and the New Biology*. San Francisco: Harper and Row, 1986. [2]

Freedom and Agency
Bishop, John. *Natural Agency*. Cambridge: Cambridge University Press, 1989. [3]
Rowe, William L. *Thomas Reid on Freedom and Morality*. Ithaca, N.Y.: Cornell
    University Press, 1991. [2]
Van Inwagen, Peter. "The Place of Chance in a World Sustained by God." In *Divine
    & Human Action*. Edited by Thomas V. Morris. Ithaca, N. Y.: Cornell University
    Press, 1988. [3]

Theistic Science, Miracles and God-of-the-Gaps
Moreland, J. P. *Christianity and the Nature of Science*. Grand Rapids, Mich.: Baker,
    1989. [2]
_____. "Creation Science and Methodological Naturalism." In *Man and Creation*.
    Edited by Michael Bauman. Hillsdale, Mich.: Hillsdale College Press, 1993. [1]
_____, ed. *The Creation Hypothesis*. Downers Grove, Ill.: InterVarsity Press, 1994.
    [1]
Van Till, Howard J. "When Faith and Reason Meet." In *Man and Creation*. Edited
    by Michael Bauman. Hillsdale, Mich.: Hillsdale College Press, 1993. [1]
Van Till, Howard J., Robert E. Snow, John H. Stek and Davis A. Young. *Portraits of
    Creation*. Grand Rapids, Mich.: Eerdmans, 1990. [2]
Van Till, Howard J., Davis A. Young and Clarence Menninga. *Science Held Hostage*.
    Downers Grove, Ill.: InterVarsity Press, 1988. [1]

Chapter 9/Beck
The Theist's Side
Adler, Mortimer. *How to Think About God*. New York: Macmillan, 1980. [1]
Craig, William Lane. *Reasonable Faith*. Rev. ed. Wheaton, Ill.: Crossway, 1994. [2]
Evans, C. Stephen. *Philosophy of Religion*. Downers Grove, Ill.: InterVarsity Press, 1985. [2]
Geisler, Norman, and Winfried Corduan. *Philosophy of Religion*. Rev. ed. Grand
    Rapids, Mich.: Baker, 1988. [2]
Geivett, R. Douglas. *Evil and the Evidence for God*. Philadelphia: Temple University
    Press, 1993. [3]
Geivett, R. Douglas, and Brendan Sweetman, eds. *Contemporary Perspectives on*

Religious Epistemology. New York: Oxford University Press, 1992. [2]

Kushner, Harold. *Who Needs God?* New York: Summit Books, 1989. [1]

Lewis, C. S. *Mere Christianity.* New York: Macmillan, 1943. [1]

Miller, Ed. *God and Reason.* New York: Macmillan, 1972. [2]

Moreland, J. P., ed. *The Creation Hypothesis.* Downers Grove, Ill.: InterVarsity Press, 1994. [2]

Swinburne, Richard. *The Existence of God.* Rev. ed. Oxford: Clarendon, 1991. [3]

The Atheist's Side

Mackie, J. L. *The Miracle of Theism.* Oxford: Clarendon, 1982. [3]

Martin, Michael. *Atheism: A Philosophical Justification.* Philadelphia: Temple University Press, 1990. [2]

Smith, George. *Atheism: The Case Against God.* Buffalo, N.Y.: Prometheus, 1979. [1]

Chapter 10/Davis

Abraham, William J. *An Introduction to the Philosophy of Religion.* Englewood Cliffs, N.J.: Prentice-Hall, 1985. [2]

Alston, William P. "Divine and Human Action" and "God's Action in the World." In *Divine Nature and Human Language: Essays in Philosophical Theology.* Ithaca, N.Y.: Cornell University Press, 1989. [2]

_____. "How to Think About Divine Action." In *Divine Action: Studies Inspired by the Philosophical Theology of Austin Farrer.* Edited by Brian Hebblethwaite and Edward Henderson. Edinburgh: T & T Clark, 1990. [2]

Davis, Stephen T. *Risen Indeed: Making Sense of the Resurrection.* Grand Rapids, Mich.: Eerdmans, 1993. [2]

Freddoso, Alfred J. "God's General Concurrence with Secondary Causes: Why Conservation Is Not Enough." In *Philosophical Perspectives,* vol. 5, *Philosophy of Religion, 1991.* Edited by James E. Tomberlin. Atascadero, Calif.: Ridgeview, 1991. [3]

Martin, Michael. *Atheism: A Philosophical Justification.* Philadelphia: Temple University Press, 1990. See especially pages 188-209. [2]

_____. "Atheistic Teleological Arguments." In *Contemporary Perspectives on Religious Epistemology.* Edited by R. Douglas Geivett and Brendan Sweetman. Oxford: Oxford University Press, 1992. [2]

Strawson, P. F. *Individuals.* Garden City, N.Y.: Anchor Books, 1959. [3]

Thomas, Owen. "Recent Thought on Divine Agency." In *Divine Action: Studies Inspired by the Philosophical Theology of Austin Farrer.* Edited by Brian Hebblethwaite and Edward Henderson. Edinburgh: T & T Clark, 1990. [2]

Tracy, Thomas. *God, Action and Embodiment.* Grand Rapids, Mich.: Eerdmans, 1984. [2]

Chapter 11/Geivett

Anglin, W. S. "Revelation." In *Free Will and the Christian Faith.* Oxford: Clarendon, 1990. [2]

Basinger, David. *Philosophy and Miracle: The Contemporary Debate.* Lewiston, N.Y.: Edwin Mellen, 1986. [3]

Basinger, David, and Randall Basinger. "Science and the Concept of Miracle." *Journal of the American Scientific Affiliation* 30 (December 1978): 164-68. [2]

Boden, Margaret. "Miracles and Scientific Explanation." *Ratio* 11 (December 1969): 137-41. [2]

Butler, Joseph. *The Analogy of Religion* [1736]. Edited by Ernest C. Mossner. New York: Frederick Ungar, 1961. [2]

Hughes, Henry. *A Critical Examination of Butler's "Analogy."* London: Kegan Paul, Trench, Trubner, 1898. Chapter 7. [2]

Lacordaire, Henri-Dominique. *God and Man.* New York: O'Shea, 1871. [2]

Larmer, Robert A. H. "Miracles and Apologetics." In *Water into Wine? An Investigation of the Concept of Miracle.* Kingston, Ont.: McGill-Queen's University Press, 1988. [2]

Locke, John. *The Reasonableness of Christianity* [1695], *with A Discourse of Miracles* [1706] *and Part of a Third Letter Concerning Toleration* [1692]. Edited by I. T. Ramsey. Stanford, Calif.: Stanford University Press, 1958. [2]

M'Ilvaine, Charles Pettit. *The Evidences of Christianity.* Philadelphia: Smith and English, 1856. Lecture 5, "Miracles." [1]

Newman, John Henry. "Critique of Hume's View of Miracles." In *Philosophical Readings in Cardinal Newman.* Edited by James Collins. Chicago: Henry Regnery, 1961. [2]

Paley, William. *A View of the Evidences of Christianity* [1794]. Annotations by Richard Whately. New York: James Miller, 1865. [2]

Penelhum, Terence. "Revelation and Miracle." In *Butler.* London: Routledge and Kegan Paul, 1985. [2]

Purtill, Richard L. "Miracles: What If They Happen?" In *Thinking About Religion.* Englewood Cliffs, N.J.: Prentice-Hall, 1978. [1]

Smart, Ninian. "On the Idea of Revealed Truth." In *The Philosophy of Religion.* New York: Oxford University Press, 1979. [2]

Swinburne, Richard. *The Existence of God.* Oxford: Clarendon, 1979. Chapter 12. [3]

_____. *Faith and Reason.* Oxford: Clarendon, 1981. Chapter 7. [2]

_____. *Revelation.* Oxford: Clarendon Press, 1992. Chapters 5-6. [2]

Wykstra, Stephen J. "The Problem of Miracle in the Apologetic from History." *Journal of the American Scientific Affiliation* 30 (December 1978): 154-63. [2]

Chapter 12/Clark

Conway, David A. "Miracles, Evidence and Contrary Religion." *Sophia* 22 (1983): 3-14. [2]

Langtry, Bruce. "Miracles and Contrary Religions." *Sophia* 14 (1975): 29-34. [2]

_____. "Miracles and Rival Systems of Religion." *Sophia* 24 (1985): 21-31. [2]

Chapter 13/Newman
Contemporary Works

Beegle, Dewey M. *Prophecy and Prediction.* Ann Arbor, Mich.: Pryor Pettengill, 1978. [2]

Bloom, John. "Truth via Prophecy." In *Evidence for Faith: Deciding the God Question.* Edited by John Warwick Montgomery. Dallas, Tex.: Probe/Word, 1991. [1]

Levine, Samuel. *You Take Jesus, I'll Take God: How to Refute Christian Missionaries.* Los Angeles, Calif.: Hamoroh, 1980. [1]

Newman, Robert C. "Israel's History Written in Advance: A Neglected Evidence for the God of the Bible." In *Evidence for Faith: Deciding the God Question*. Edited by John Warwick Montgomery. Dallas, Tex.: Probe/Word, 1991. [1]

_____. "The Testimony of Messianic Prophecy." In *Evidence for Faith: Deciding the God Question*. Edited by John Warwick Montgomery. Dallas, Tex.: Probe/Word, 1991. [1]

_____, ed. *The Evidence of Prophecy: Fulfilled Prediction as a Testimony to the Truth of Christianity*. Hatfield, Penn.: Interdisciplinary Biblical Research Institute, 1988. [2]

Oxtoby, Gurdon C. *Prediction and Fulfillment in the Bible*. Philadelphia: Westminster, 1956. [2]

Payne, J. Barton. *The Encyclopedia of Biblical Prophecy*. New York: Harper and Row, 1973. [2]

Van Groningen, Gerard. *Messianic Revelation in the Old Testament*. Grand Rapids, Mich.: Baker, 1990. [3]

Classic Works

Keith, Alexander. *Evidence of the Truth of the Christian Religion Derived from the Literal Fulfillment of Prophecy*. 36th ed. Edinburgh: William Whyte, 1848. [2]

Kellogg, Samuel H. *The Jews, or Prediction and Fulfillment: An Argument for the Times*. New ed. New York: Anson Randolph, 1887. [2]

Newton, Thomas. *Dissertations on the Prophecies Which Have Been Remarkably Fulfilled, and at This Time Are Fulfilling in the World*. London: J. F. Dove; Philadelphia: Crissy and Markley, 1853. [2]

Pember, G. H. *The Great Prophecies of the Centuries Concerning Israel and the Gentiles*. 5th ed. London: Hodder and Stoughton, 1902. [2]

Urquhart, John. *The Wonders of Prophecy*. Harrisburg, Penn.: Christian Publications, 1887. [2]

Chapter 14/Feinberg

Brown, David. *The Divine Trinity*. London: Duckworth, 1985. [3]

Davis, Stephen T. *Logic and the Nature of God*. London: Macmillan, 1983. Chapter 8. [3]

Feenstra, R. J., and C. Plantinga, eds. *Trinity, Incarnation and Atonement*. Notre Dame, Ind.: University of Notre Dame Press, 1989. [2]

Freddoso, Alfred J. "Human Nature, Potency and the Incarnation." *Faith and Philosophy* 3 (1986): 27-53. [3]

Hick, John. *The Metaphor of God Incarnate*. Louisville, Ky.: Westminster/John Knox, 1993. [2]

_____, ed. *The Myth of God Incarnate*. London: SCM Press, 1977. [2]

Morris, Thomas V. *The Logic of God Incarnate*. Ithaca, N.Y.: Cornell University Press, 1986. [3]

Swinburne, Richard. *The Christian God*. Oxford: Clarendon, 1994. Chapters 9-10. [2]

Chapter 15/Craig

Bode, Edward Lynn. *The First Easter Morning*. Analecta Biblia 45. Rome: Pontifical Biblical Institute, 1970. [3]

Craig, William Lane. *Assessing the New Testament Evidence for the Historicity of the*

Resurrection of Jesus. Lewiston, N.Y.: Edwin Mellen, 1989. [3]

_____. *The Historical Argument for the Resurrection of Jesus.* Lewiston, N.Y.: Edwin Mellen, 1985. [3]

_____. *Knowing the Truth About the Resurrection.* Ann Arbor, Mich.: Servant, 1988. [1]

_____. *The Son Rises.* Chicago: Moody Press, 1981. [1]

Chapter 16/Habermas

Alsup, John. *The Post-resurrection Appearances of the Gospel Tradition.* Stuttgart: Calwer Verlag, 1975. [3]

Brown, Raymond. *The Virginal Conception and Bodily Resurrection of Jesus.* New York: Paulist, 1973. [2]

Craig, William Lane. See bibliography for chapter 15.

Davis, Stephen T. *Risen Indeed: Making Sense of the Resurrection* (Grand Rapids, Mich.: Eerdmans, 1993. [2]

_____. "'Seeing' the Risen Jesus." In *Resurrection 2000: An Interdisciplinary Symposium on the Resurrection of Jesus.* Edited by Stephen T. Davis, Dan Kendall and Gerald O'Collins. Oxford: Oxford University Press, 1997. [2]

Dodd, C. H. "The Appearances of the Risen Christ: An Essay in Form Criticism." In *More New Testament Essays.* Grand Rapids, Mich.: Eerdmans, 1968. [2]

Fuller, Reginald. *The Formation of the Resurrection Narratives.* New York: Macmillan, 1971. [2]

Grass, Hans. *Ostergeschehen und Osterberichte.* 2d ed. Göttingen: Vandenhoeck und Ruprecht, 1962. [2]

Gundry, Robert H. *Soma in Biblical Theology: With Emphasis on Pauline Anthropology.* Cambridge: Cambridge University Press, 1976; Grand Rapids, Mich.: Zondervan, 1987. [2]

Habermas, Gary R. *The Historical Jesus: Ancient Evidence for the Life of Christ.* Joplin, Mo.: College Press, 1996. [2]

_____. *The Resurrection of Jesus.* Grand Rapids, Mich.: Baker, 1980. [1]

Habermas, Gary R., and Antony Flew. *Did Jesus Rise from the Dead? The Resurrection Debate.* Edited by Terry Miethe. San Francisco: Harper and Row, 1987. [2]

Lapide, Pinchas. *The Resurrection of Jesus: A Jewish Perspective.* Minneapolis: Augsburg, 1983. [1]

O'Collins, Gerald. "Luminous Appearances of the Risen Christ." *The Catholic Biblical Quarterly* 46 (1984): 247-54. [2]

Osborne, Grant. *The Resurrection Narratives: A Redactional Study.* Grand Rapids, Mich.: Baker, 1984. [2]

Contributors

W. David Beck (Ph.D., Boston University) is professor of philosophy and associate vice president for faculty development at Liberty University and has edited *Opening the American Mind* (Baker, 1991) and written "Agnosticism: Kant" in *Biblical Errancy*, Norman L. Geisler, editor (Zondervan, 1981).

Francis J. Beckwith (Ph.D., Fordham University) is assistant professor of philosophy at Whittier College and author of *David Hume's Argument Against Miracles: A Critical Analysis* (University Press of America, 1989) and *Politically Correct Death: Answering Arguments for Abortion Rights* (Baker, 1993).

David K. Clark (Ph.D., Northwestern University and Garrett-Evangelical Theological Seminary) is professor of theology at Bethel Theological Seminary and author of *The Pantheism of Alan Watts* (InterVarsity Press, 1978) and *Dialogical Apologetics: A Person-Centered Approach to Christian Defense* (Baker, 1993).

Winfried Corduan (Ph.D., Rice University) is professor of philosophy and religion at Taylor University, coauthor (with Norman L. Geisler) of *Philosophy of Religion* (Baker, 1988) and author of *Reasonable Faith* (Broadman and Holman, 1993).

William Lane Craig (Ph.D., University of Birmingham, England; D.Theol., University of Munich, Germany) is research professor at Talbot School of Theology, Biola University, and author of *The Historical Argument for the Resurrection of Jesus* (Edwin Mellen, 1985) and *Assessing the New Testament Evidence for the Historicity of the Resurrection of Jesus* (Edwin Mellen, 1989).

Stephen T. Davis (Ph.D., Claremont Graduate School) is professor of philosophy at Claremont McKenna College and author of *Logic and the Nature of God* (Macmillan, 1983) and *Risen Indeed: Making Sense of the Resurrection* (Eerdmans, 1993).

John S. Feinberg (Ph.D., University of Chicago) is professor of biblical and systematic theology at Trinity Evangelical Divinity School, and coauthor (with Paul D. Feinberg) of *Ethics for a Brave New World* (Crossway, 1993) and author of *The Many Faces of Evil: Theological Systems and the Problem of Evil* (Zondervan, 1994).

Antony G. N. Flew (D.Litt., University of Keele, England) is professor emeritus of philosophy at the University of Reading, England, and is the author of *Hume's*

Philosophy of Belief (Routledge and Kegan Paul, 1961) and *God and Philosophy* (Dell, 1966).

Norman L. Geisler (Ph.D., Loyola University of Chicago) is dean of Southern Evangelical Seminary, author of *Miracles and the Modern Mind* (Baker, 1992) and coauthor (with Winfried Corduan) of *Philosophy of Religion* (Baker, 1988).

R. Douglas Geivett (Ph.D., University of Southern California) is associate professor of philosophy at Talbot School of Theology, Biola University, author of *Evil and the Evidence for God* (Temple University Press, 1993) and coeditor of *Contemporary Perspectives on Religious Epistemology* (Oxford University Press, 1992).

Gary R. Habermas (Ph.D., Michigan State University; D.D., Emmanuel College, Oxford, England) is distinguished professor and chairman of the department of philosophy and theology at Liberty University, coauthor (with Antony Flew) of *Did Jesus Rise from the Dead?* (Harper and Row, 1987) and author of *The Historical Jesus* (College Press, 1996).

David Hume (1711-1776) studied at the University of Edinburgh, Scotland, without taking a degree and was turned down for academic posts at Edinburgh and Glasgow, but authored several influential essays, including *An Enquiry Concerning Human Understanding* (1748), *The Natural History of Religion* (1757) and *Dialogues Concerning Natural Religion* (published posthumously in 1779).

J. P. Moreland (Ph.D., University of Southern California) is professor of philosophy at Talbot School of Theology, Biola University, author of *Christianity and the Nature of Science* (Baker, 1989) and editor of *The Creation Hypothesis* (InterVarsity Press, 1994).

Ronald H. Nash (Ph.D., Syracuse University) is professor of philosophy and theology at Reformed Theological Seminary and author of *Faith and Reason: Searching for a Rational Faith* (Zondervan, 1988) and *Worldviews in Conflict* (Zondervan, 1992).

Robert C. Newman (Ph.D., Cornell University) is professor of New Testament at Biblical Theological Seminary, coauthor (with Peter W. Stoner) of *Science Speaks* (Moody, 1976) and editor of *The Evidence of Prophecy* (Interdisciplinary Biblical Research Institute, 1988).

Richard L. Purtill (Ph.D., University of Chicago) is professor of philosophy at Western Washington University and author of *Thinking About Religion: A Philosophical Introduction to Religion* (Prentice-Hall, 1978) and *C. S. Lewis's Case for the Christian Faith* (Harper and Row, 1981).